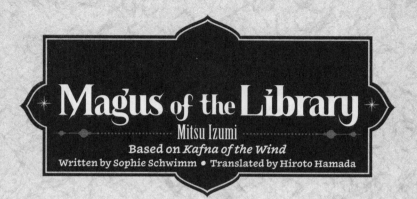

Magus of the Library

Mitsu Izumi

Based on *Kafna of the Wind*

Written by Sophie Schwimm • Translated by Hiroto Hamada

4

Magus of the Library

Magus of the Library 4

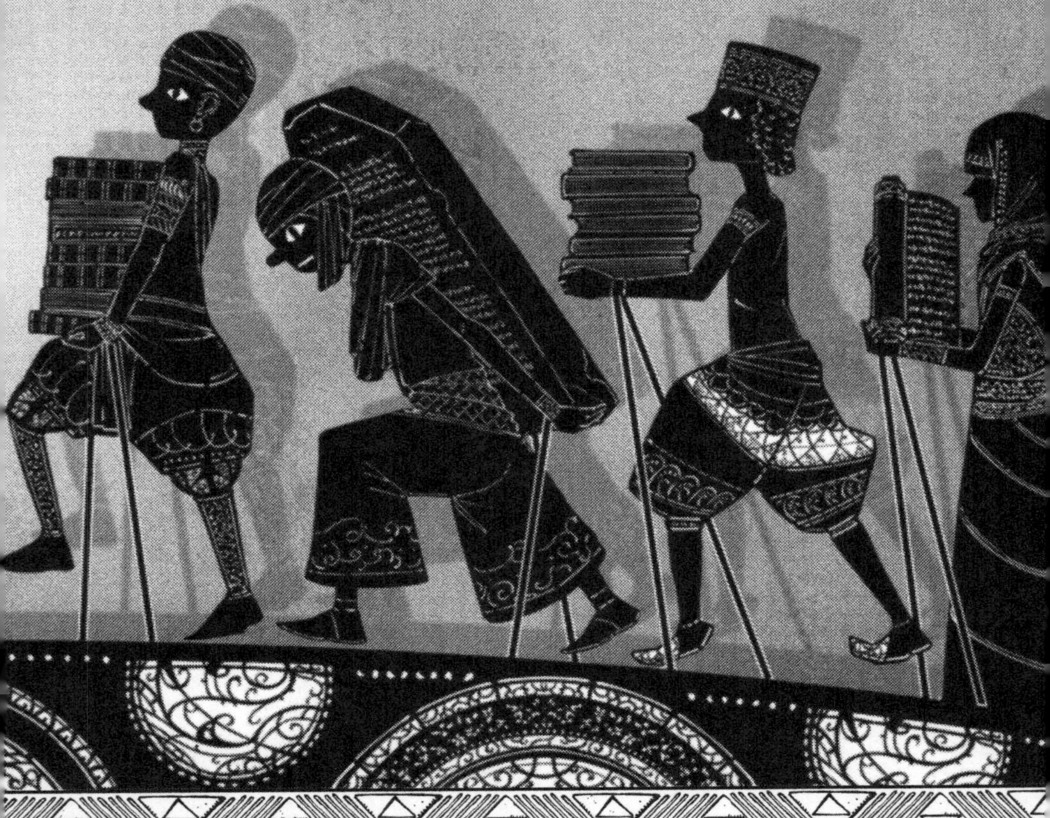

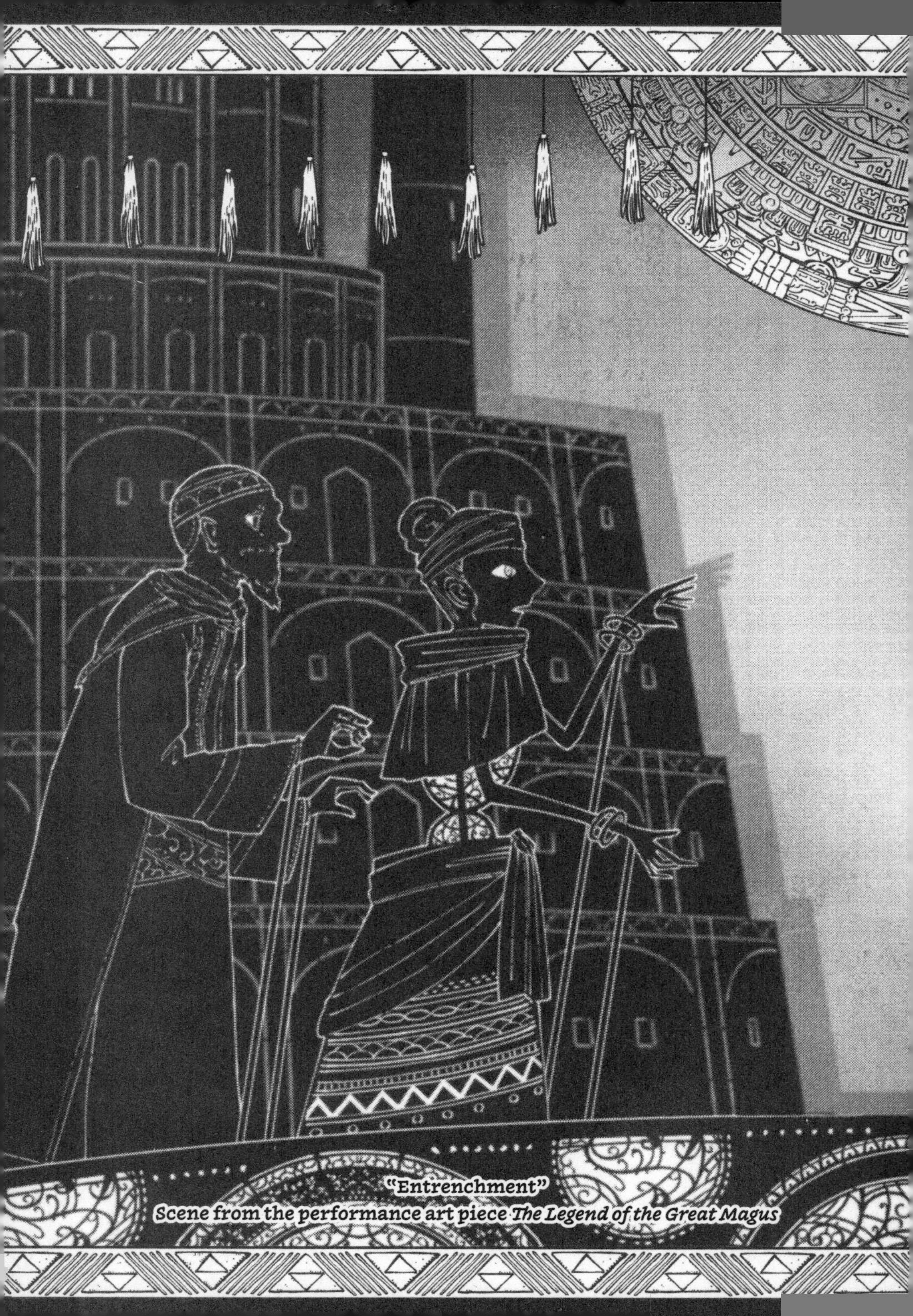

"Entrenchment"
Scene from the performance art piece *The Legend of the Great Magus*

*"No theft a crime if Haupi purse,
no trespass wrong if Haupi shamed,
no murder sin if Haupi blood."*

—Zarama Ingare'i
From *The Words of Justice*

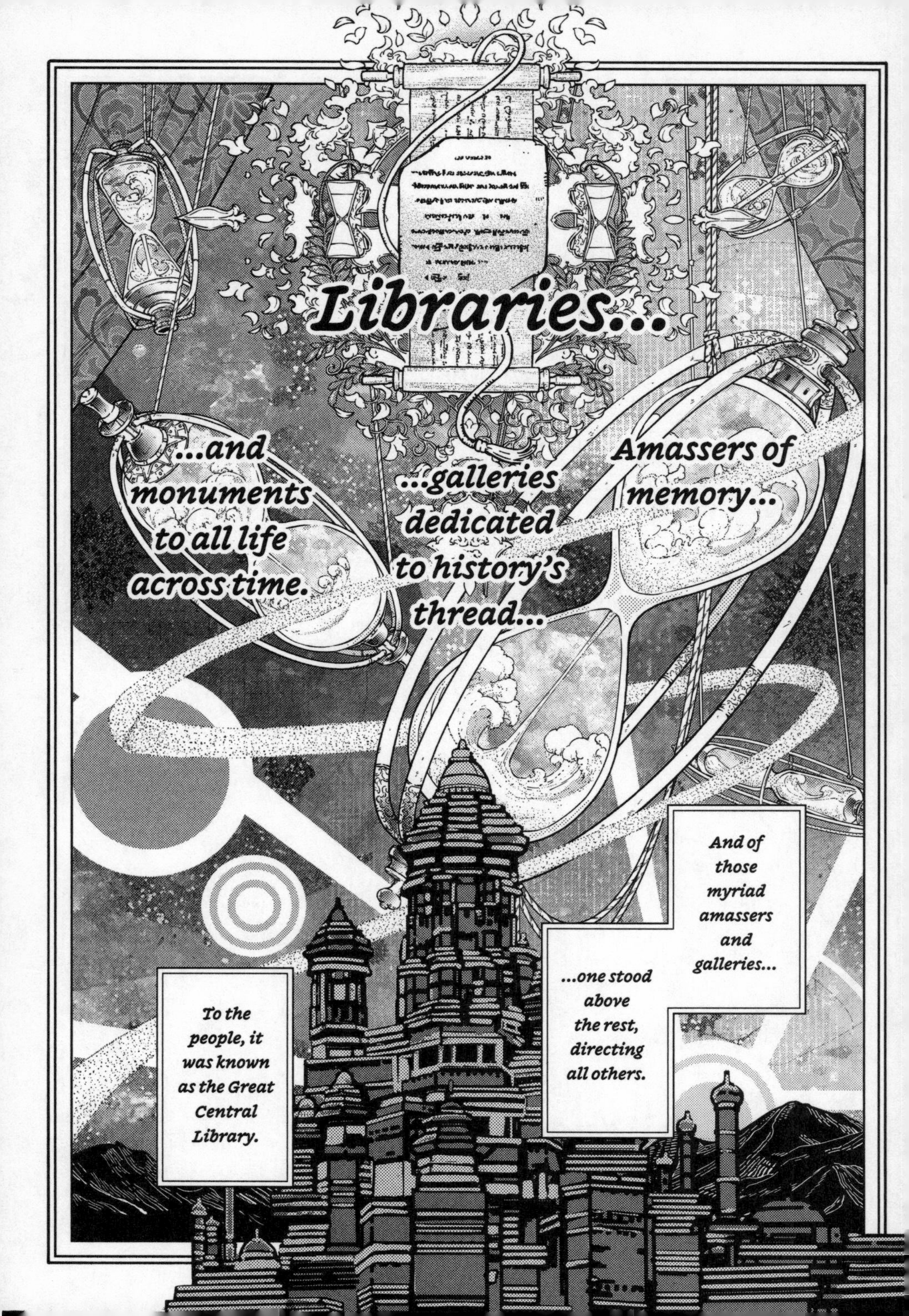
Libraries...
Amassers of memory...
...galleries dedicated to history's thread...
...and monuments to all life across time.
And of those myriad amassers and galleries...
...one stood above the rest, directing all others.
To the people, it was known as the Great Central Library.

15 The Continent is Small, Fly on Syrrana

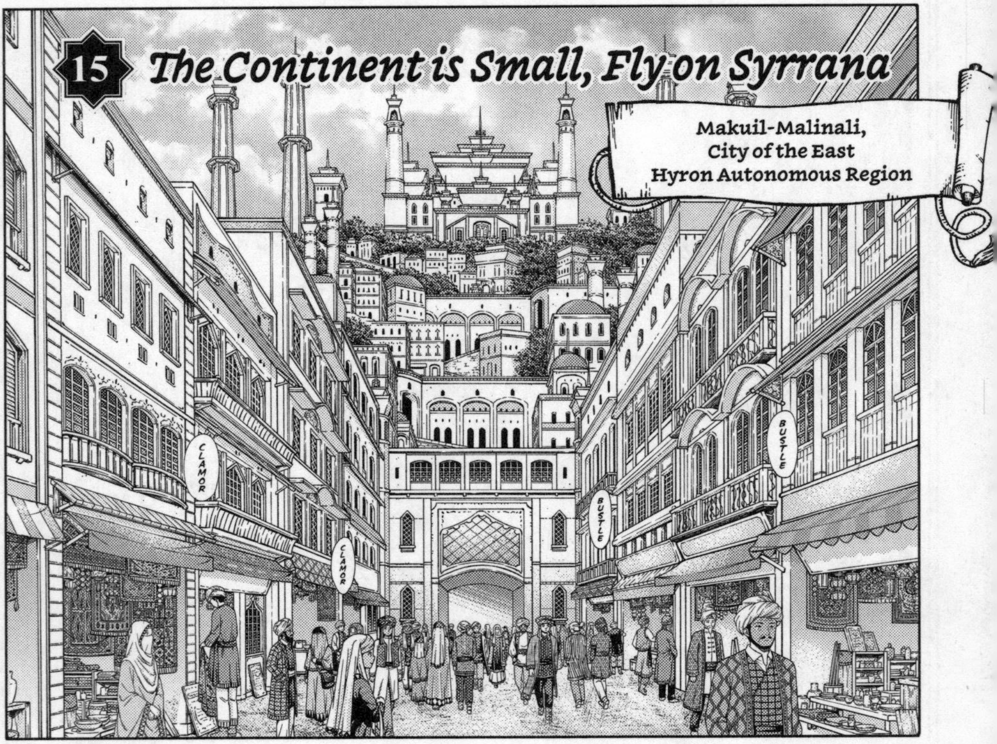
Makuil-Malinali,
City of the East
Hyron Autonomous Region
BUSTLE
BUSTLE
CLAMOR
CLAMOR

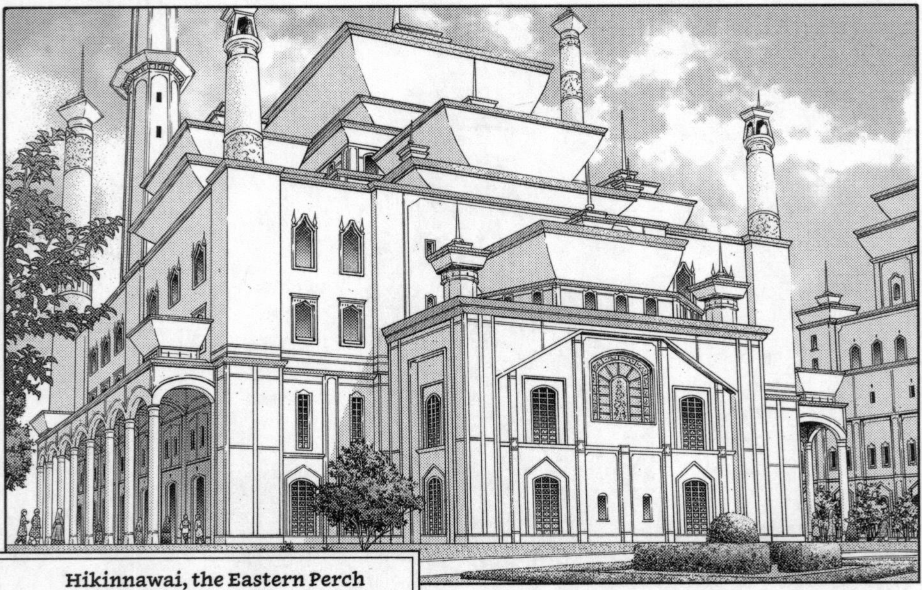
Hikinnawai, the Eastern Perch
Temple of the Asin Faith

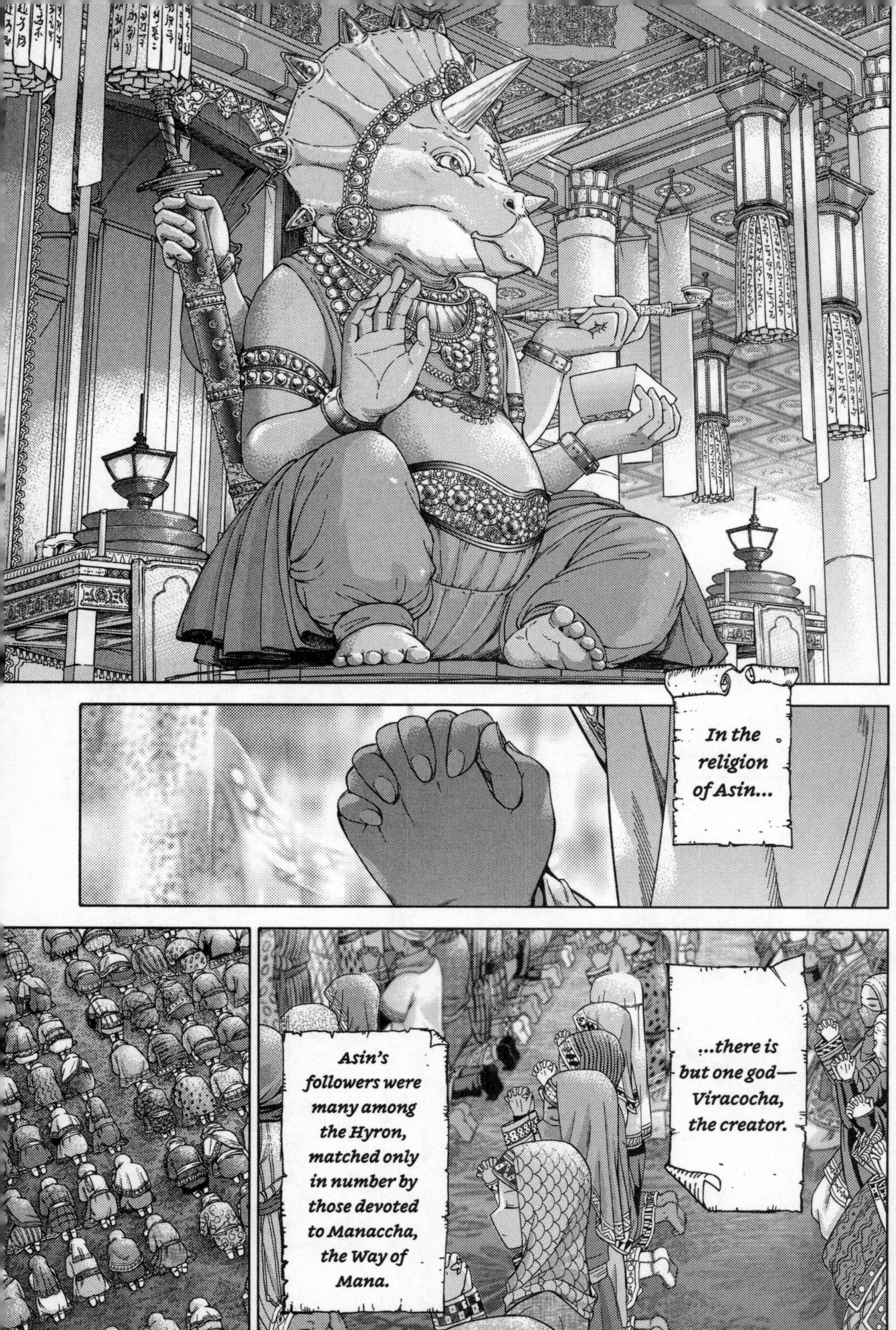
In the religion of Asin...
...there is but one god—Viracocha, the creator.
Asin's followers were many among the Hyron, matched only in number by those devoted to Manaccha, the Way of Mana.

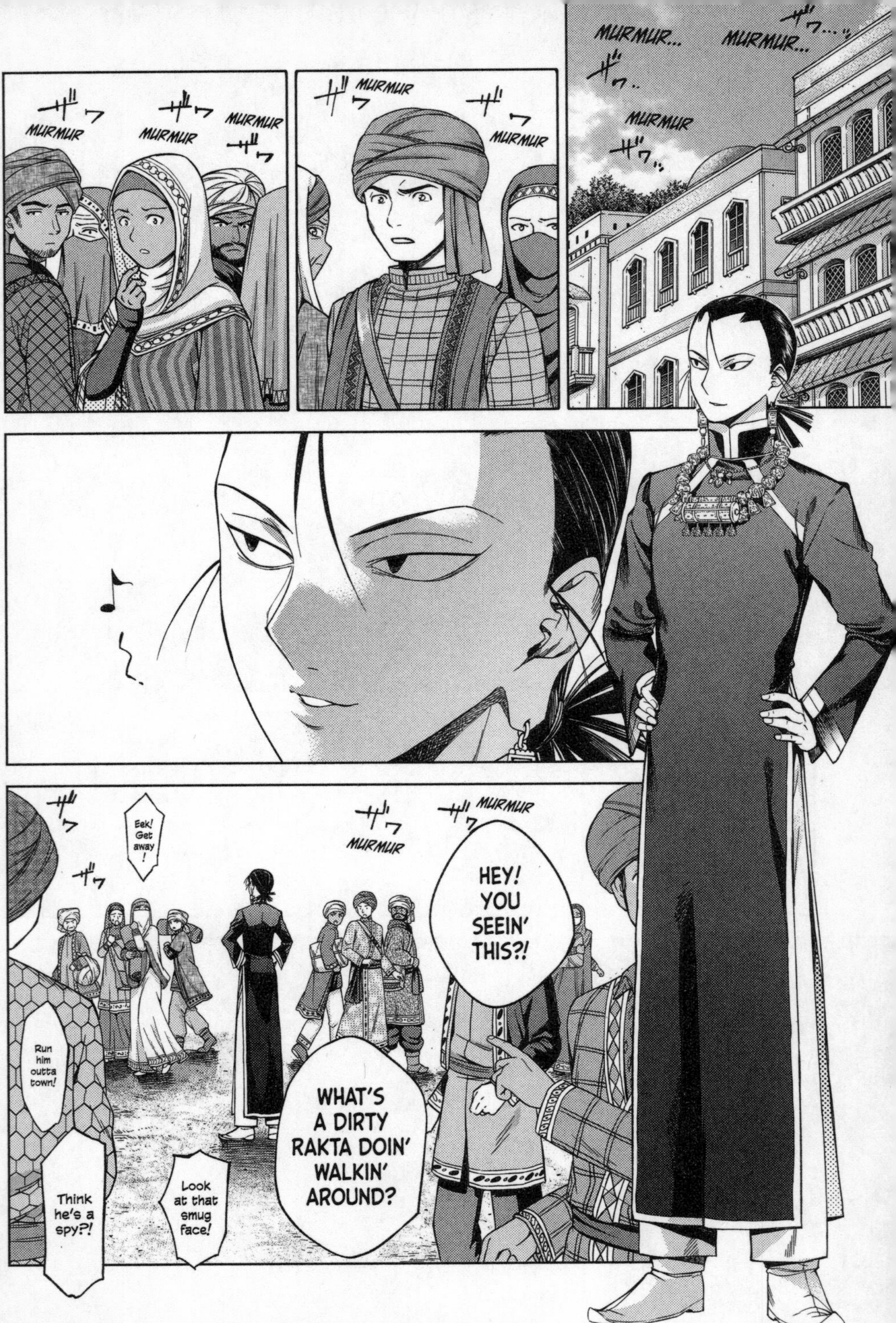

ザワ…
MURMUR...
MURMUR...
ザワ…
MURMUR
ザワ…
ザワ
MURMUR
ザワ
MURMUR
MURMUR
ザワ
MURMUR
ザワ
MURMUR
ザワ
MURMUR
HEY! YOU SEEIN' THIS?!
WHAT'S A DIRTY RAKTA DOIN' WALKIN' AROUND?
ザワ
MURMUR
ザワ
Eek! Get away!
Look at that smug face!
ザワ
ザワ
Run him outta town!
Think he's a spy?!

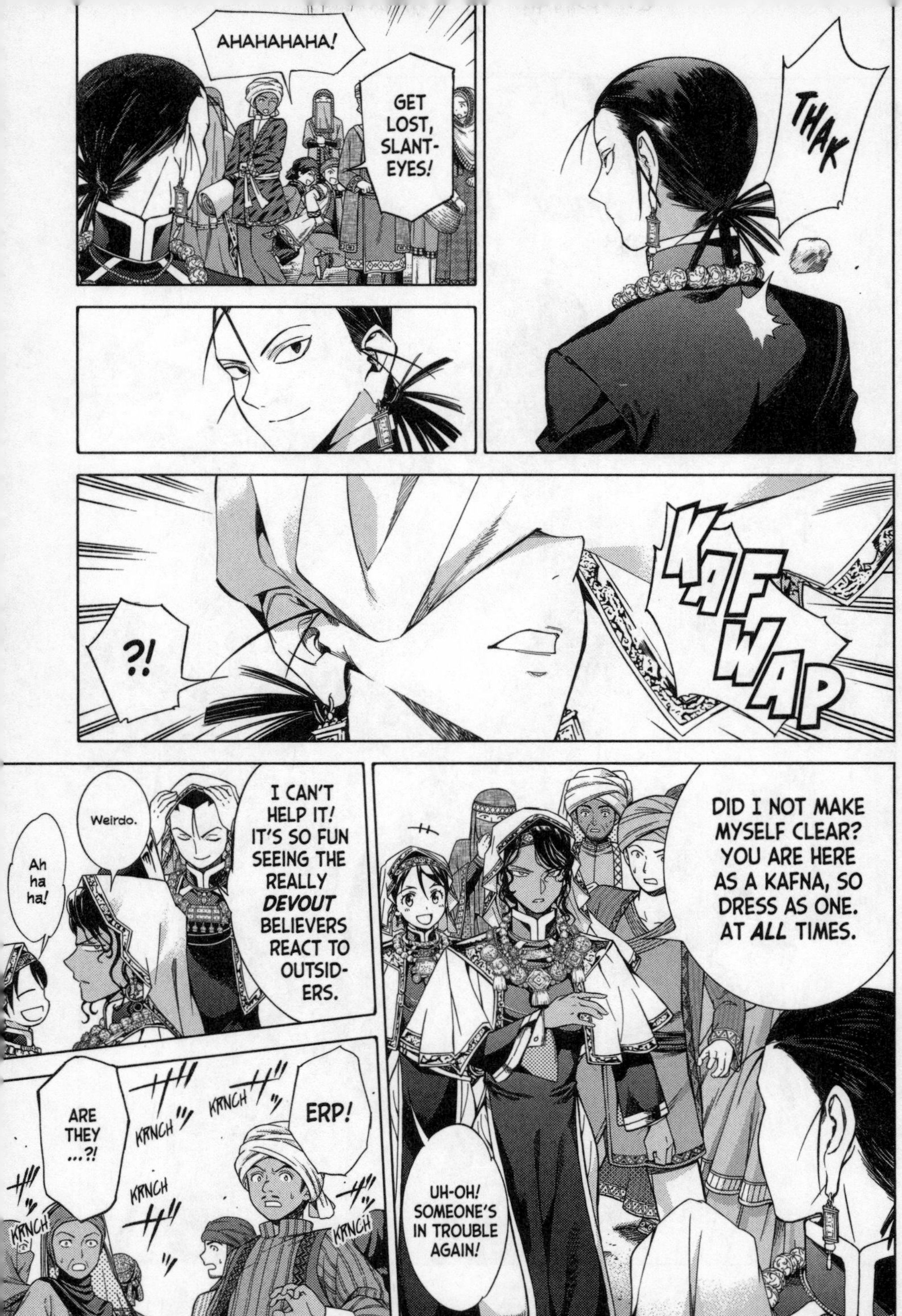
THAK
AHAHAHAHA!
GET LOST, SLANT-EYES!
KAF WAP
?!
DID I NOT MAKE MYSELF CLEAR? YOU ARE HERE AS A KAFNA, SO DRESS AS ONE. AT ALL TIMES.
UH-OH! SOMEONE'S IN TROUBLE AGAIN!
I CAN'T HELP IT! IT'S SO FUN SEEING THE REALLY DEVOUT BELIEVERS REACT TO OUTSIDERS.
Weirdo.
Ah ha ha!
ERP!
KRNCH
KRNCH
ARE THEY ...?!
KRNCH
KRNCH
KRNCH

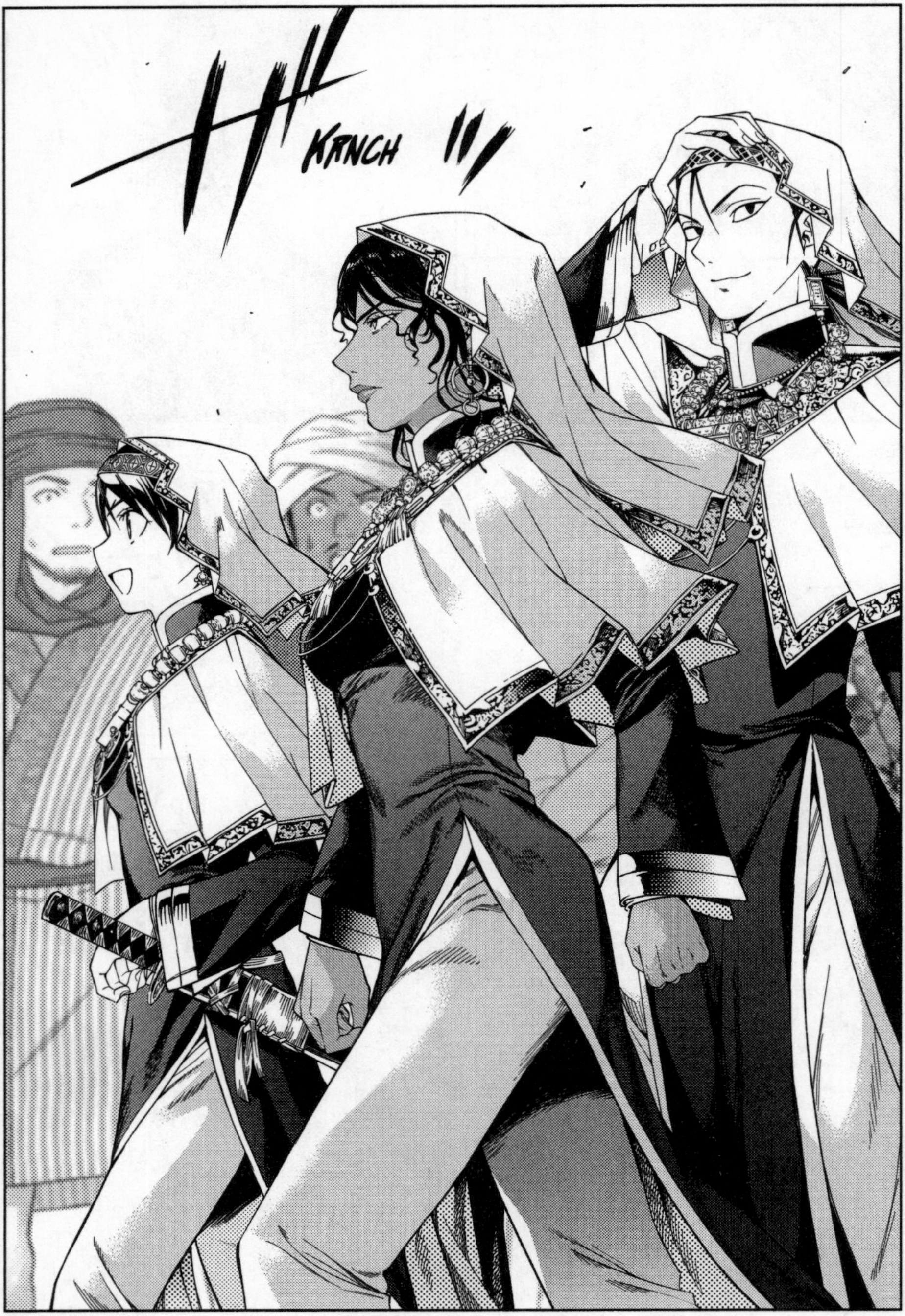
KRNCH

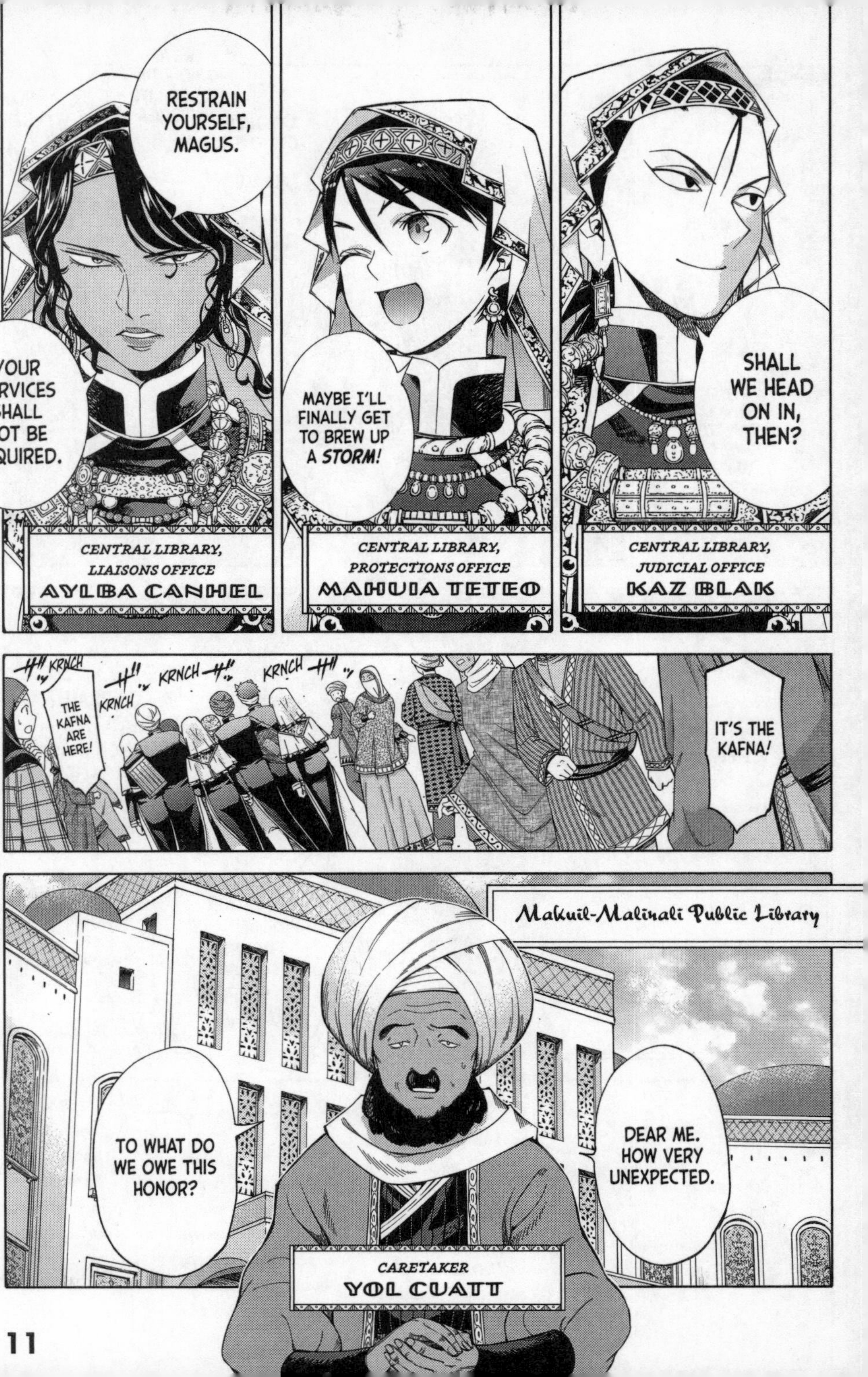

SHALL WE HEAD ON IN, THEN?
CENTRAL LIBRARY, JUDICIAL OFFICE
KAZ BLAK
MAYBE I'LL FINALLY GET TO BREW UP A *STORM!*
CENTRAL LIBRARY, PROTECTIONS OFFICE
MAHUIA TETEO
RESTRAIN YOURSELF, MAGUS.
YOUR SERVICES SHALL NOT BE REQUIRED.
CENTRAL LIBRARY, LIAISONS OFFICE
AYLBA CANHEL
IT'S THE KAFNA!
KRNCH
KRNCH
KRNCH
KRNCH
THE KAFNA ARE HERE!
Makuil-Malinali Public Library
DEAR ME. HOW VERY UNEXPECTED.
TO WHAT DO WE OWE THIS HONOR?
CARETAKER
YOL CUATT

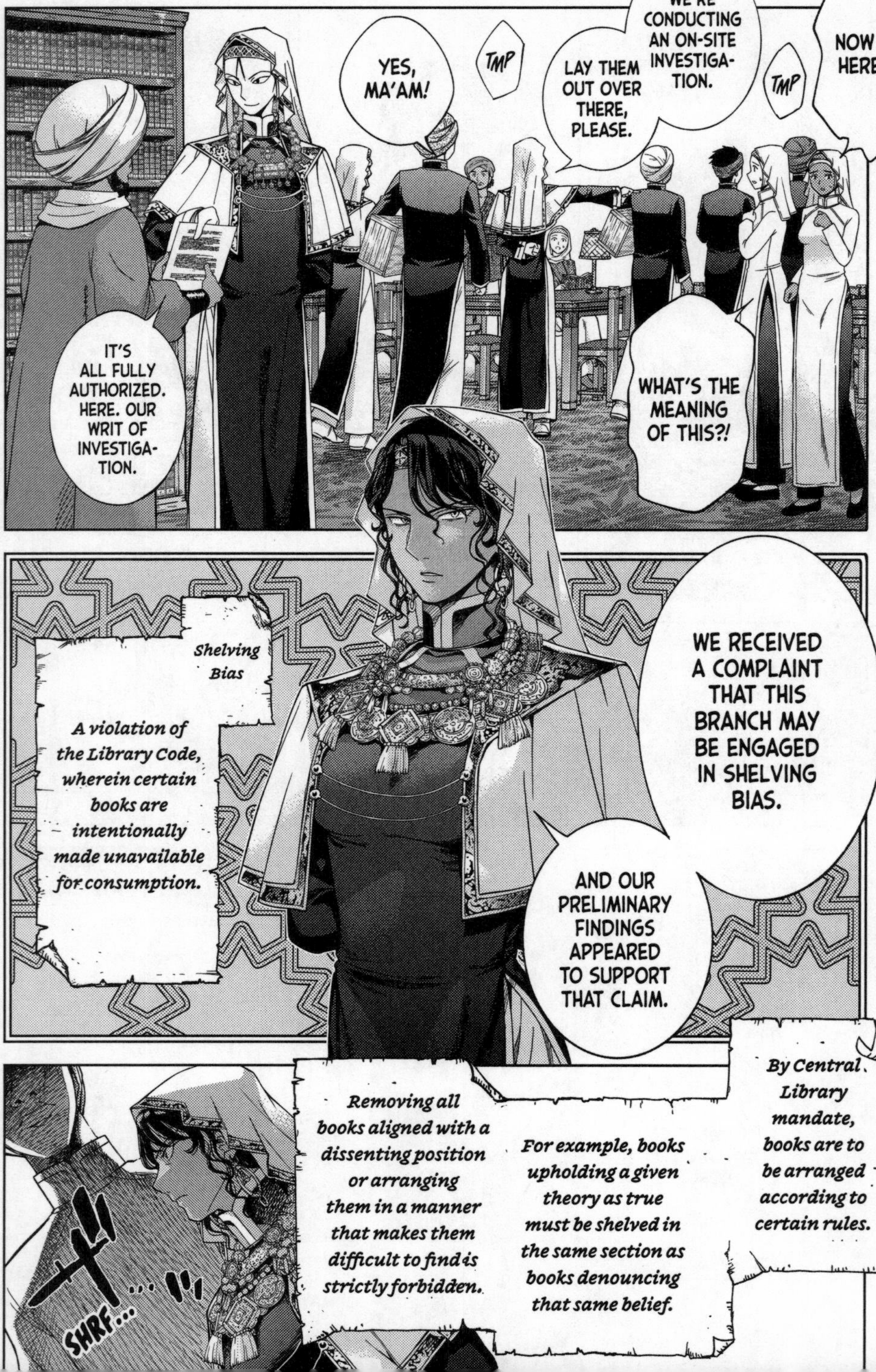
NOW SEE HERE...!
TMP
WE'RE CONDUCTING AN ON-SITE INVESTIGATION.
LAY THEM OUT OVER THERE, PLEASE.
TMP
YES, MA'AM!
WHAT'S THE MEANING OF THIS?!
IT'S ALL FULLY AUTHORIZED. HERE. OUR WRIT OF INVESTIGATION.
WE RECEIVED A COMPLAINT THAT THIS BRANCH MAY BE ENGAGED IN SHELVING BIAS.
AND OUR PRELIMINARY FINDINGS APPEARED TO SUPPORT THAT CLAIM.
Shelving Bias
A violation of the Library Code, wherein certain books are intentionally made unavailable for consumption.
By Central Library mandate, books are to be arranged according to certain rules.
For example, books upholding a given theory as true must be shelved in the same section as books denouncing that same belief.
Removing all books aligned with a dissenting position or arranging them in a manner that makes them difficult to find is strictly forbidden.
SHRF...

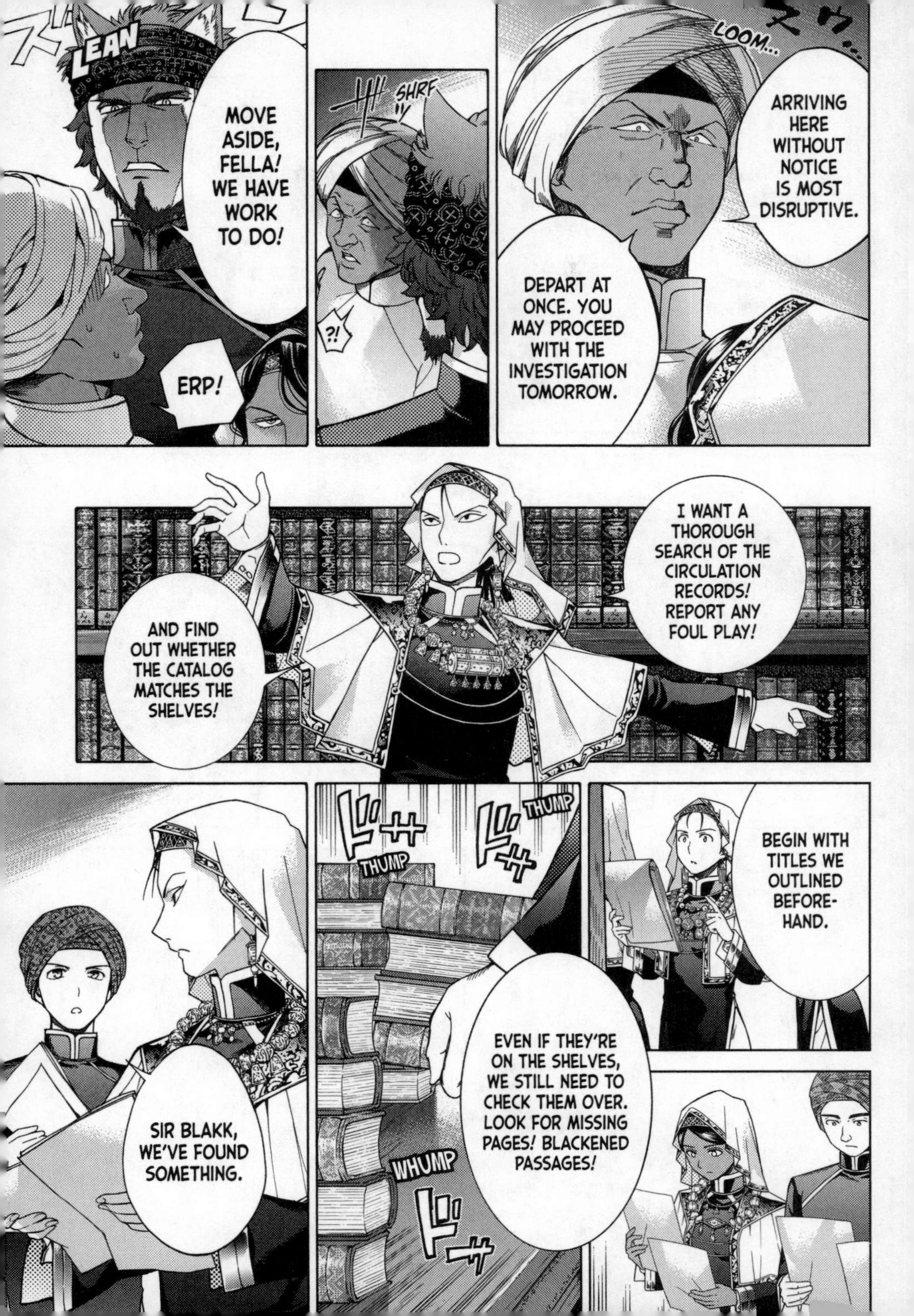
LOOM...
ARRIVING HERE WITHOUT NOTICE IS MOST DISRUPTIVE.
DEPART AT ONCE. YOU MAY PROCEED WITH THE INVESTIGATION TOMORROW.
SHRF
?!
LEAN
MOVE ASIDE, FELLA! WE HAVE WORK TO DO!
ERP!
I WANT A THOROUGH SEARCH OF THE CIRCULATION RECORDS! REPORT ANY FOUL PLAY!
AND FIND OUT WHETHER THE CATALOG MATCHES THE SHELVES!
BEGIN WITH TITLES WE OUTLINED BEFORE-HAND.
THUMP
THUMP
EVEN IF THEY'RE ON THE SHELVES, WE STILL NEED TO CHECK THEM OVER. LOOK FOR MISSING PAGES! BLACKENED PASSAGES!
WHUMP
SIR BLAKK, WE'VE FOUND SOMETHING.

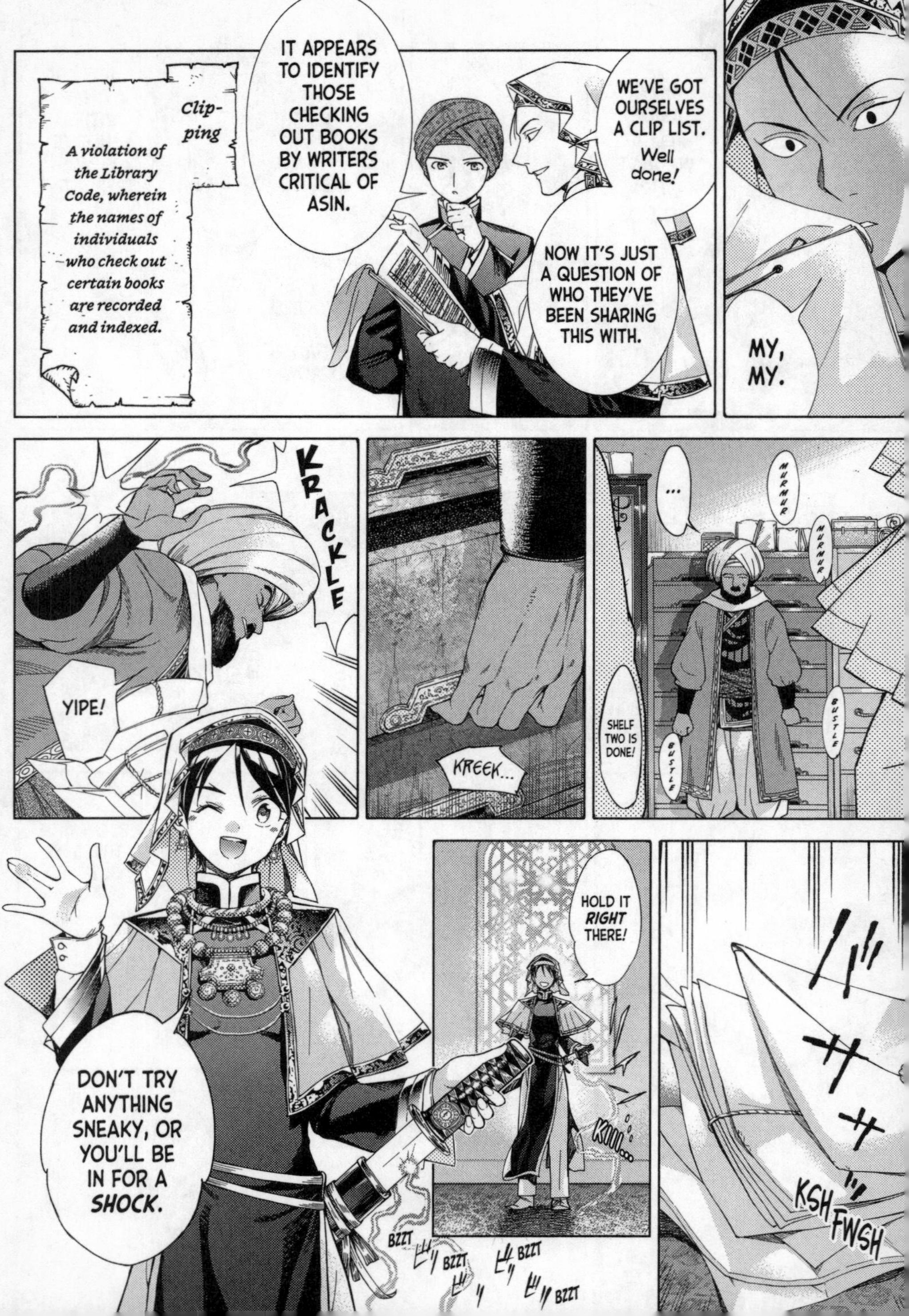
MY, MY.
WE'VE GOT OURSELVES A CLIP LIST.
Well done!
IT APPEARS TO IDENTIFY THOSE CHECKING OUT BOOKS BY WRITERS CRITICAL OF ASIN.
NOW IT'S JUST A QUESTION OF WHO THEY'VE BEEN SHARING THIS WITH.
Clip-ping
A violation of the Library Code, wherein the names of individuals who check out certain books are recorded and indexed.
...
MURMUR
MURMUR
SHELF TWO IS DONE!
BUSTLE
BUSTLE
KREEK...
KRACKLE
YIPE!
KSH
FWSH
HOLD IT RIGHT THERE!
KOOO...
DON'T TRY ANYTHING SNEAKY, OR YOU'LL BE IN FOR A SHOCK.
BZZT
BZZT
BZZT
BZZT

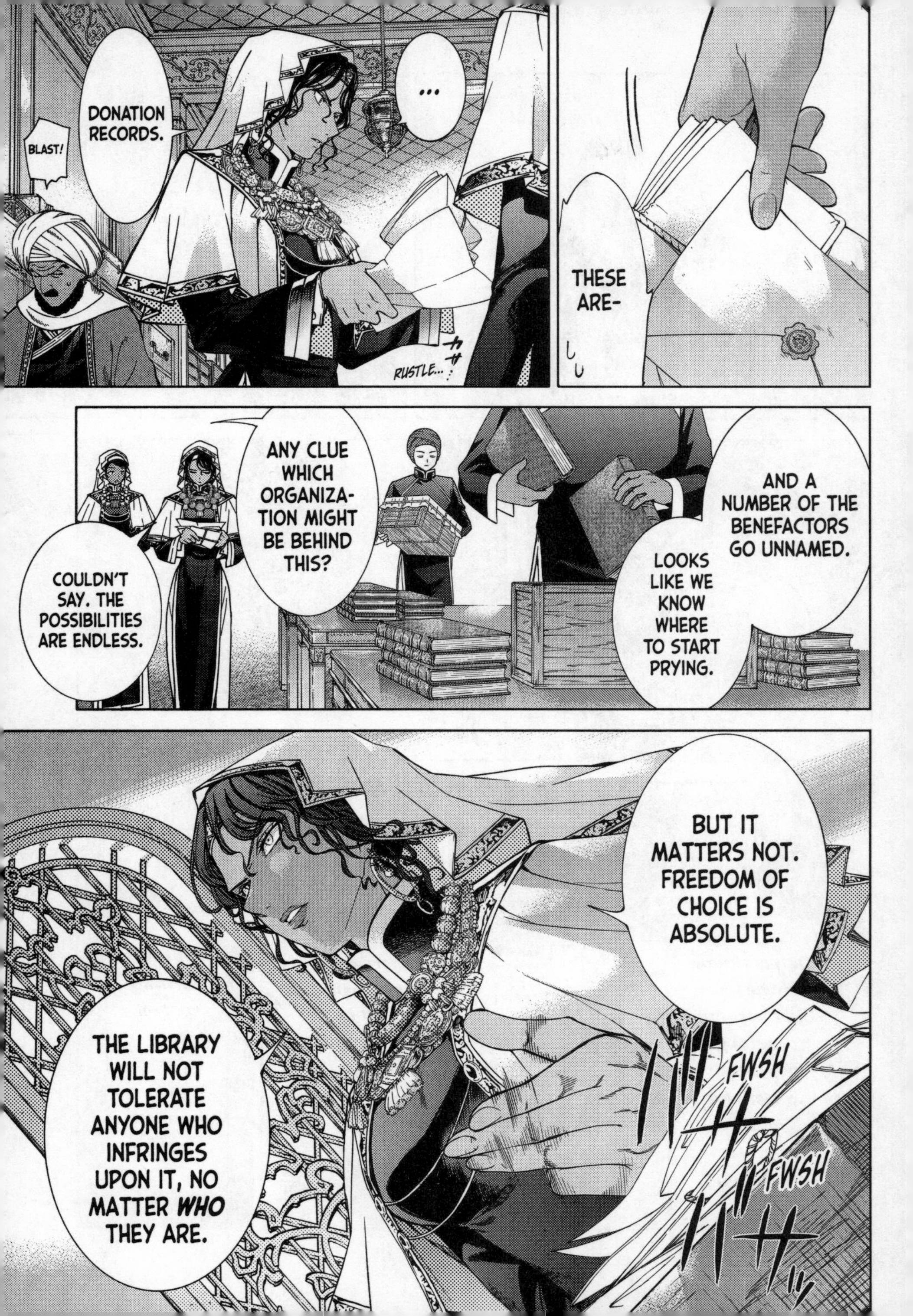
THESE ARE-
...
DONATION RECORDS.
BLAST!
RUSTLE...
AND A NUMBER OF THE BENEFACTORS GO UNNAMED.
LOOKS LIKE WE KNOW WHERE TO START PRYING.
ANY CLUE WHICH ORGANIZATION MIGHT BE BEHIND THIS?
COULDN'T SAY. THE POSSIBILITIES ARE ENDLESS.
BUT IT MATTERS NOT. FREEDOM OF CHOICE IS ABSOLUTE.
THE LIBRARY WILL NOT TOLERATE ANYONE WHO INFRINGES UPON IT, NO MATTER *WHO* THEY ARE.
FWSH
FWSH

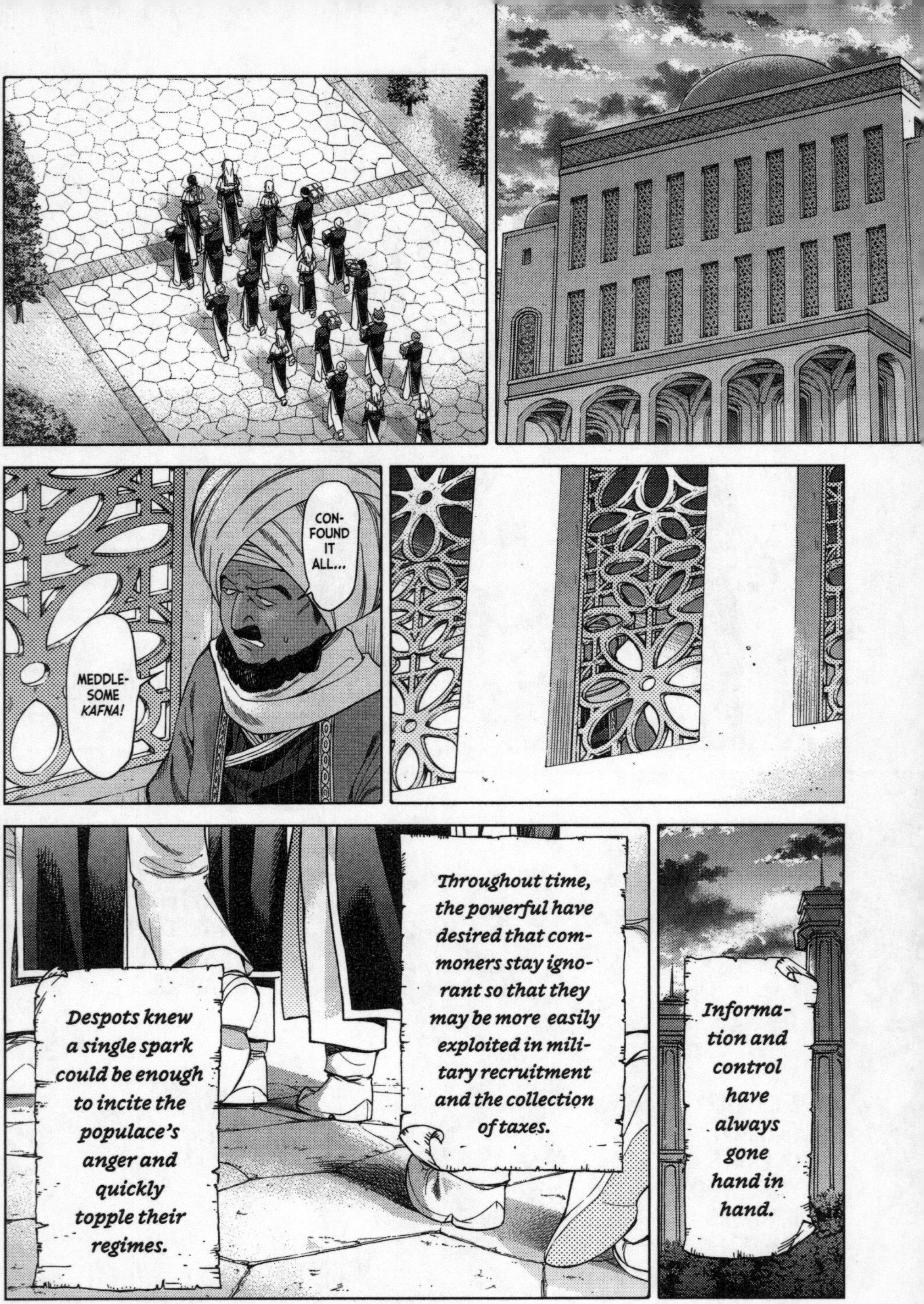
CON-FOUND IT ALL...
MEDDLE-SOME KAFNA!
Informa-tion and control have always gone hand in hand.
Throughout time, the powerful have desired that com-moners stay igno-rant so that they may be more easily exploited in mili-tary recruitment and the collection of taxes.
Despots knew a single spark could be enough to incite the populace's anger and quickly topple their regimes.

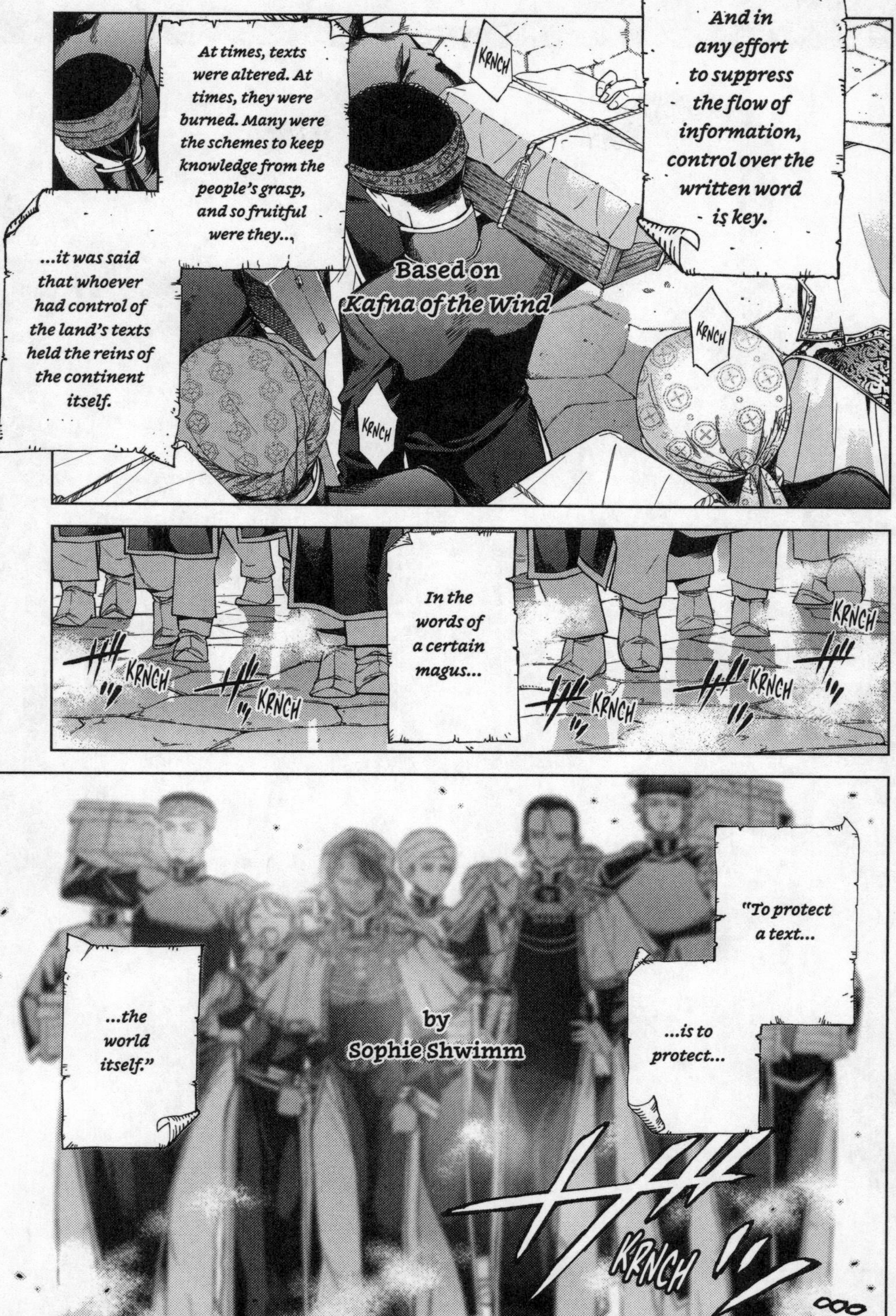
And in any effort to suppress the flow of information, control over the written word is key.
KRNCH
At times, texts were altered. At times, they were burned. Many were the schemes to keep knowledge from the people's grasp, and so fruitful were they...
KRNCH
Based on Kafna of the Wind
...it was said that whoever had control of the land's texts held the reins of the continent itself.
KRNCH
KRNCH
KRNCH
KRNCH
In the words of a certain magus...
KRNCH
KRNCH
"To protect a text...
...is to protect...
KRNCH
by Sophie Shwimm
...the world itself."

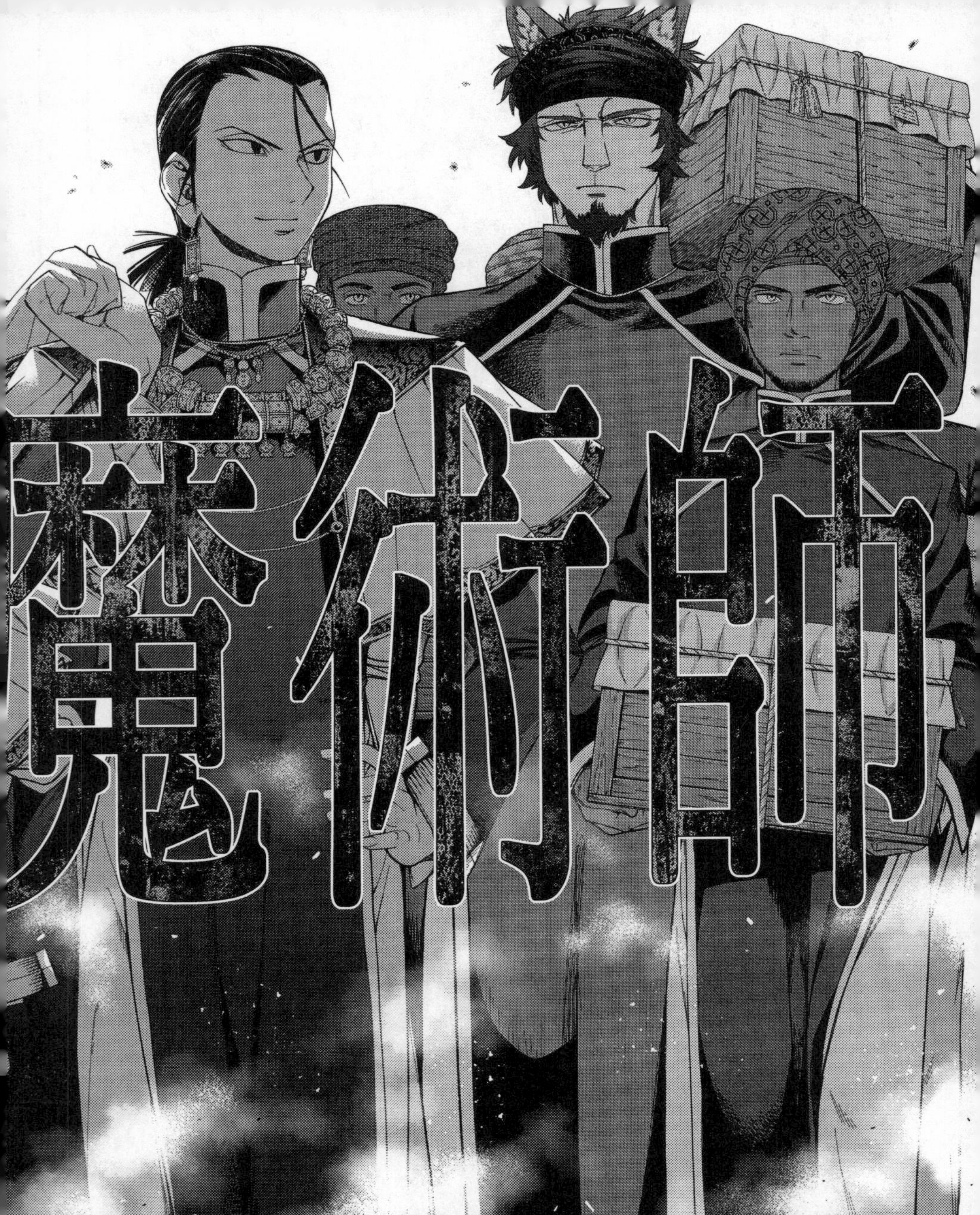
魔術師

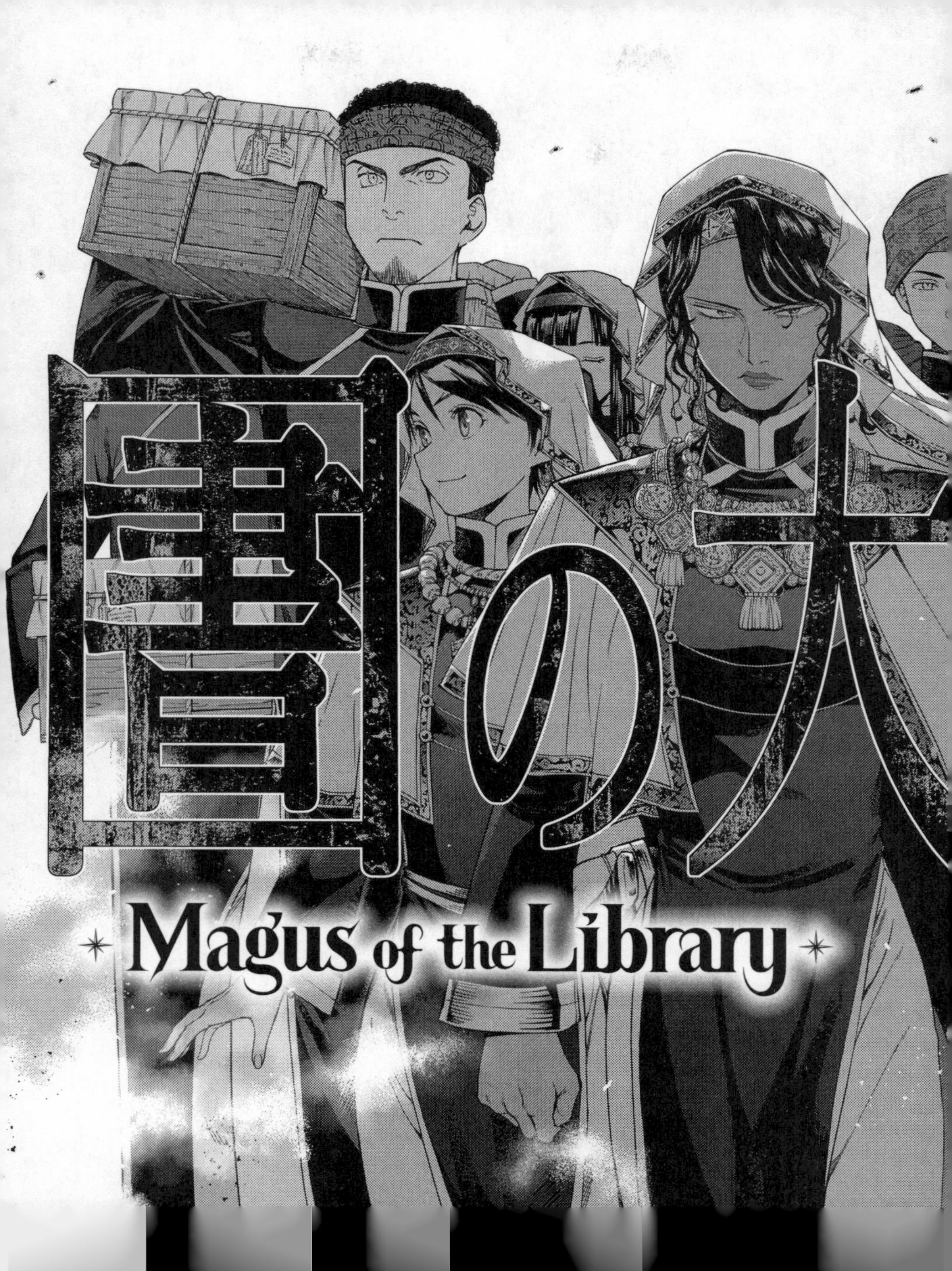
圕の大
Magus of the Library

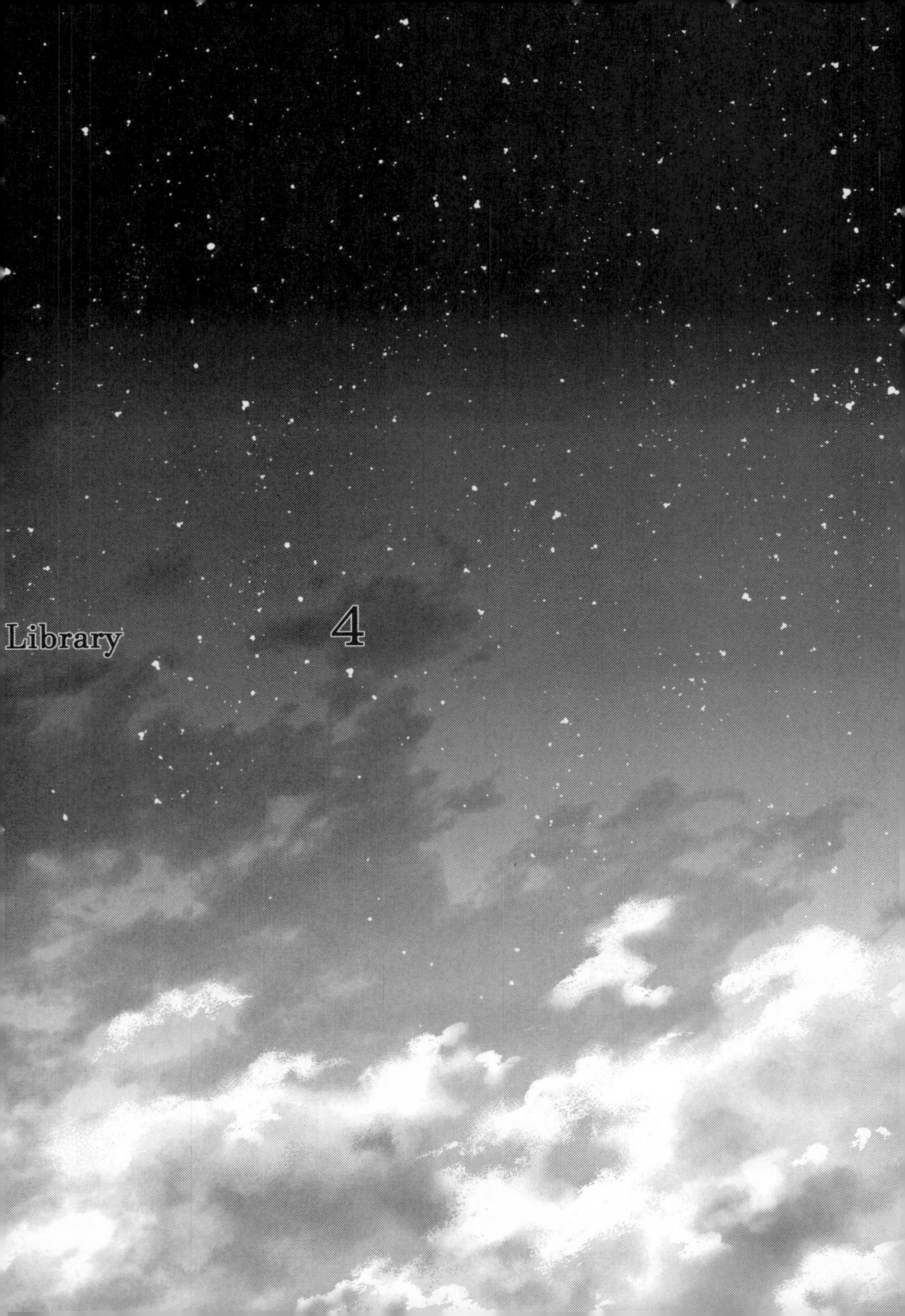
Library
4

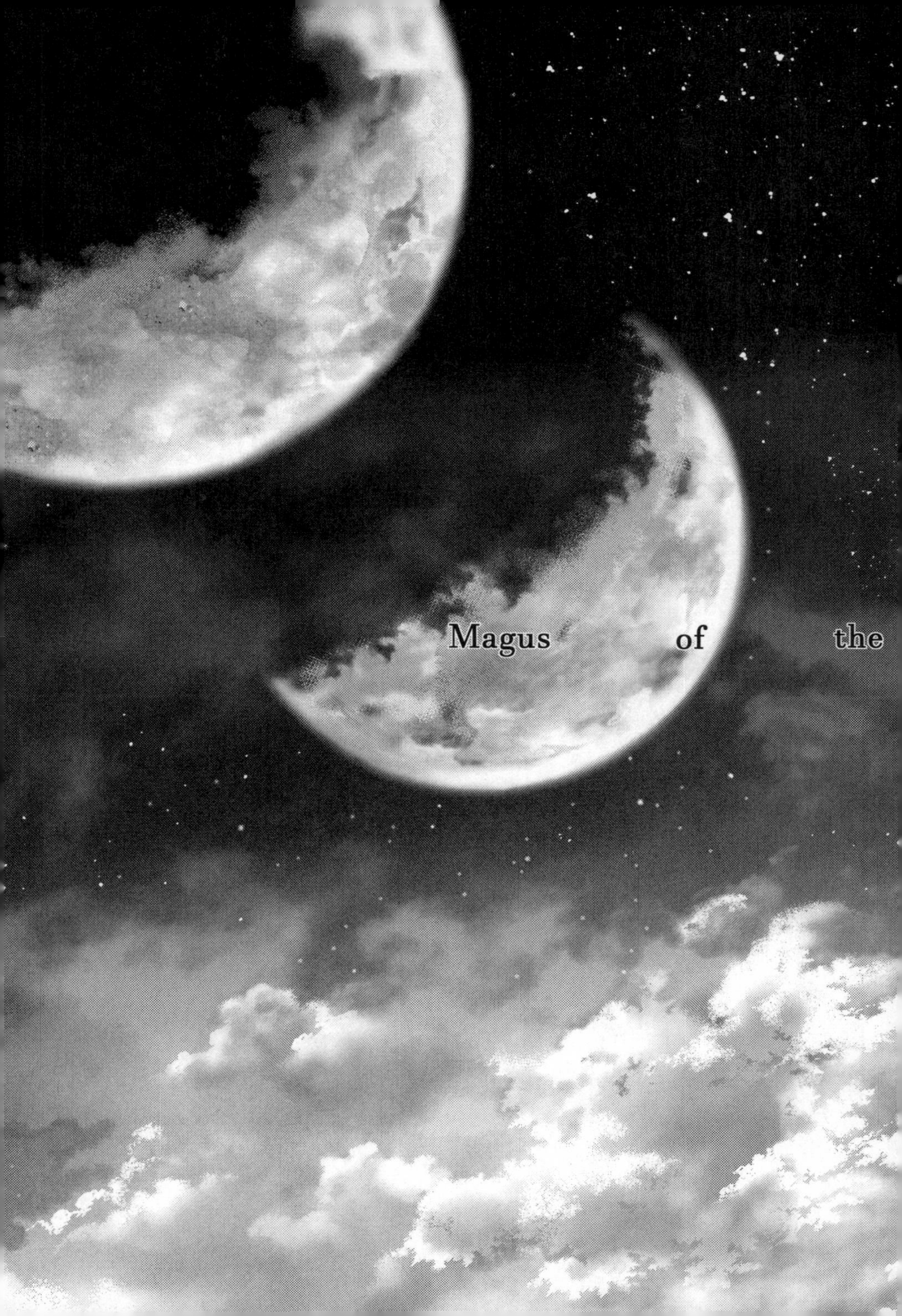
Magus of the

[redacted]

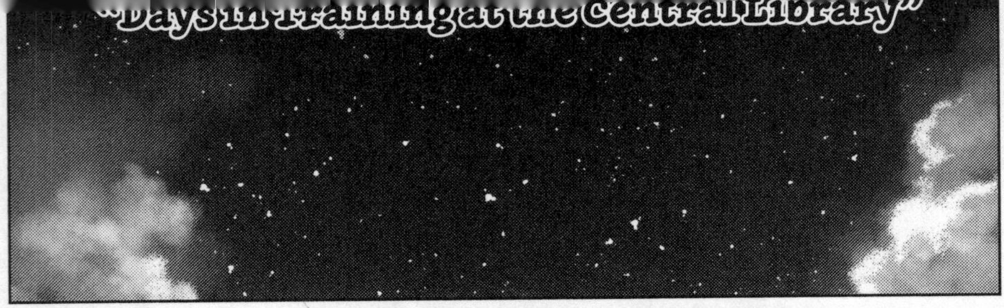

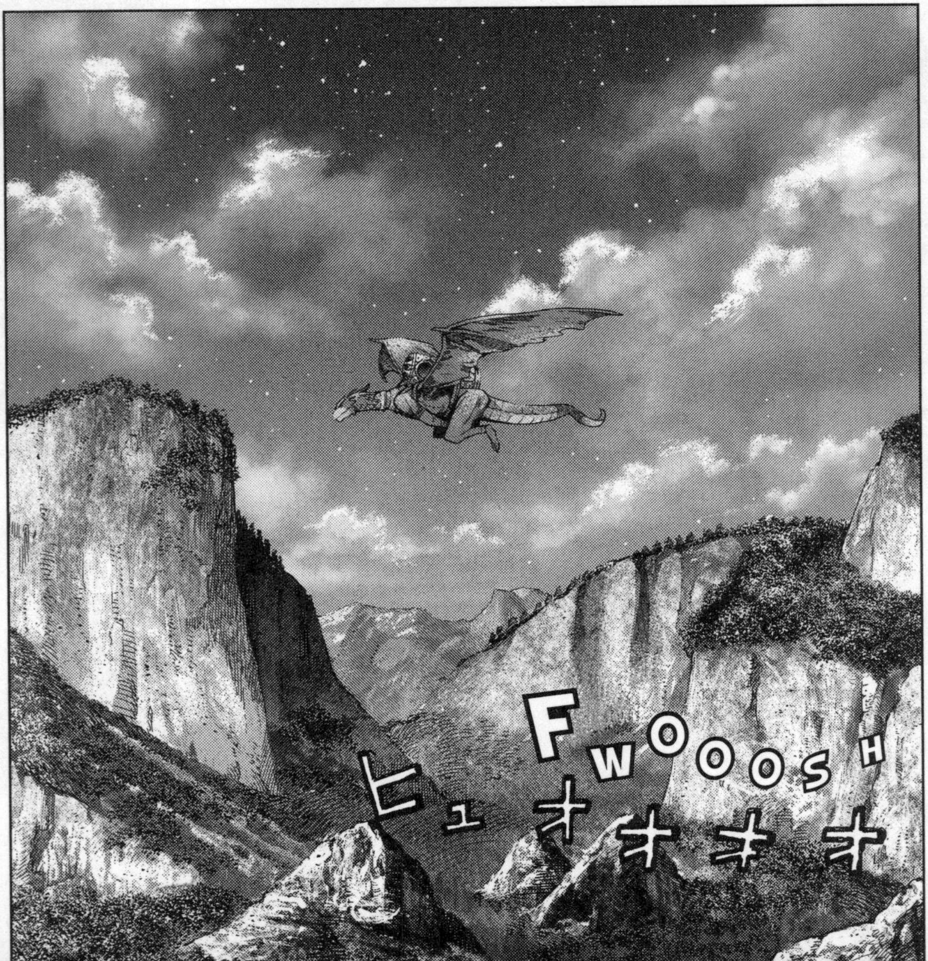
ヒュオオオオ
FWOOOSH

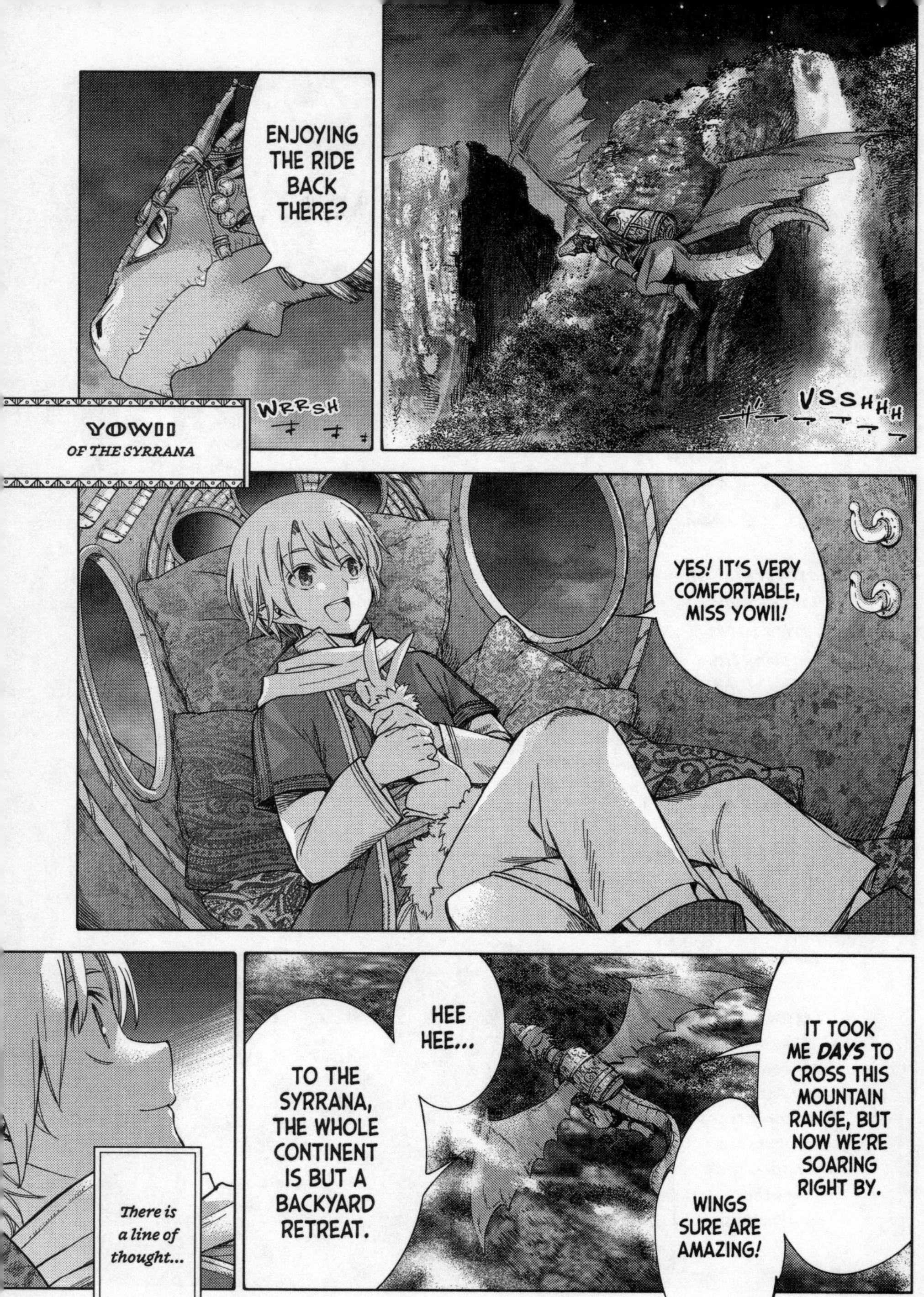
VSSHHH
ENJOYING THE RIDE BACK THERE?
WRRSH
YOWII
OF THE SYRRANA
YES! IT'S VERY COMFORTABLE, MISS YOWII!
IT TOOK ME *DAYS* TO CROSS THIS MOUNTAIN RANGE, BUT NOW WE'RE SOARING RIGHT BY.
WINGS SURE ARE AMAZING!
HEE HEE...
TO THE SYRRANA, THE WHOLE CONTINENT IS BUT A BACKYARD RETREAT.
There is a line of thought...

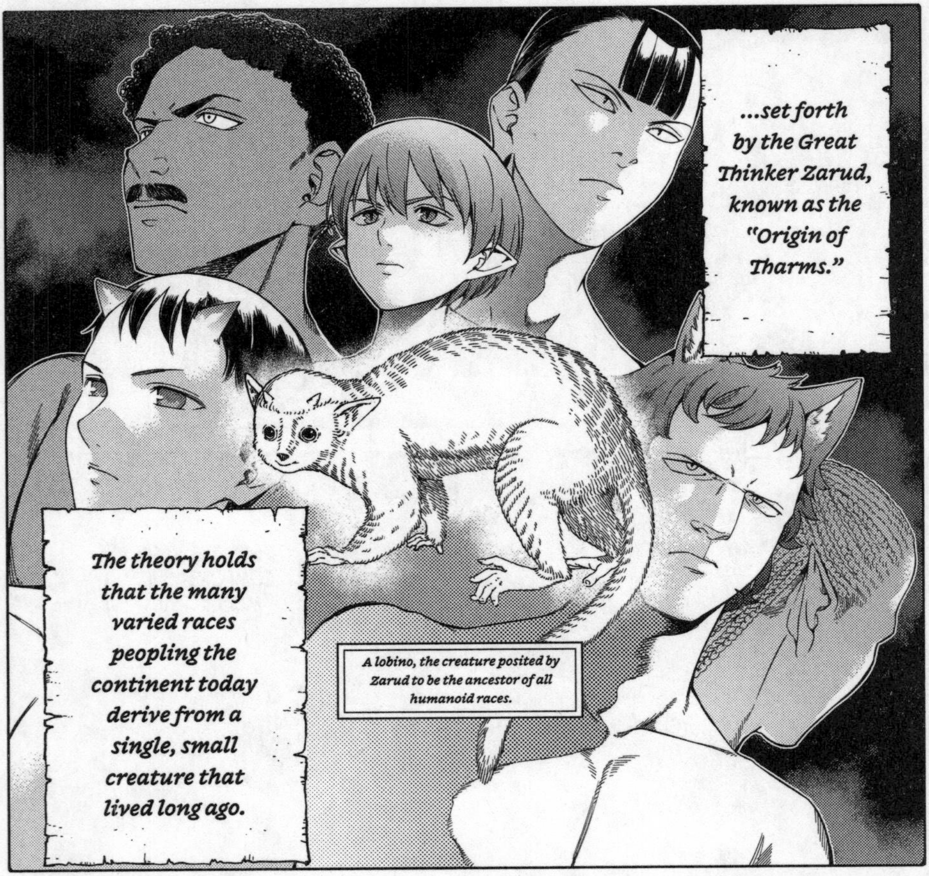
...set forth by the Great Thinker Zarud, known as the "Origin of Tharms."
The theory holds that the many varied races peopling the continent today derive from a single, small creature that lived long ago.
A lobino, the creature posited by Zarud to be the ancestor of all humanoid races.

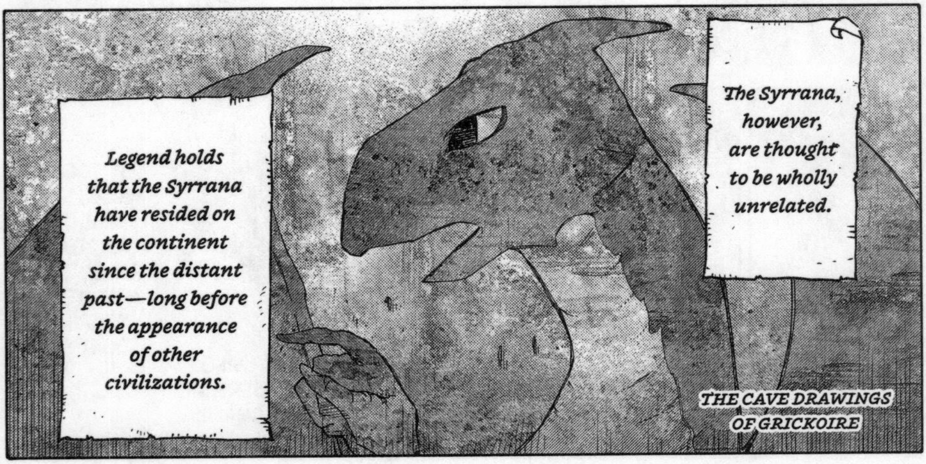
The Syrrana, however, are thought to be wholly unrelated.
Legend holds that the Syrrana have resided on the continent since the distant past—long before the appearance of other civilizations.
THE CAVE DRAWINGS OF GRICKOIRE

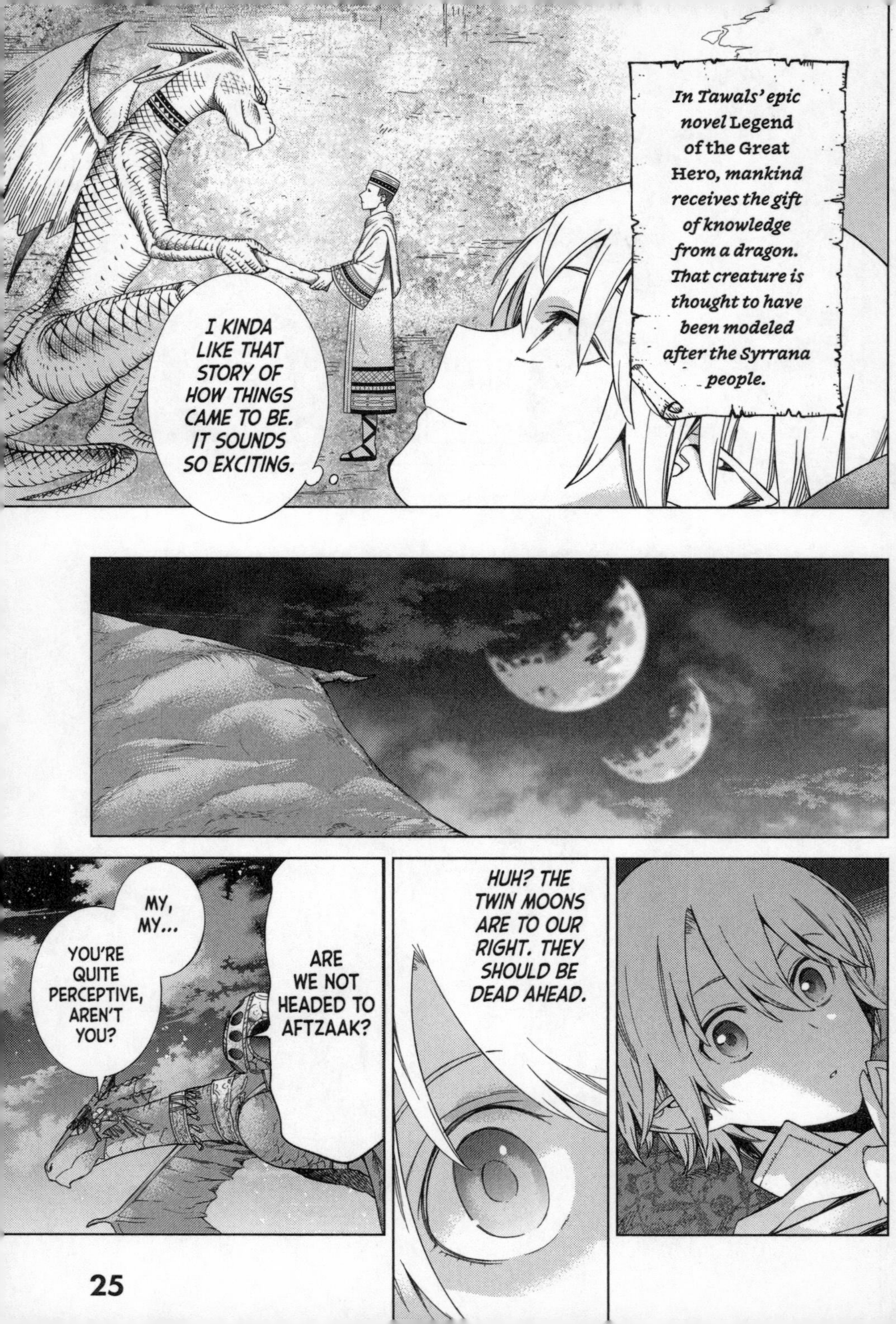
In Tawals' epic novel Legend of the Great Hero, mankind receives the gift of knowledge from a dragon. That creature is thought to have been modeled after the Syrrana people.
I KINDA LIKE THAT STORY OF HOW THINGS CAME TO BE. IT SOUNDS SO EXCITING.
HUH? THE TWIN MOONS ARE TO OUR RIGHT. THEY SHOULD BE DEAD AHEAD.
ARE WE NOT HEADED TO AFTZAAK?
MY, MY...
YOU'RE QUITE PERCEPTIVE, AREN'T YOU?

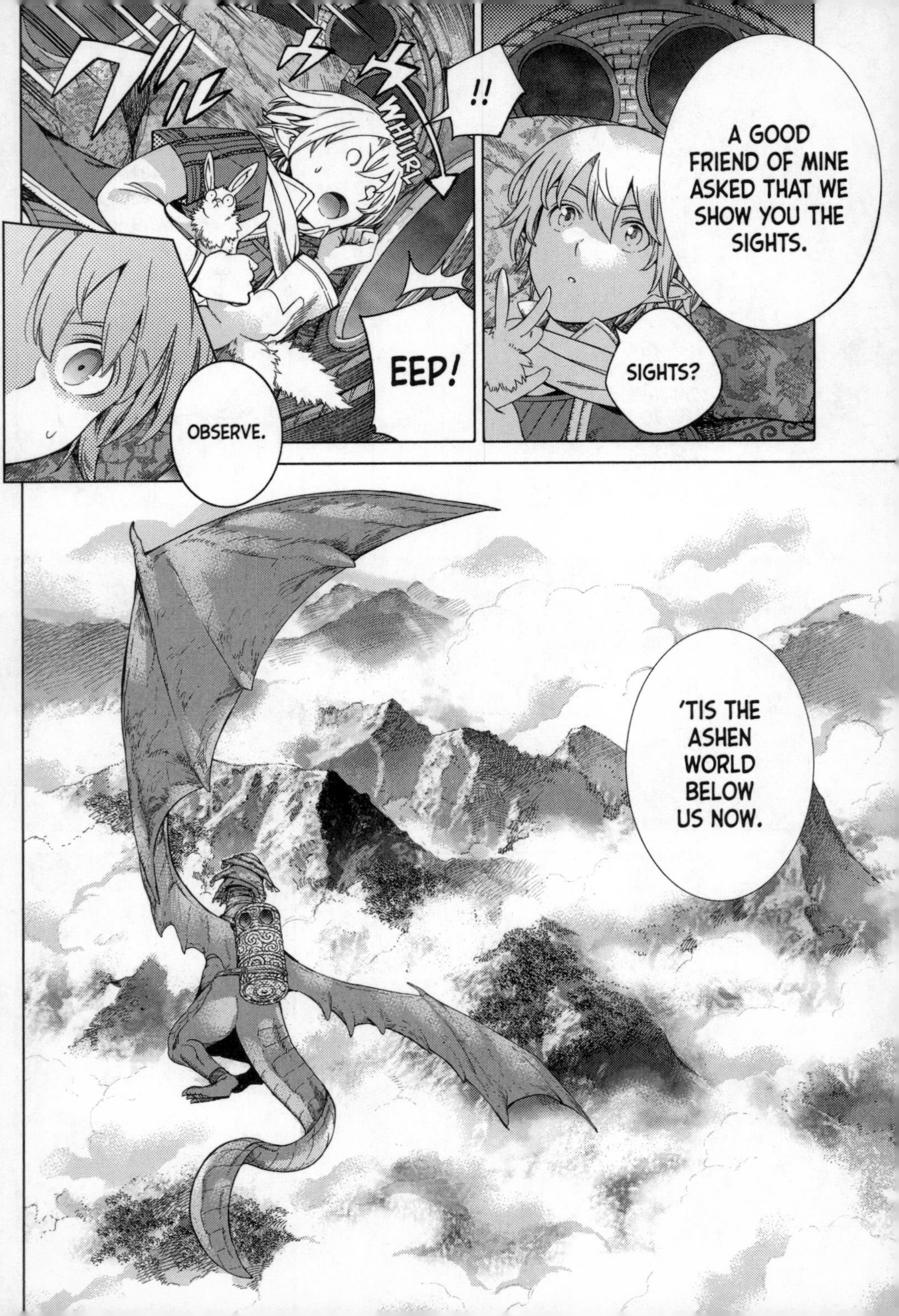
A GOOD FRIEND OF MINE ASKED THAT WE SHOW YOU THE SIGHTS.
SIGHTS?
!!
WHIIRL
EEP!
OBSERVE.
'TIS THE ASHEN WORLD BELOW US NOW.

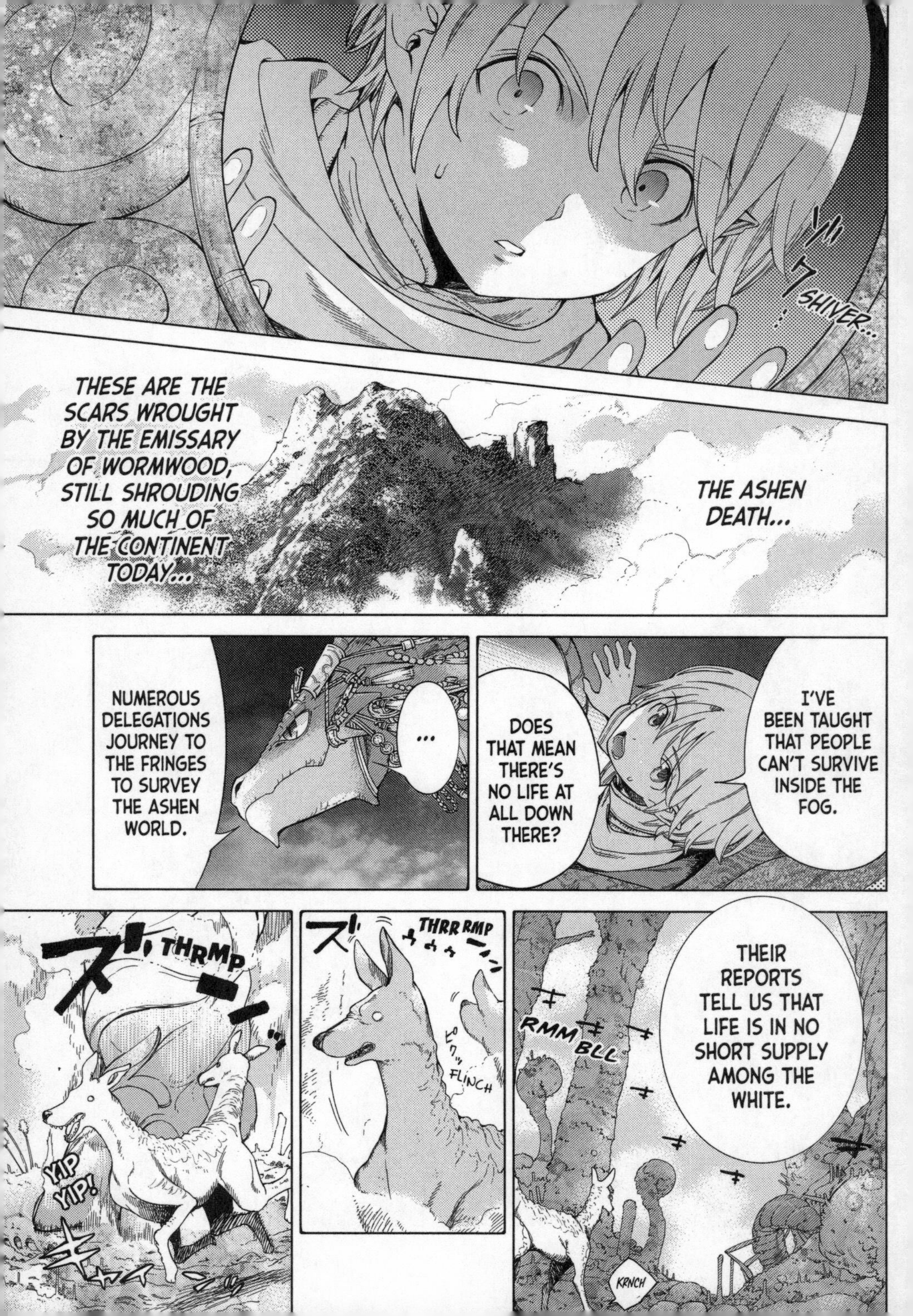
SHIVER...
THESE ARE THE SCARS WROUGHT BY THE EMISSARY OF WORMWOOD, STILL SHROUDING SO MUCH OF THE CONTINENT TODAY...
THE ASHEN DEATH...
I'VE BEEN TAUGHT THAT PEOPLE CAN'T SURVIVE INSIDE THE FOG.
DOES THAT MEAN THERE'S NO LIFE AT ALL DOWN THERE?
...
NUMEROUS DELEGATIONS JOURNEY TO THE FRINGES TO SURVEY THE ASHEN WORLD.
THEIR REPORTS TELL US THAT LIFE IS IN NO SHORT SUPPLY AMONG THE WHITE.
RMM BLL
KRNCH
THRR RMP
FLINCH
THRMP
YIP YIP!

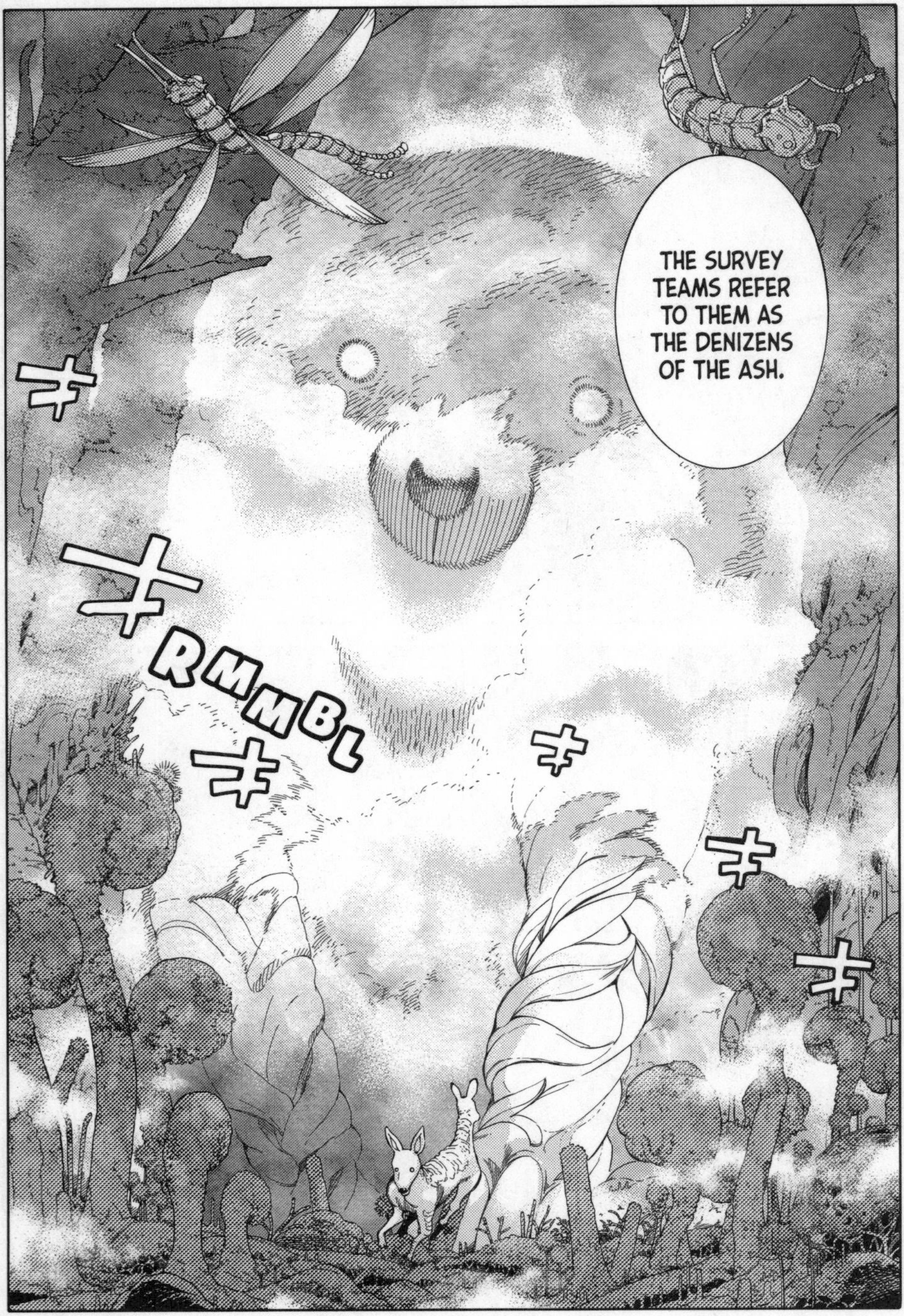
THE SURVEY TEAMS REFER TO THEM AS THE DENIZENS OF THE ASH.
RMMBL

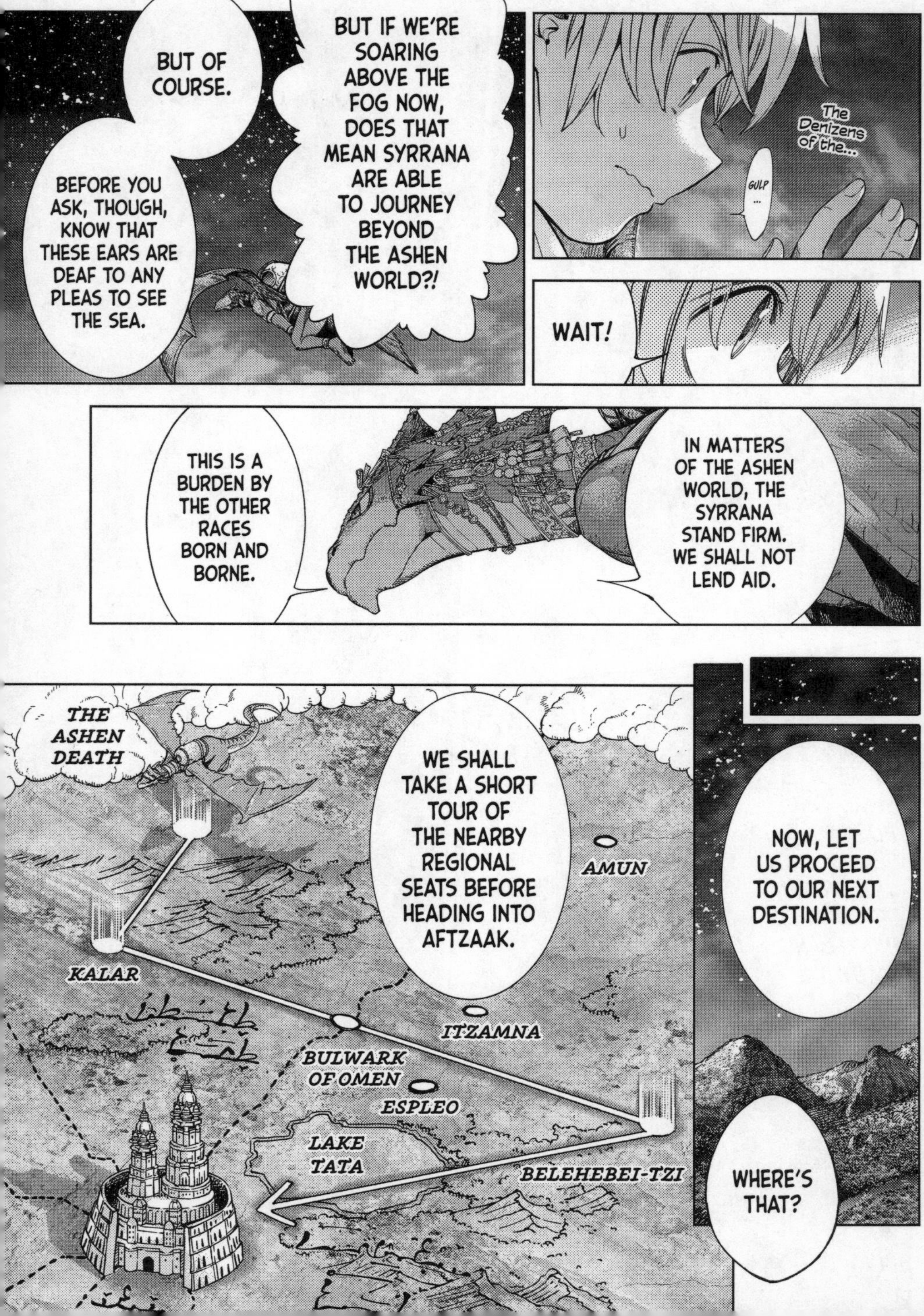
The Denizens of the...
GULP ...
WAIT!
BUT IF WE'RE SOARING ABOVE THE FOG NOW, DOES THAT MEAN SYRRANA ARE ABLE TO JOURNEY BEYOND THE ASHEN WORLD?!
BUT OF COURSE.
BEFORE YOU ASK, THOUGH, KNOW THAT THESE EARS ARE DEAF TO ANY PLEAS TO SEE THE SEA.
IN MATTERS OF THE ASHEN WORLD, THE SYRRANA STAND FIRM. WE SHALL NOT LEND AID.
THIS IS A BURDEN BY THE OTHER RACES BORN AND BORNE.
NOW, LET US PROCEED TO OUR NEXT DESTINATION.
WHERE'S THAT?
WE SHALL TAKE A SHORT TOUR OF THE NEARBY REGIONAL SEATS BEFORE HEADING INTO AFTZAAK.
THE ASHEN DEATH
AMUN
KALAR
ITZAMNA
BULWARK OF OMEN
ESPLEO
LAKE TATA
BELEHEBEI-TZI

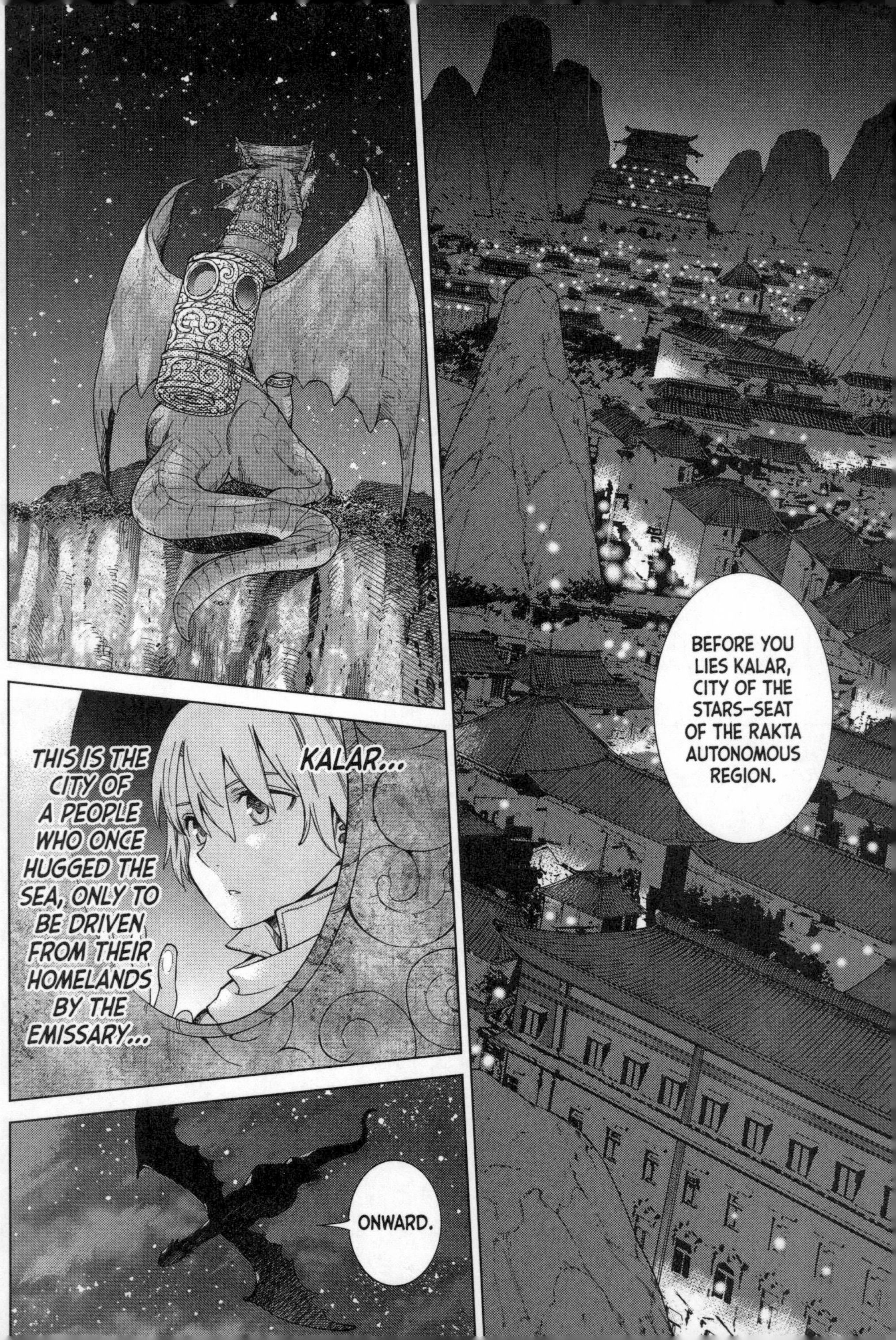
BEFORE YOU LIES KALAR, CITY OF THE STARS—SEAT OF THE RAKTA AUTONOMOUS REGION.
KALAR...
THIS IS THE CITY OF A PEOPLE WHO ONCE HUGGED THE SEA, ONLY TO BE DRIVEN FROM THEIR HOMELANDS BY THE EMISSARY...
ONWARD.

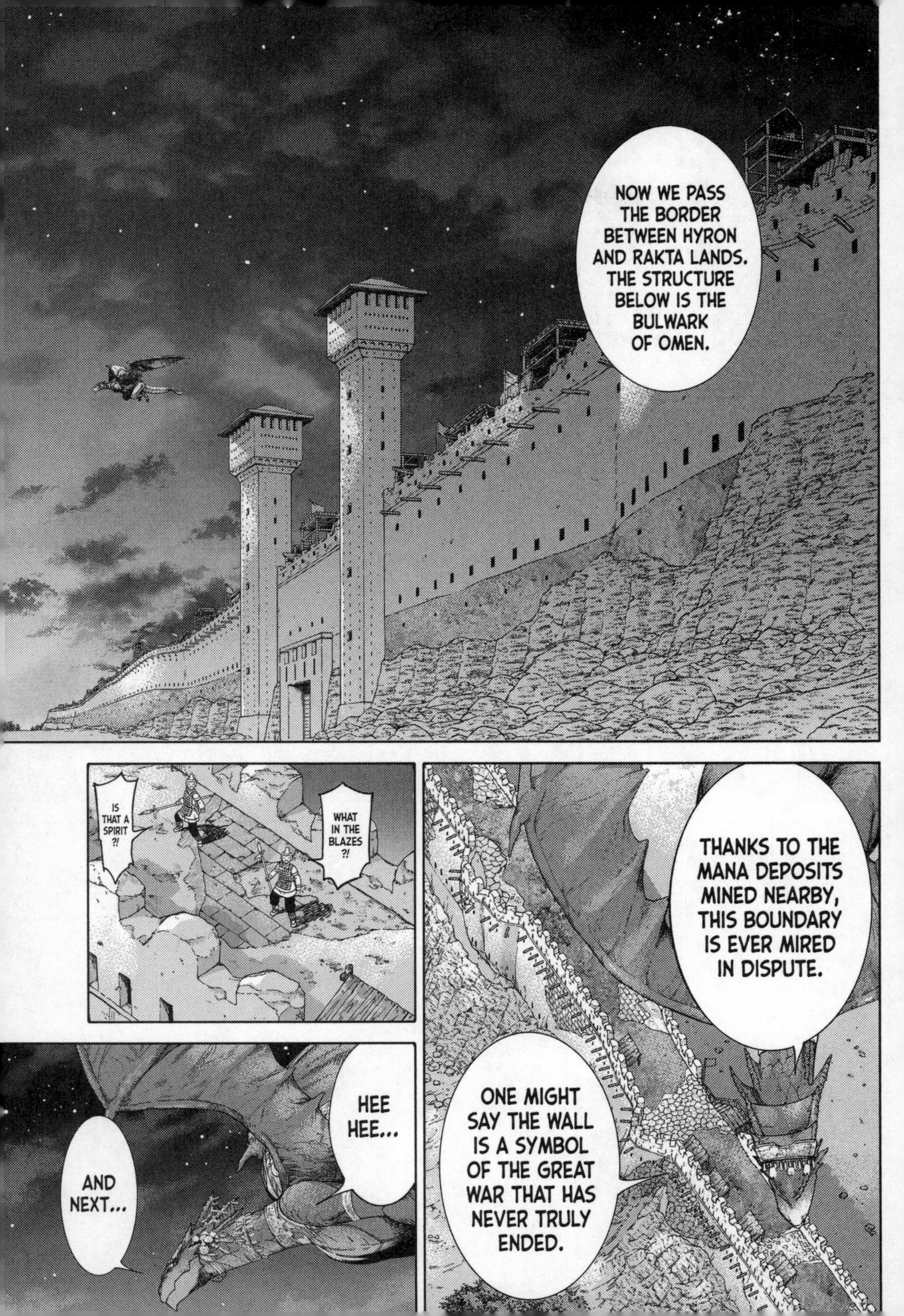
NOW WE PASS THE BORDER BETWEEN HYRON AND RAKTA LANDS. THE STRUCTURE BELOW IS THE BULWARK OF OMEN.
THANKS TO THE MANA DEPOSITS MINED NEARBY, THIS BOUNDARY IS EVER MIRED IN DISPUTE.
ONE MIGHT SAY THE WALL IS A SYMBOL OF THE GREAT WAR THAT HAS NEVER TRULY ENDED.
WHAT IN THE BLAZES ?!
IS THAT A SPIRIT ?!
HEE HEE...
AND NEXT...

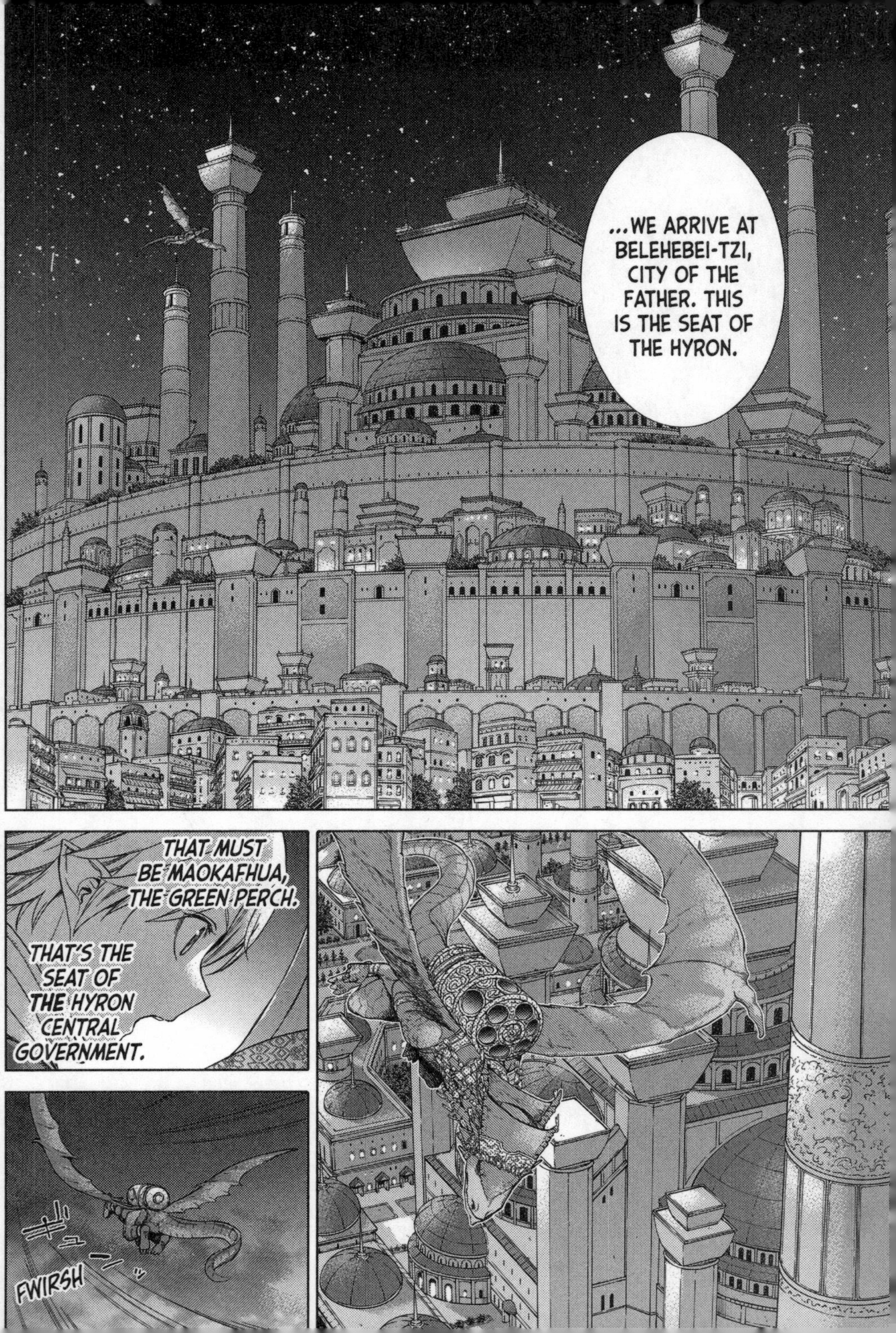
...WE ARRIVE AT BELEHEBEI-TZI, CITY OF THE FATHER. THIS IS THE SEAT OF THE HYRON.
THAT MUST BE MAOKAFHUA, THE GREEN PERCH.
THAT'S THE SEAT OF THE HYRON CENTRAL GOVERNMENT.
FWIRSH

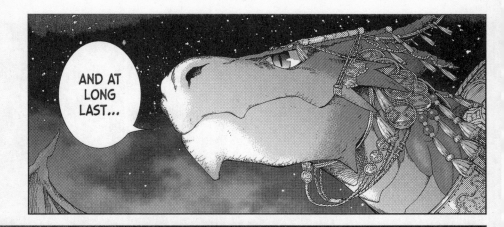

AND AT LONG LAST...

AFTZAAK, THE CITY OF BOOKS.

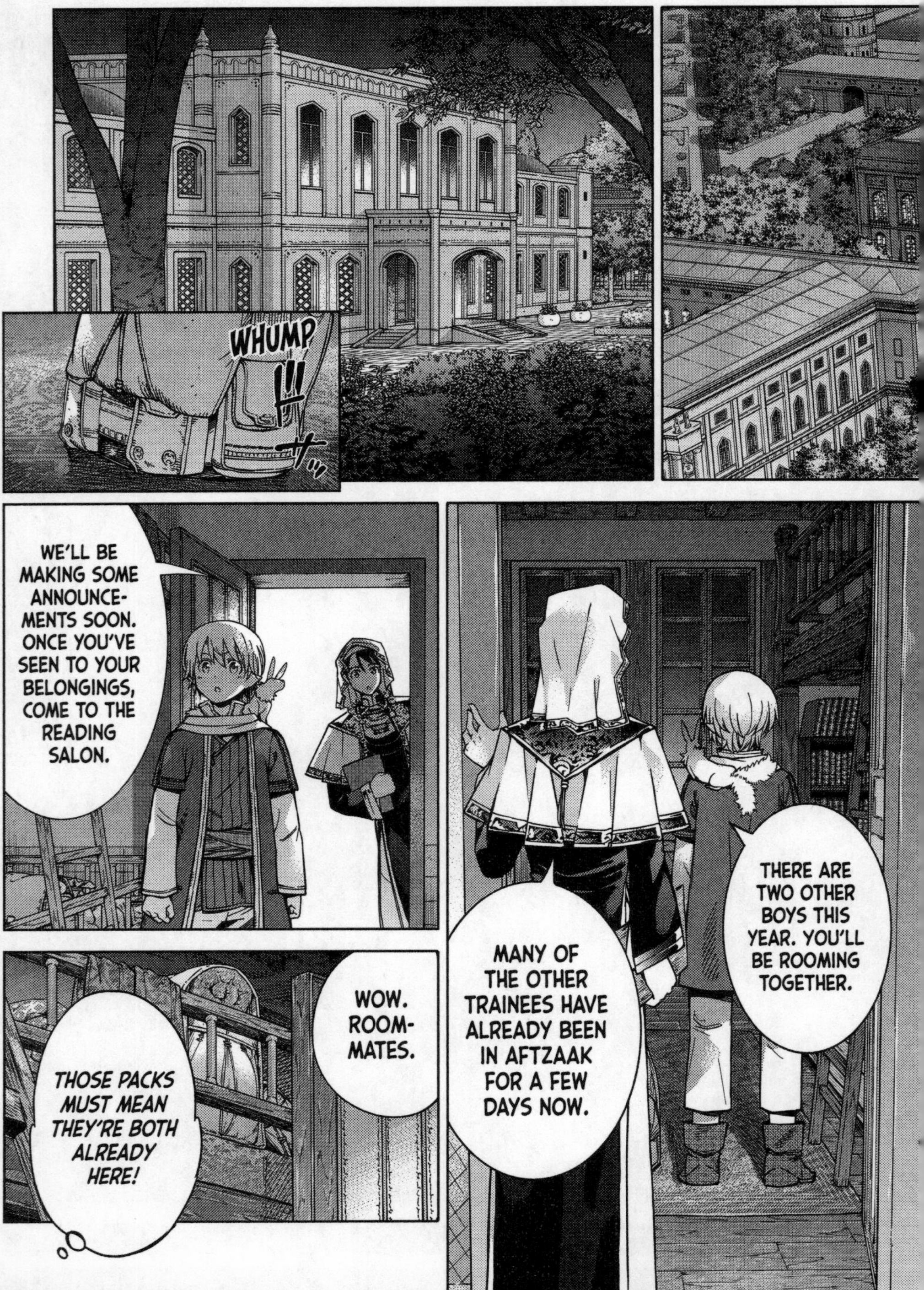
WHUMP
THERE ARE TWO OTHER BOYS THIS YEAR. YOU'LL BE ROOMING TOGETHER.
MANY OF THE OTHER TRAINEES HAVE ALREADY BEEN IN AFTZAAK FOR A FEW DAYS NOW.
WE'LL BE MAKING SOME ANNOUNCE-MENTS SOON. ONCE YOU'VE SEEN TO YOUR BELONGINGS, COME TO THE READING SALON.
WOW. ROOM-MATES.
THOSE PACKS MUST MEAN THEY'RE BOTH ALREADY HERE!

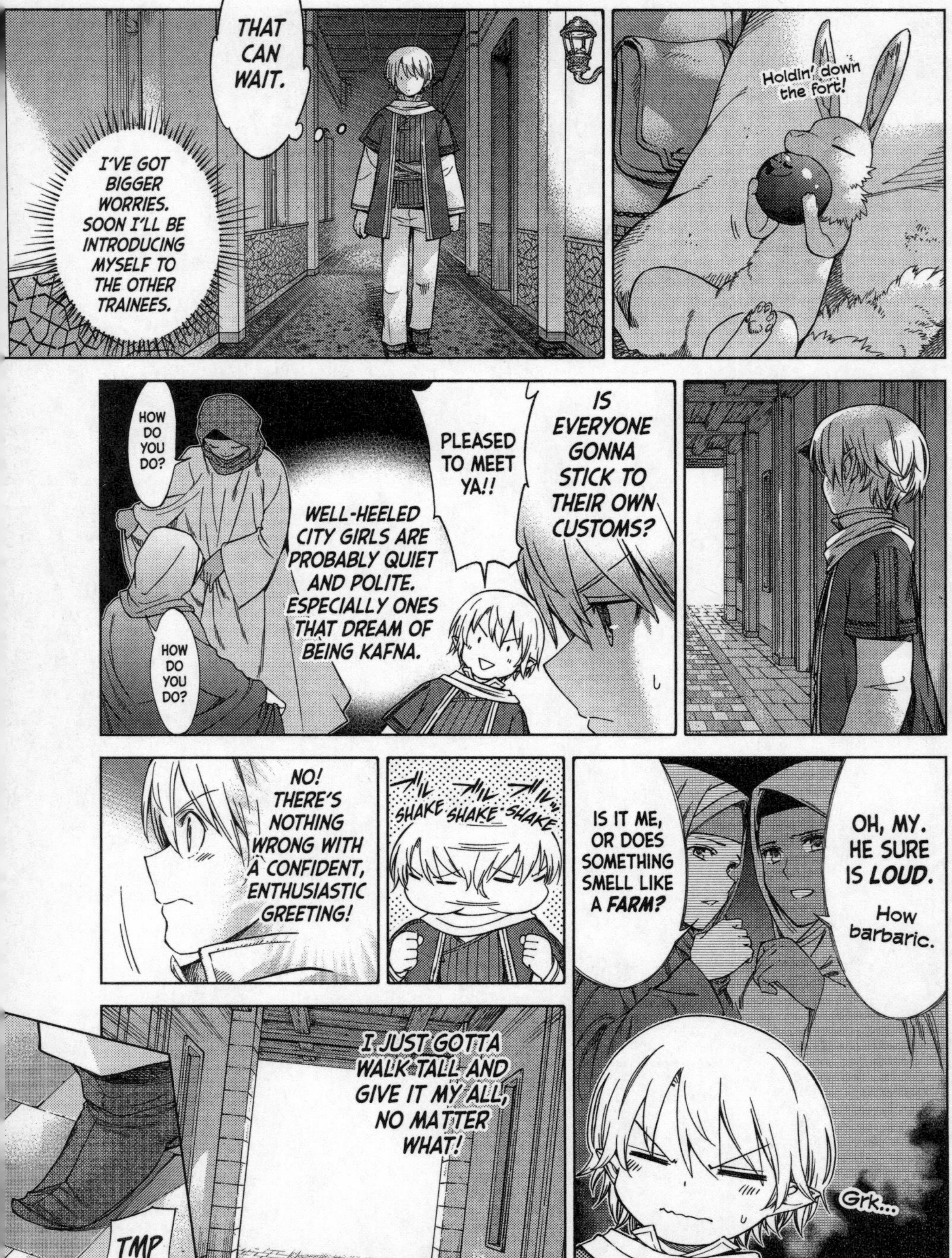
Holdin' down the fort!
THAT CAN WAIT.
I'VE GOT BIGGER WORRIES. SOON I'LL BE INTRODUCING MYSELF TO THE OTHER TRAINEES.
IS EVERYONE GONNA STICK TO THEIR OWN CUSTOMS?
PLEASED TO MEET YA!!
WELL-HEELED CITY GIRLS ARE PROBABLY QUIET AND POLITE. ESPECIALLY ONES THAT DREAM OF BEING KAFNA.
HOW DO YOU DO?
HOW DO YOU DO?
OH, MY. HE SURE IS **LOUD**.
How barbaric.
IS IT ME, OR DOES SOMETHING SMELL LIKE A **FARM**?
SHAKE SHAKE SHAKE
NO! THERE'S NOTHING WRONG WITH A CONFIDENT, ENTHUSIASTIC GREETING!
Grk...
I JUST GOTTA WALK TALL AND GIVE IT MY ALL, NO MATTER WHAT!
TMP

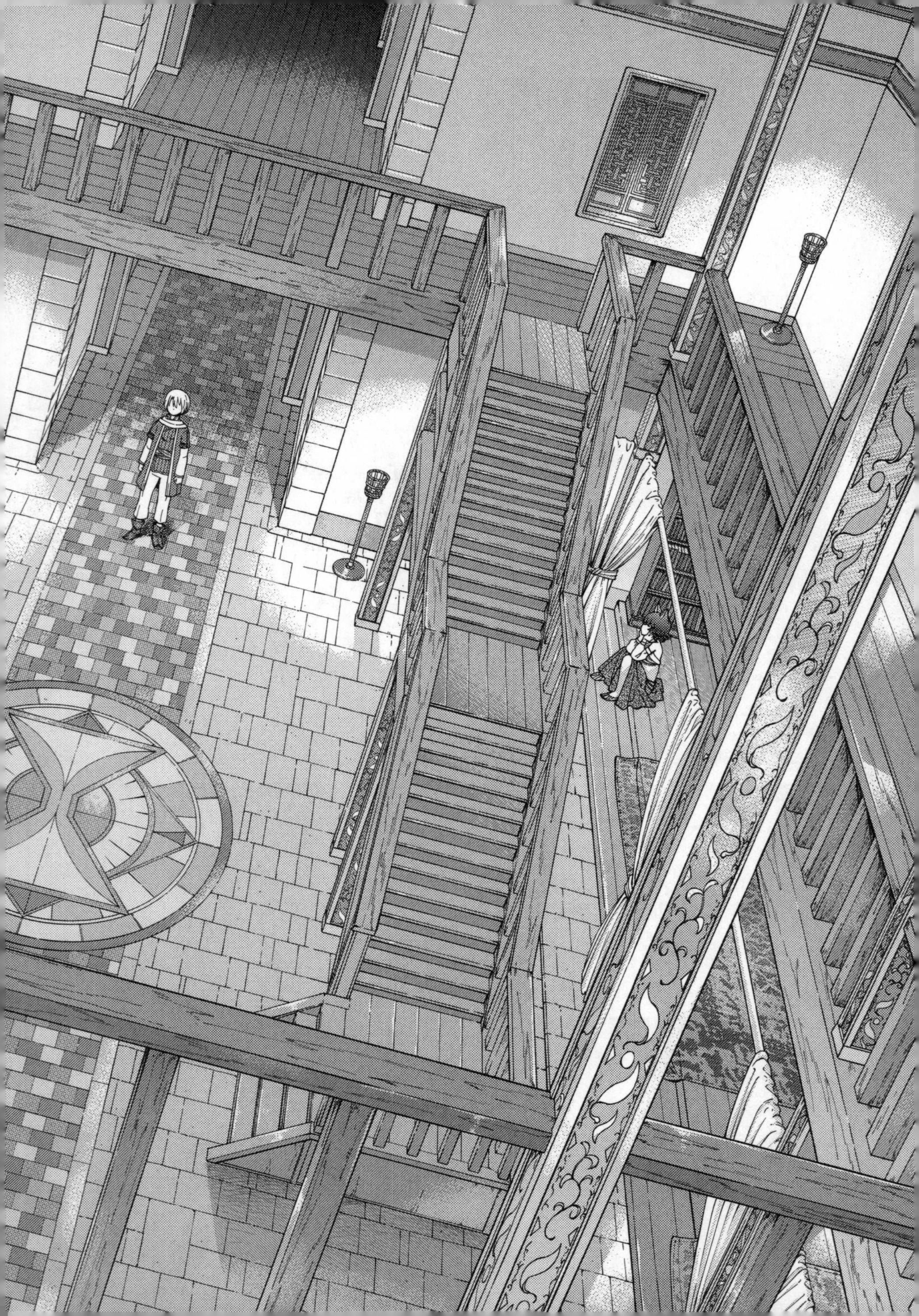

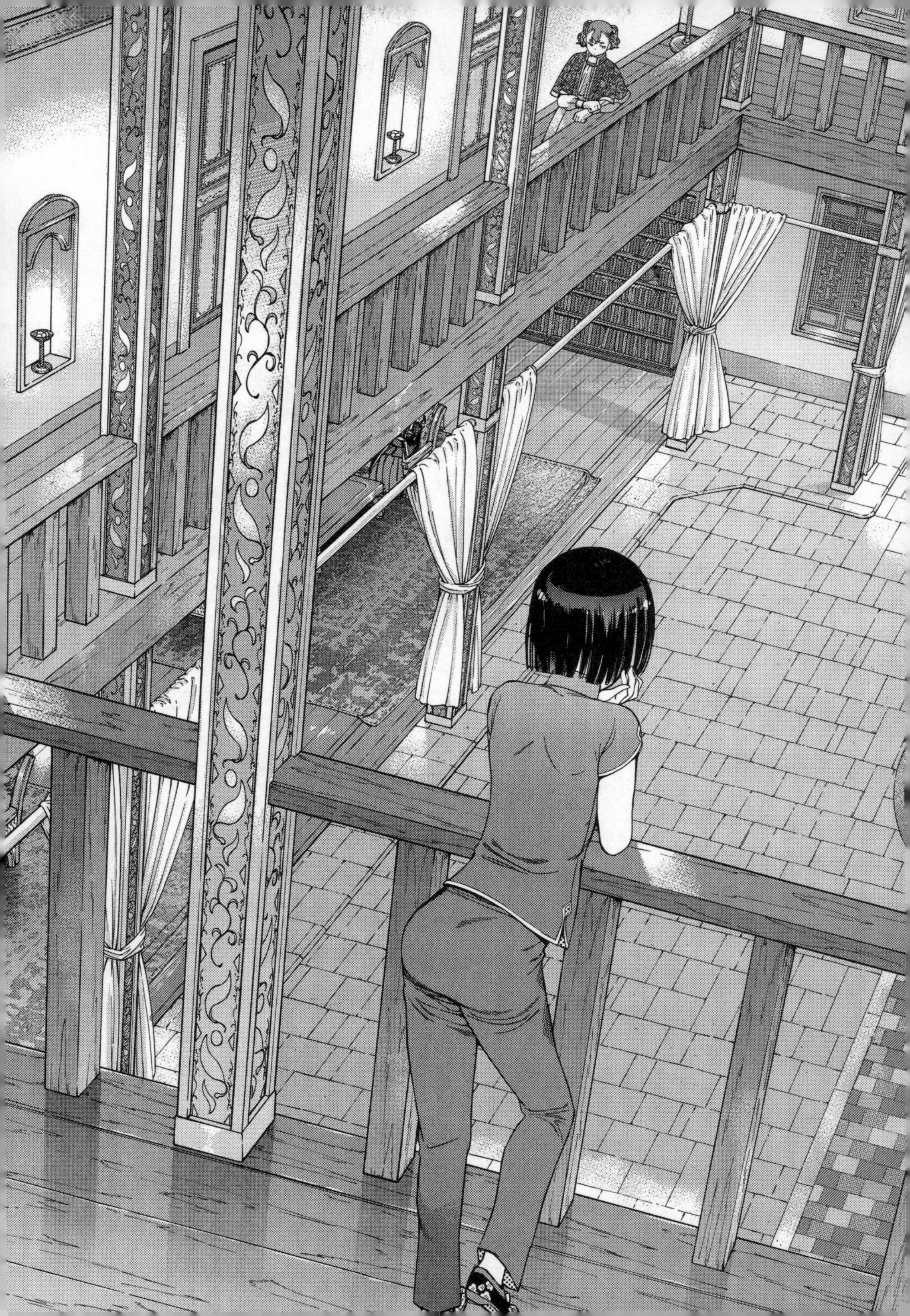

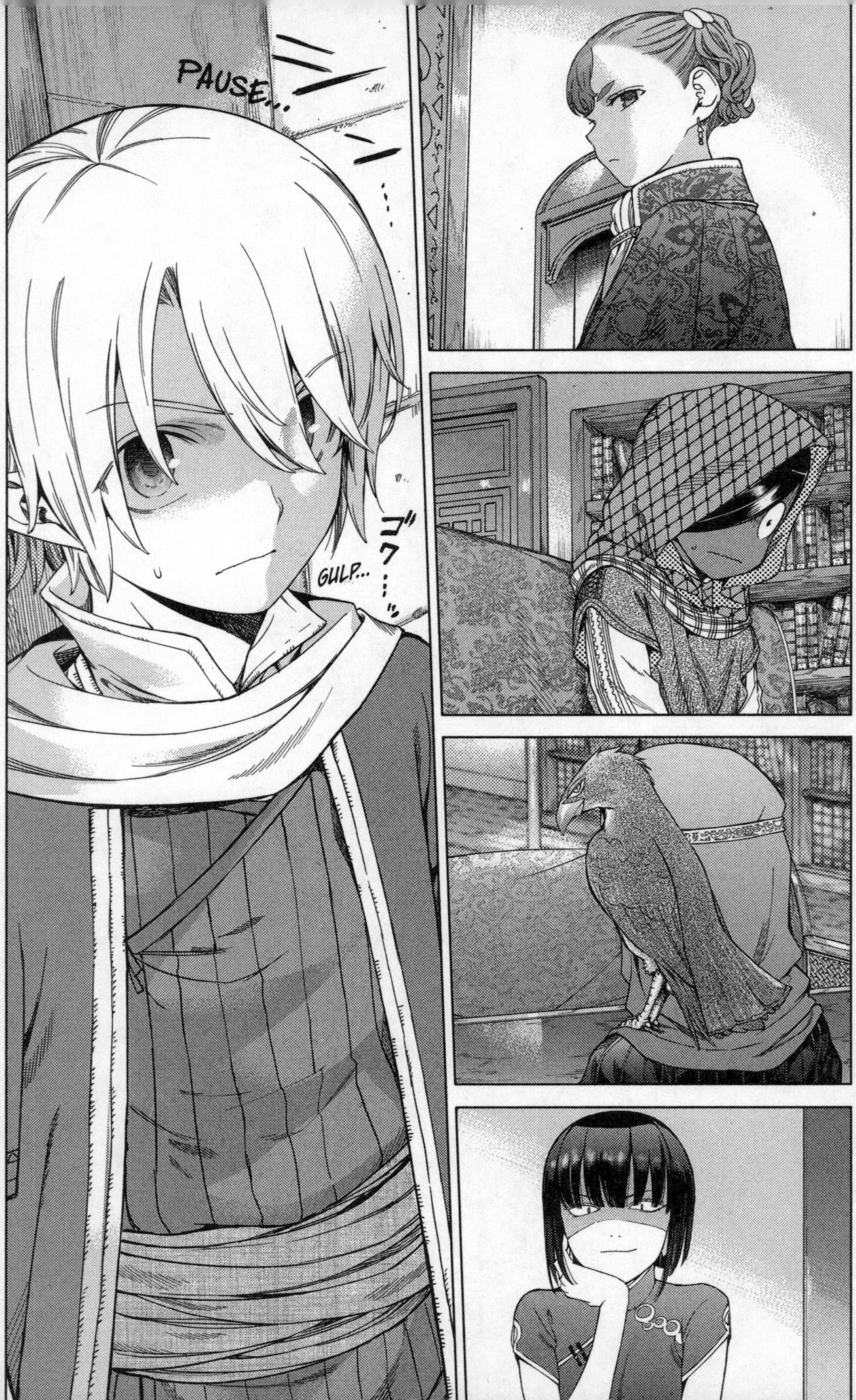
PAUSE...
...
ゴク...
GULP...

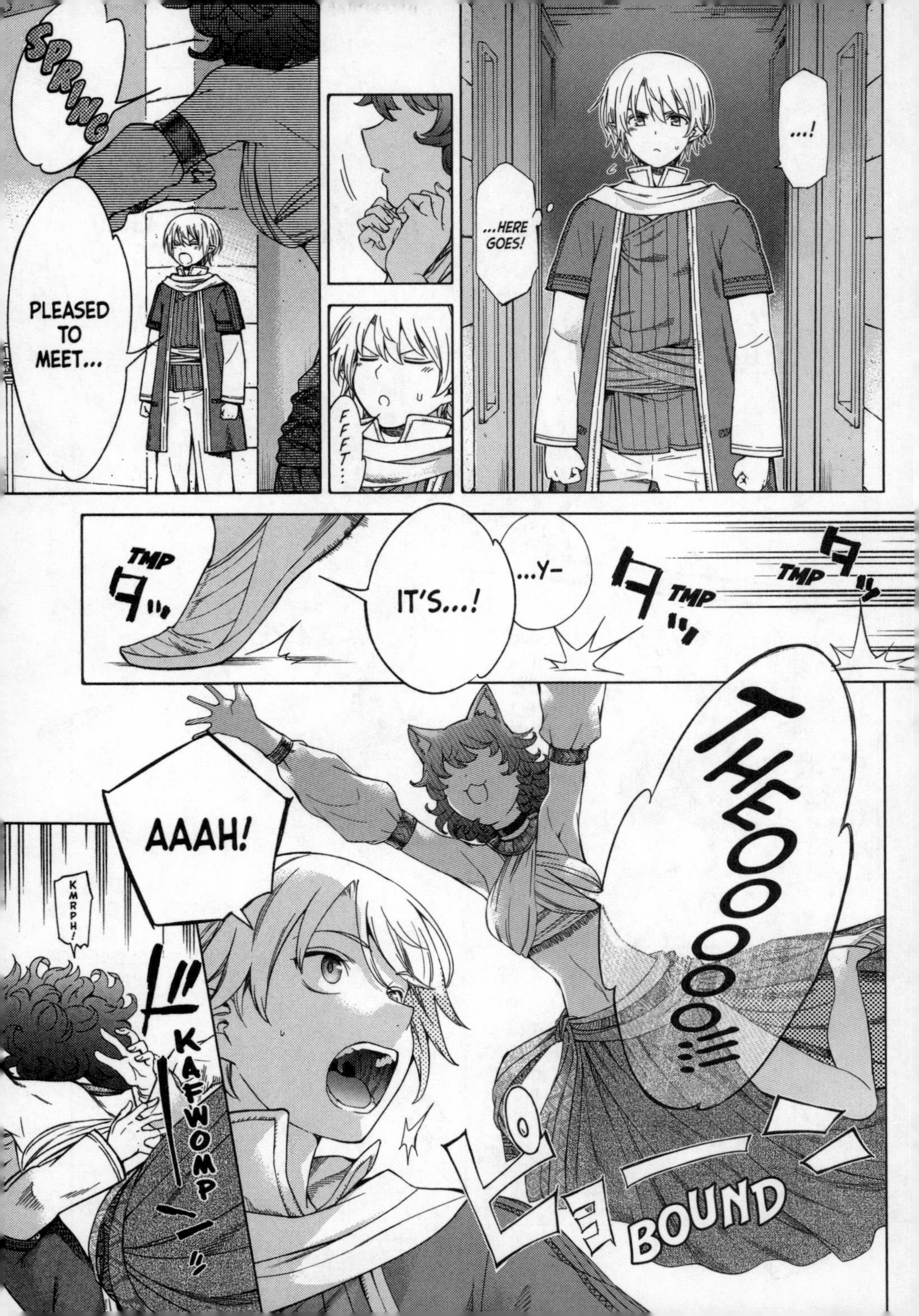
...!
...HERE GOES!
FFFT...
SPRING
PLEASED TO MEET...
TMP
TMP
...Y-
IT'S...!
TMP
THEOOOOO!!!!
AAAH!
KMRPH!
KAFWOMP
BOUND

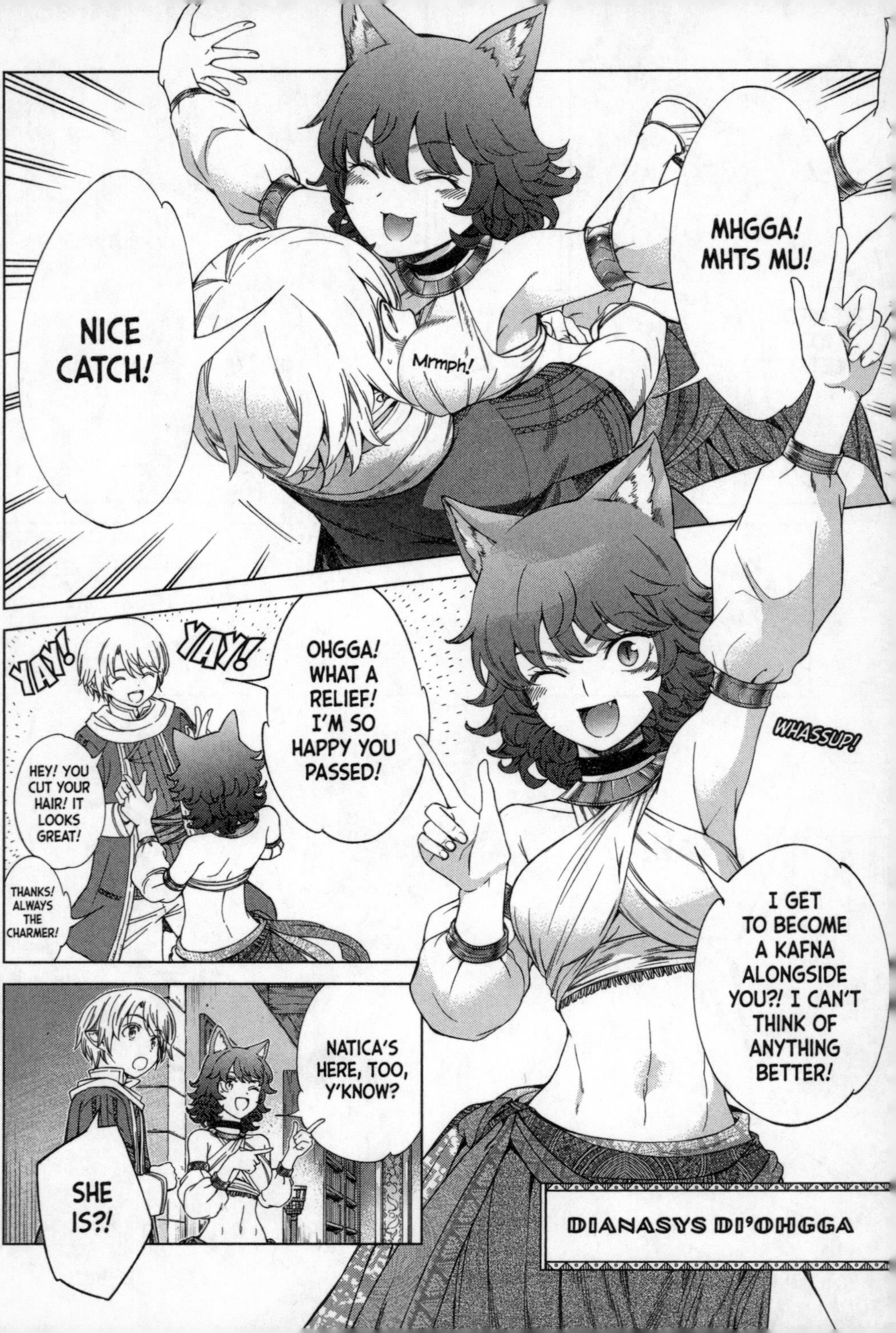
MHGGA! MHTS MU!
Mrmph!
NICE CATCH!
WHASSUP!
I GET TO BECOME A KAFNA ALONGSIDE YOU?! I CAN'T THINK OF ANYTHING BETTER!
DIANASYS DI'OHGGA
YAY!
YAY!
OHGGA! WHAT A RELIEF! I'M SO HAPPY YOU PASSED!
HEY! YOU CUT YOUR HAIR! IT LOOKS GREAT!
THANKS! ALWAYS THE CHARMER!
NATICA'S HERE, TOO, Y'KNOW?
SHE IS?!

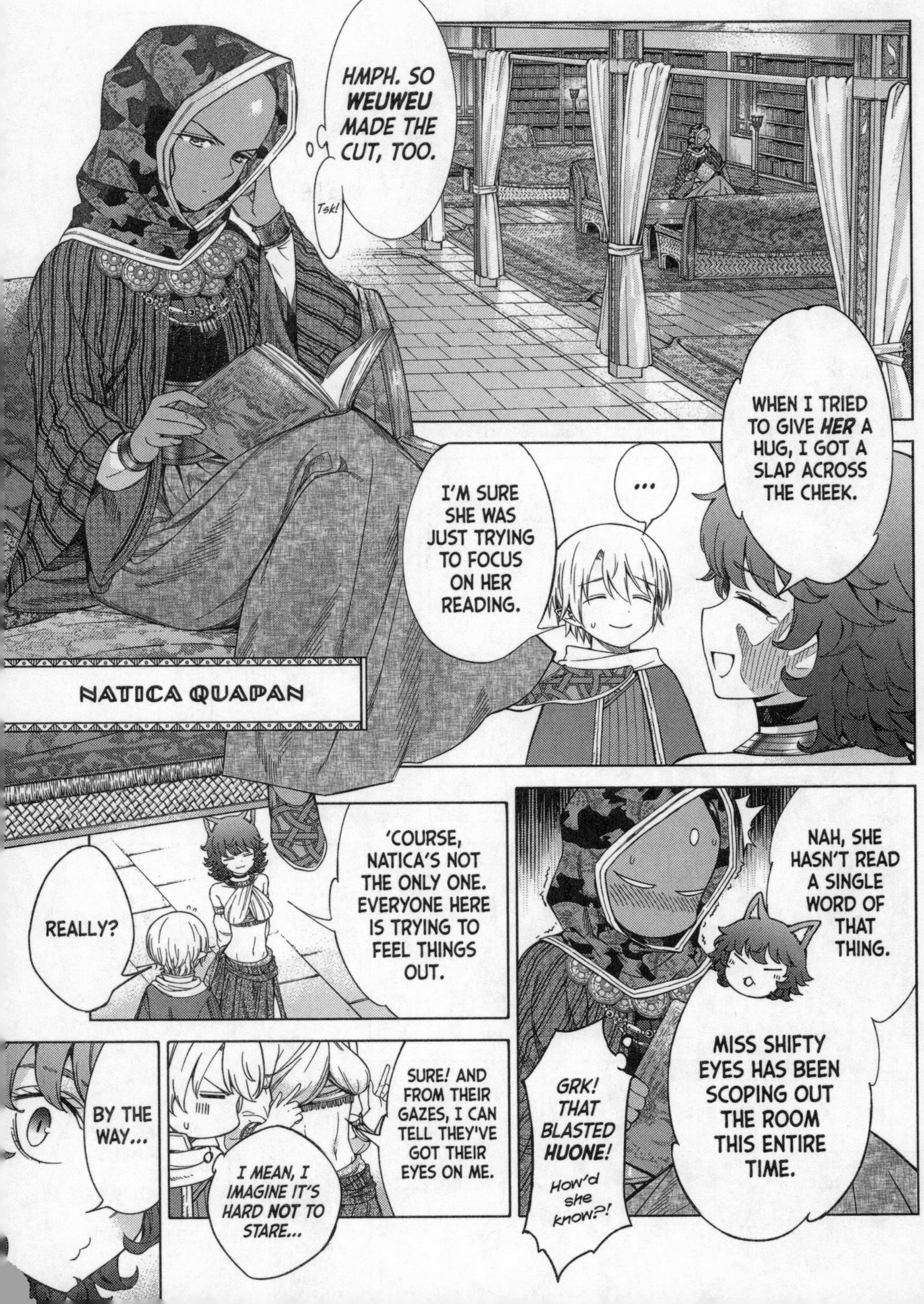
HMPH. SO **WEUWEU** MADE THE CUT, TOO.
Tsk!
NATICA QUAPAN
WHEN I TRIED TO GIVE ***HER*** A HUG, I GOT A SLAP ACROSS THE CHEEK.
...
I'M SURE SHE WAS JUST TRYING TO FOCUS ON HER READING.
NAH, SHE HASN'T READ A SINGLE WORD OF THAT THING.
MISS SHIFTY EYES HAS BEEN SCOPING OUT THE ROOM THIS ENTIRE TIME.
GRK! THAT BLASTED ***HUONE!***
How'd she know?!
'COURSE, NATICA'S NOT THE ONLY ONE. EVERYONE HERE IS TRYING TO FEEL THINGS OUT.
REALLY?
SURE! AND FROM THEIR GAZES, I CAN TELL THEY'VE GOT THEIR EYES ON ME.
I MEAN, I IMAGINE IT'S HARD ***NOT*** TO STARE...
BY THE WAY...

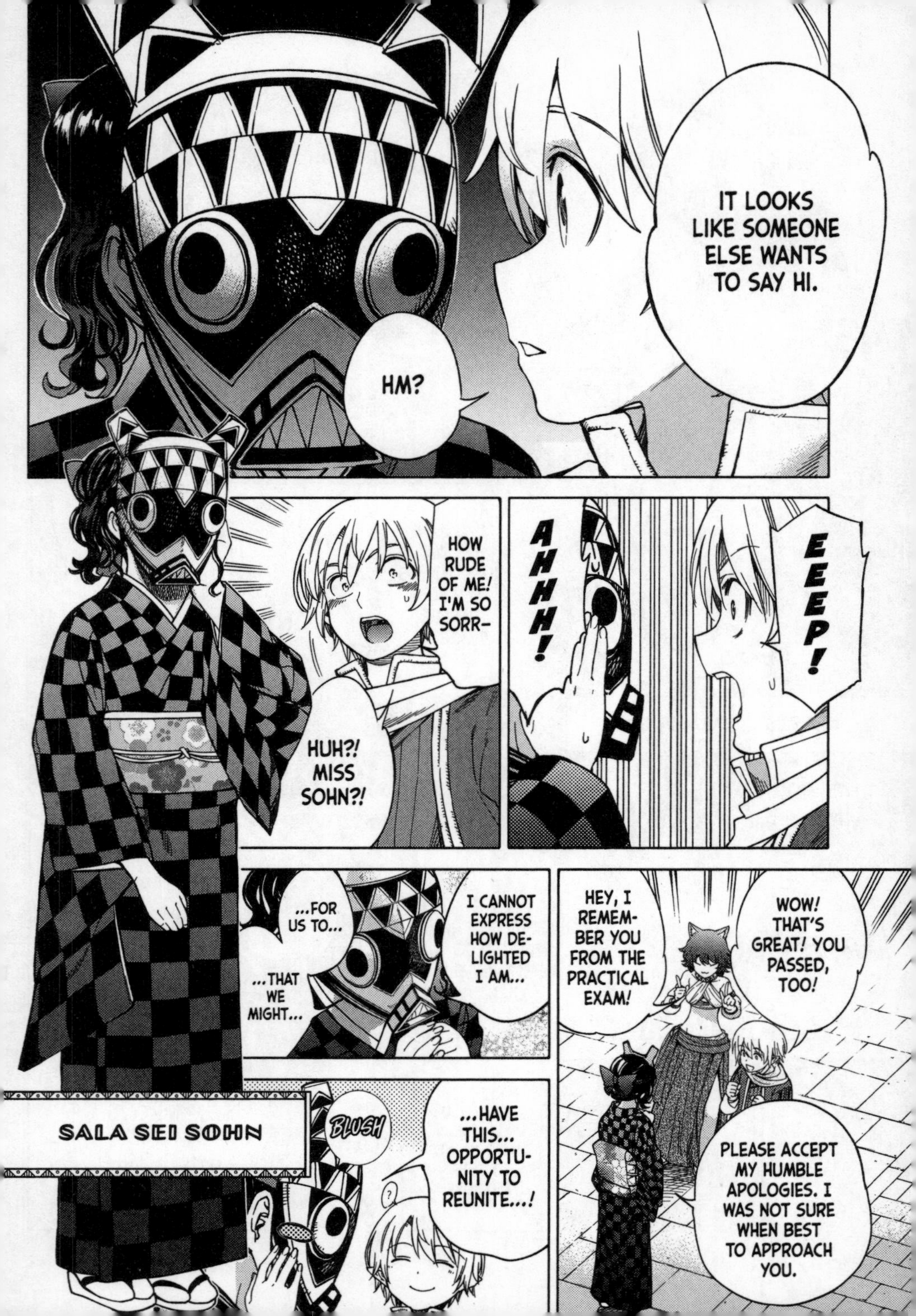
IT LOOKS LIKE SOMEONE ELSE WANTS TO SAY HI.
HM?
EEEP!
AHHHH!
HOW RUDE OF ME! I'M SO SORR–
HUH?! MISS SOHN?!
WOW! THAT'S GREAT! YOU PASSED, TOO!
HEY, I REMEMBER YOU FROM THE PRACTICAL EXAM!
PLEASE ACCEPT MY HUMBLE APOLOGIES. I WAS NOT SURE WHEN BEST TO APPROACH YOU.
I CANNOT EXPRESS HOW DELIGHTED I AM...
...FOR US TO...
...THAT WE MIGHT...
BLUSH
...HAVE THIS... OPPORTUNITY TO REUNITE...!
?
SALA SEI SOHN

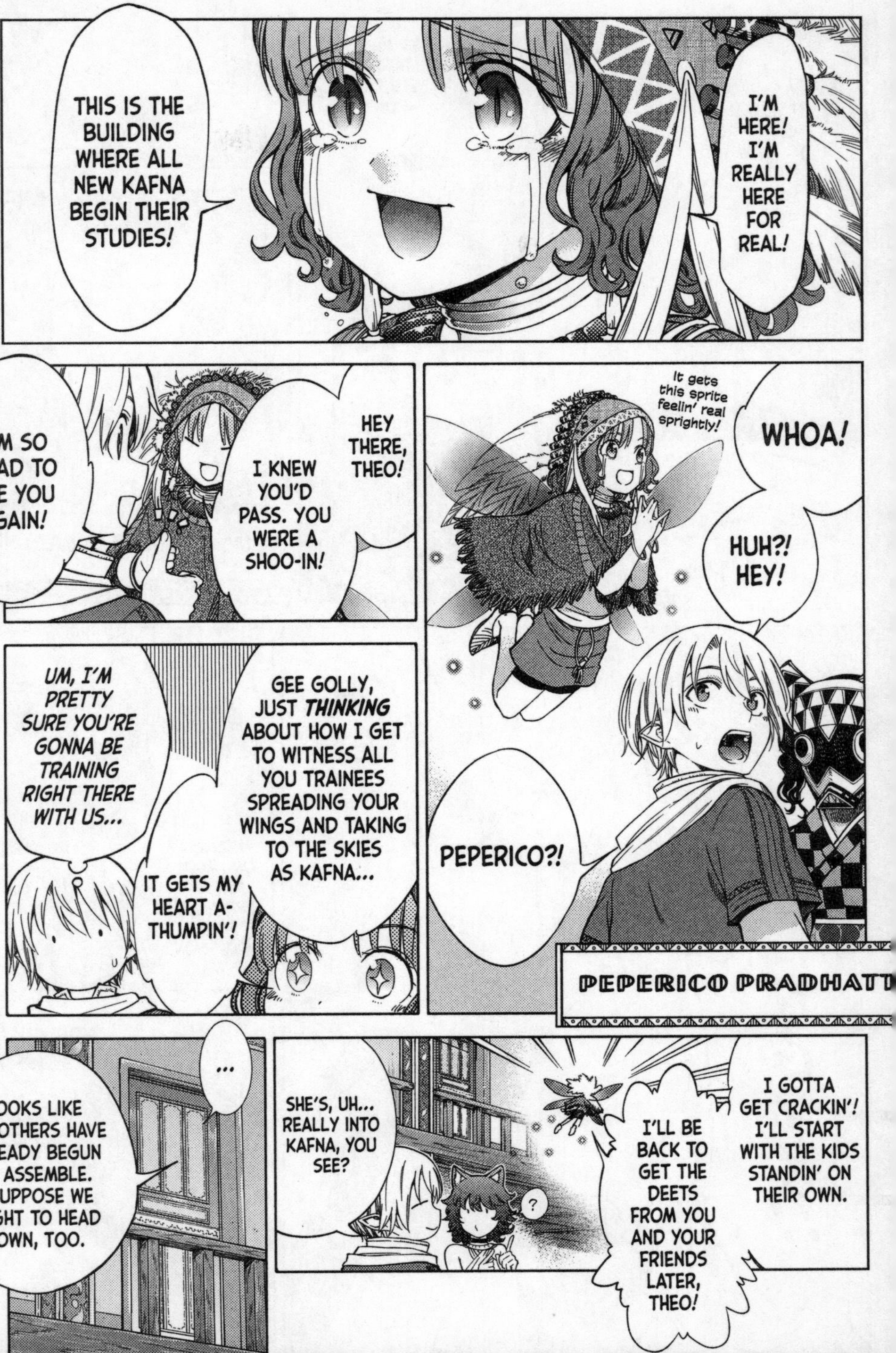
I'M HERE! I'M REALLY HERE FOR REAL!
THIS IS THE BUILDING WHERE ALL NEW KAFNA BEGIN THEIR STUDIES!
It gets this sprite feelin' real sprightly!
WHOA!
HUH?! HEY!
PEPERICO?!
PEPERICO PRADHATT
HEY THERE, THEO!
I KNEW YOU'D PASS. YOU WERE A SHOO-IN!
I'M SO GLAD TO SEE YOU AGAIN!
GEE GOLLY, JUST *THINKING* ABOUT HOW I GET TO WITNESS ALL YOU TRAINEES SPREADING YOUR WINGS AND TAKING TO THE SKIES AS KAFNA...
IT GETS MY HEART A-THUMPIN'!
UM, I'M PRETTY SURE YOU'RE GONNA BE TRAINING RIGHT THERE WITH US...
I GOTTA GET CRACKIN'! I'LL START WITH THE KIDS STANDIN' ON THEIR OWN.
I'LL BE BACK TO GET THE DEETS FROM YOU AND YOUR FRIENDS LATER, THEO!
?
SHE'S, UH... REALLY INTO KAFNA, YOU SEE?
...
LOOKS LIKE THE OTHERS HAVE ALREADY BEGUN TO ASSEMBLE. I SUPPOSE WE OUGHT TO HEAD DOWN, TOO.

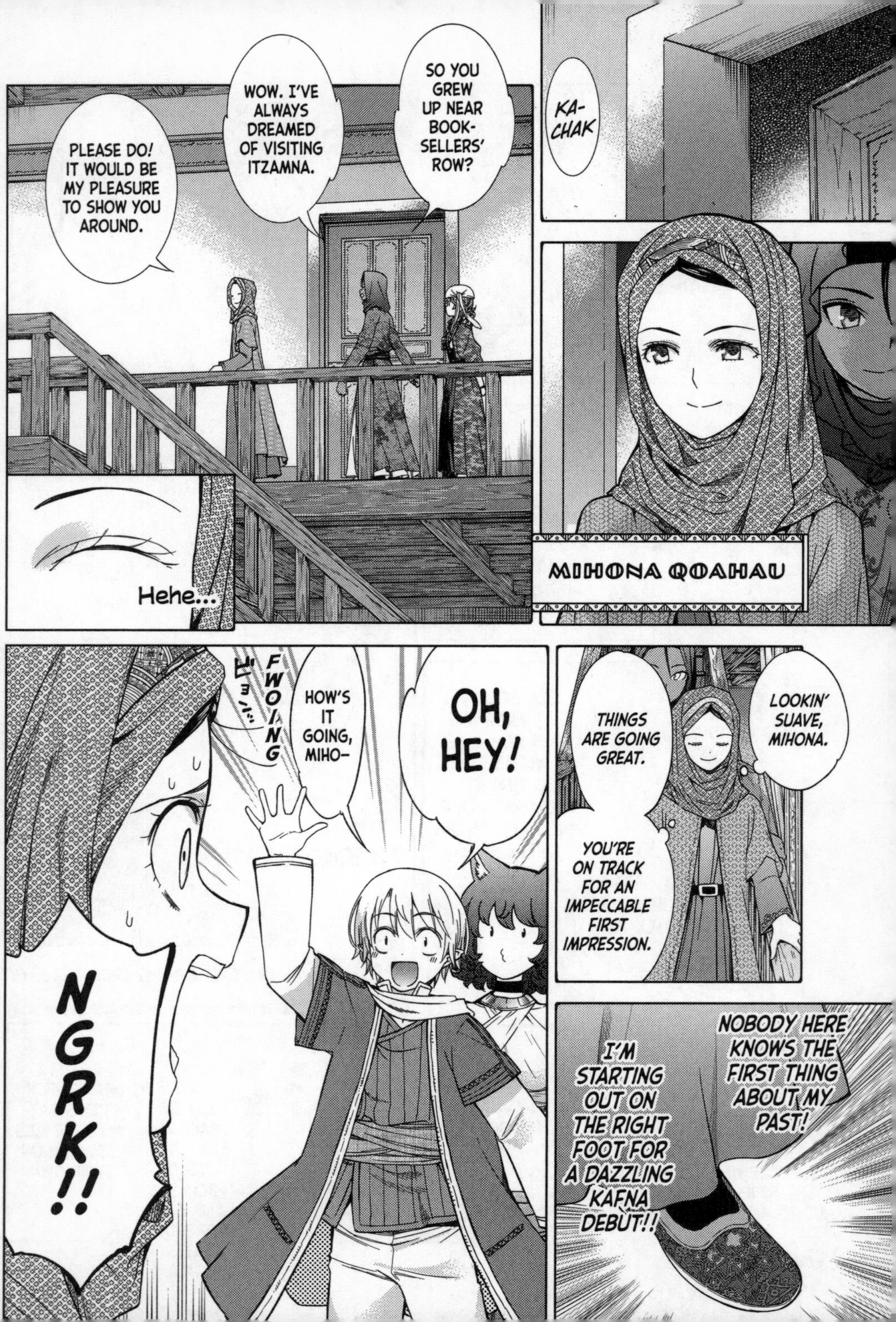
KA-CHAK
MIHONA QOAHAU
SO YOU GREW UP NEAR BOOKSELLERS' ROW?
WOW. I'VE ALWAYS DREAMED OF VISITING ITZAMNA.
PLEASE DO! IT WOULD BE MY PLEASURE TO SHOW YOU AROUND.
Hehe...
LOOKIN' SUAVE, MIHONA.
THINGS ARE GOING GREAT.
YOU'RE ON TRACK FOR AN IMPECCABLE FIRST IMPRESSION.
NOBODY HERE KNOWS THE FIRST THING ABOUT MY PAST!
I'M STARTING OUT ON THE RIGHT FOOT FOR A DAZZLING KAFNA DEBUT!!
OH, HEY!
HOW'S IT GOING, MIHO-
FWOING
NGRK!!

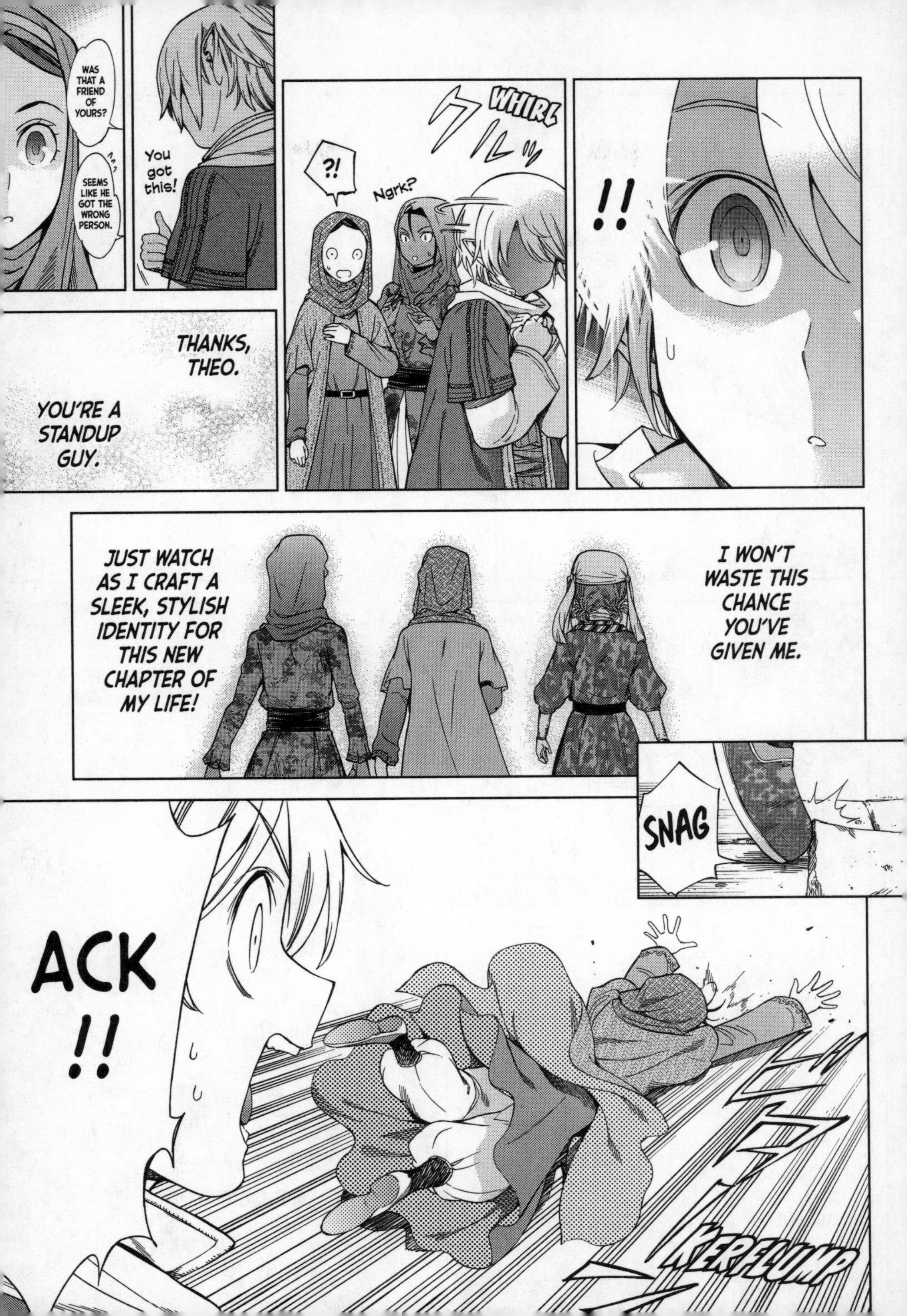
!!
WHIRL
Ngrk?
?!
You got this!
WAS THAT A FRIEND OF YOURS?
SEEMS LIKE HE GOT THE WRONG PERSON.
THANKS, THEO.
YOU'RE A STANDUP GUY.
I WON'T WASTE THIS CHANCE YOU'VE GIVEN ME.
JUST WATCH AS I CRAFT A SLEEK, STYLISH IDENTITY FOR THIS NEW CHAPTER OF MY LIFE!
SNAG
ACK !!
KERFLUMP

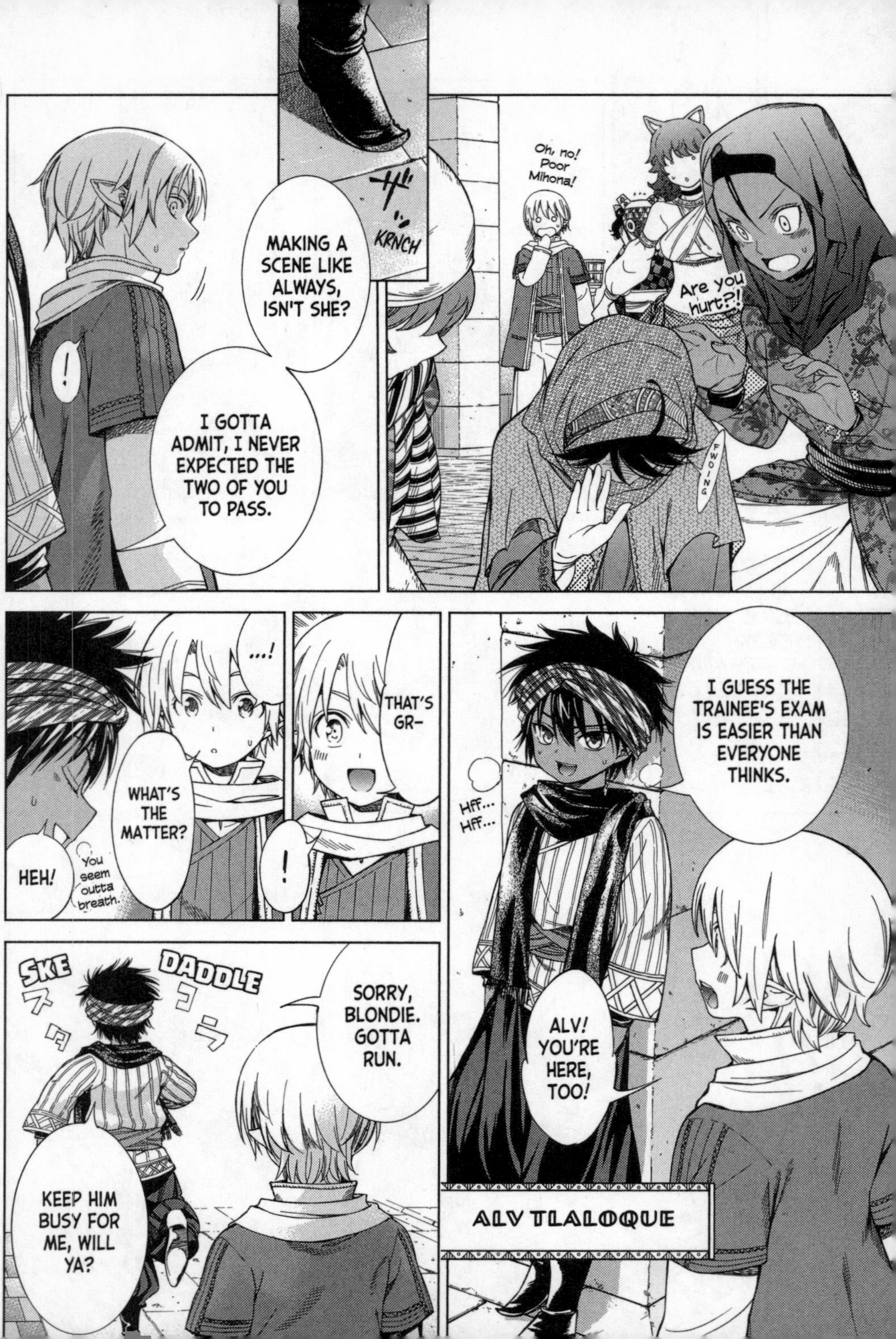
Oh, no! Poor Mihona!
Are you hurt?!
FWOING
KRNCH
MAKING A SCENE LIKE ALWAYS, ISN'T SHE?
!
I GOTTA ADMIT, I NEVER EXPECTED THE TWO OF YOU TO PASS.
I GUESS THE TRAINEE'S EXAM IS EASIER THAN EVERYONE THINKS.
HFF... HFF...
ALV! YOU'RE HERE, TOO!
ALV TLALOQUE
THAT'S GR-
!
...!
WHAT'S THE MATTER?
You seem outta breath.
HEH!
SORRY, BLONDIE. GOTTA RUN.
SKE
DADDLE
KEEP HIM BUSY FOR ME, WILL YA?

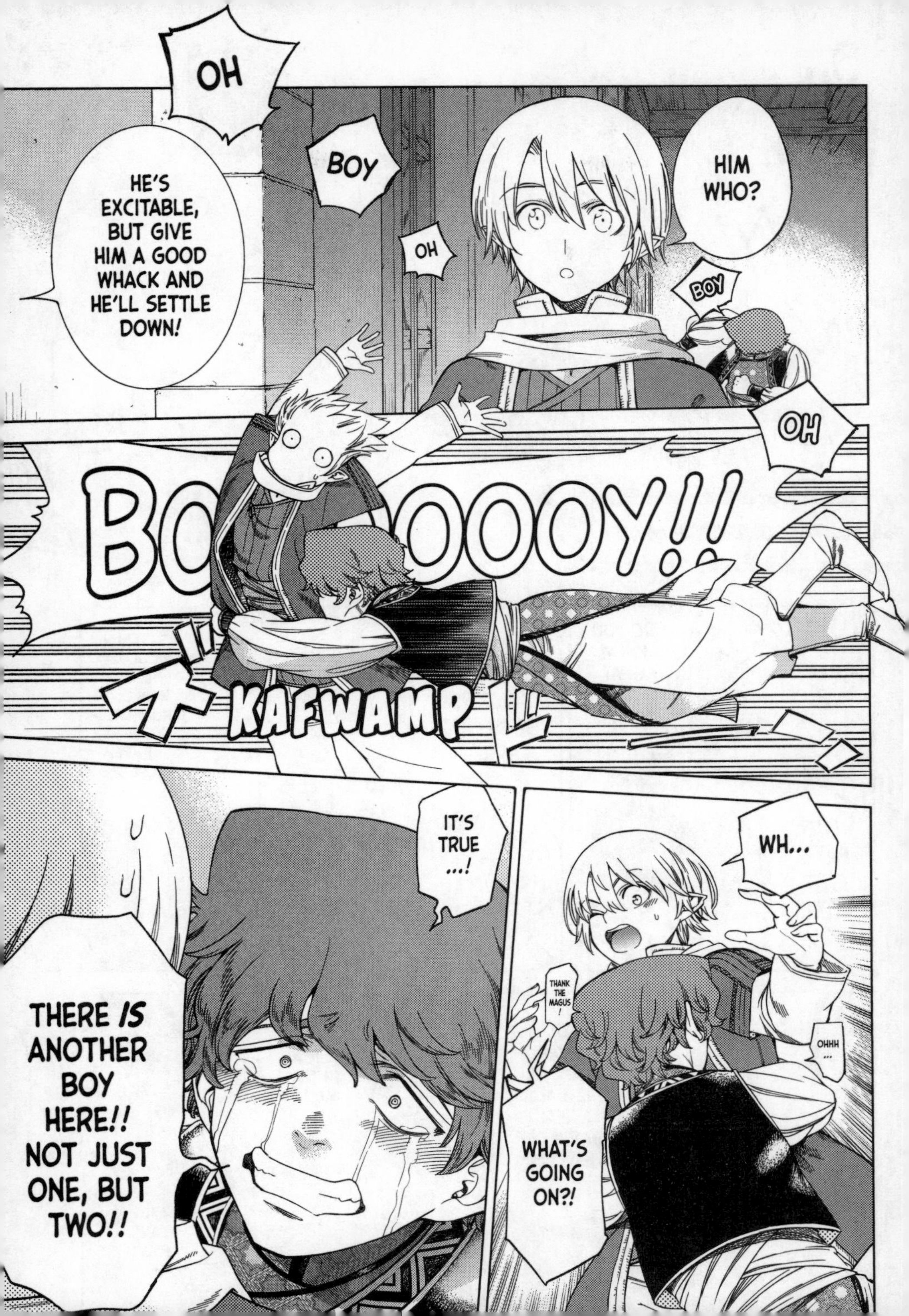

HIM WHO?
HE'S EXCITABLE, BUT GIVE HIM A GOOD WHACK AND HE'LL SETTLE DOWN!
OH
BOY
OH
BOY
OH
BOOOOOY!!
KAFWAMP
WH...
THANK THE MAGUS!
OHHH...
WHAT'S GOING ON?!
IT'S TRUE...!
THERE *IS* ANOTHER BOY HERE!! NOT JUST ONE, BUT TWO!!

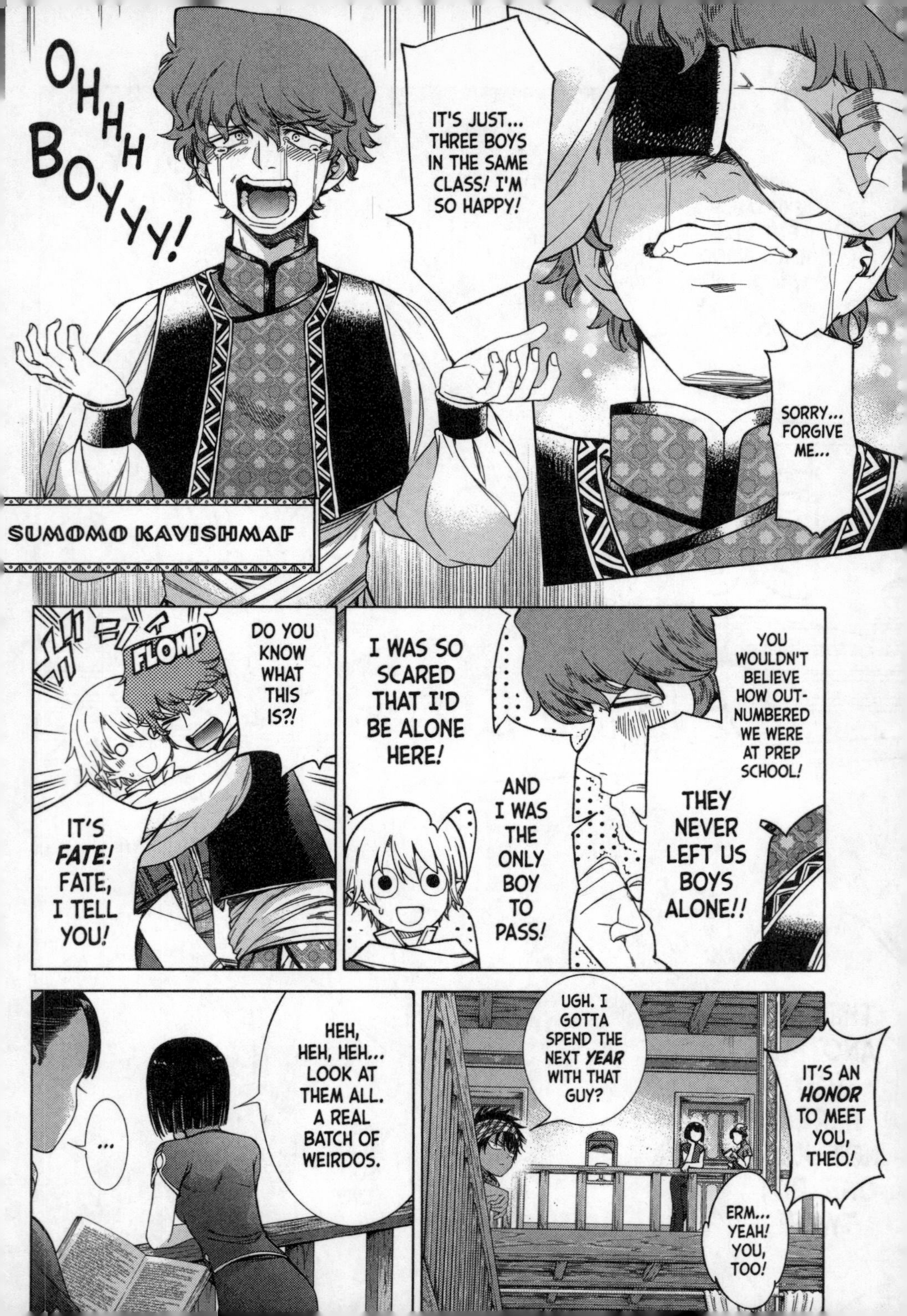
IT'S JUST... THREE BOYS IN THE SAME CLASS! I'M SO HAPPY!
SORRY... FORGIVE ME...
OHHHH BOYYYY!
SUMOMO KAVISHMAF
YOU WOULDN'T BELIEVE HOW OUT-NUMBERED WE WERE AT PREP SCHOOL!
I WAS SO SCARED THAT I'D BE ALONE HERE!
THEY NEVER LEFT US BOYS ALONE!!
AND I WAS THE ONLY BOY TO PASS!
FLOMP
DO YOU KNOW WHAT THIS IS?!
IT'S *FATE*! FATE, I TELL YOU!
IT'S AN *HONOR* TO MEET YOU, THEO!
ERM... YEAH! YOU, TOO!
UGH. I GOTTA SPEND THE NEXT *YEAR* WITH THAT GUY?
HEH, HEH, HEH... LOOK AT THEM ALL. A REAL BATCH OF WEIRDOS.
...

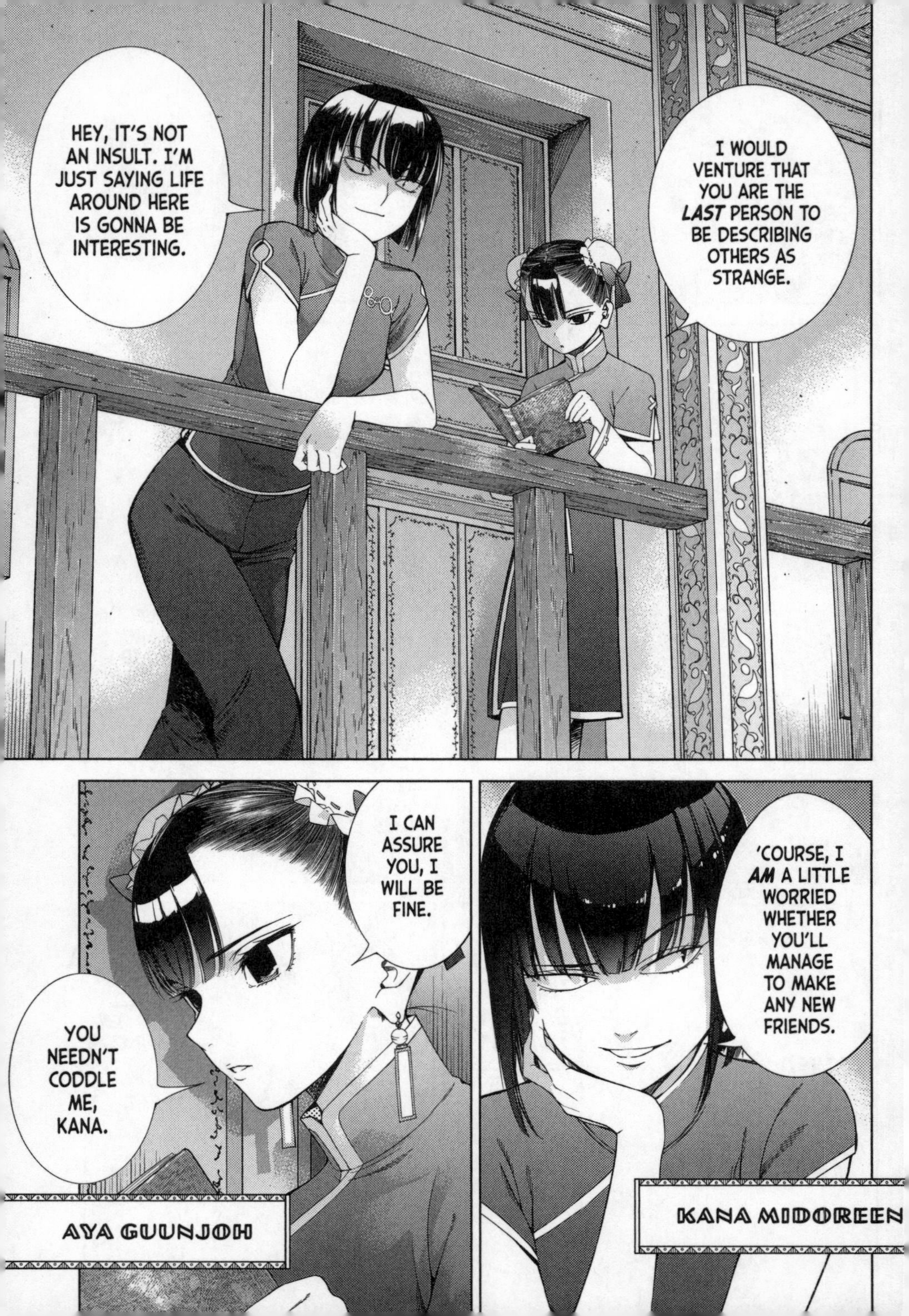
I WOULD VENTURE THAT YOU ARE THE LAST PERSON TO BE DESCRIBING OTHERS AS STRANGE.
HEY, IT'S NOT AN INSULT. I'M JUST SAYING LIFE AROUND HERE IS GONNA BE INTERESTING.
'COURSE, I AM A LITTLE WORRIED WHETHER YOU'LL MANAGE TO MAKE ANY NEW FRIENDS.
KANA MIDOREEN
I CAN ASSURE YOU, I WILL BE FINE.
YOU NEEDN'T CODDLE ME, KANA.
AYA GUUNJOH

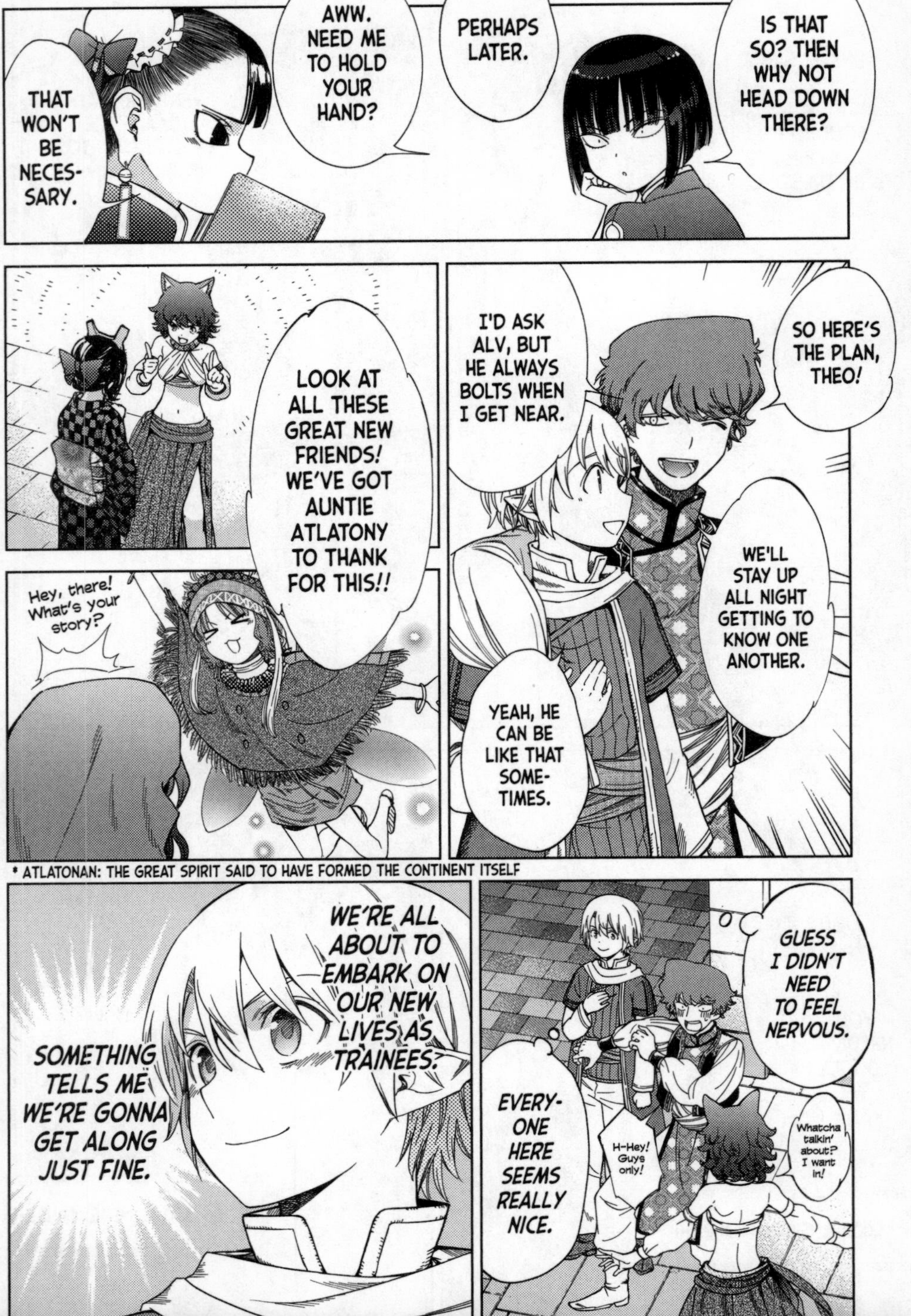
IS THAT SO? THEN WHY NOT HEAD DOWN THERE?
PERHAPS LATER.
AWW. NEED ME TO HOLD YOUR HAND?
THAT WON'T BE NECES-SARY.
SO HERE'S THE PLAN, THEO!
I'D ASK ALV, BUT HE ALWAYS BOLTS WHEN I GET NEAR.
WE'LL STAY UP ALL NIGHT GETTING TO KNOW ONE ANOTHER.
YEAH, HE CAN BE LIKE THAT SOME-TIMES.
LOOK AT ALL THESE GREAT NEW FRIENDS! WE'VE GOT AUNTIE ATLATONY TO THANK FOR THIS!!
Hey, there! What's your story?
GUESS I DIDN'T NEED TO FEEL NERVOUS.
EVERY-ONE HERE SEEMS REALLY NICE.
Whatcha talkin' about? I want in!
H-Hey! Guys only!
WE'RE ALL ABOUT TO EMBARK ON OUR NEW LIVES AS TRAINEES.
SOMETHING TELLS ME WE'RE GONNA GET ALONG JUST FINE.

* ATLATONAN: THE GREAT SPIRIT SAID TO HAVE FORMED THE CONTINENT ITSELF

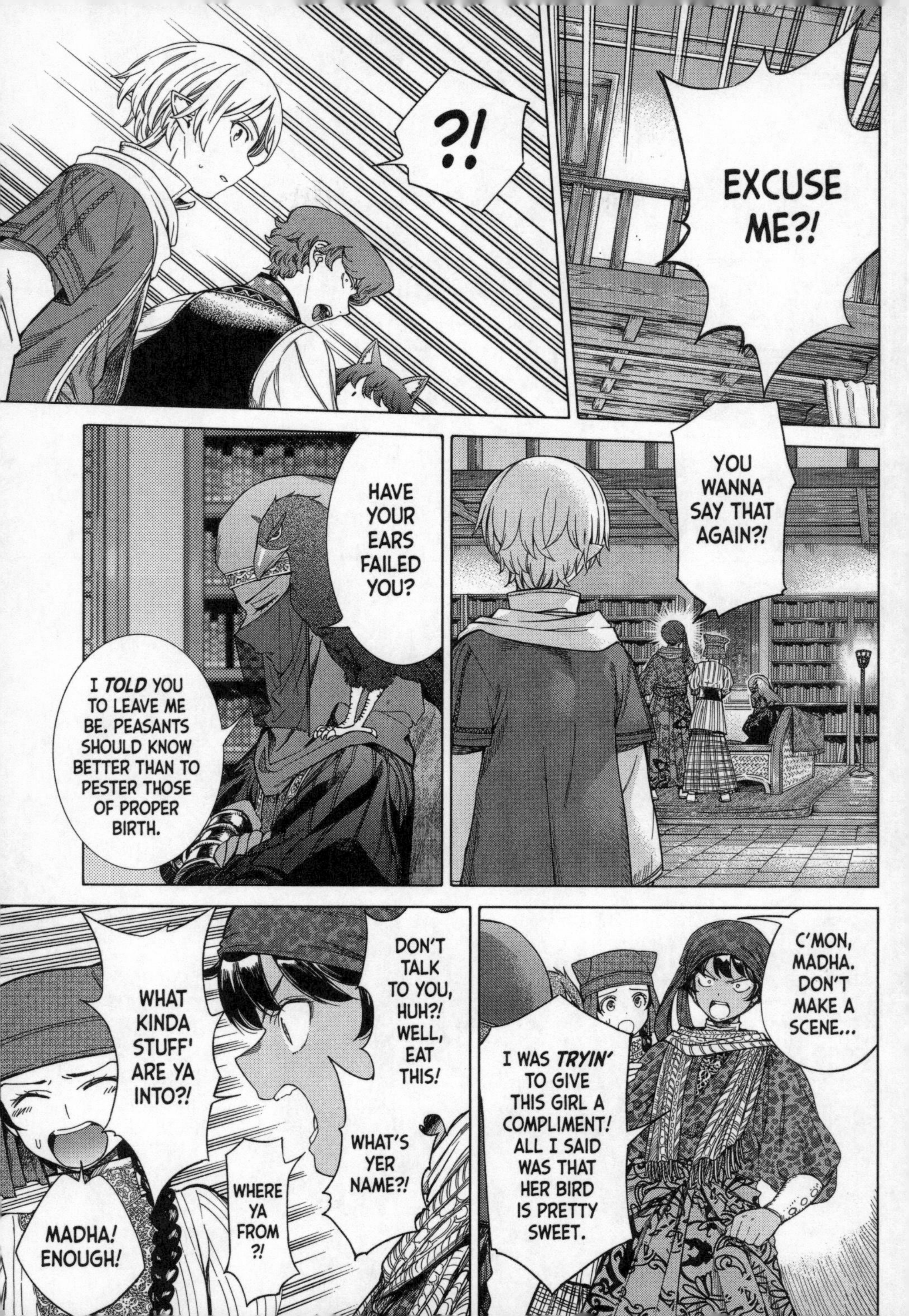
EXCUSE ME?!
?!
YOU WANNA SAY THAT AGAIN?!
HAVE YOUR EARS FAILED YOU?
I TOLD YOU TO LEAVE ME BE. PEASANTS SHOULD KNOW BETTER THAN TO PESTER THOSE OF PROPER BIRTH.
C'MON, MADHA. DON'T MAKE A SCENE...
I WAS TRYIN' TO GIVE THIS GIRL A COMPLIMENT! ALL I SAID WAS THAT HER BIRD IS PRETTY SWEET.
DON'T TALK TO YOU, HUH?! WELL, EAT THIS!
WHAT KINDA STUFF' ARE YA INTO?!
WHAT'S YER NAME?!
WHERE YA FROM ?!
MADHA! ENOUGH!

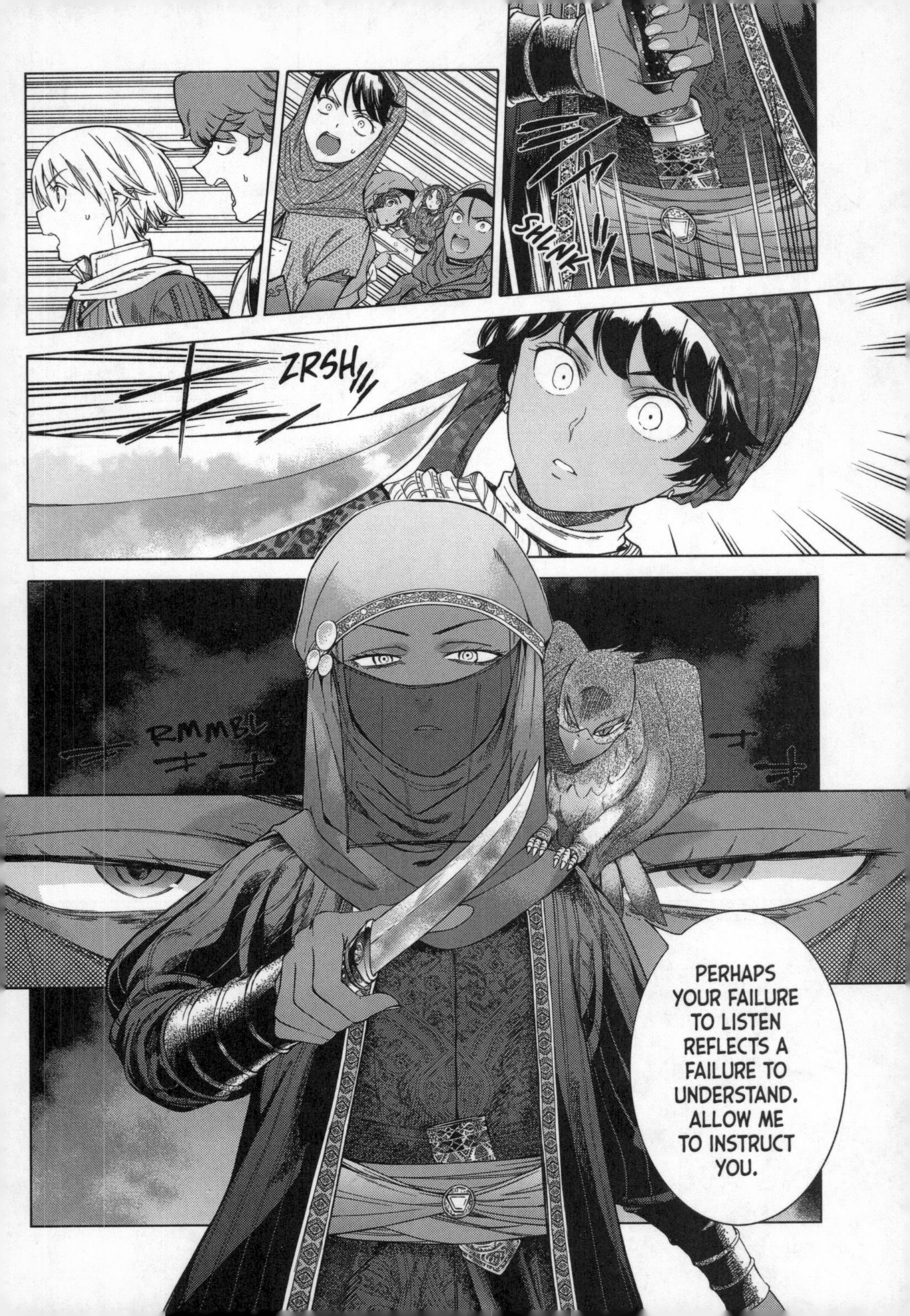
SHINK
ZRSH
RMMBL
PERHAPS YOUR FAILURE TO LISTEN REFLECTS A FAILURE TO UNDERSTAND. ALLOW ME TO INSTRUCT YOU.

The Kafna-in-Training

The Banded Few

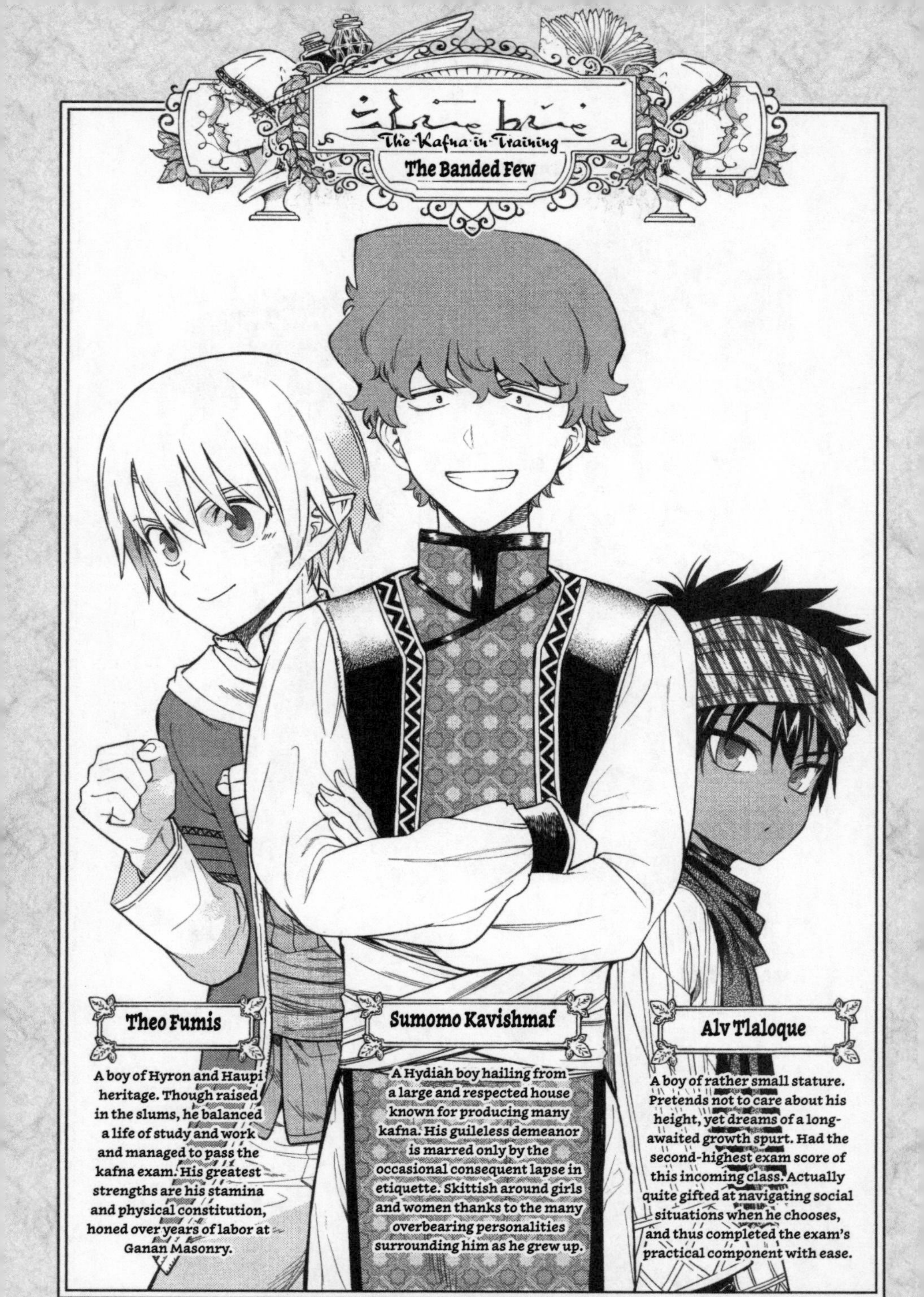

Theo Fumis

A boy of Hyron and Haupi heritage. Though raised in the slums, he balanced a life of study and work and managed to pass the kafna exam. His greatest strengths are his stamina and physical constitution, honed over years of labor at Ganan Masonry.

Sumomo Kavishmaf

A Hydiah boy hailing from a large and respected house known for producing many kafna. His guileless demeanor is marred only by the occasional consequent lapse in etiquette. Skittish around girls and women thanks to the many overbearing personalities surrounding him as he grew up.

Alv Tlaloque

A boy of rather small stature. Pretends not to care about his height, yet dreams of a long-awaited growth spurt. Had the second-highest exam score of this incoming class. Actually quite gifted at navigating social situations when he chooses, and thus completed the exam's practical component with ease.

The Kafra in Training

The Seaborn Souls

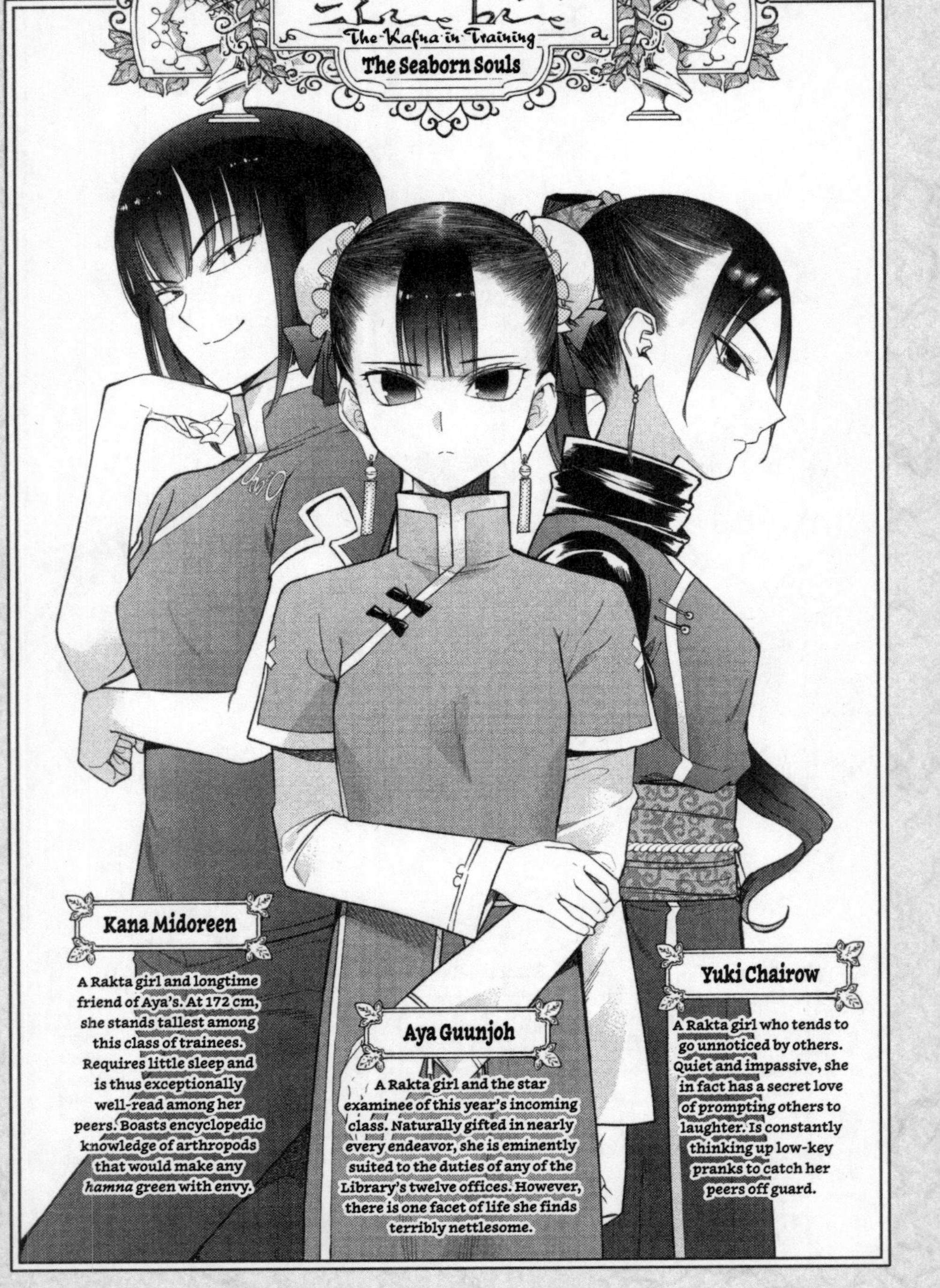

Kana Midoreen

A Rakta girl and longtime friend of Aya's. At 172 cm, she stands tallest among this class of trainees. Requires little sleep and is thus exceptionally well-read among her peers. Boasts encyclopedic knowledge of arthropods that would make any *hamna* green with envy.

Aya Guunjoh

A Rakta girl and the star examinee of this year's incoming class. Naturally gifted in nearly every endeavor, she is eminently suited to the duties of any of the Library's twelve offices. However, there is one facet of life she finds terribly nettlesome.

Yuki Chairow

A Rakta girl who tends to go unnoticed by others. Quiet and impassive, she in fact has a secret love of prompting others to laughter. Is constantly thinking up low-key pranks to catch her peers off guard.

16 Blood Will Be Drawn When Nobles Draw Forth

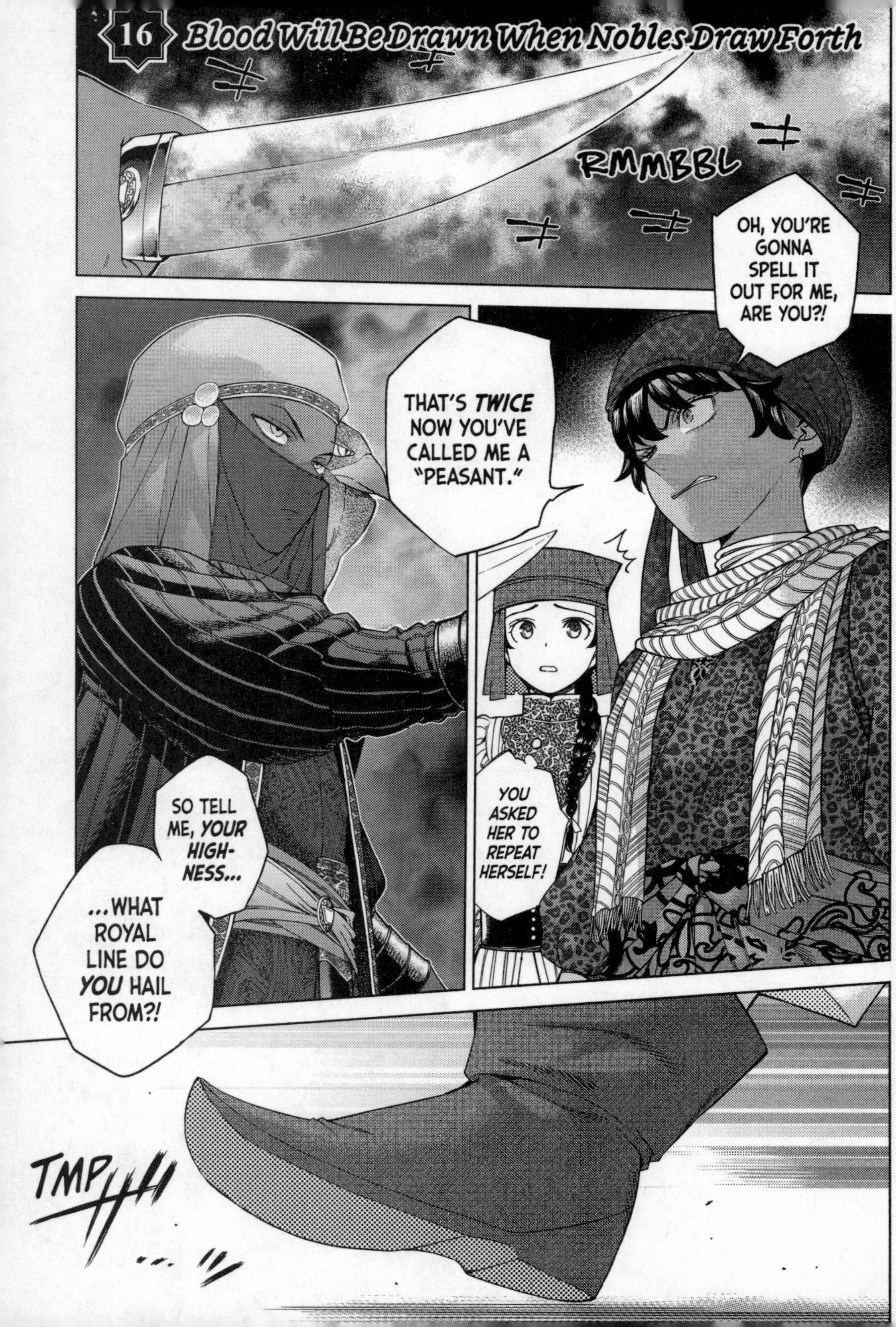
RMMBBL
OH, YOU'RE GONNA SPELL IT OUT FOR ME, ARE YOU?!
YOU ASKED HER TO REPEAT HERSELF!
THAT'S *TWICE* NOW YOU'VE CALLED ME A "PEASANT."
SO TELL ME, *YOUR HIGHNESS...*
...WHAT ROYAL LINE DO *YOU* HAIL FROM?!
TMP

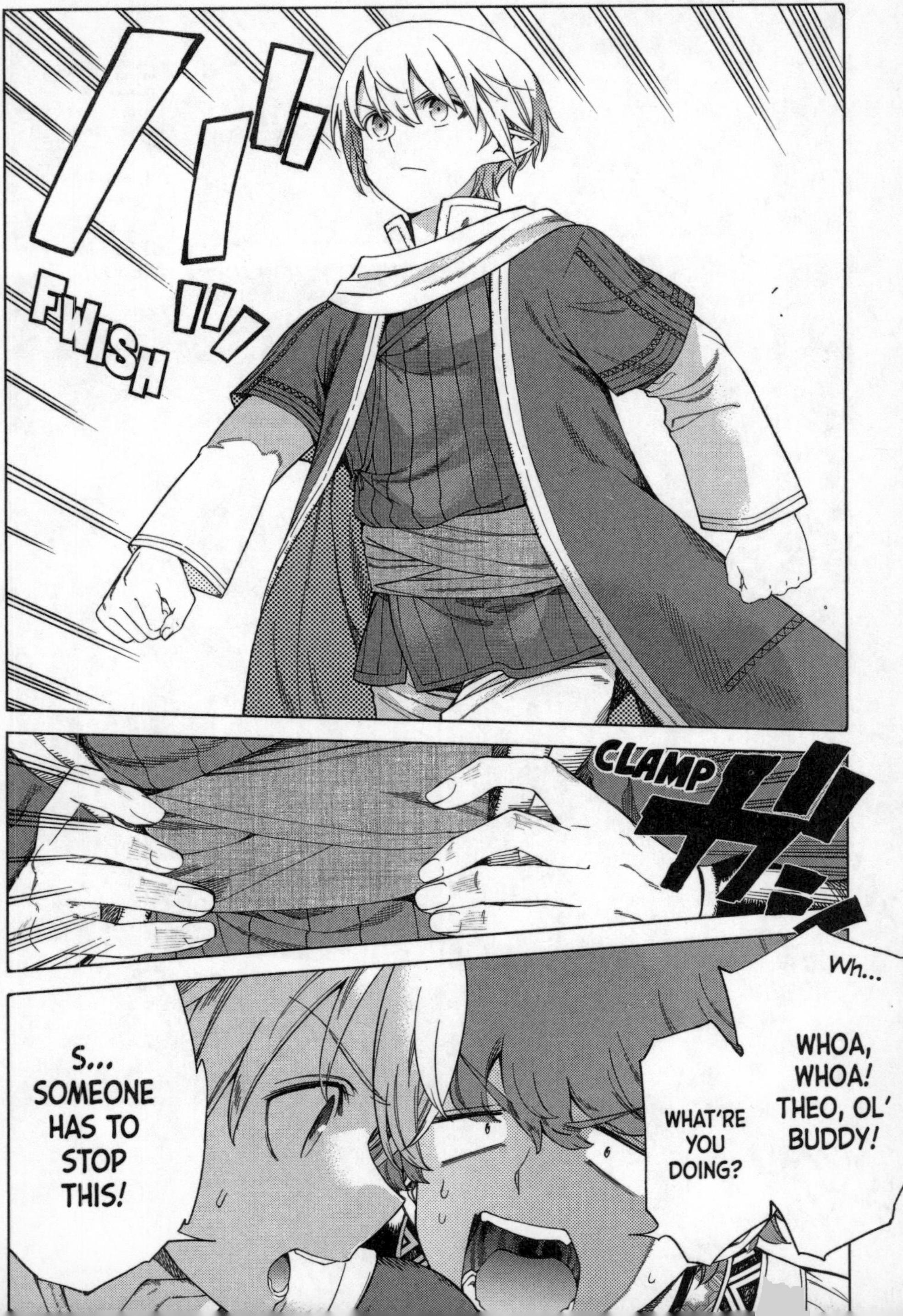
FWISH
CLAMP
Wh...
WHOA, WHOA! THEO, OL' BUDDY!
WHAT'RE YOU DOING?
S... SOMEONE HAS TO STOP THIS!

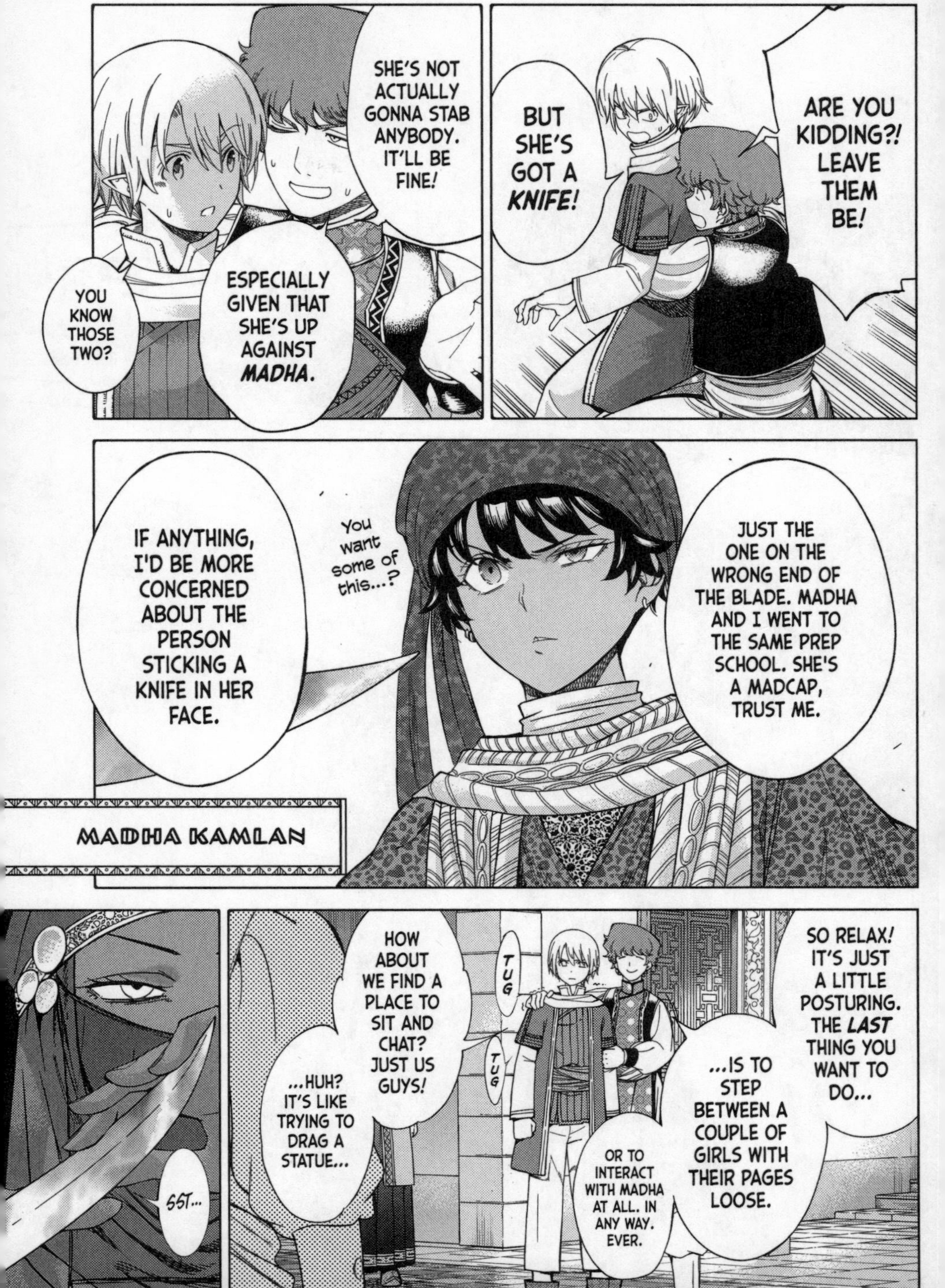
ARE YOU KIDDING?! LEAVE THEM BE!
BUT SHE'S GOT A KNIFE!
SHE'S NOT ACTUALLY GONNA STAB ANYBODY. IT'LL BE FINE!
ESPECIALLY GIVEN THAT SHE'S UP AGAINST MADHA.
YOU KNOW THOSE TWO?
JUST THE ONE ON THE WRONG END OF THE BLADE. MADHA AND I WENT TO THE SAME PREP SCHOOL. SHE'S A MADCAP, TRUST ME.
You want some of this...?
IF ANYTHING, I'D BE MORE CONCERNED ABOUT THE PERSON STICKING A KNIFE IN HER FACE.
MADHA KAMLAN
SO RELAX! IT'S JUST A LITTLE POSTURING. THE LAST THING YOU WANT TO DO...
...IS TO STEP BETWEEN A COUPLE OF GIRLS WITH THEIR PAGES LOOSE.
OR TO INTERACT WITH MADHA AT ALL. IN ANY WAY. EVER.
TUG
TUG
HOW ABOUT WE FIND A PLACE TO SIT AND CHAT? JUST US GUYS!
...HUH? IT'S LIKE TRYING TO DRAG A STATUE...
SST...

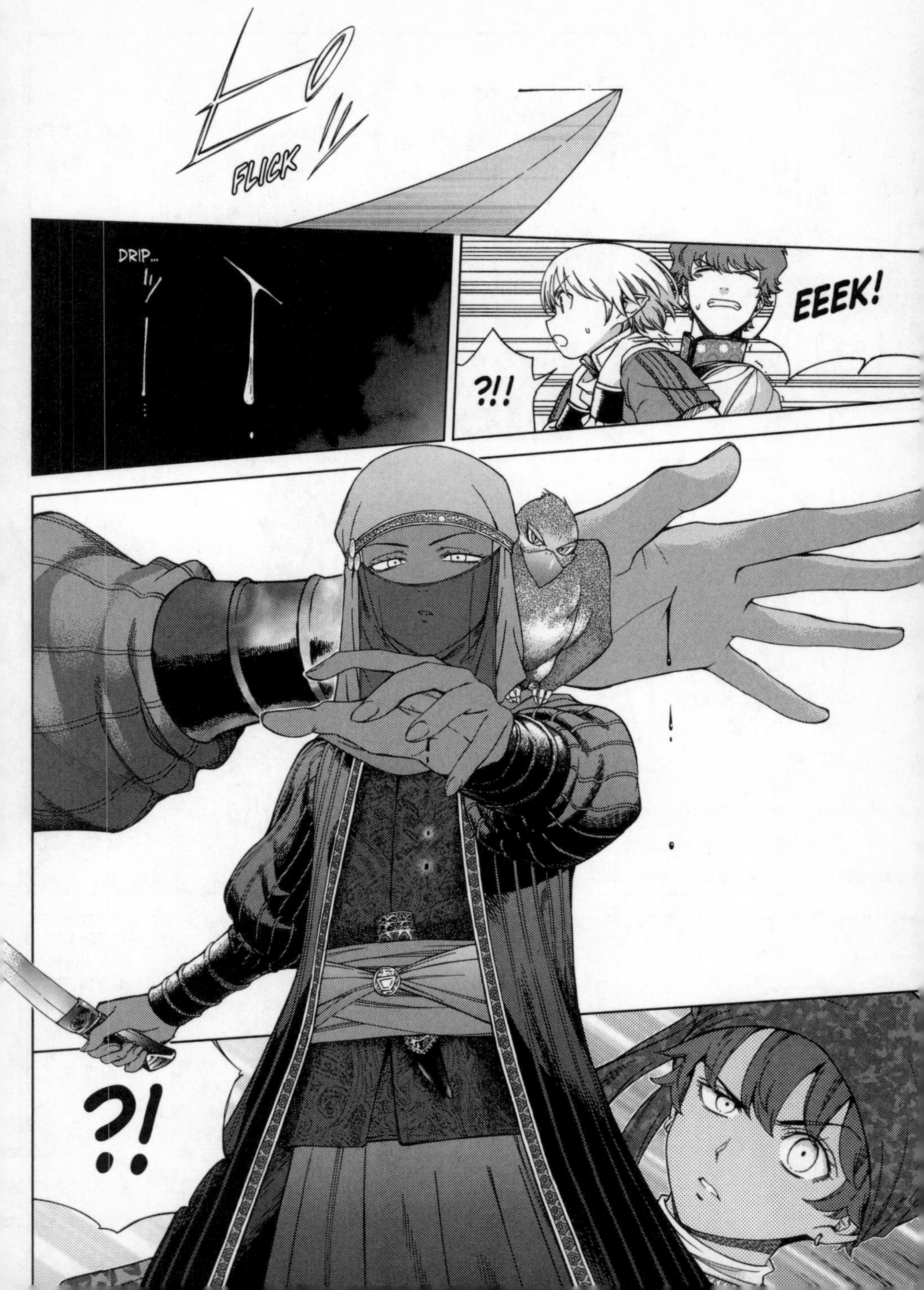
FLICK
EEEK!
?!!
DRIP...
?!

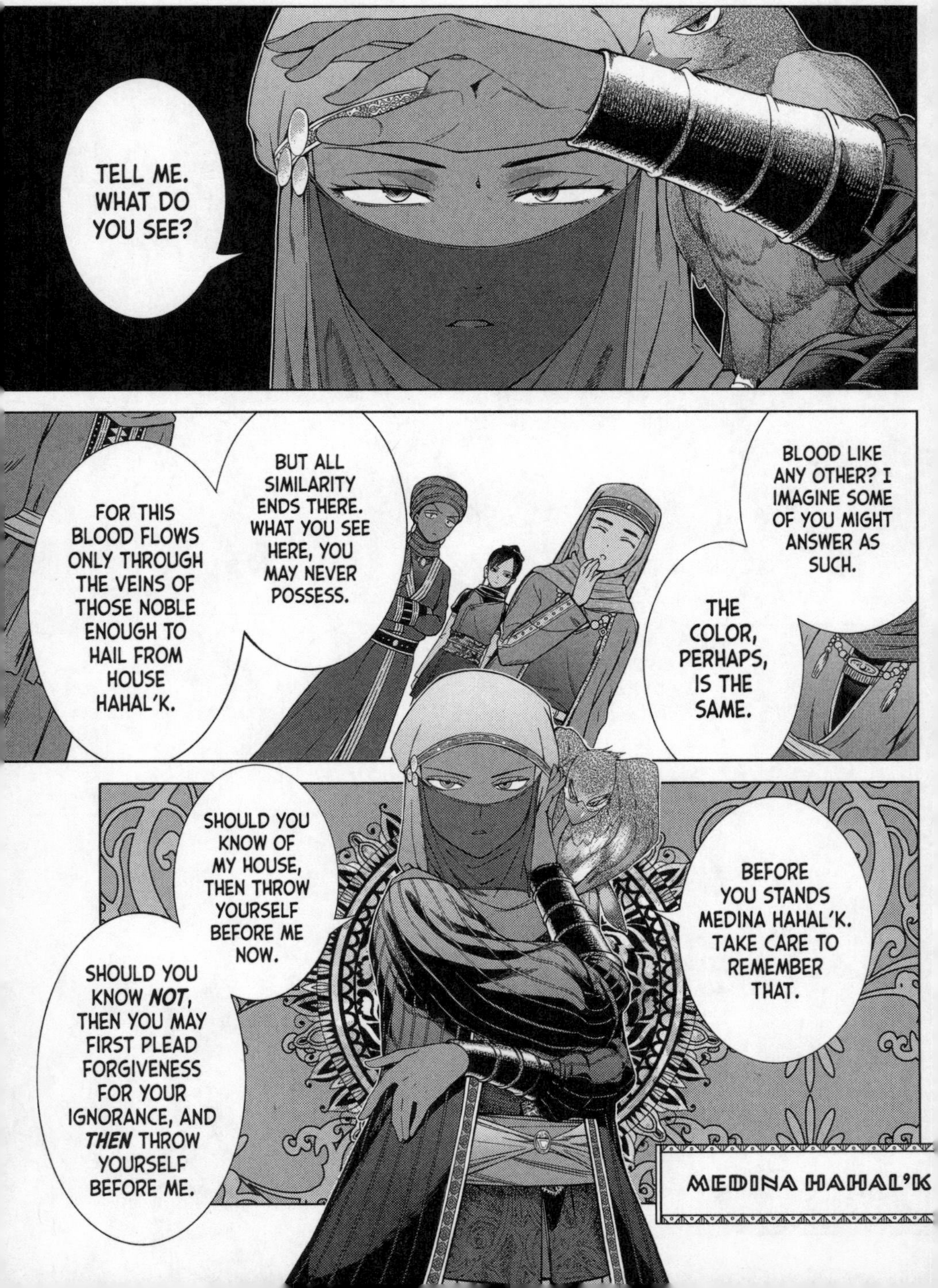
TELL ME. WHAT DO YOU SEE?
BLOOD LIKE ANY OTHER? I IMAGINE SOME OF YOU MIGHT ANSWER AS SUCH.
THE COLOR, PERHAPS, IS THE SAME.
BUT ALL SIMILARITY ENDS THERE. WHAT YOU SEE HERE, YOU MAY NEVER POSSESS.
FOR THIS BLOOD FLOWS ONLY THROUGH THE VEINS OF THOSE NOBLE ENOUGH TO HAIL FROM HOUSE HAHAL'K.
BEFORE YOU STANDS MEDINA HAHAL'K. TAKE CARE TO REMEMBER THAT.
MEDINA HAHAL'K
SHOULD YOU KNOW OF MY HOUSE, THEN THROW YOURSELF BEFORE ME NOW.
SHOULD YOU KNOW ***NOT***, THEN YOU MAY FIRST PLEAD FORGIVENESS FOR YOUR IGNORANCE, AND ***THEN*** THROW YOURSELF BEFORE ME.

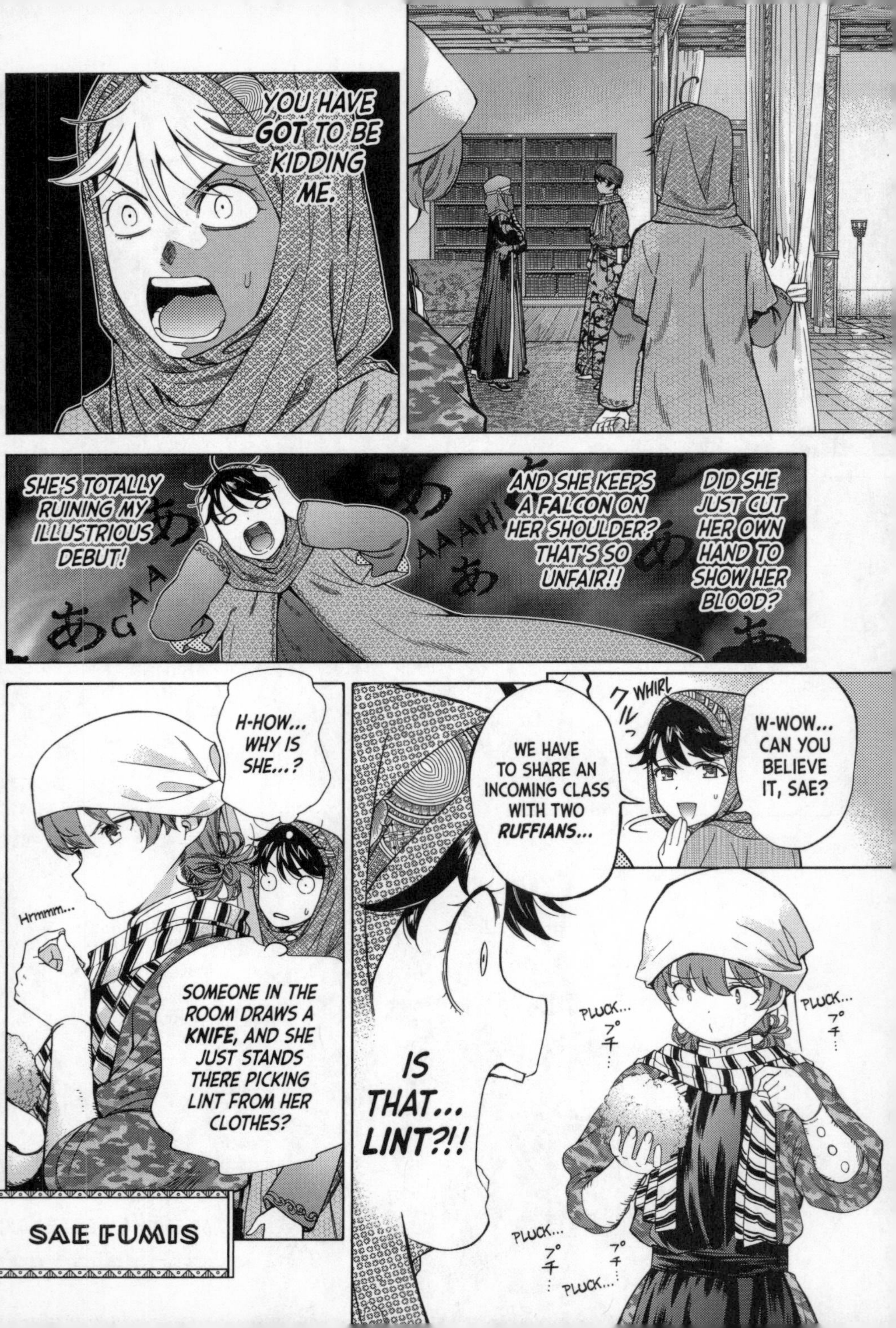
YOU HAVE GOT TO BE KIDDING ME.
DID SHE JUST CUT HER OWN HAND TO SHOW HER BLOOD?
AND SHE KEEPS A **FALCON** ON HER SHOULDER? THAT'S SO UNFAIR!!
AAAH!
SHE'S TOTALLY RUINING MY ILLUSTRIOUS DEBUT!
W-WOW... CAN YOU BELIEVE IT, SAE?
クルッ WHIRL
WE HAVE TO SHARE AN INCOMING CLASS WITH TWO *RUFFIANS*...
PLUCK... プチ...
PLUCK... プチ...
IS THAT... LINT?!!
PLUCK... プチ...
PLUCK... プチ...
H-HOW... WHY IS SHE...?
Hrmmm...
SOMEONE IN THE ROOM DRAWS A **KNIFE,** AND SHE JUST STANDS THERE PICKING LINT FROM HER CLOTHES?
SAE FUMIS

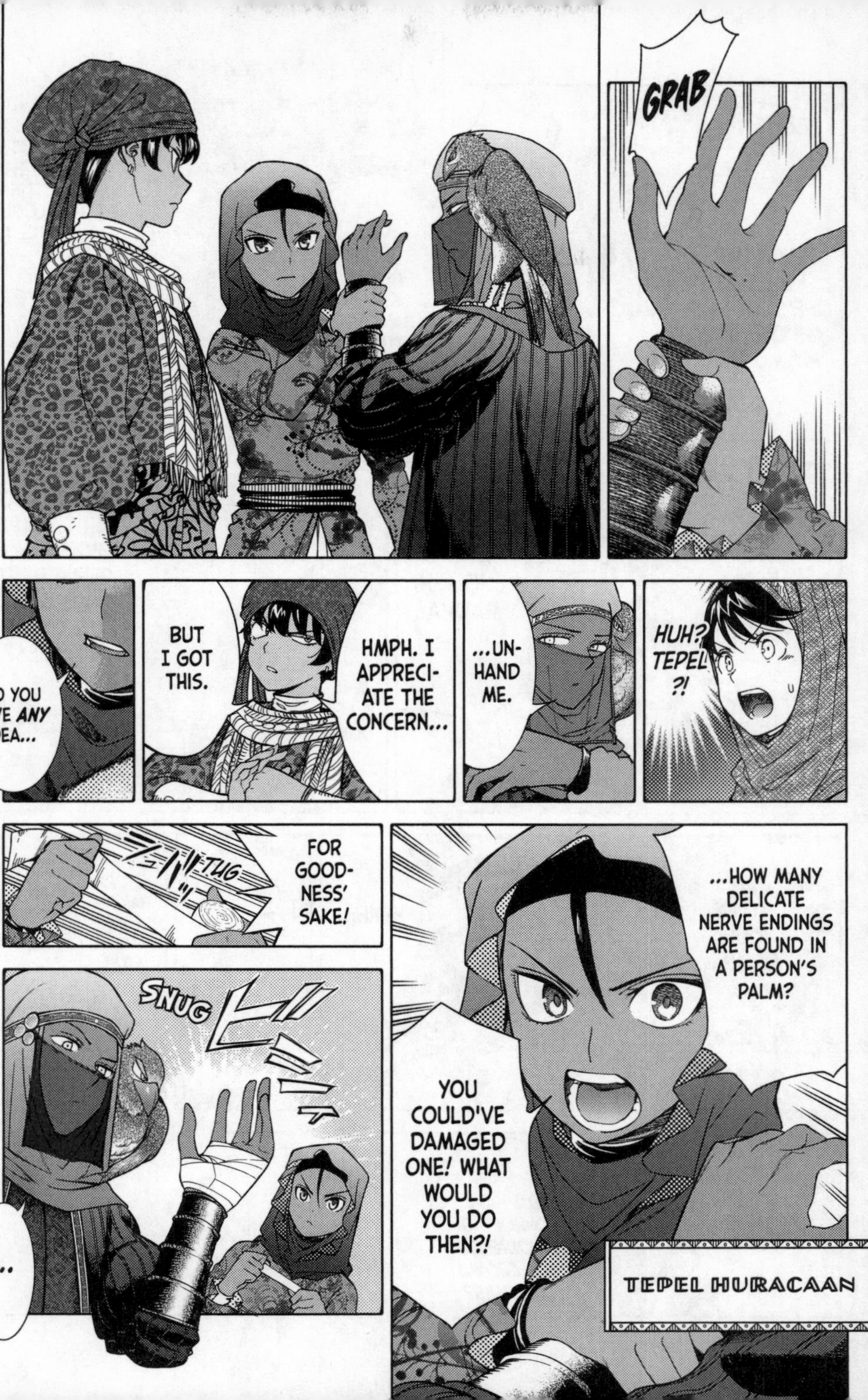
GRAB
HUH? TEPEL ?!
...UN-HAND ME.
HMPH. I APPRECI-ATE THE CONCERN...
BUT I GOT THIS.
DO YOU HAVE ANY IDEA...
...HOW MANY DELICATE NERVE ENDINGS ARE FOUND IN A PERSON'S PALM?
YOU COULD'VE DAMAGED ONE! WHAT WOULD YOU DO THEN?!
TEPEL HURACAAN
TUG
FOR GOOD-NESS' SAKE!
SNUG
...

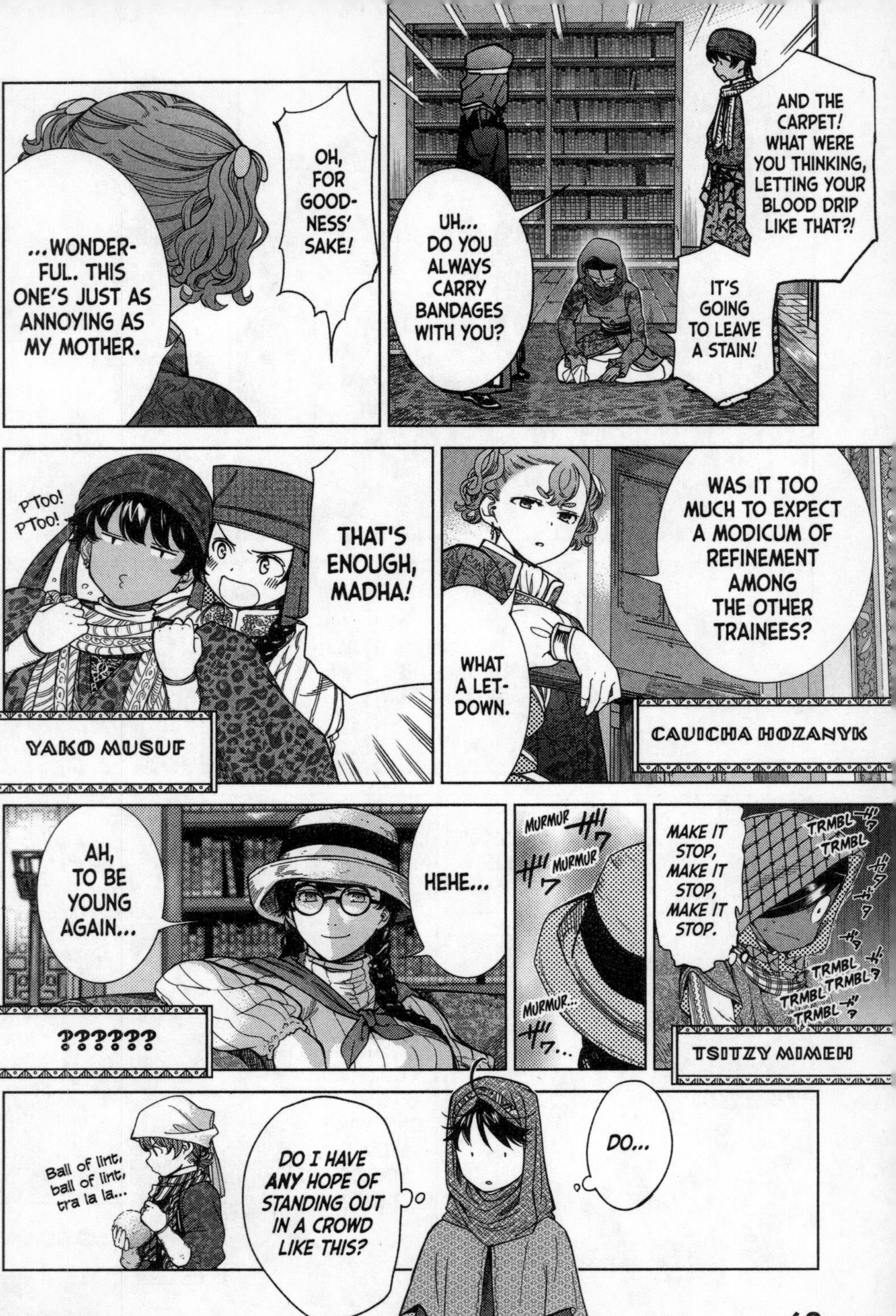
AND THE CARPET! WHAT WERE YOU THINKING, LETTING YOUR BLOOD DRIP LIKE THAT?!
IT'S GOING TO LEAVE A STAIN!
UH... DO YOU ALWAYS CARRY BANDAGES WITH YOU?
OH, FOR GOODNESS' SAKE!
...WONDERFUL. THIS ONE'S JUST AS ANNOYING AS MY MOTHER.
WAS IT TOO MUCH TO EXPECT A MODICUM OF REFINEMENT AMONG THE OTHER TRAINEES?
WHAT A LETDOWN.
CAUICHA HOZANYK
THAT'S ENOUGH, MADHA!
PTOO! PTOO!
YAKO MUSUF
MAKE IT STOP, MAKE IT STOP, MAKE IT STOP.
TRMBL TRMBL
TRMBL TRMBL TRMBL TRMBL
TSITZY MIMEH
MURMUR
MURMUR
MURMUR...
HEHE...
AH, TO BE YOUNG AGAIN...
??????
DO...
DO I HAVE ANY HOPE OF STANDING OUT IN A CROWD LIKE THIS?
Ball of lint, ball of lint, tra la la...

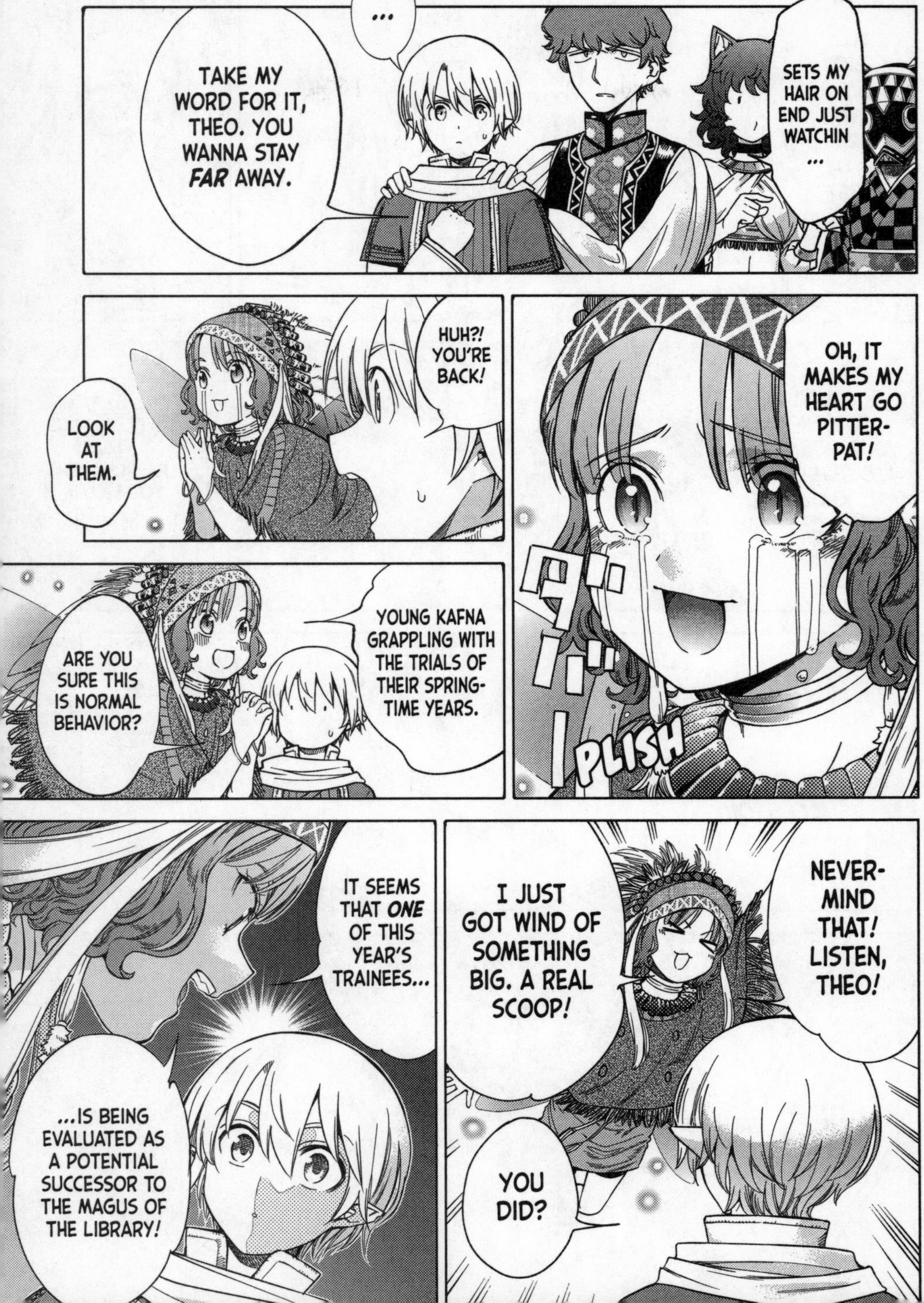
SETS MY HAIR ON END JUST WATCHIN...
...
TAKE MY WORD FOR IT, THEO. YOU WANNA STAY FAR AWAY.
OH, IT MAKES MY HEART GO PITTER-PAT!
PLISH
HUH?! YOU'RE BACK!
LOOK AT THEM.
YOUNG KAFNA GRAPPLING WITH THE TRIALS OF THEIR SPRING-TIME YEARS.
ARE YOU SURE THIS IS NORMAL BEHAVIOR?
NEVER-MIND THAT! LISTEN, THEO!
I JUST GOT WIND OF SOMETHING BIG. A REAL SCOOP!
YOU DID?
IT SEEMS THAT ONE OF THIS YEAR'S TRAINEES...
...IS BEING EVALUATED AS A POTENTIAL SUCCESSOR TO THE MAGUS OF THE LIBRARY!

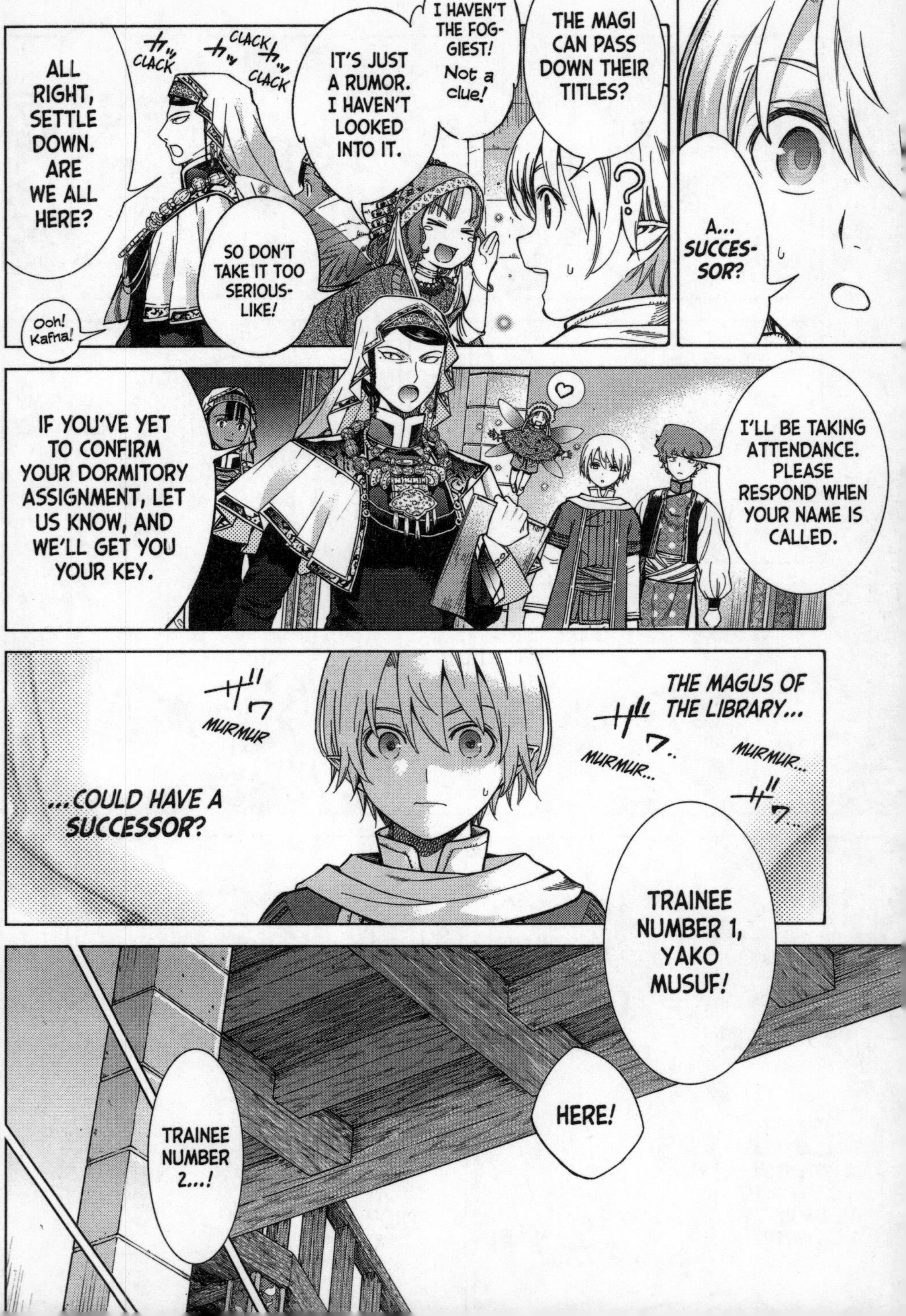
A... SUCCESSOR?
THE MAGI CAN PASS DOWN THEIR TITLES?
I HAVEN'T THE FOGGIEST! Not a clue!
IT'S JUST A RUMOR. I HAVEN'T LOOKED INTO IT.
SO DON'T TAKE IT TOO SERIOUS-LIKE!
CLACK CLACK CLACK
ALL RIGHT, SETTLE DOWN. ARE WE ALL HERE?
Ooh! Kafna!
I'LL BE TAKING ATTENDANCE. PLEASE RESPOND WHEN YOUR NAME IS CALLED.
IF YOU'VE YET TO CONFIRM YOUR DORMITORY ASSIGNMENT, LET US KNOW, AND WE'LL GET YOU YOUR KEY.
THE MAGUS OF THE LIBRARY...
MURMUR... MURMUR... MURMUR
...COULD HAVE A SUCCESSOR?
TRAINEE NUMBER 1, YAKO MUSUF!
HERE!
TRAINEE NUMBER 2...!

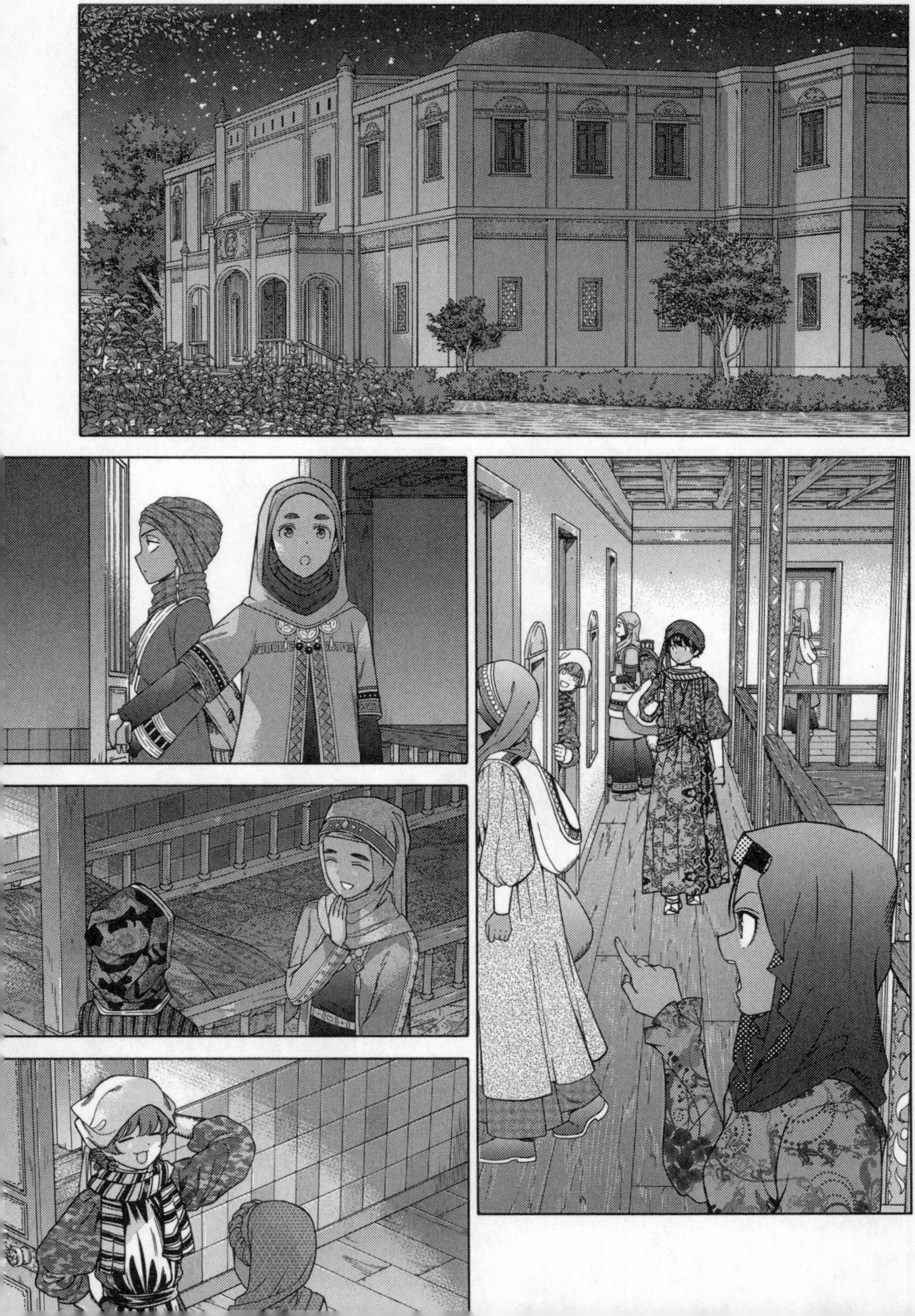

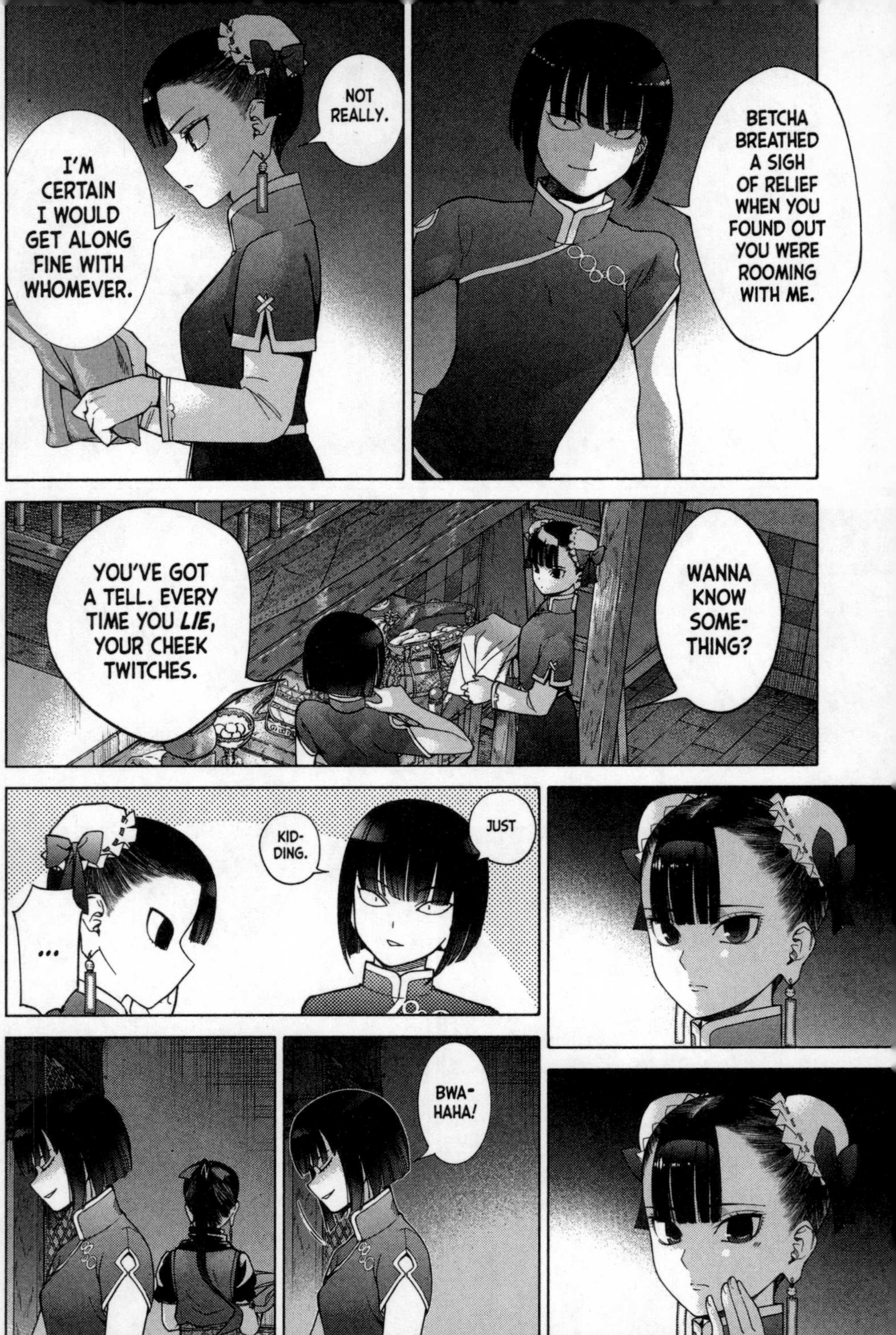
BETCHA BREATHED A SIGH OF RELIEF WHEN YOU FOUND OUT YOU WERE ROOMING WITH ME.
NOT REALLY.
I'M CERTAIN I WOULD GET ALONG FINE WITH WHOMEVER.
WANNA KNOW SOME-THING?
YOU'VE GOT A TELL. EVERY TIME YOU *LIE*, YOUR CHEEK TWITCHES.
JUST KID-DING.
...
BWA-HAHA!

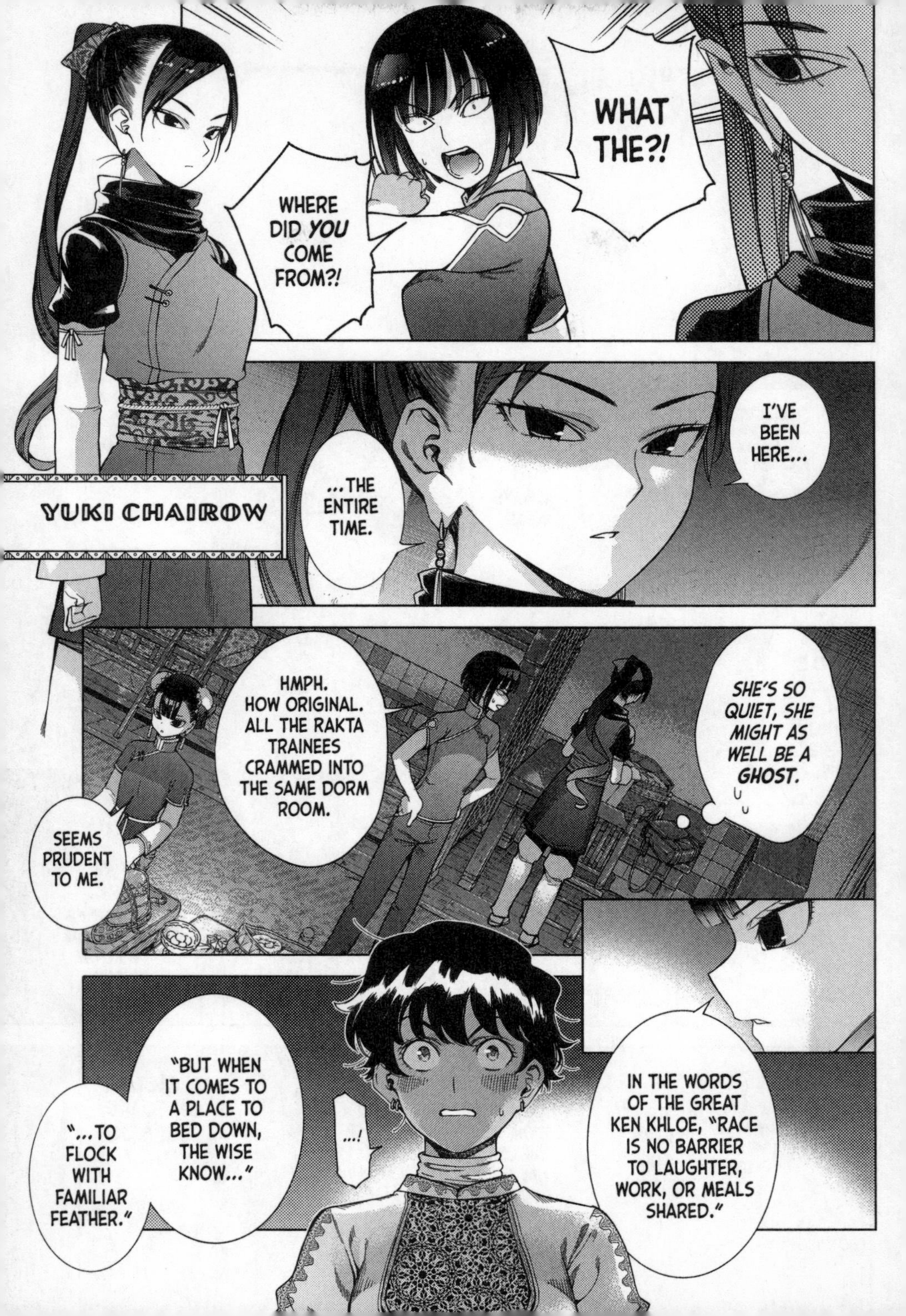
WHAT THE?!
WHERE DID YOU COME FROM?!
I'VE BEEN HERE...
...THE ENTIRE TIME.
YUKI CHAIROW
SHE'S SO QUIET, SHE MIGHT AS WELL BE A GHOST.
HMPH. HOW ORIGINAL. ALL THE RAKTA TRAINEES CRAMMED INTO THE SAME DORM ROOM.
SEEMS PRUDENT TO ME.
IN THE WORDS OF THE GREAT KEN KHLOE, "RACE IS NO BARRIER TO LAUGHTER, WORK, OR MEALS SHARED."
...!
"BUT WHEN IT COMES TO A PLACE TO BED DOWN, THE WISE KNOW..."
"...TO FLOCK WITH FAMILIAR FEATHER."

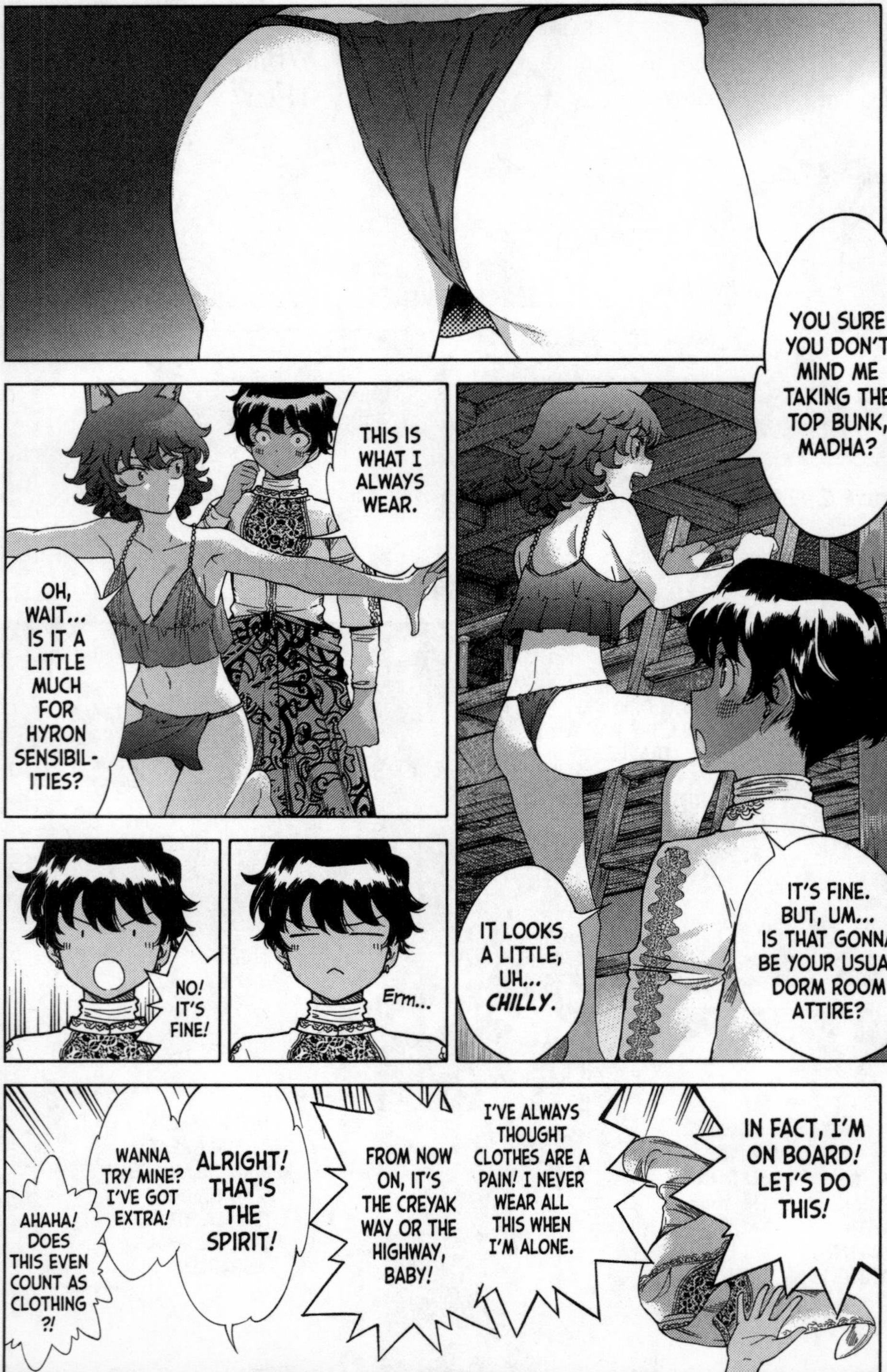
YOU SURE YOU DON'T MIND ME TAKING THE TOP BUNK, MADHA?
IT'S FINE. BUT, UM... IS THAT GONNA BE YOUR USUAL DORM ROOM ATTIRE?
IT LOOKS A LITTLE, UH... *CHILLY.*
THIS IS WHAT I ALWAYS WEAR.
OH, WAIT... IS IT A LITTLE MUCH FOR HYRON SENSIBIL-ITIES?
Erm...
NO! IT'S FINE!
IN FACT, I'M ON BOARD! LET'S DO THIS!
I'VE ALWAYS THOUGHT CLOTHES ARE A PAIN! I NEVER WEAR ALL THIS WHEN I'M ALONE.
FROM NOW ON, IT'S THE CREYAK WAY OR THE HIGHWAY, BABY!
ALRIGHT! THAT'S THE SPIRIT!
WANNA TRY MINE? I'VE GOT EXTRA!
AHAHA! DOES THIS EVEN COUNT AS CLOTHING?!

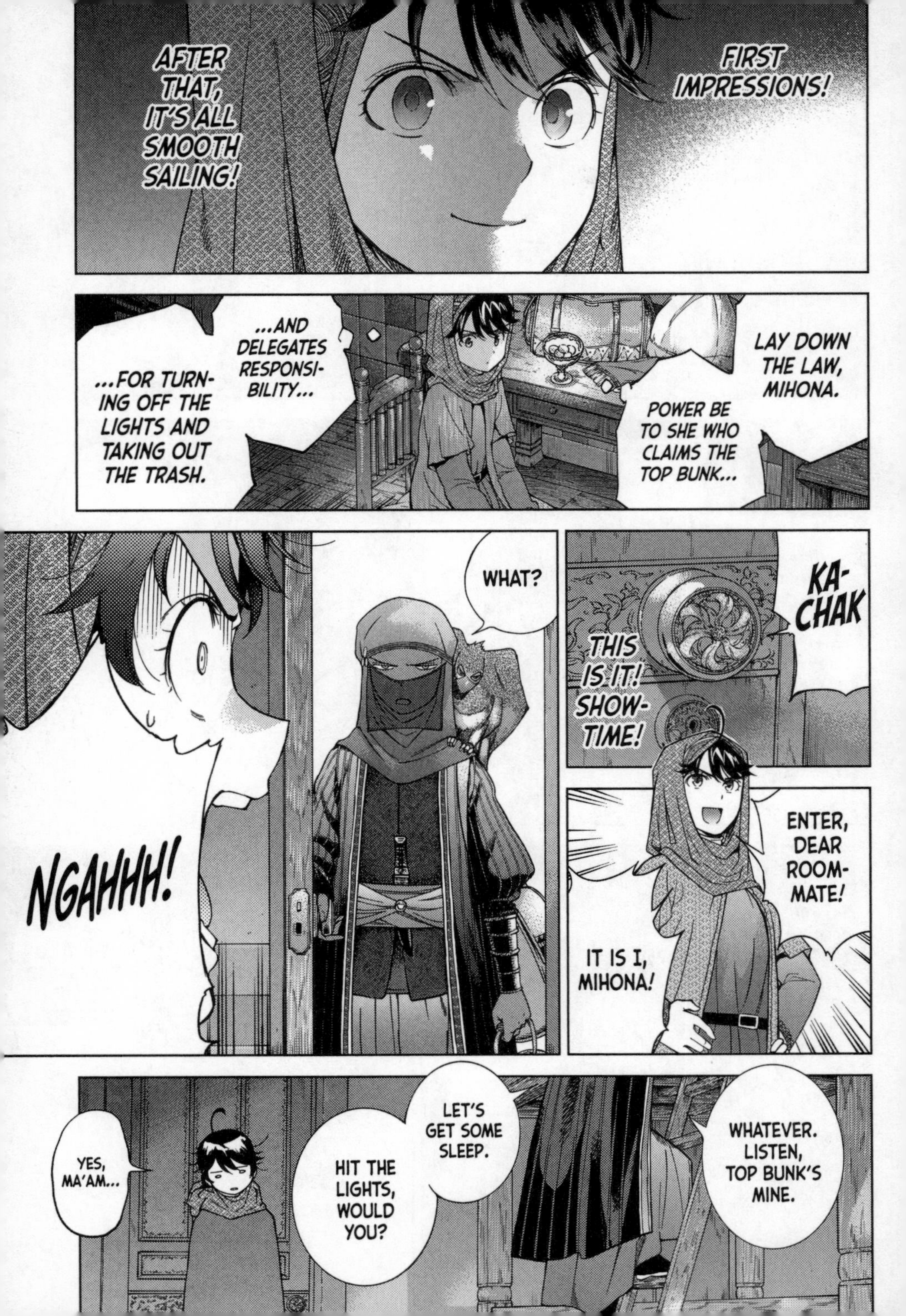
FIRST IMPRESSIONS!
AFTER THAT, IT'S ALL SMOOTH SAILING!
LAY DOWN THE LAW, MIHONA.
POWER BE TO SHE WHO CLAIMS THE TOP BUNK...
...AND DELEGATES RESPONSIBILITY...
...FOR TURNING OFF THE LIGHTS AND TAKING OUT THE TRASH.
KA-CHAK
THIS IS IT! SHOWTIME!
ENTER, DEAR ROOMMATE!
IT IS I, MIHONA!
WHAT?
NGAHHH!
WHATEVER. LISTEN, TOP BUNK'S MINE.
LET'S GET SOME SLEEP.
HIT THE LIGHTS, WOULD YOU?
YES, MA'AM...

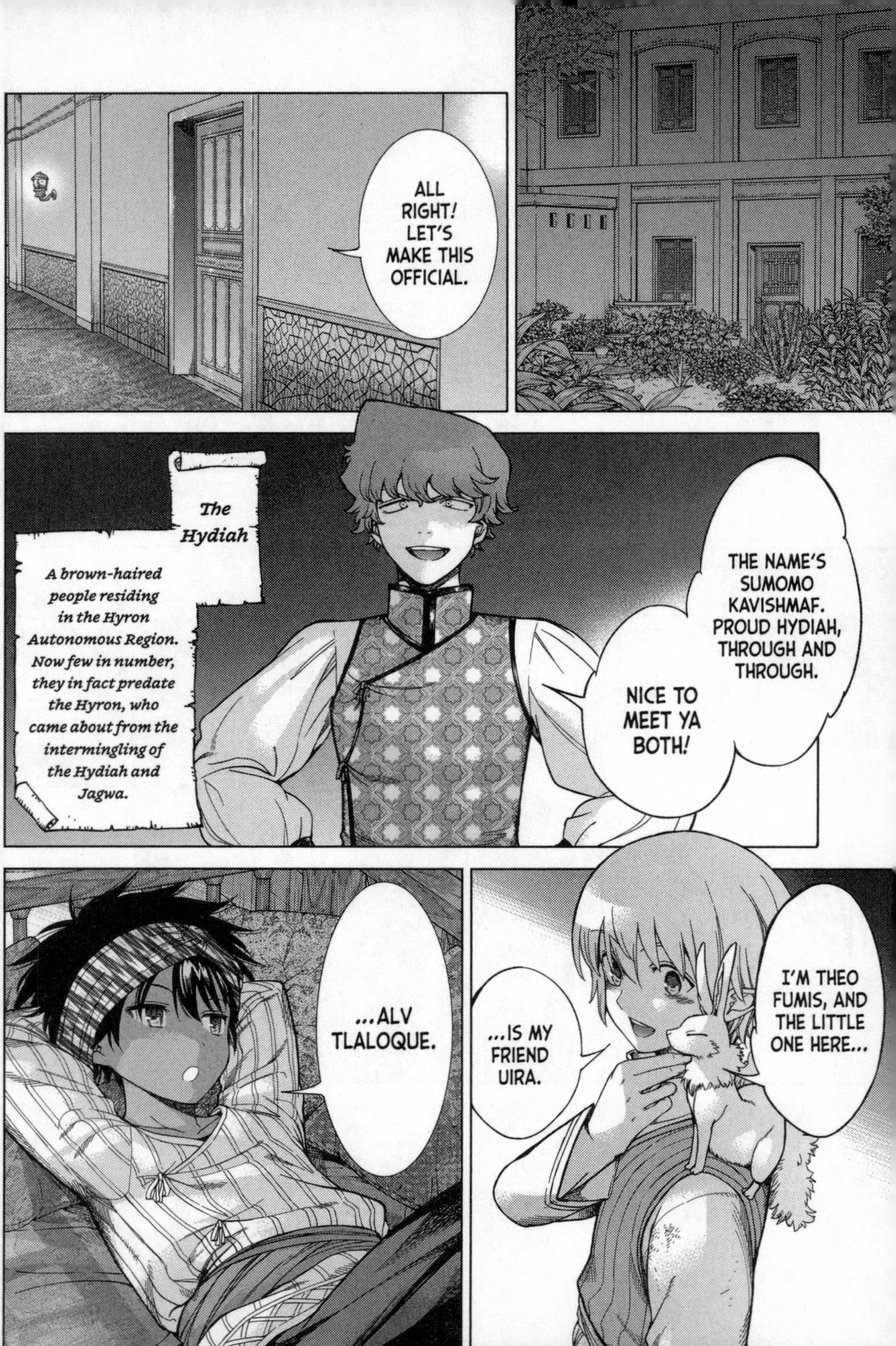
ALL RIGHT! LET'S MAKE THIS OFFICIAL.
THE NAME'S SUMOMO KAVISHMAF. PROUD HYDIAH, THROUGH AND THROUGH.
NICE TO MEET YA BOTH!
The Hydiah
A brown-haired people residing in the Hyron Autonomous Region. Now few in number, they in fact predate the Hyron, who came about from the intermingling of the Hydiah and Jagwa.
I'M THEO FUMIS, AND THE LITTLE ONE HERE...
...IS MY FRIEND UIRA.
...ALV TLALOQUE.

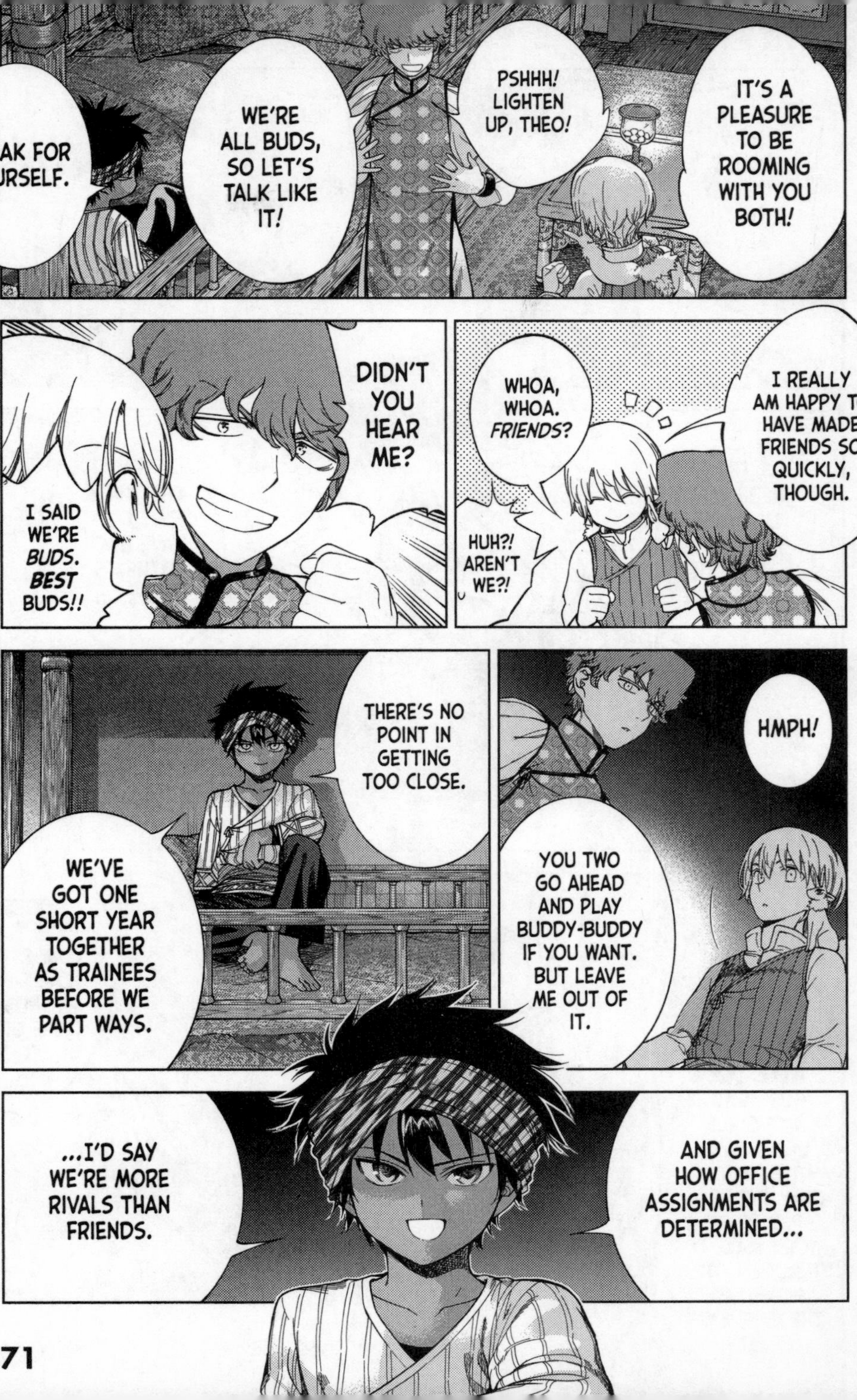
IT'S A PLEASURE TO BE ROOMING WITH YOU BOTH!
PSHHH! LIGHTEN UP, THEO!
WE'RE ALL BUDS, SO LET'S TALK LIKE IT!
SPEAK FOR YOURSELF.
I REALLY AM HAPPY TO HAVE MADE FRIENDS SO QUICKLY, THOUGH.
WHOA, WHOA. *FRIENDS*?
HUH?! AREN'T WE?!
DIDN'T YOU HEAR ME?
I SAID WE'RE *BUDS*. ***BEST*** BUDS!!
HMPH!
YOU TWO GO AHEAD AND PLAY BUDDY-BUDDY IF YOU WANT. BUT LEAVE ME OUT OF IT.
THERE'S NO POINT IN GETTING TOO CLOSE.
WE'VE GOT ONE SHORT YEAR TOGETHER AS TRAINEES BEFORE WE PART WAYS.
AND GIVEN HOW OFFICE ASSIGNMENTS ARE DETERMINED...
...I'D SAY WE'RE MORE RIVALS THAN FRIENDS.

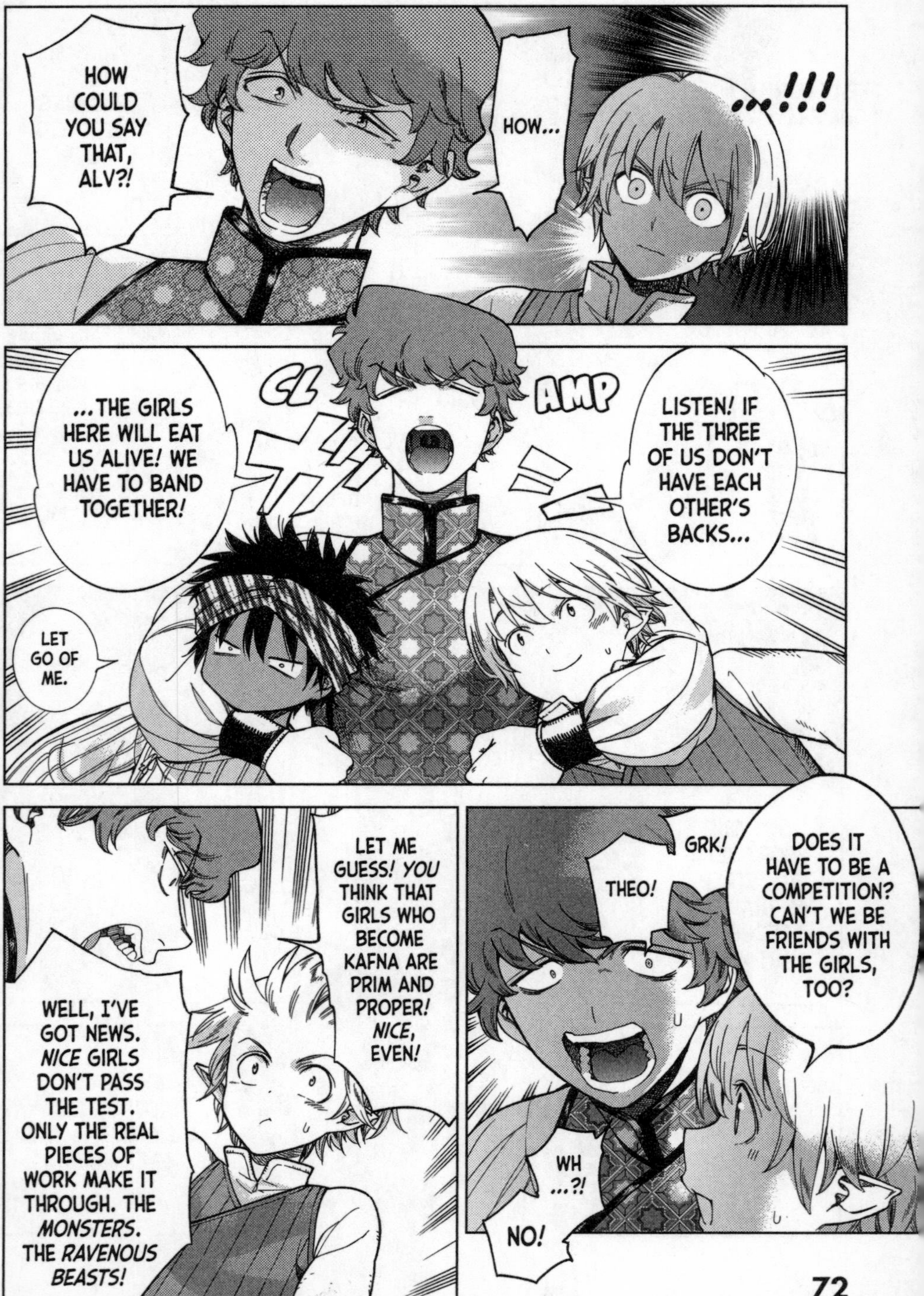
...!!!
HOW...
HOW COULD YOU SAY THAT, ALV?!
CLAMP
LISTEN! IF THE THREE OF US DON'T HAVE EACH OTHER'S BACKS...
...THE GIRLS HERE WILL EAT US ALIVE! WE HAVE TO BAND TOGETHER!
LET GO OF ME.
DOES IT HAVE TO BE A COMPETITION? CAN'T WE BE FRIENDS WITH THE GIRLS, TOO?
GRK!
THEO!
WH ...?!
NO!
LET ME GUESS! *YOU* THINK THAT GIRLS WHO BECOME KAFNA ARE PRIM AND PROPER! *NICE*, EVEN!
WELL, I'VE GOT NEWS. *NICE* GIRLS DON'T PASS THE TEST. ONLY THE REAL PIECES OF WORK MAKE IT THROUGH. THE *MONSTERS*. THE *RAVENOUS* *BEASTS*!

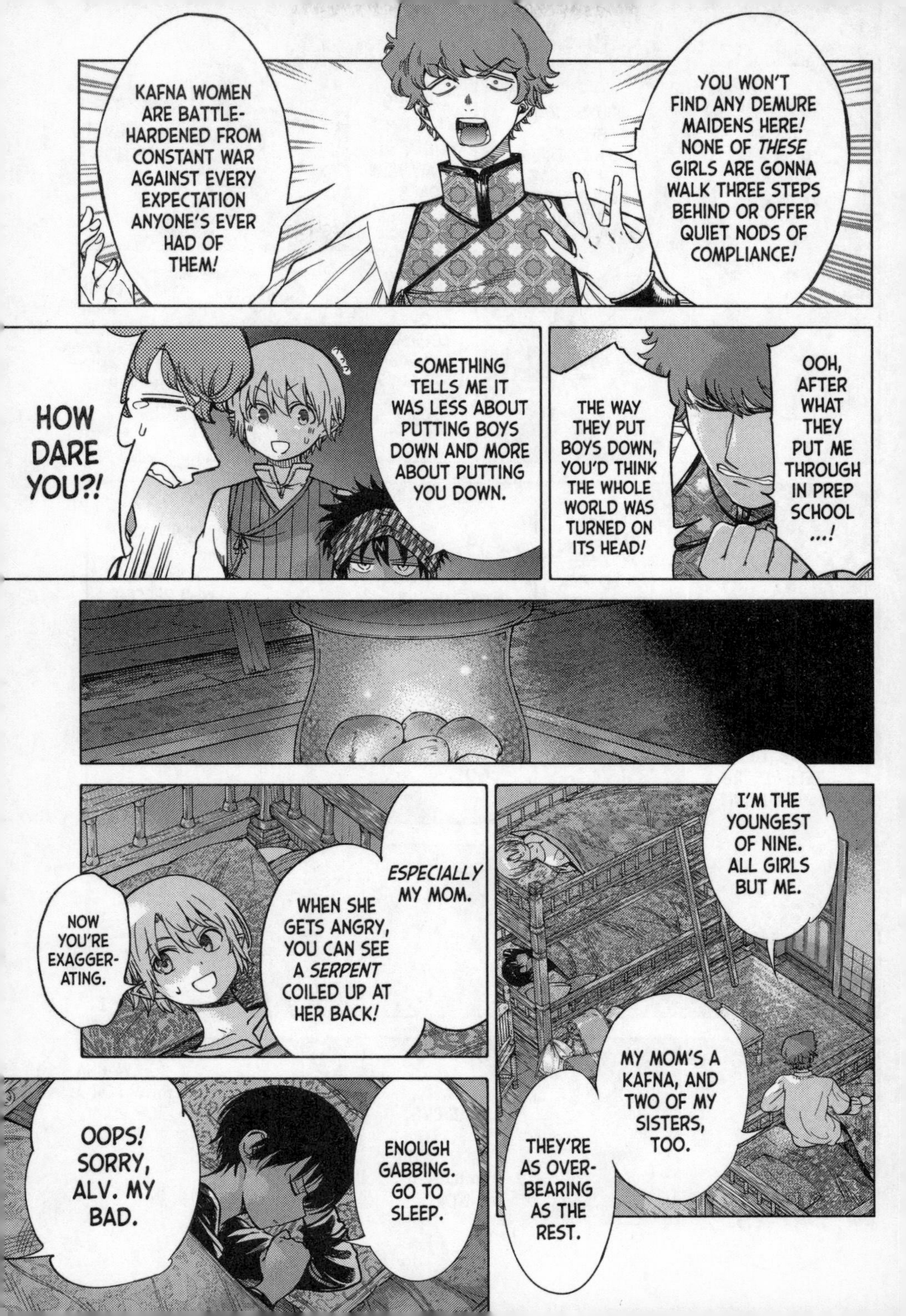
YOU WON'T FIND ANY DEMURE MAIDENS HERE! NONE OF *THESE* GIRLS ARE GONNA WALK THREE STEPS BEHIND OR OFFER QUIET NODS OF COMPLIANCE!
KAFNA WOMEN ARE BATTLE-HARDENED FROM CONSTANT WAR AGAINST EVERY EXPECTATION ANYONE'S EVER HAD OF THEM!
OOH, AFTER WHAT THEY PUT ME THROUGH IN PREP SCHOOL ...!
THE WAY THEY PUT BOYS DOWN, YOU'D THINK THE WHOLE WORLD WAS TURNED ON ITS HEAD!
SOMETHING TELLS ME IT WAS LESS ABOUT PUTTING BOYS DOWN AND MORE ABOUT PUTTING YOU DOWN.
HOW DARE YOU?!
I'M THE YOUNGEST OF NINE. ALL GIRLS BUT ME.
MY MOM'S A KAFNA, AND TWO OF MY SISTERS, TOO.
THEY'RE AS OVER-BEARING AS THE REST.
ESPECIALLY MY MOM.
WHEN SHE GETS ANGRY, YOU CAN SEE A *SERPENT* COILED UP AT HER BACK!
NOW YOU'RE EXAGGER-ATING.
ENOUGH GABBING. GO TO SLEEP.
OOPS! SORRY, ALV. MY BAD.

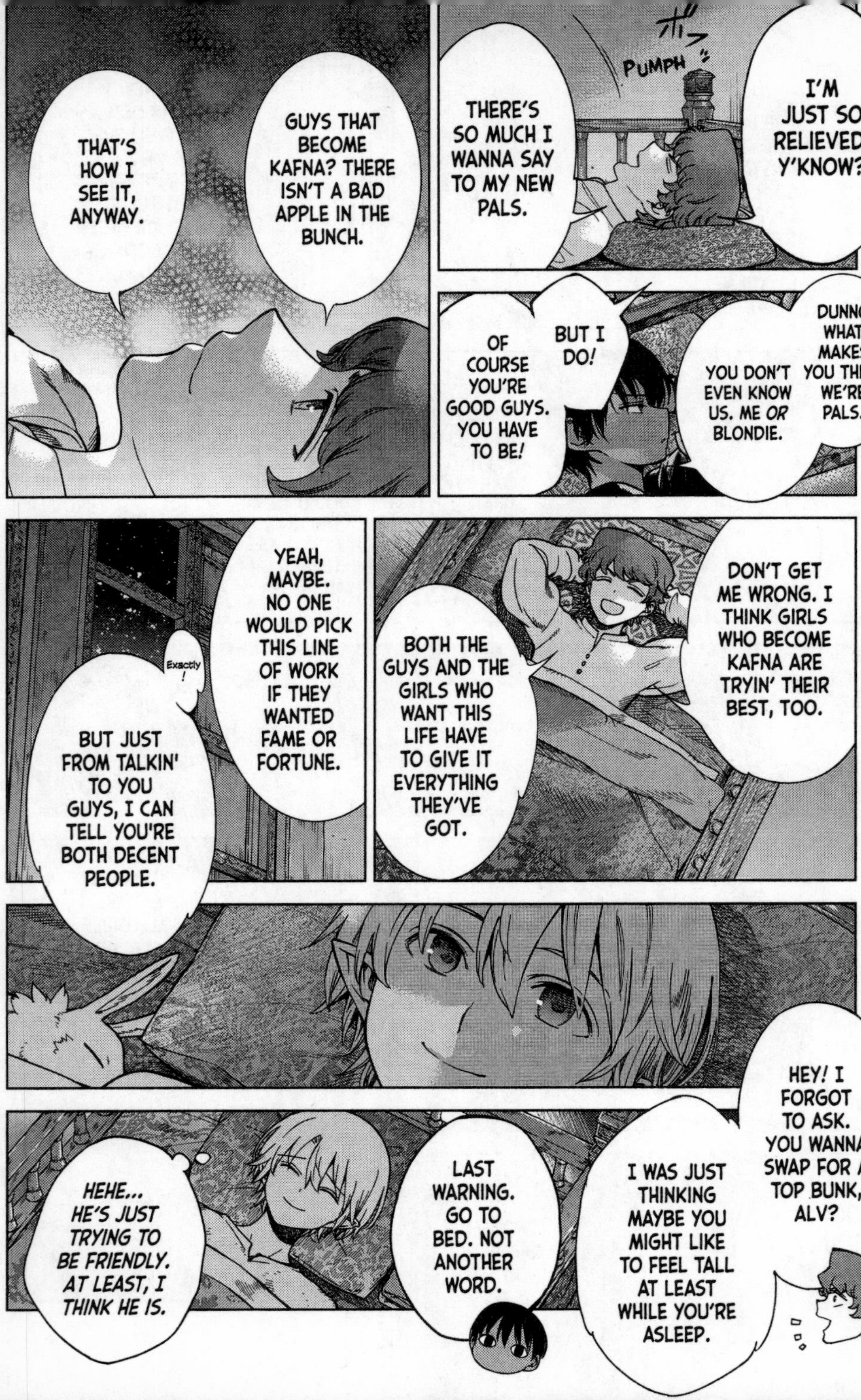
PUMPH
I'M JUST SO RELIEVED, Y'KNOW?
THERE'S SO MUCH I WANNA SAY TO MY NEW PALS.
DUNNO WHAT MAKES YOU THINK WE'RE PALS.
YOU DON'T EVEN KNOW US. ME *OR* BLONDIE.
BUT I DO!
OF COURSE YOU'RE GOOD GUYS. YOU HAVE TO BE!
GUYS THAT BECOME KAFNA? THERE ISN'T A BAD APPLE IN THE BUNCH.
THAT'S HOW I SEE IT, ANYWAY.
DON'T GET ME WRONG. I THINK GIRLS WHO BECOME KAFNA ARE TRYIN' THEIR BEST, TOO.
BOTH THE GUYS AND THE GIRLS WHO WANT THIS LIFE HAVE TO GIVE IT EVERYTHING THEY'VE GOT.
YEAH, MAYBE. NO ONE WOULD PICK THIS LINE OF WORK IF THEY WANTED FAME OR FORTUNE.
Exactly!
BUT JUST FROM TALKIN' TO YOU GUYS, I CAN TELL YOU'RE BOTH DECENT PEOPLE.
HEY! I FORGOT TO ASK. YOU WANNA SWAP FOR A TOP BUNK, ALV?
I WAS JUST THINKING MAYBE YOU MIGHT LIKE TO FEEL TALL AT LEAST WHILE YOU'RE ASLEEP.
LAST WARNING. GO TO BED. NOT ANOTHER WORD.
HEHE... HE'S JUST TRYING TO BE FRIENDLY. AT LEAST, I THINK HE IS.

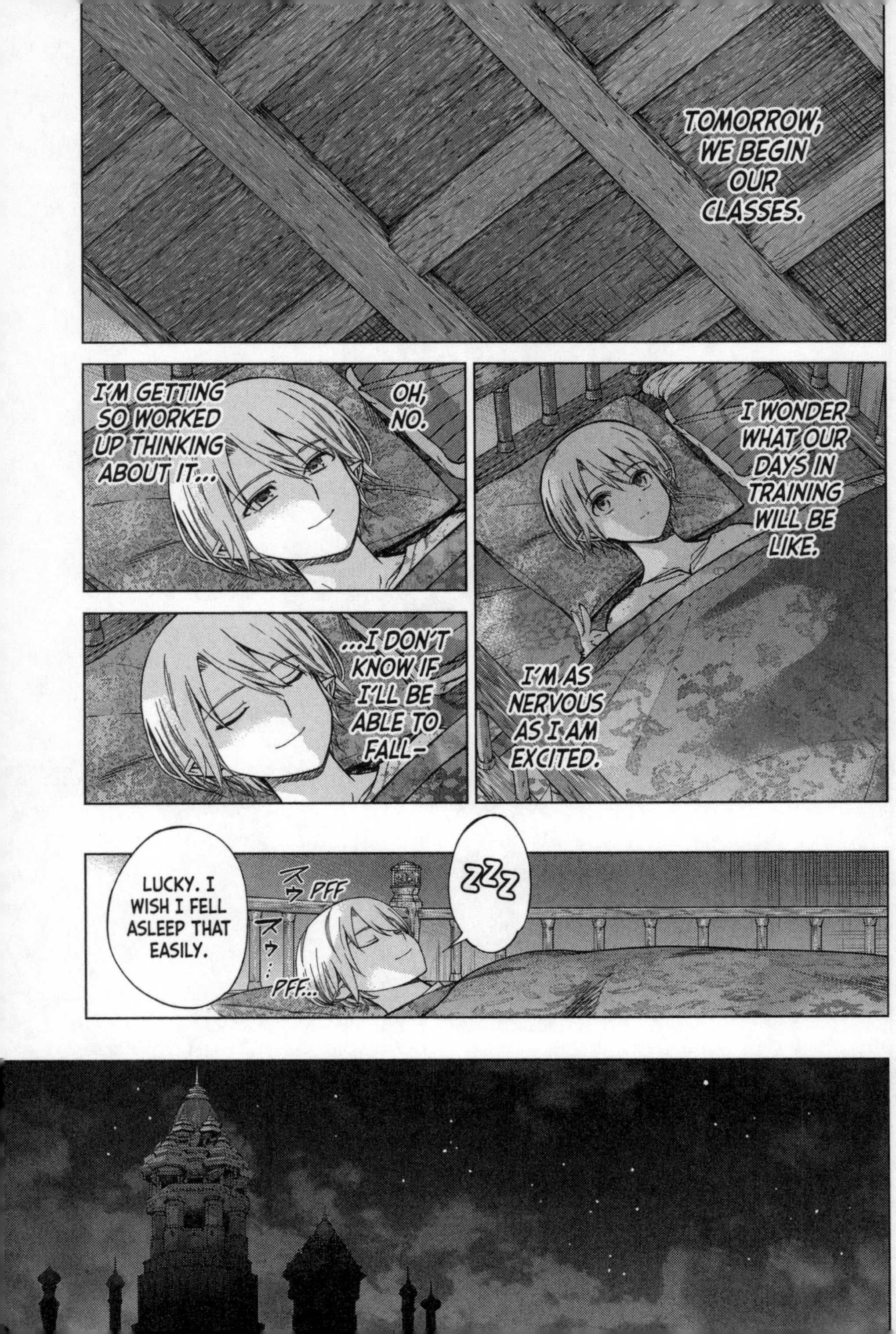
TOMORROW, WE BEGIN OUR CLASSES.
I WONDER WHAT OUR DAYS IN TRAINING WILL BE LIKE.
I'M AS NERVOUS AS I AM EXCITED.
OH, NO.
I'M GETTING SO WORKED UP THINKING ABOUT IT...
...I DON'T KNOW IF I'LL BE ABLE TO FALL–
ZZZ
スゥ PFF
スゥ… PFF...
LUCKY. I WISH I FELL ASLEEP THAT EASILY.

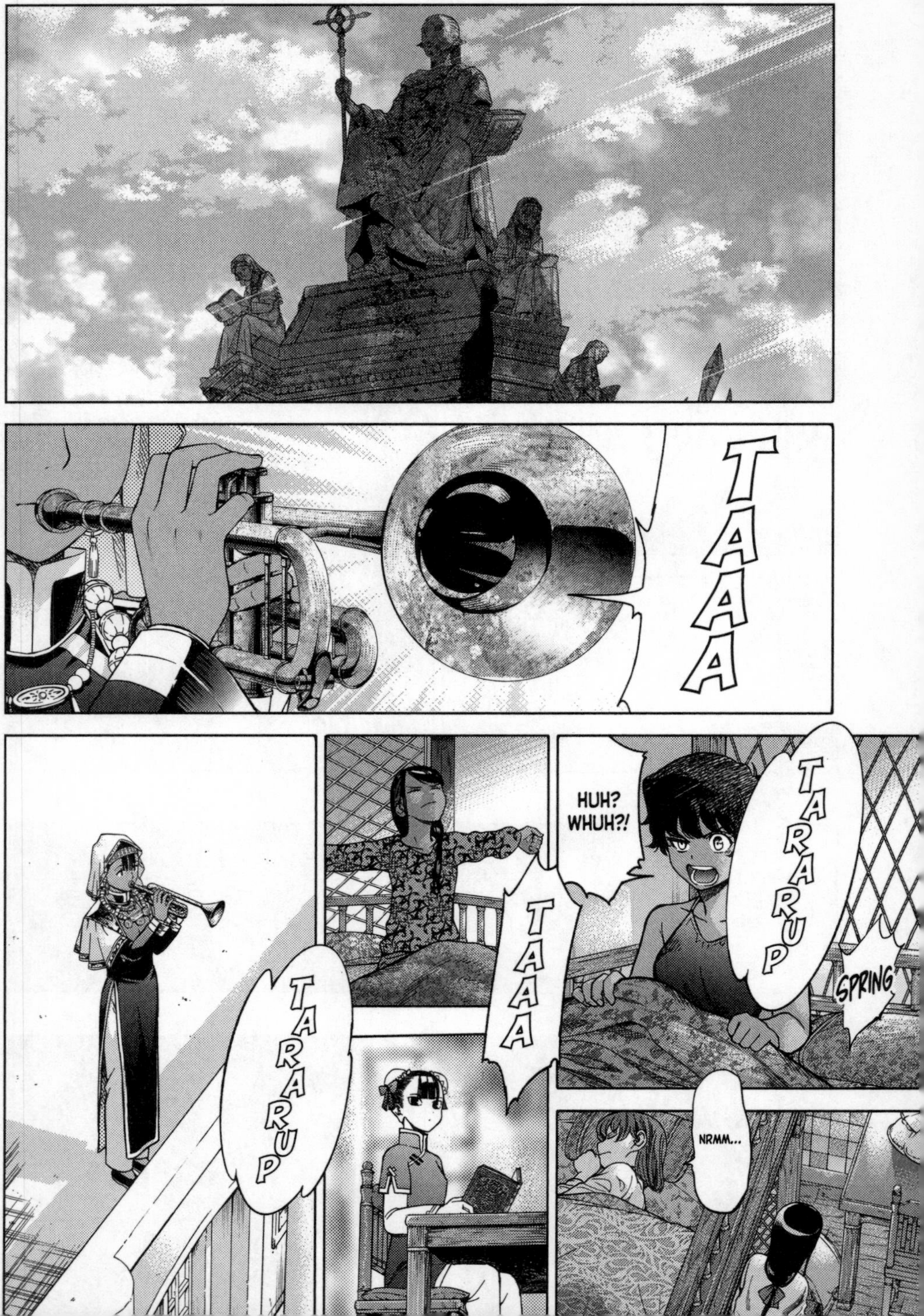
TAAAA
TARARUP
HUH? WHUH?!
SPRING
TAAAA
NRMM...
TARARUP

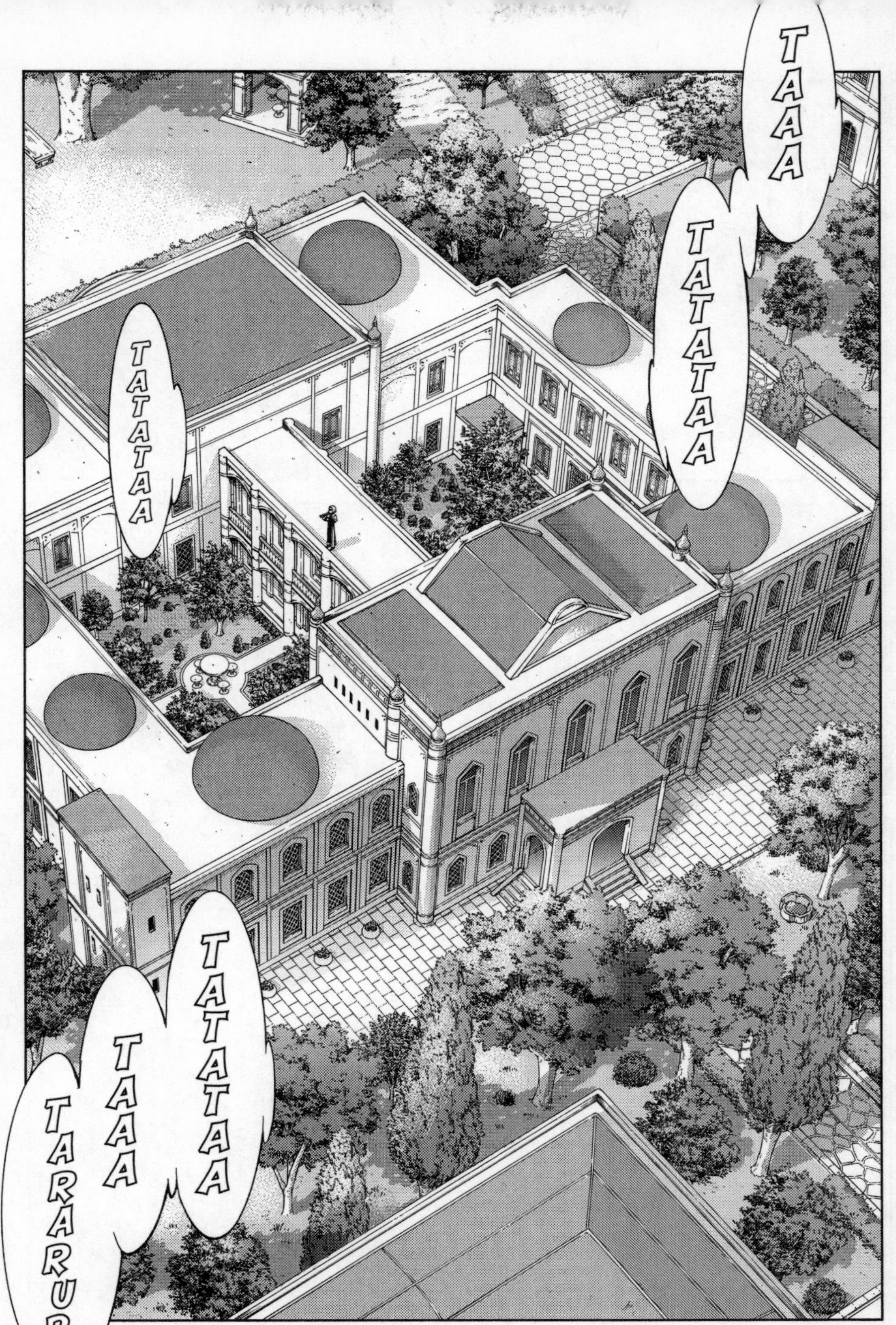
TAAA
TATATAA
TATATAA
TATATAA
TAAA
TARARUP

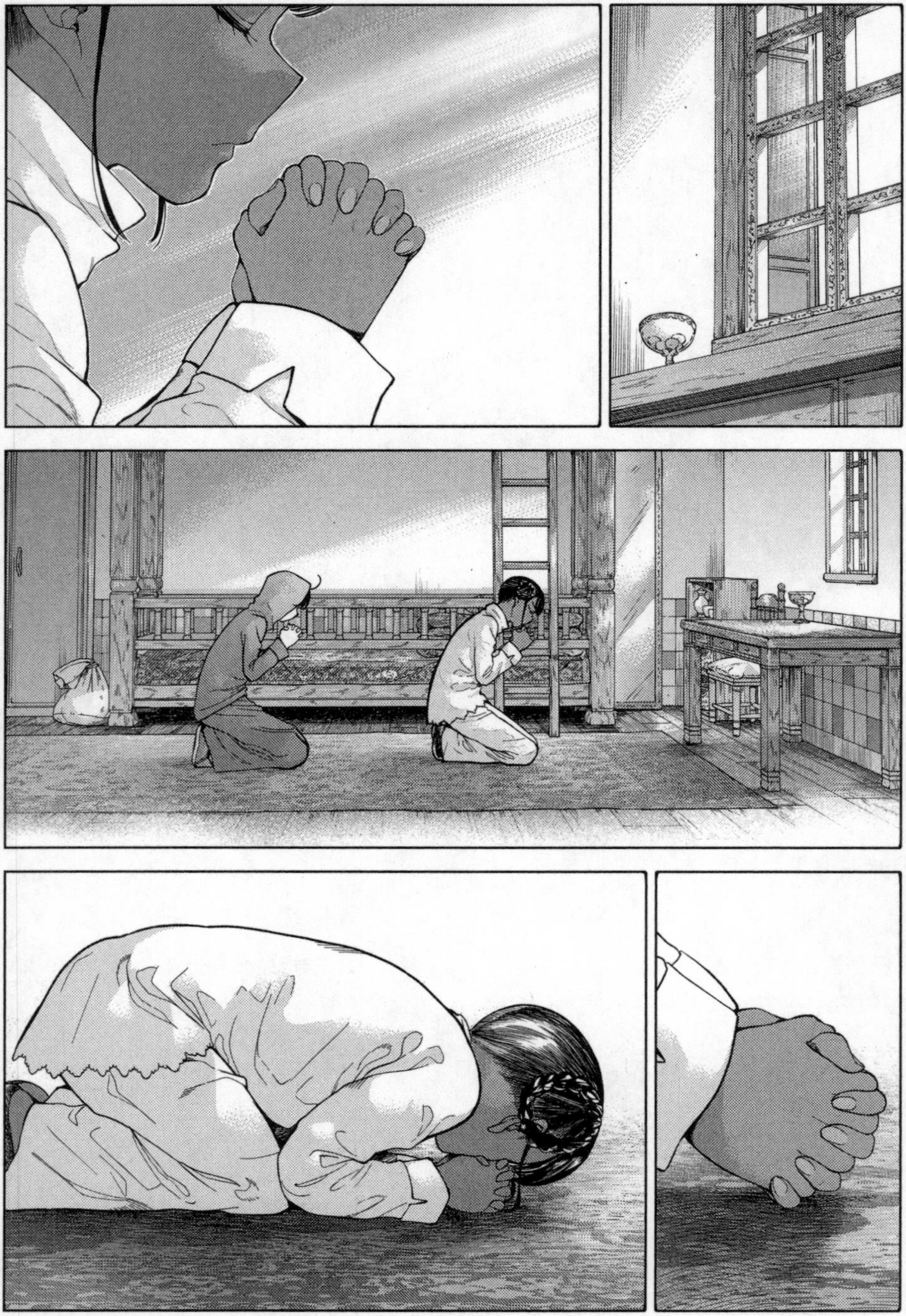

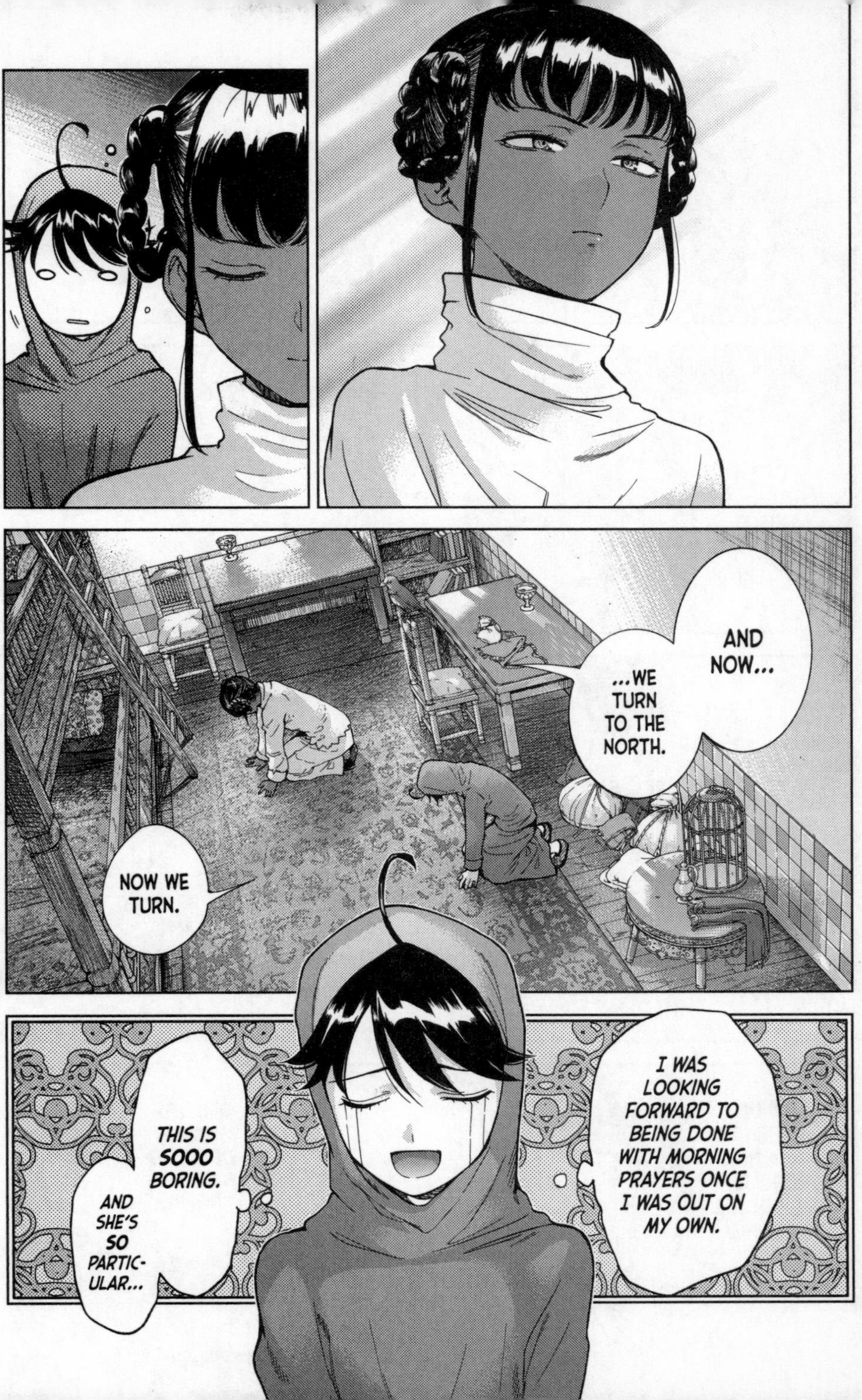
AND NOW...
...WE TURN TO THE NORTH.
NOW WE TURN.
I WAS LOOKING FORWARD TO BEING DONE WITH MORNING PRAYERS ONCE I WAS OUT ON MY OWN.
THIS IS SOOO BORING.
AND SHE'S SO PARTIC-ULAR...

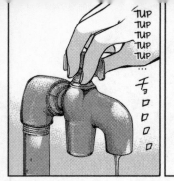

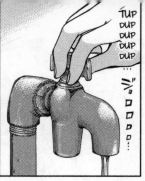

TUP DUP DUP DUP DUP ...
ジョロロロロロ...
SQRK
TUP TUP TUP TUP TUP ...
チョロロロロロ
WOOOOOW...
TUP TUP TUP TUP TUP ...
ロロロロロロ...
CAREFUL. IF YOU GET CAUGHT WASTING WATER, YOU'RE GONNA GET AN EARFUL.
SORRY. IT'S JUST SO AMAZING...
AFTZAAK MIGHT BE BLESSED WITH PLENTY OF WATER FROM LAKE TATA AND ELSE-WHERE...
...BUT IN A CITY OF OVER A MILLION, WE ALL GOTTA DO OUR PART TO MAKE SURE IT DOESN'T RUN OUT.
VSSHHH
ジャアアアア
SPLSH SPLSH
VSSSSS
シャアアアア
IN OTHER WORDS, *DON'T* DO WHAT HE'S DOING.
AHHH! NOTHING LIKE A NICE, THOROUGH WASH IN THE MORNING!
SHH

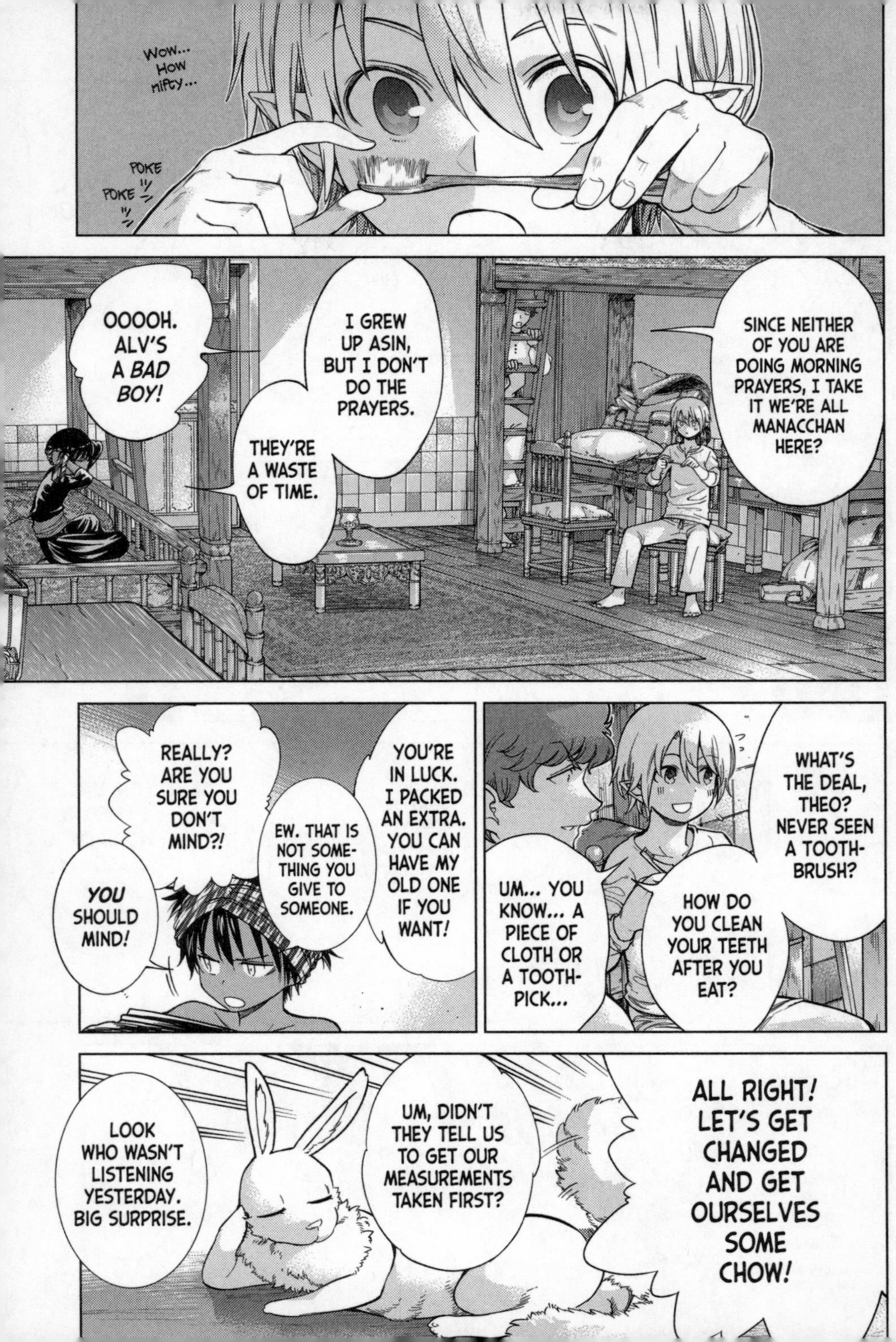
Wow... How nifty...
POKE POKE
SINCE NEITHER OF YOU ARE DOING MORNING PRAYERS, I TAKE IT WE'RE ALL MANACCHAN HERE?
I GREW UP ASIN, BUT I DON'T DO THE PRAYERS.
THEY'RE A WASTE OF TIME.
OOOOH. ALV'S A *BAD BOY!*
WHAT'S THE DEAL, THEO? NEVER SEEN A TOOTH-BRUSH?
HOW DO YOU CLEAN YOUR TEETH AFTER YOU EAT?
UM... YOU KNOW... A PIECE OF CLOTH OR A TOOTH-PICK...
YOU'RE IN LUCK. I PACKED AN EXTRA. YOU CAN HAVE MY OLD ONE IF YOU WANT!
EW. THAT IS NOT SOME-THING YOU GIVE TO SOMEONE.
REALLY? ARE YOU SURE YOU DON'T MIND?!
YOU SHOULD MIND!
ALL RIGHT! LET'S GET CHANGED AND GET OURSELVES SOME CHOW!
UM, DIDN'T THEY TELL US TO GET OUR MEASUREMENTS TAKEN FIRST?
LOOK WHO WASN'T LISTENING YESTERDAY. BIG SURPRISE.

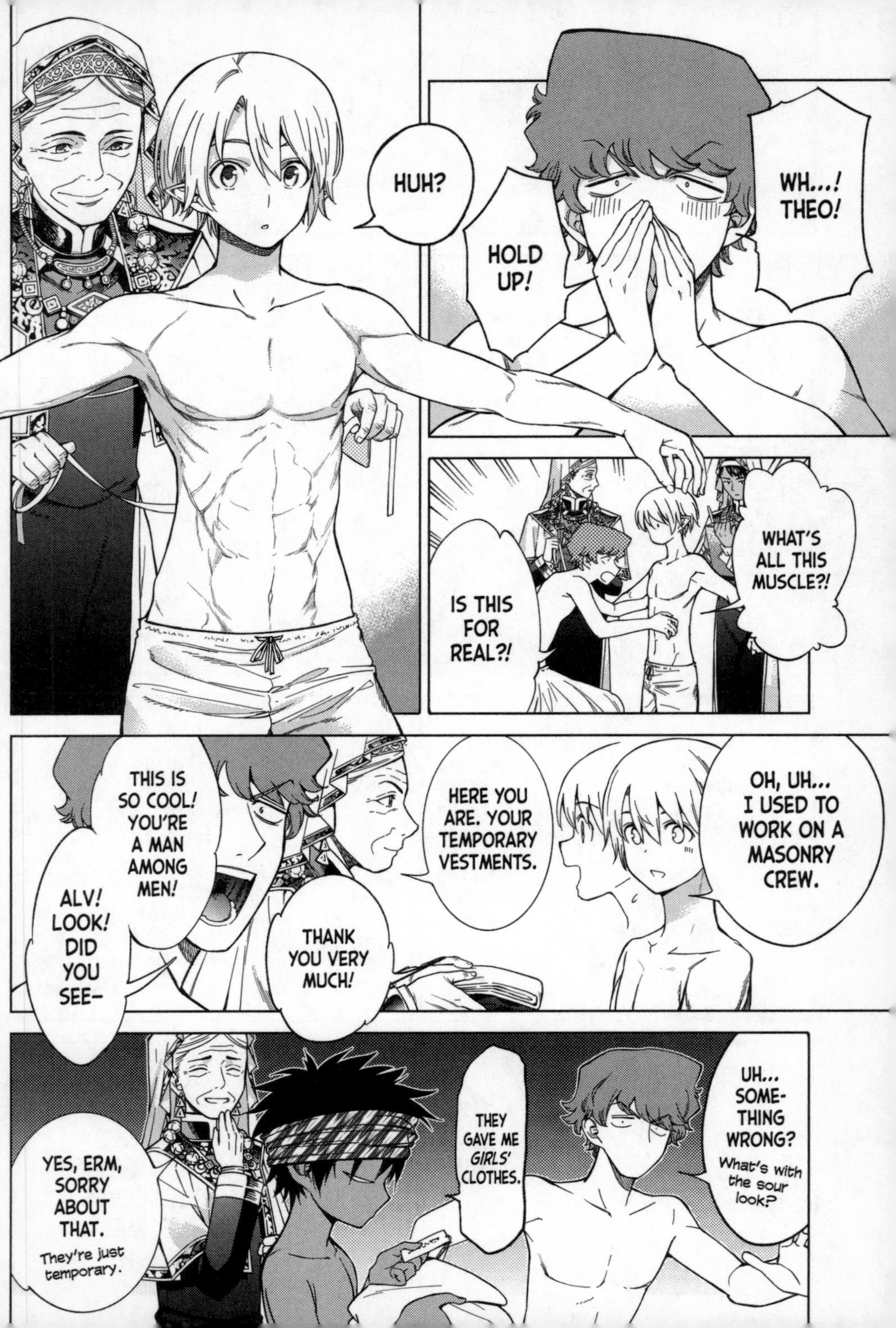
WH...! THEO!
HOLD UP!
WHAT'S ALL THIS MUSCLE?!
IS THIS FOR REAL?!
HUH?
OH, UH... I USED TO WORK ON A MASONRY CREW.
HERE YOU ARE. YOUR TEMPORARY VESTMENTS.
THIS IS SO COOL! YOU'RE A MAN AMONG MEN!
THANK YOU VERY MUCH!
ALV! LOOK! DID YOU SEE–
UH... SOME-THING WRONG?
What's with the sour look?
THEY GAVE ME *GIRLS'* CLOTHES.
YES, ERM, SORRY ABOUT THAT.
They're just temporary.

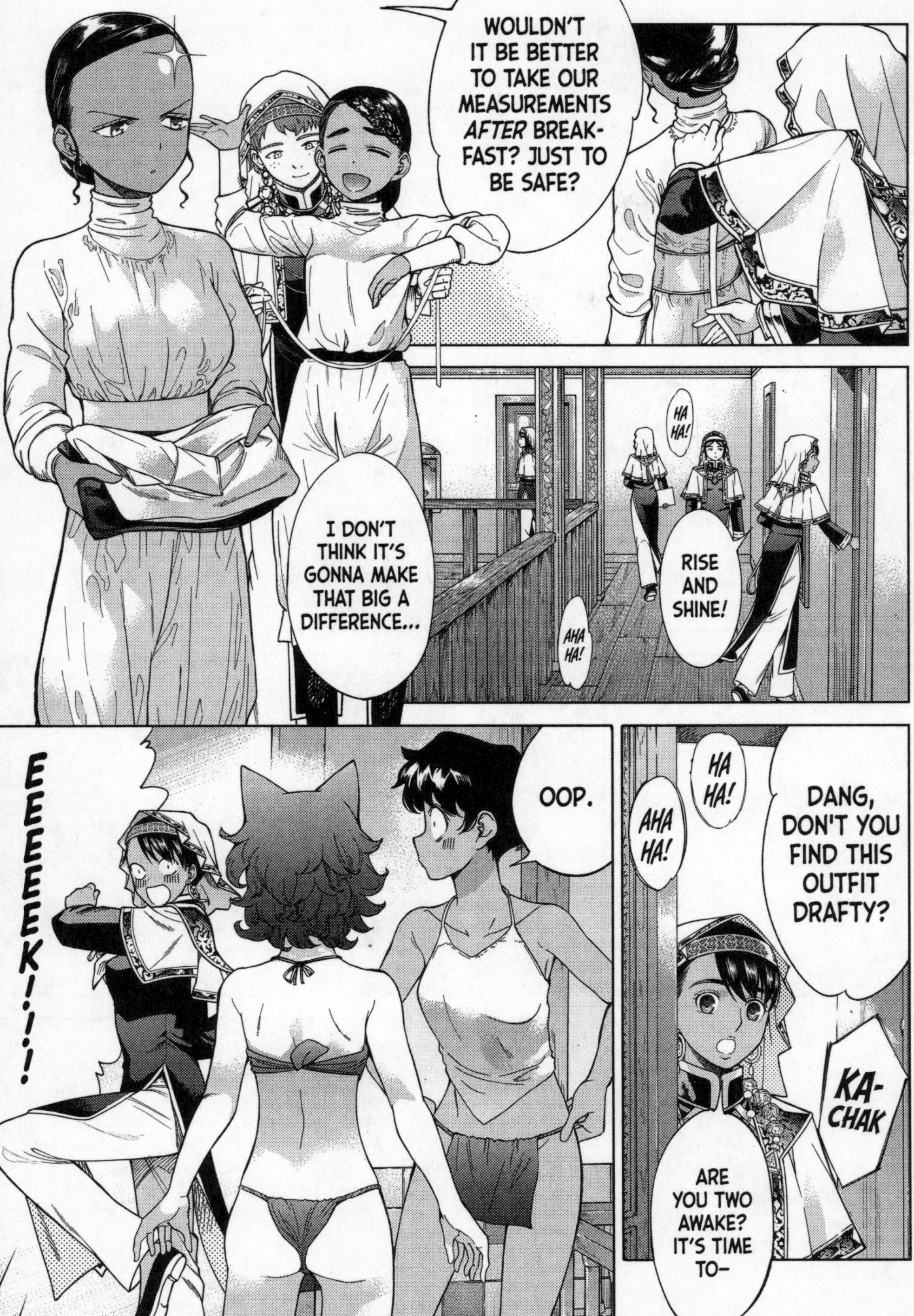
WOULDN'T IT BE BETTER TO TAKE OUR MEASUREMENTS *AFTER* BREAKFAST? JUST TO BE SAFE?
I DON'T THINK IT'S GONNA MAKE THAT BIG A DIFFERENCE...
HA HA!
RISE AND SHINE!
AHA HA!
HA HA!
AHA HA!
DANG, DON'T YOU FIND THIS OUTFIT DRAFTY?
KA-CHAK
ARE YOU TWO AWAKE? IT'S TIME TO—
OOP.
EEEEEEEK!!!!!

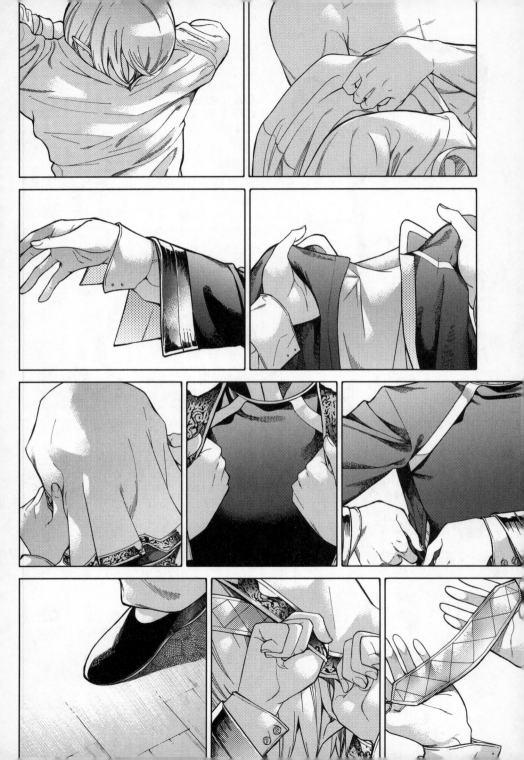

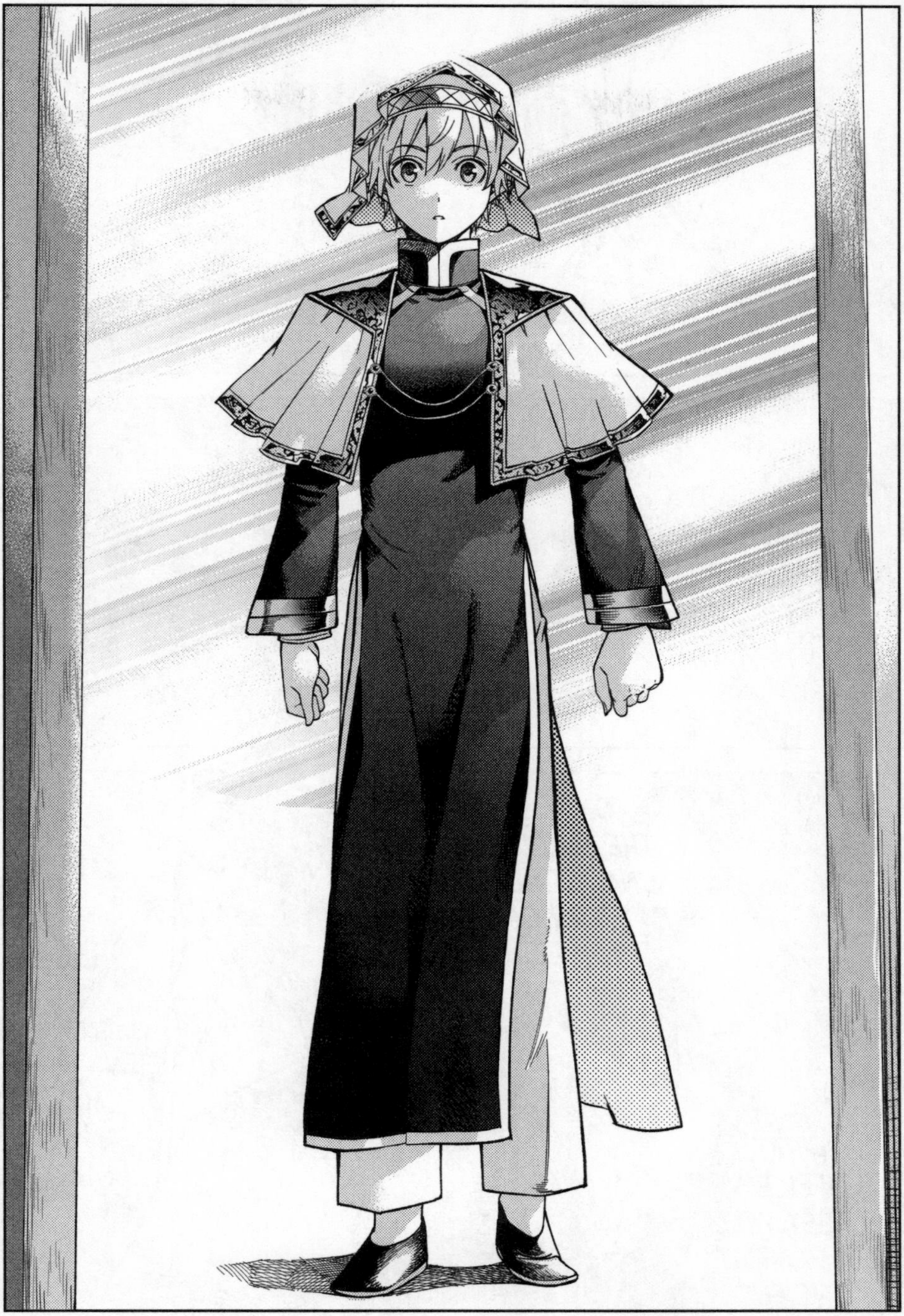

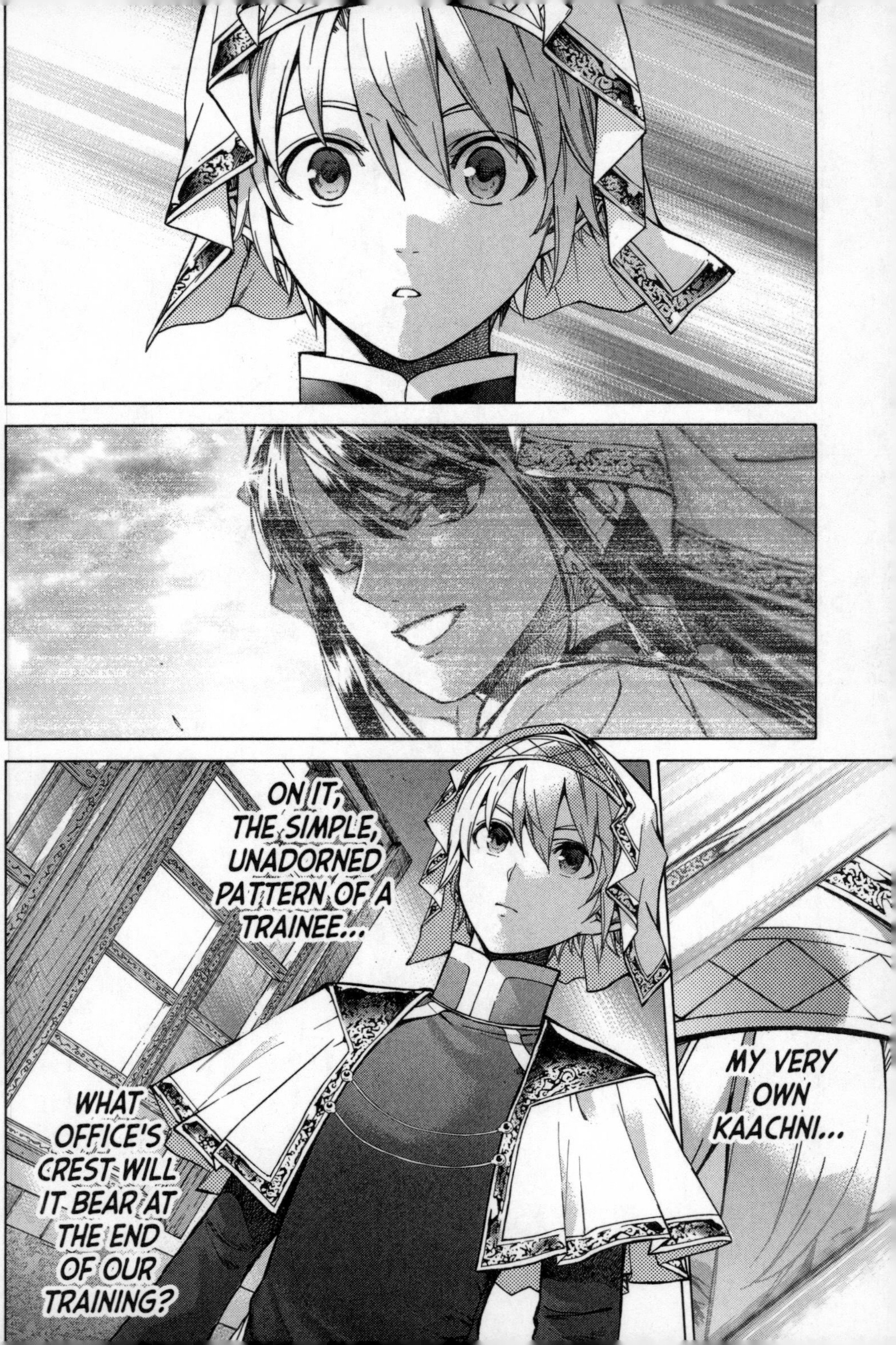
MY VERY OWN KAACHNI...
ON IT, THE SIMPLE, UNADORNED PATTERN OF A TRAINEE...
WHAT OFFICE'S CREST WILL IT BEAR AT THE END OF OUR TRAINING?

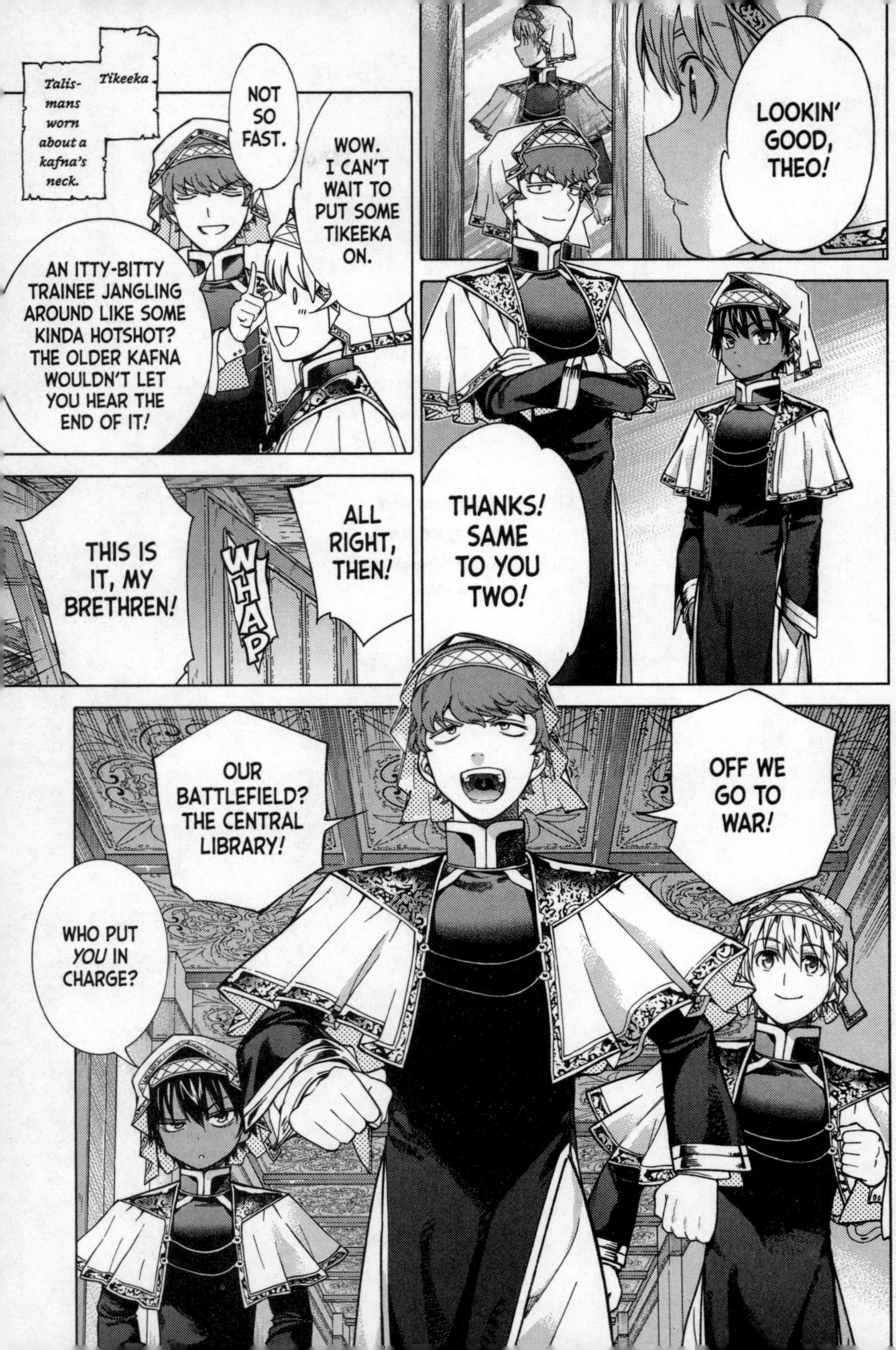
LOOKIN' GOOD, THEO!
WOW. I CAN'T WAIT TO PUT SOME TIKEEKA ON.
NOT SO FAST.
AN ITTY-BITTY TRAINEE JANGLING AROUND LIKE SOME KINDA HOTSHOT? THE OLDER KAFNA WOULDN'T LET YOU HEAR THE END OF IT!
Tikeeka
Talis-mans worn about a kafna's neck.
THANKS! SAME TO YOU TWO!
ALL RIGHT, THEN!
WHAP
THIS IS IT, MY BRETHREN!
OFF WE GO TO WAR!
OUR BATTLEFIELD? THE CENTRAL LIBRARY!
WHO PUT *YOU* IN CHARGE?

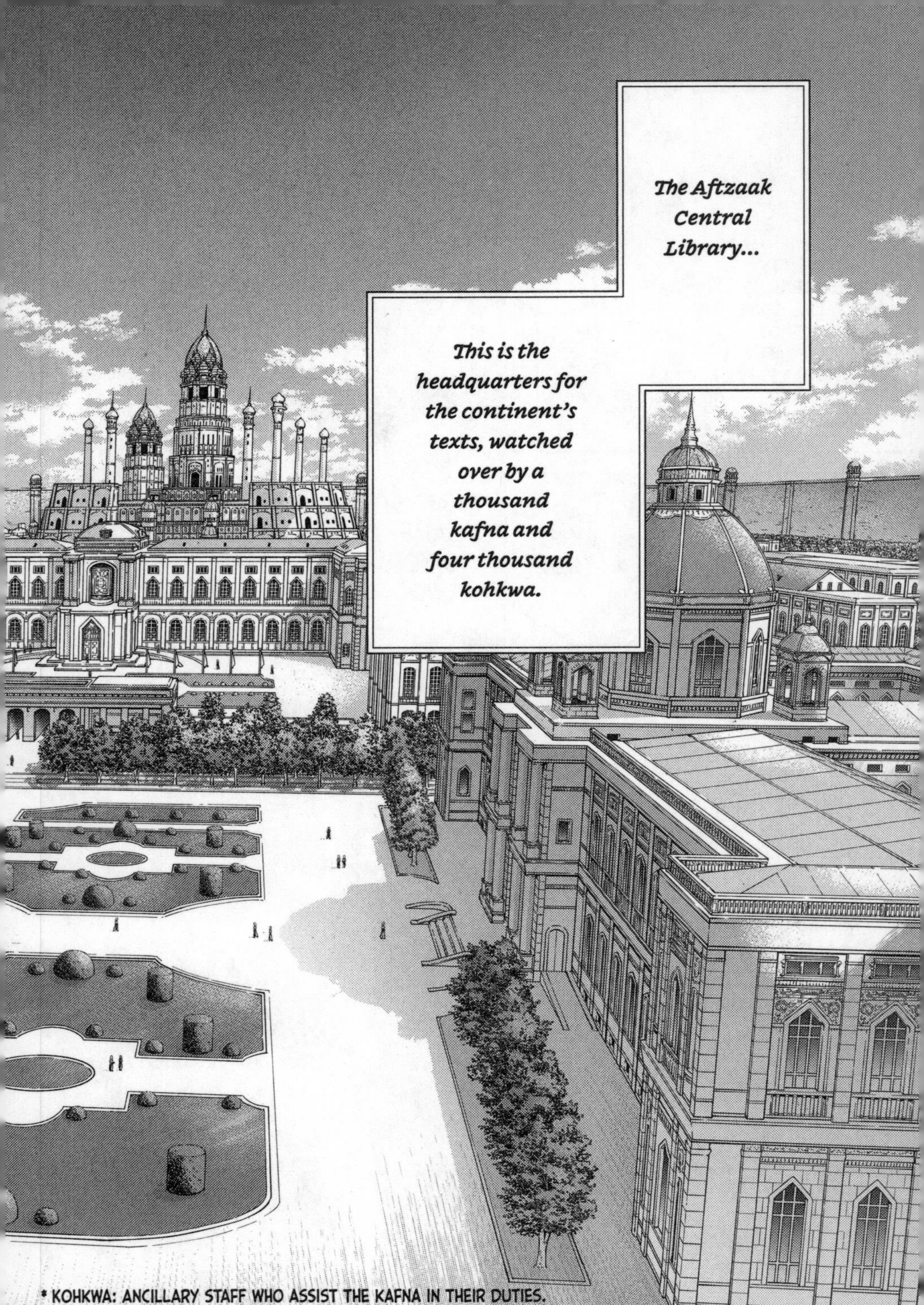
The Aftzaak Central Library...
This is the headquarters for the continent's texts, watched over by a thousand kafna and four thousand kohkwa.

* KOHKWA: ANCILLARY STAFF WHO ASSIST THE KAFNA IN THEIR DUTIES.

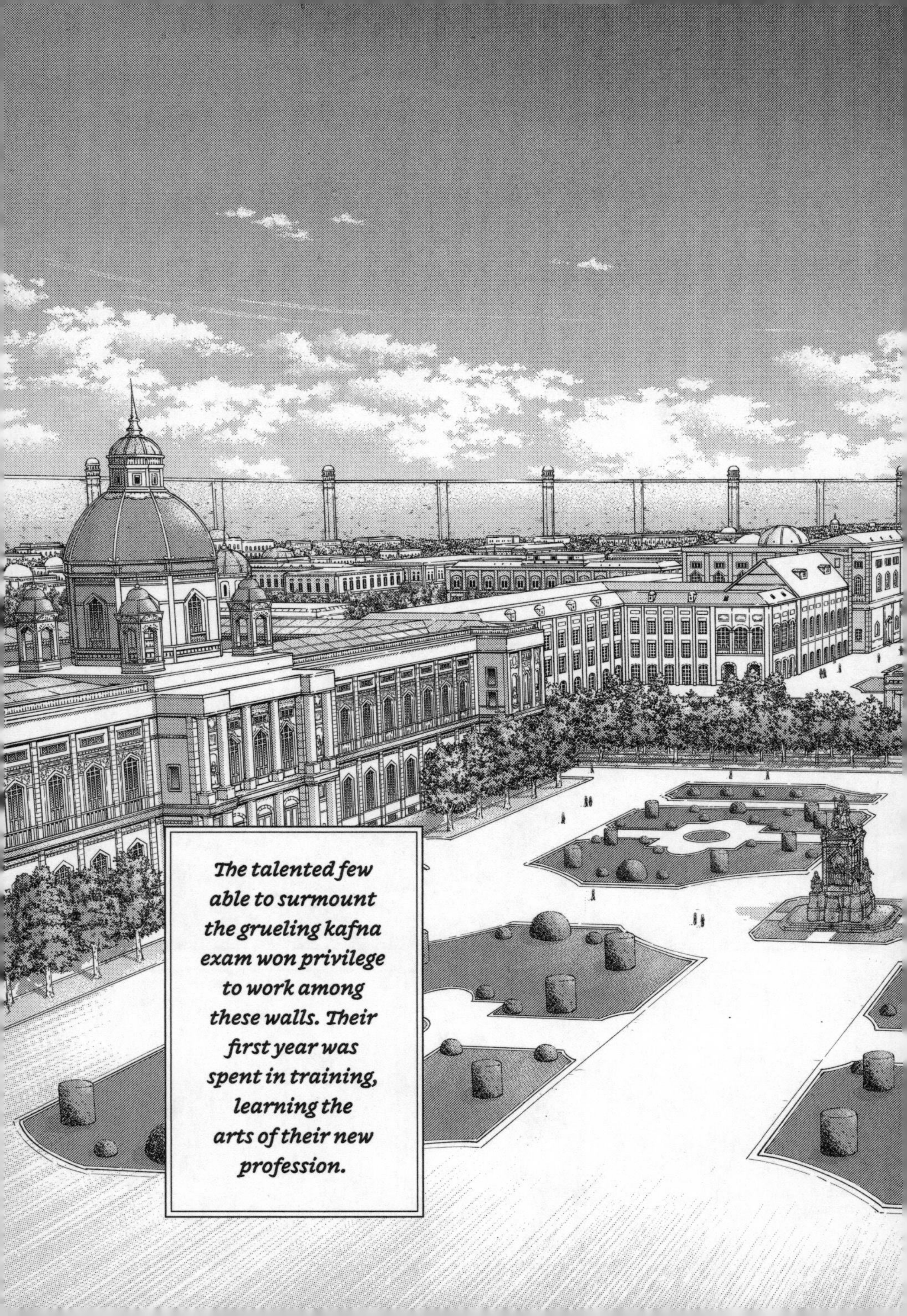
The talented few able to surmount the grueling kafna exam won privilege to work among these walls. Their first year was spent in training, learning the arts of their new profession.

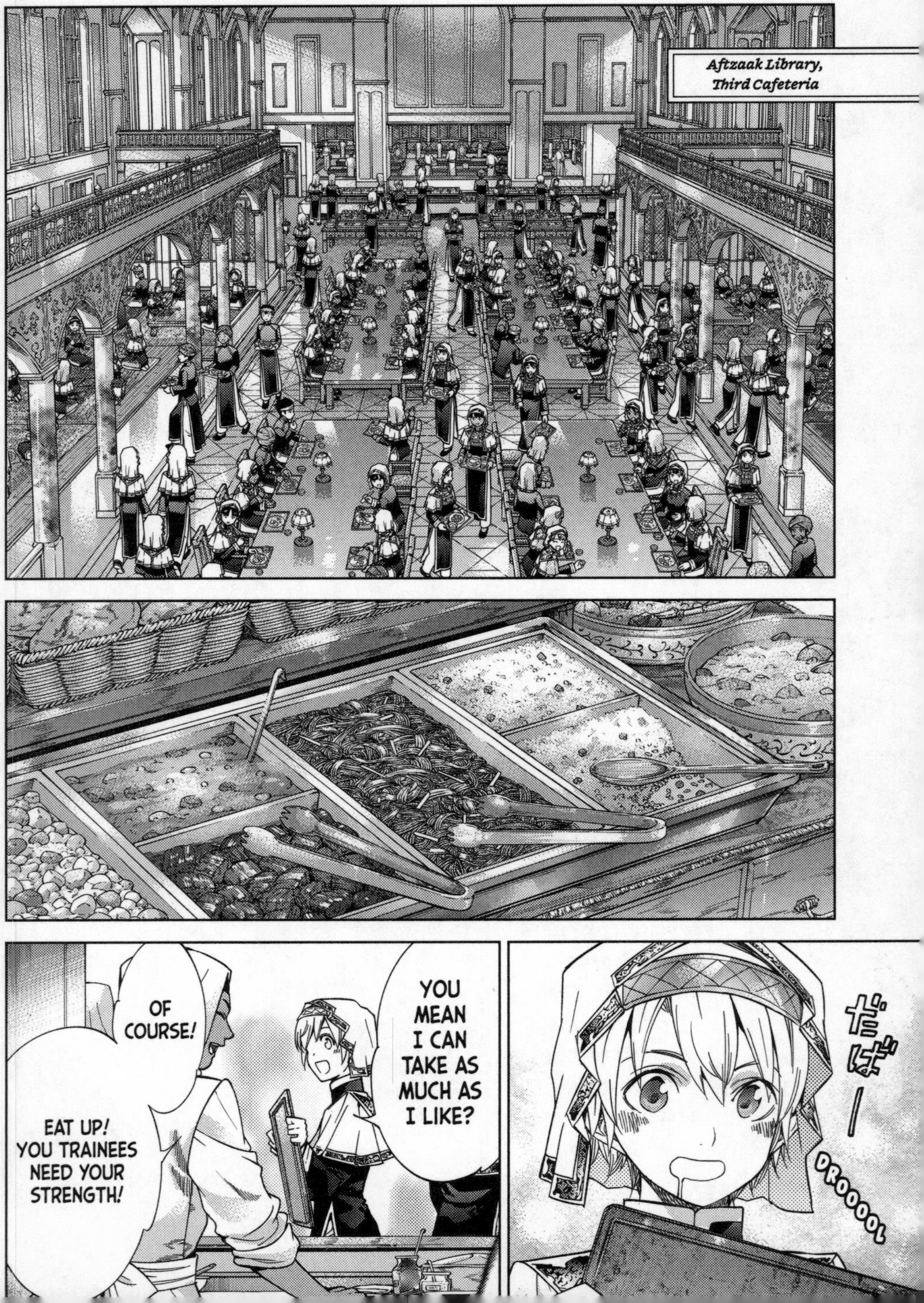
Aftzaak Library, Third Cafeteria
だばー
DROOOOOL
YOU MEAN I CAN TAKE AS MUCH AS I LIKE?
OF COURSE!
EAT UP! YOU TRAINEES NEED YOUR STRENGTH!

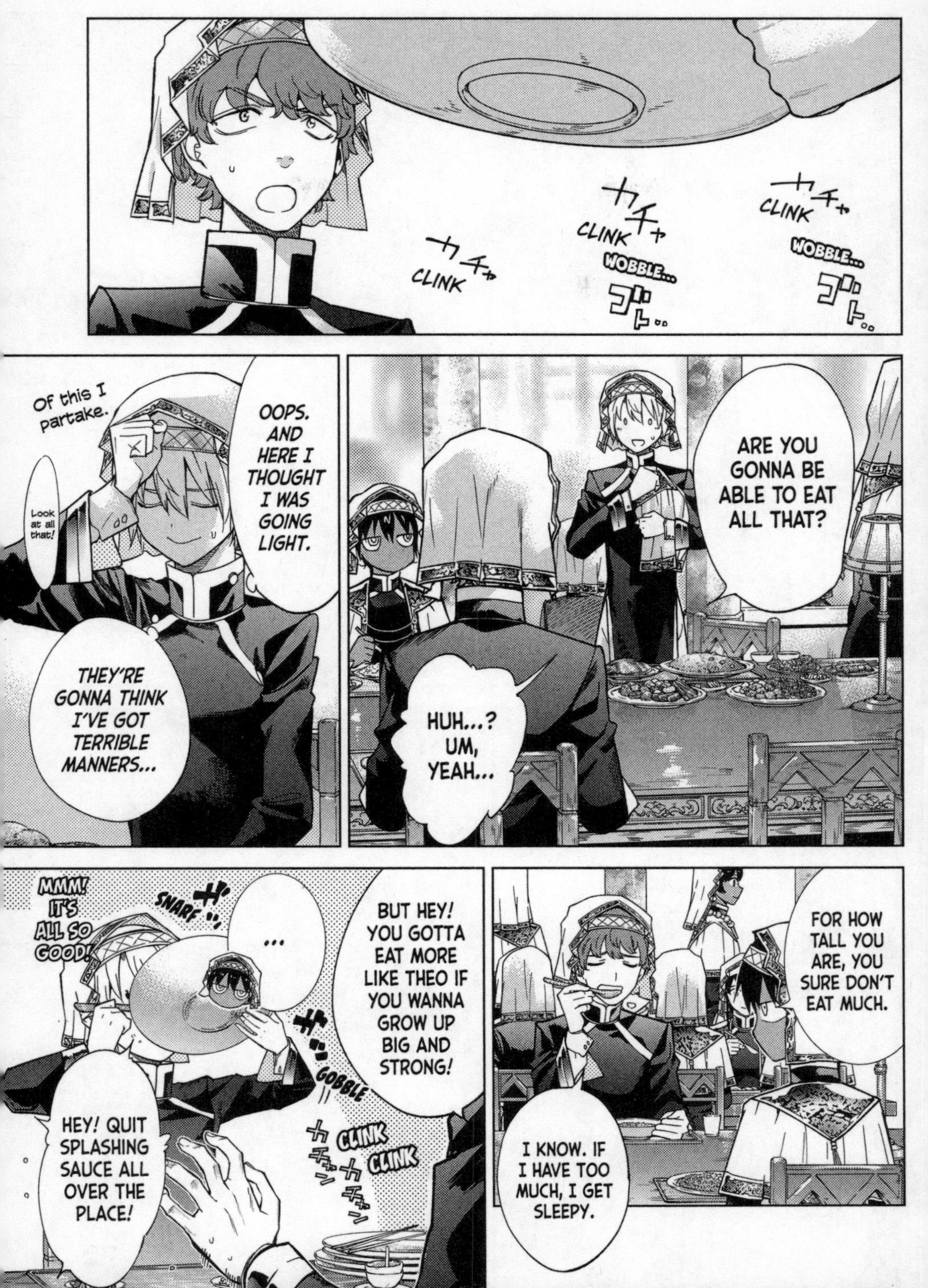
カチャ
CLINK
WOBBLE...
ゴト..
カチャ
CLINK
WOBBLE...
ゴト..
カチャ
CLINK
ARE YOU GONNA BE ABLE TO EAT ALL THAT?
HUH...? UM, YEAH...
OOPS. AND HERE I THOUGHT I WAS GOING LIGHT.
Of this I partake.
Look at all that!
THEY'RE GONNA THINK I'VE GOT TERRIBLE MANNERS...
FOR HOW TALL YOU ARE, YOU SURE DON'T EAT MUCH.
I KNOW. IF I HAVE TOO MUCH, I GET SLEEPY.
BUT HEY! YOU GOTTA EAT MORE LIKE THEO IF YOU WANNA GROW UP BIG AND STRONG!
...
ガツ
SNARF
MMM! IT'S ALL SO GOOD!
ガツ
GOBBLE
カチャン
CLINK
カチャン
CLINK
HEY! QUIT SPLASHING SAUCE ALL OVER THE PLACE!

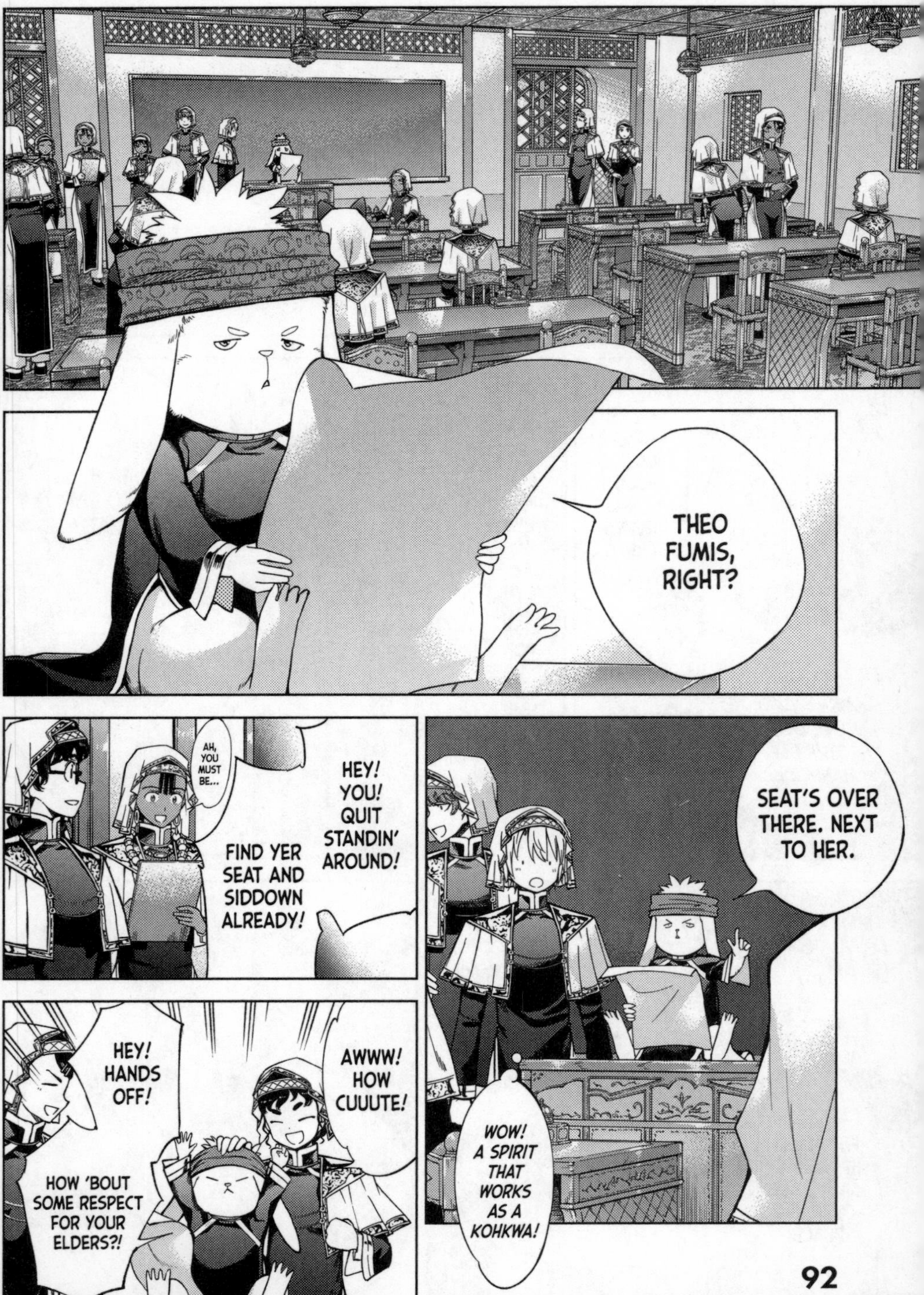
THEO FUMIS, RIGHT?
SEAT'S OVER THERE. NEXT TO HER.
WOW! A SPIRIT THAT WORKS AS A KOHKWA!
HEY! YOU! QUIT STANDIN' AROUND!
FIND YER SEAT AND SIDDOWN ALREADY!
AH, YOU MUST BE...
AWWW! HOW CUUUTE!
HEY! HANDS OFF!
HOW 'BOUT SOME RESPECT FOR YOUR ELDERS?!

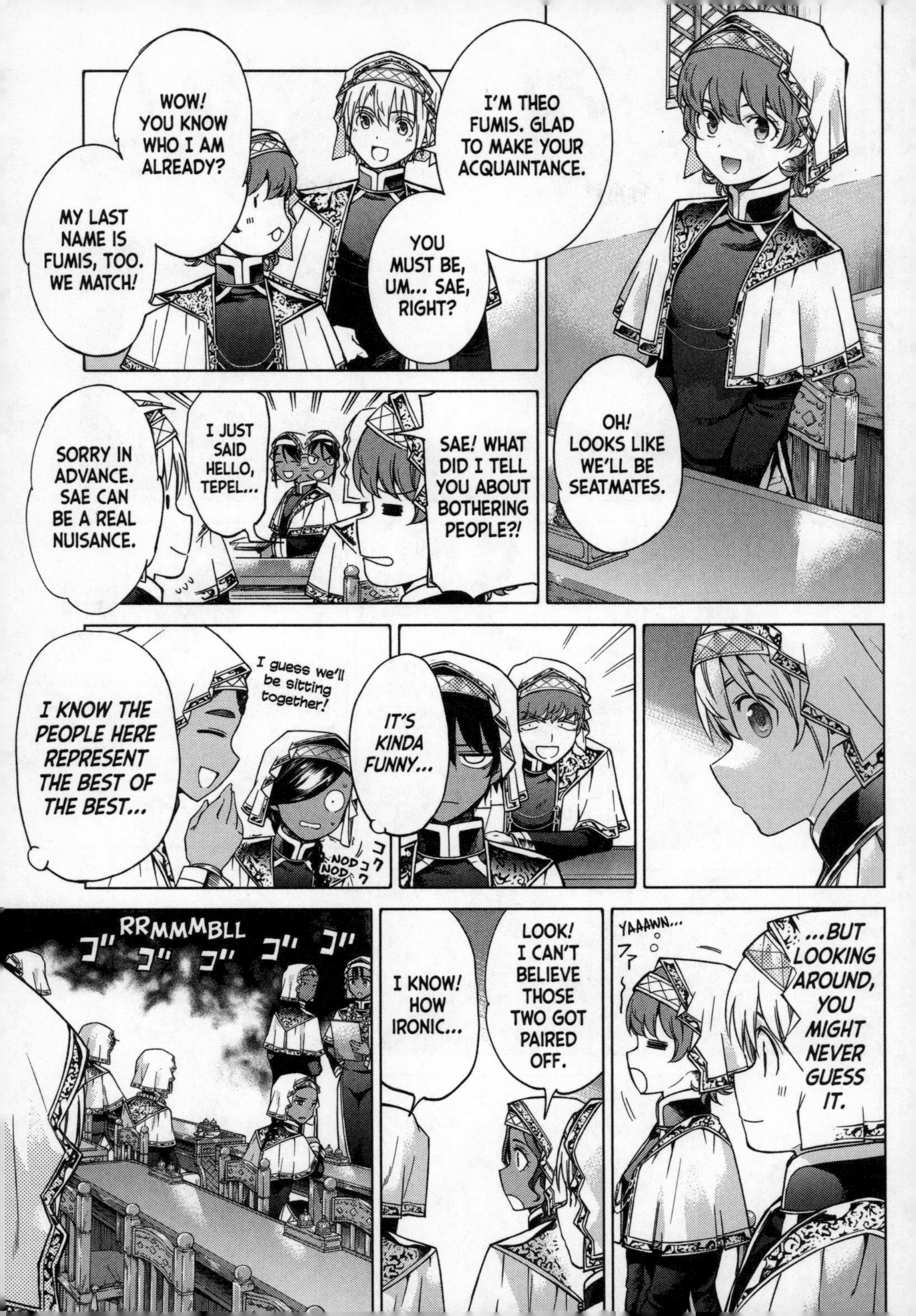
OH! LOOKS LIKE WE'LL BE SEATMATES.
I'M THEO FUMIS. GLAD TO MAKE YOUR ACQUAINTANCE.
YOU MUST BE, UM... SAE, RIGHT?
WOW! YOU KNOW WHO I AM ALREADY?
MY LAST NAME IS FUMIS, TOO. WE MATCH!
SAE! WHAT DID I TELL YOU ABOUT BOTHERING PEOPLE?!
I JUST SAID HELLO, TEPEL...
SORRY IN ADVANCE. SAE CAN BE A REAL NUISANCE.
IT'S KINDA FUNNY...
I guess we'll be sitting together!
I KNOW THE PEOPLE HERE REPRESENT THE BEST OF THE BEST...
コク コク
NOD NOD
...BUT LOOKING AROUND, YOU MIGHT NEVER GUESS IT.
YAAAWN...
ファ
LOOK! I CAN'T BELIEVE THOSE TWO GOT PAIRED OFF.
I KNOW! HOW IRONIC...
RRMMMBLL
ゴ" ゴ" ゴ" ゴ" ゴ"

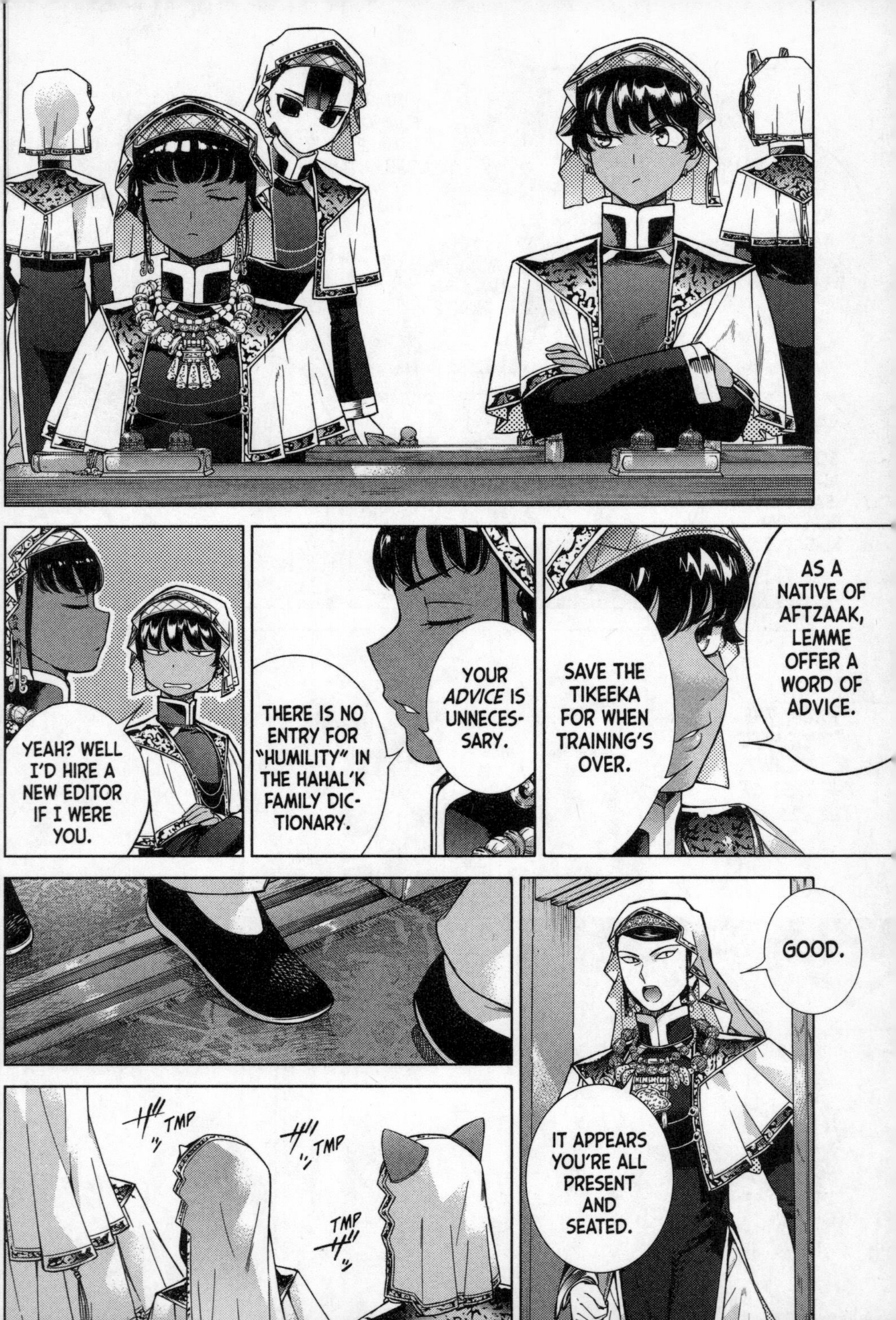
AS A NATIVE OF AFTZAAK, LEMME OFFER A WORD OF ADVICE.
SAVE THE TIKEEKA FOR WHEN TRAINING'S OVER.
YOUR *ADVICE* IS UNNECES-SARY.
THERE IS NO ENTRY FOR "HUMILITY" IN THE HAHAL'K FAMILY DIC-TIONARY.
YEAH? WELL I'D HIRE A NEW EDITOR IF I WERE YOU.
GOOD.
IT APPEARS YOU'RE ALL PRESENT AND SEATED.
TMP
TMP
TMP

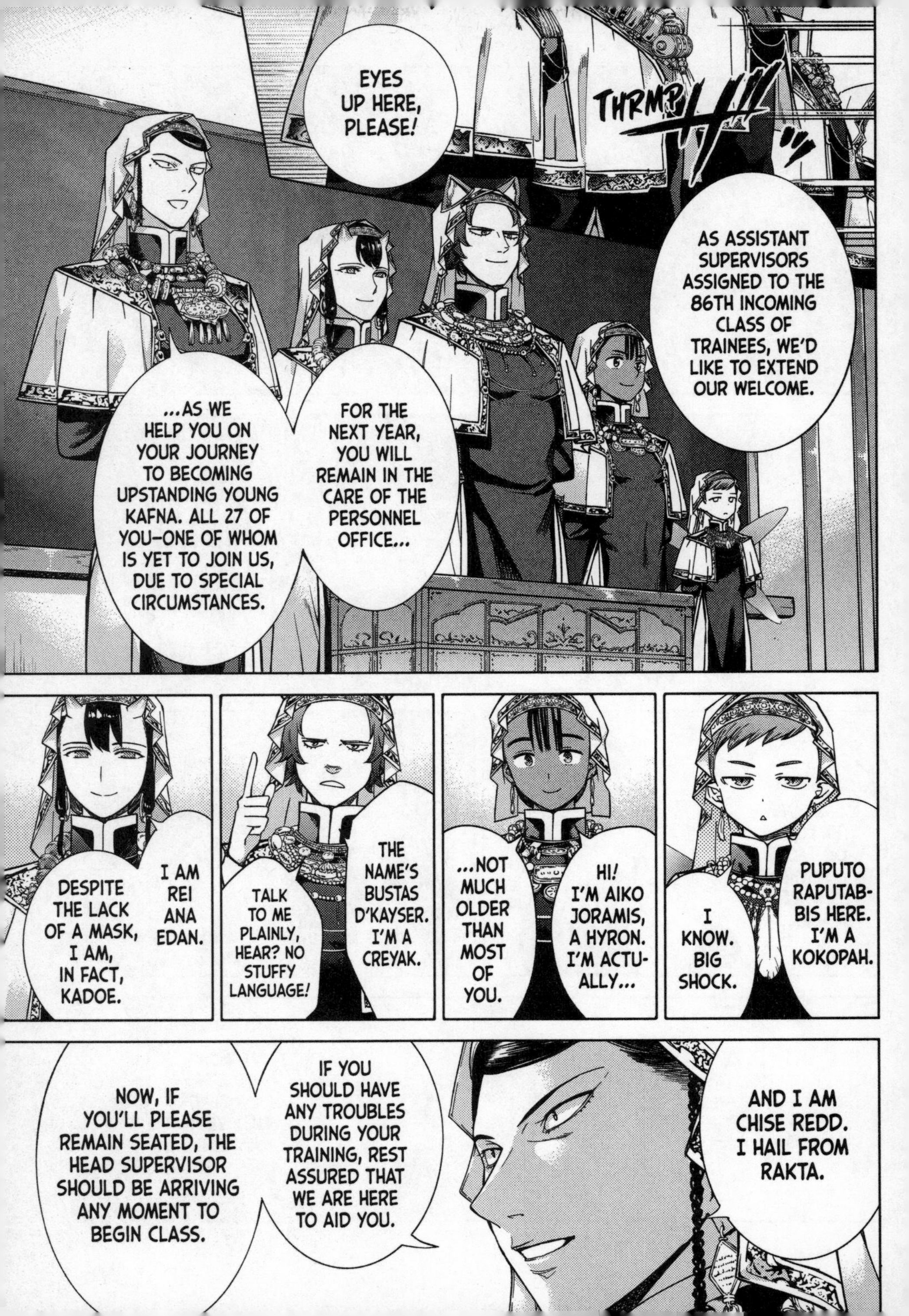
EYES UP HERE, PLEASE!
THRMP
AS ASSISTANT SUPERVISORS ASSIGNED TO THE 86TH INCOMING CLASS OF TRAINEES, WE'D LIKE TO EXTEND OUR WELCOME.
FOR THE NEXT YEAR, YOU WILL REMAIN IN THE CARE OF THE PERSONNEL OFFICE...
...AS WE HELP YOU ON YOUR JOURNEY TO BECOMING UPSTANDING YOUNG KAFNA. ALL 27 OF YOU–ONE OF WHOM IS YET TO JOIN US, DUE TO SPECIAL CIRCUMSTANCES.
PUPUTO RAPUTABBIS HERE. I'M A KOKOPAH.
I KNOW. BIG SHOCK.
HI! I'M AIKO JORAMIS, A HYRON. I'M ACTUALLY...
...NOT MUCH OLDER THAN MOST OF YOU.
THE NAME'S BUSTAS D'KAYSER. I'M A CREYAK.
TALK TO ME PLAINLY, HEAR? NO STUFFY LANGUAGE!
I AM REI ANA EDAN.
DESPITE THE LACK OF A MASK, I AM, IN FACT, KADOE.
AND I AM CHISE REDD. I HAIL FROM RAKTA.
IF YOU SHOULD HAVE ANY TROUBLES DURING YOUR TRAINING, REST ASSURED THAT WE ARE HERE TO AID YOU.
NOW, IF YOU'LL PLEASE REMAIN SEATED, THE HEAD SUPERVISOR SHOULD BE ARRIVING ANY MOMENT TO BEGIN CLASS.

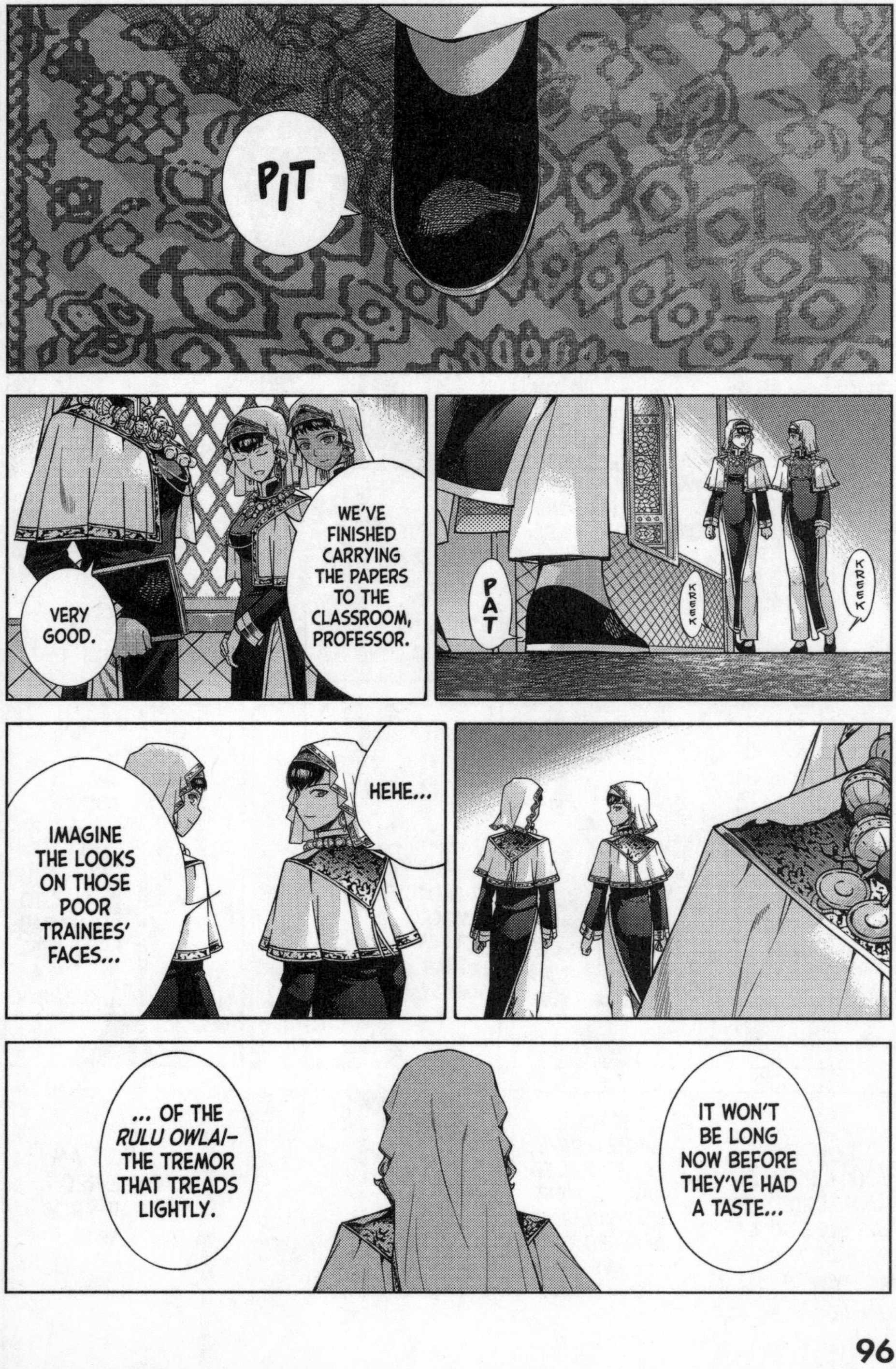
PIT
PAT
KREEK
KREEK
WE'VE FINISHED CARRYING THE PAPERS TO THE CLASSROOM, PROFESSOR.
VERY GOOD.
HEHE...
IMAGINE THE LOOKS ON THOSE POOR TRAINEES' FACES...
IT WON'T BE LONG NOW BEFORE THEY'VE HAD A TASTE...
... OF THE *RULU OWLAI*—THE TREMOR THAT TREADS LIGHTLY.

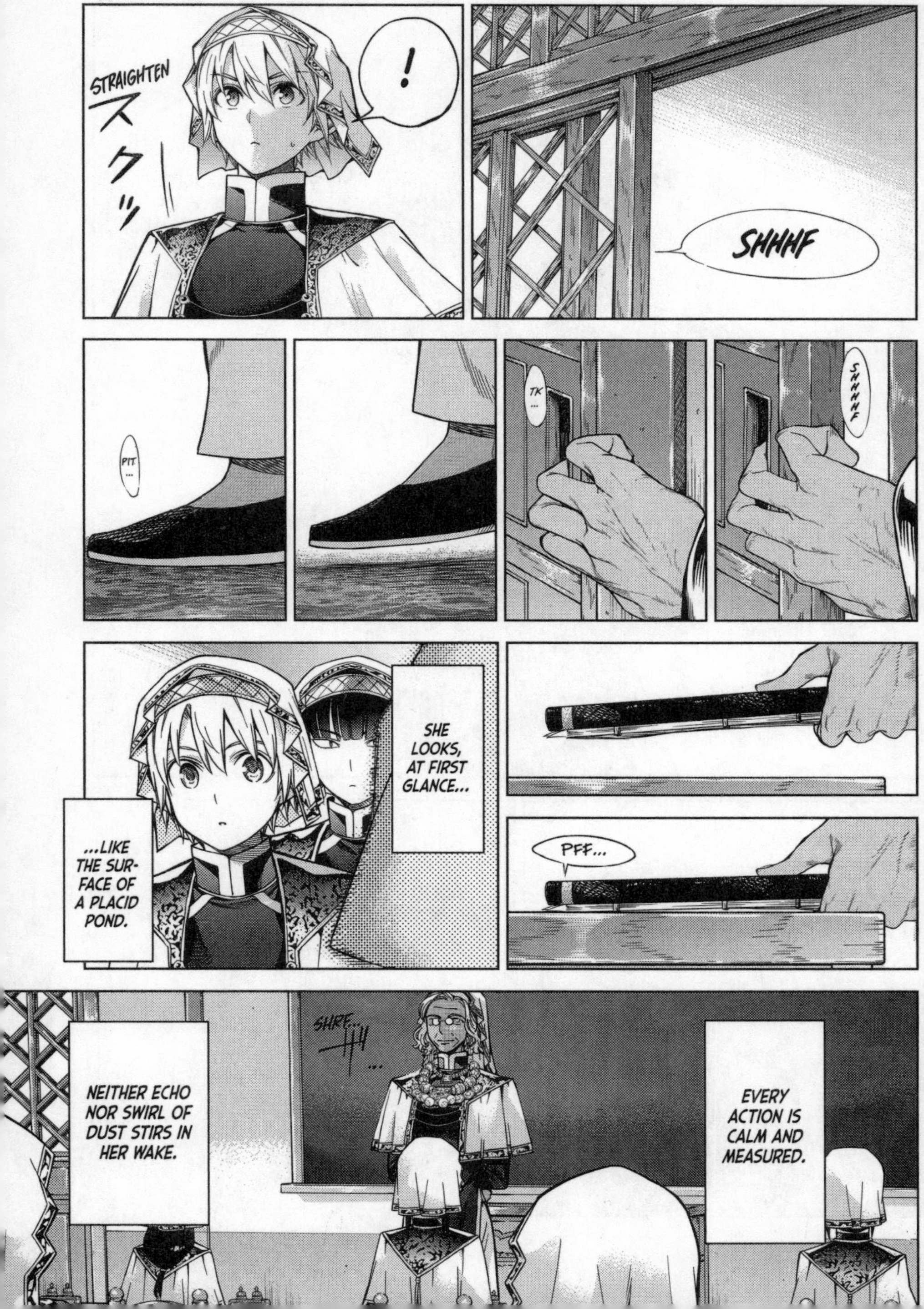
SHHHF
!
STRAIGHTEN
スクッ
SHHHHF
TK...
PIT...
PFF...
SHE LOOKS, AT FIRST GLANCE...
...LIKE THE SURFACE OF A PLACID POND.
EVERY ACTION IS CALM AND MEASURED.
SHRF...
NEITHER ECHO NOR SWIRL OF DUST STIRS IN HER WAKE.

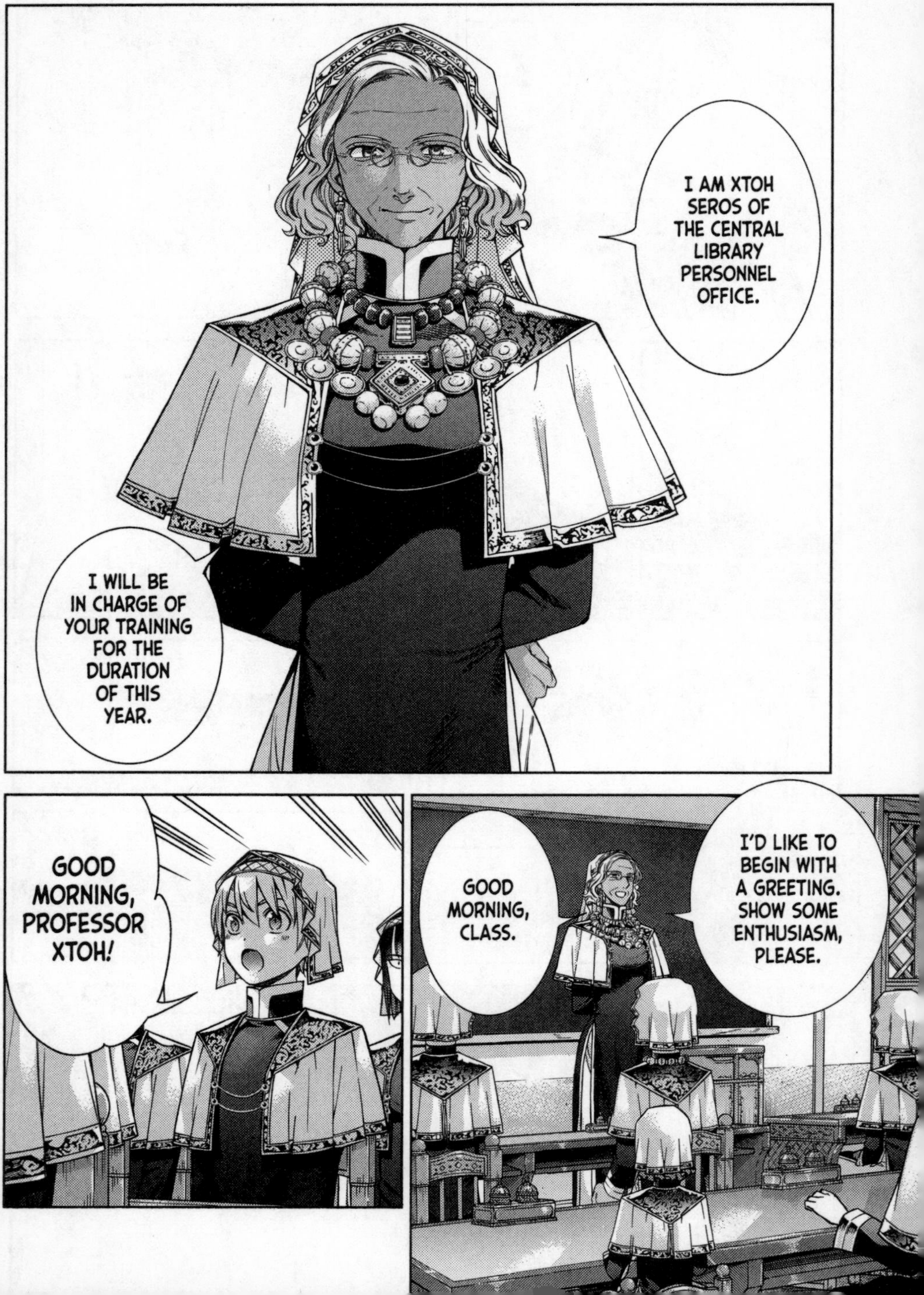
I AM XTOH SEROS OF THE CENTRAL LIBRARY PERSONNEL OFFICE.
I WILL BE IN CHARGE OF YOUR TRAINING FOR THE DURATION OF THIS YEAR.
I'D LIKE TO BEGIN WITH A GREETING. SHOW SOME ENTHUSIASM, PLEASE.
GOOD MORNING, CLASS.
GOOD MORNING, PROFESSOR XTOH!

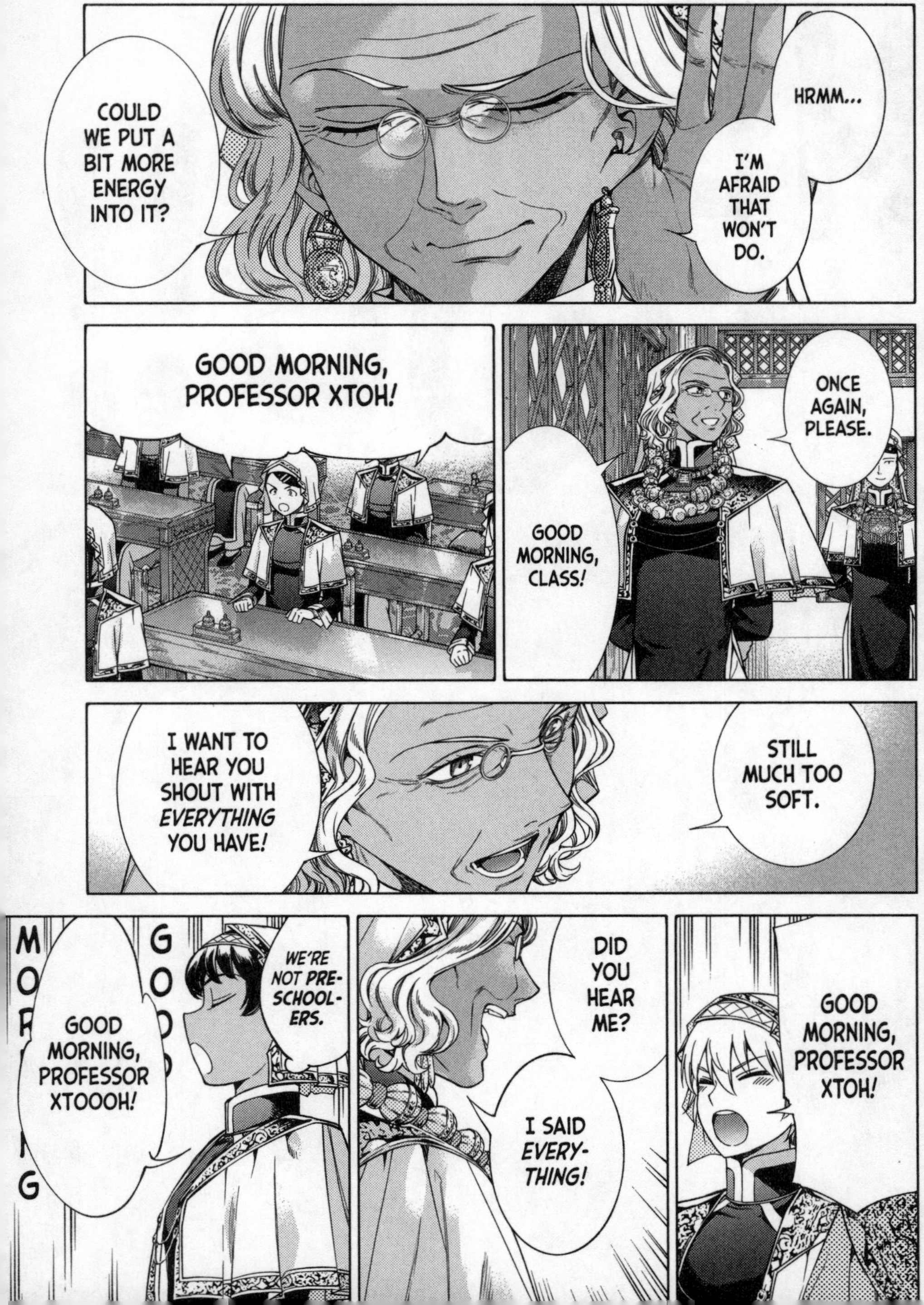
HRMM...
I'M AFRAID THAT WON'T DO.
COULD WE PUT A BIT MORE ENERGY INTO IT?
ONCE AGAIN, PLEASE.
GOOD MORNING, CLASS!
GOOD MORNING, PROFESSOR XTOH!
STILL MUCH TOO SOFT.
I WANT TO HEAR YOU SHOUT WITH *EVERYTHING* YOU HAVE!
GOOD MORNING, PROFESSOR XTOH!
DID YOU HEAR ME?
I SAID *EVERY-THING!*
WE'RE NOT PRE-SCHOOL-ERS.
GOOD MORNING, PROFESSOR XTOOOH!

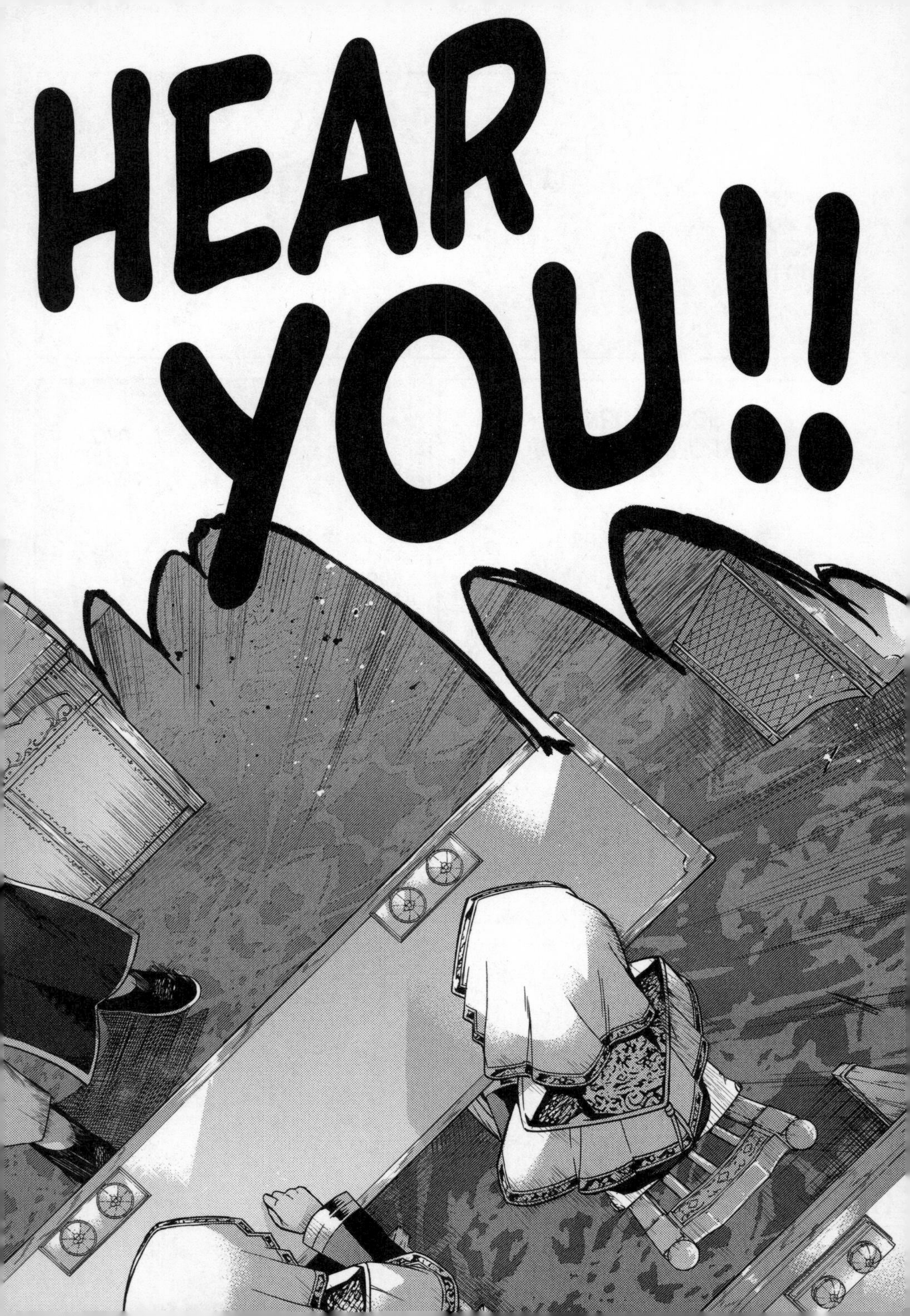
HEAR YOU!!

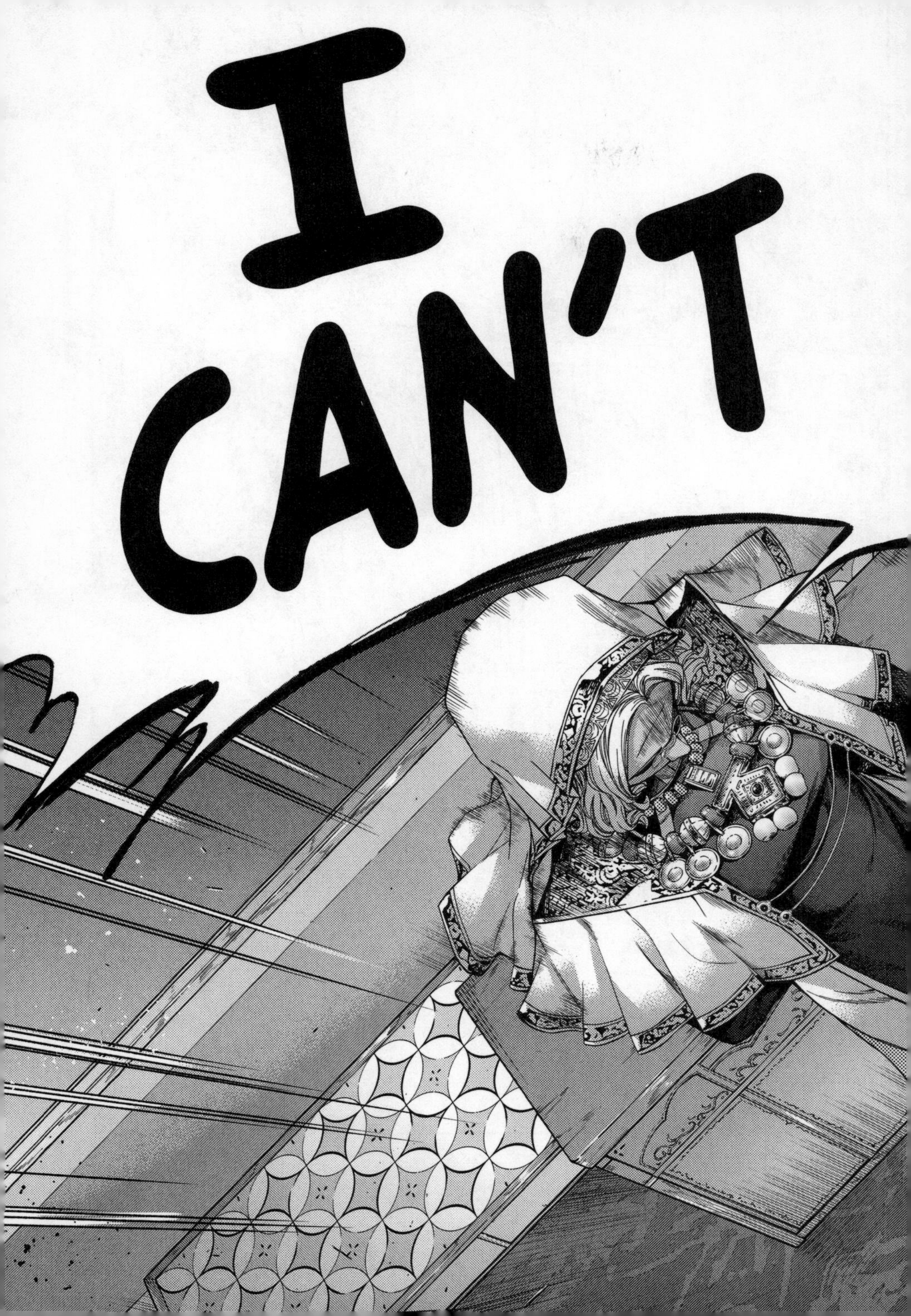
I CAN'T

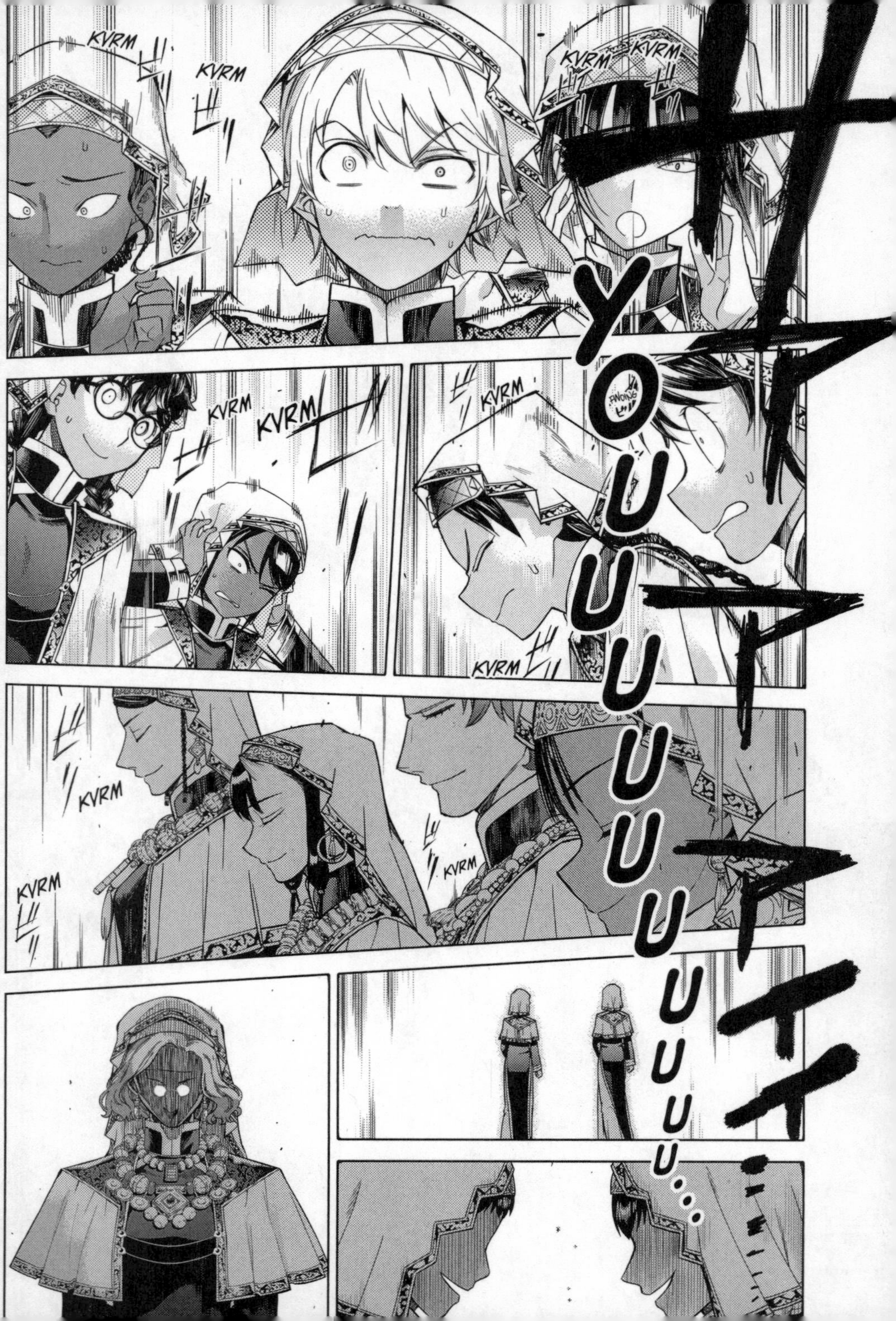
KVRM
KVRM
KVRM
KVRM
YOUUUUUUUUUUUU...
FWOING
KVRM
KVRM
KVRM
KVRM
KVRM
KVRM

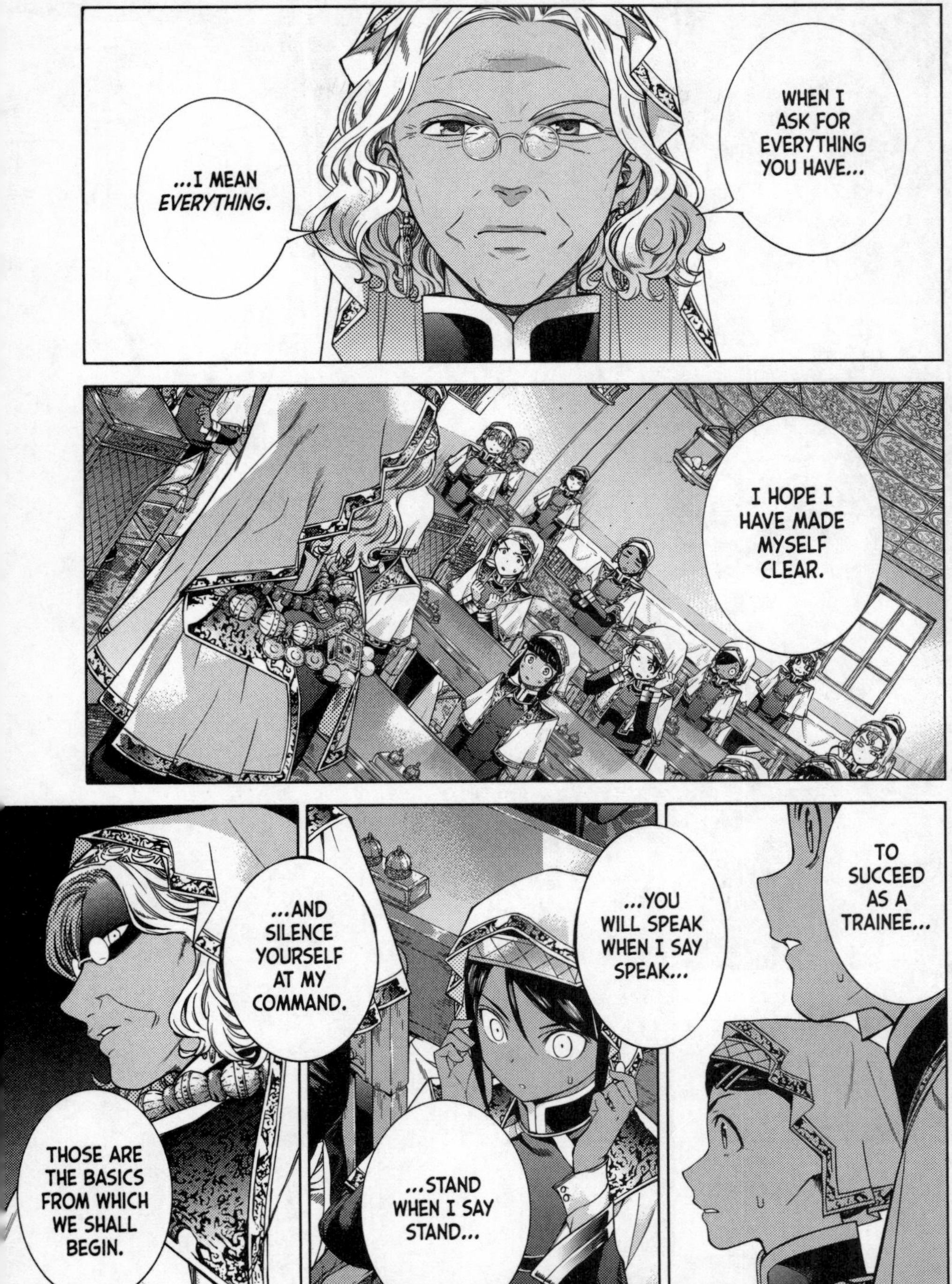
WHEN I ASK FOR EVERYTHING YOU HAVE...
...I MEAN *EVERYTHING*.
I HOPE I HAVE MADE MYSELF CLEAR.
TO SUCCEED AS A TRAINEE...
...YOU WILL SPEAK WHEN I SAY SPEAK...
...STAND WHEN I SAY STAND...
...AND SILENCE YOURSELF AT MY COMMAND.
THOSE ARE THE BASICS FROM WHICH WE SHALL BEGIN.

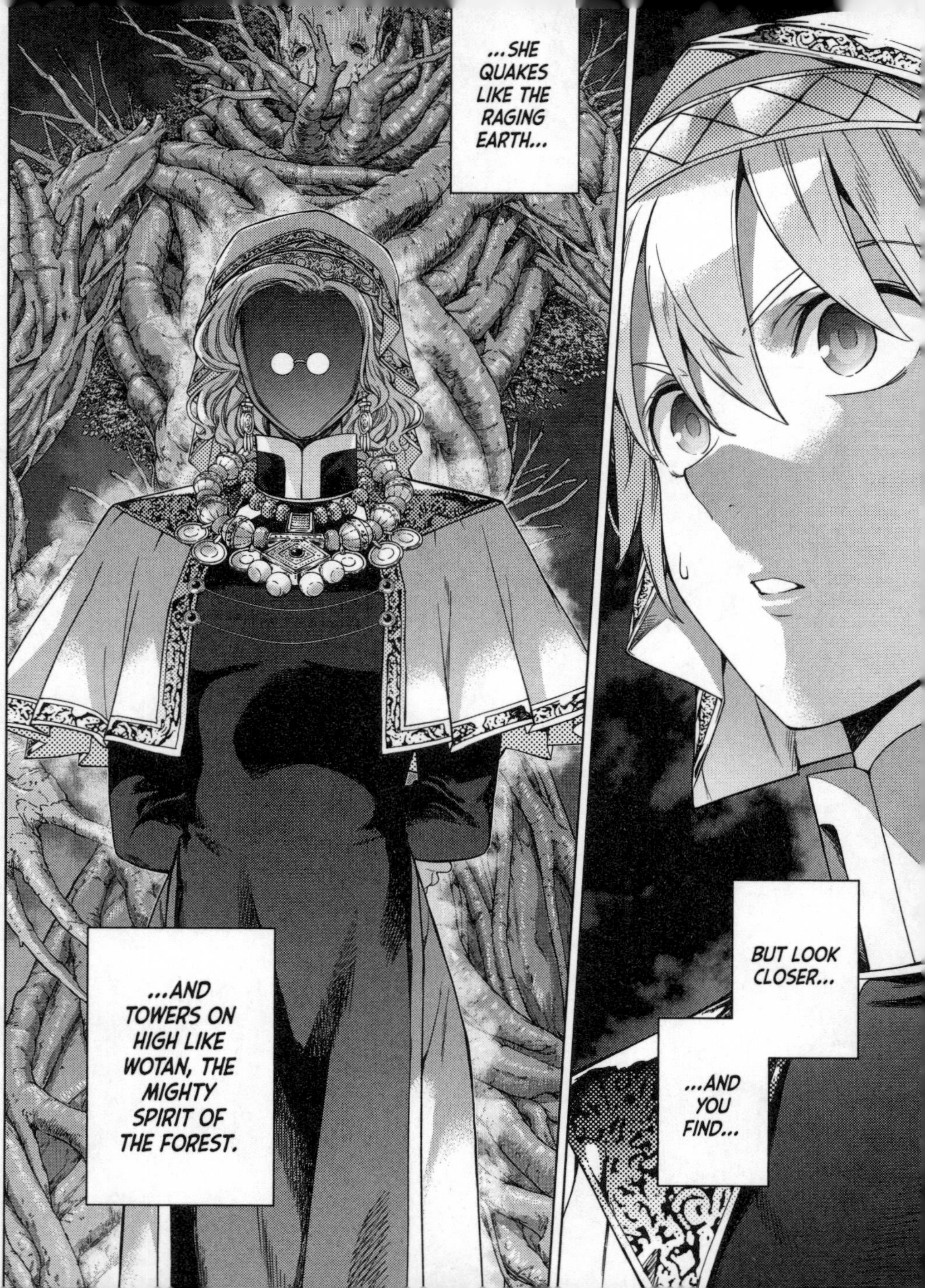
...SHE QUAKES LIKE THE RAGING EARTH...
...AND TOWERS ON HIGH LIKE WOTAN, THE MIGHTY SPIRIT OF THE FOREST.
BUT LOOK CLOSER...
...AND YOU FIND...

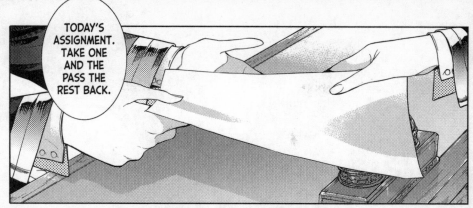

TODAY'S ASSIGNMENT. TAKE ONE AND THE PASS THE REST BACK.
I IMAGINE YOU WEREN'T EXPECTING A TEST ON DAY ONE.
CONSIDER IT MY WAY OF WELCOMING YOU, AS WE EMBARK ON THE YEAR OF RIGOROUS STUDY AHEAD.
SOMETHING *LIGHT* TO WARM UP WITH.
YOUR TIME STARTS NOW. BEGIN.
THINK OF IT AS AN EXTENSION OF THE KAFNA EXAM.
I'VE GOT THIS!
PLING...
...!!

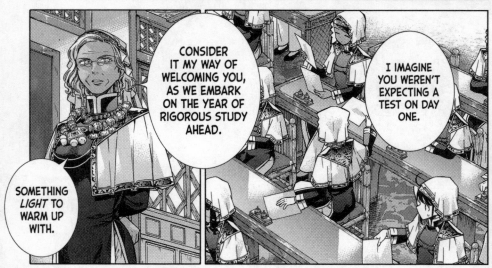

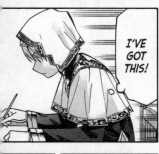

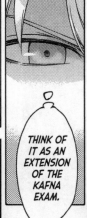

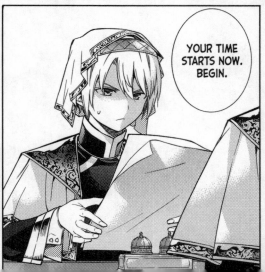

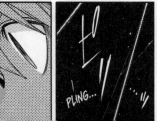

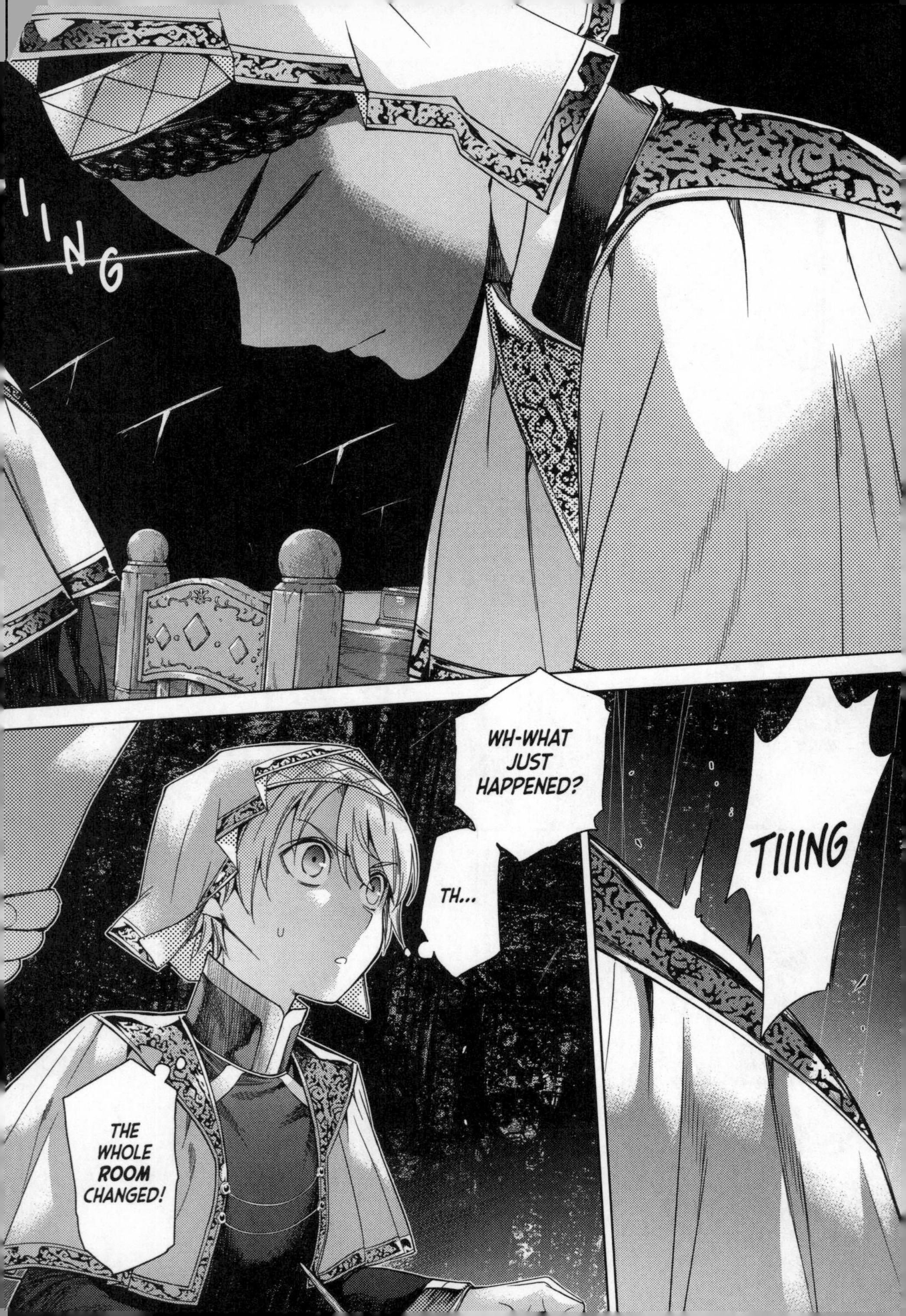
IING
TIIING
WH-WHAT JUST HAPPENED?
TH...
THE WHOLE ROOM CHANGED!

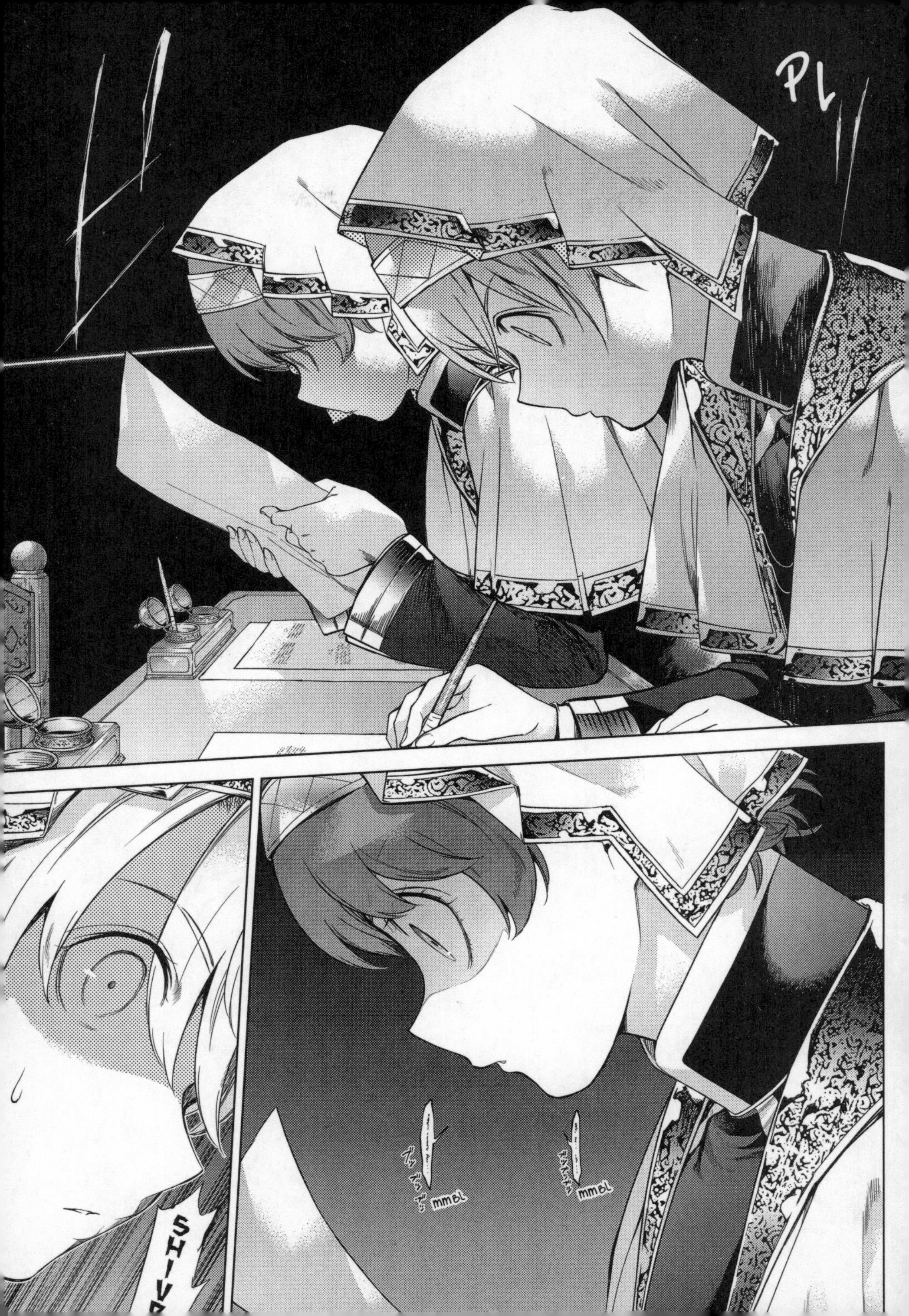
PL
mmbl
mmbl
SHIV

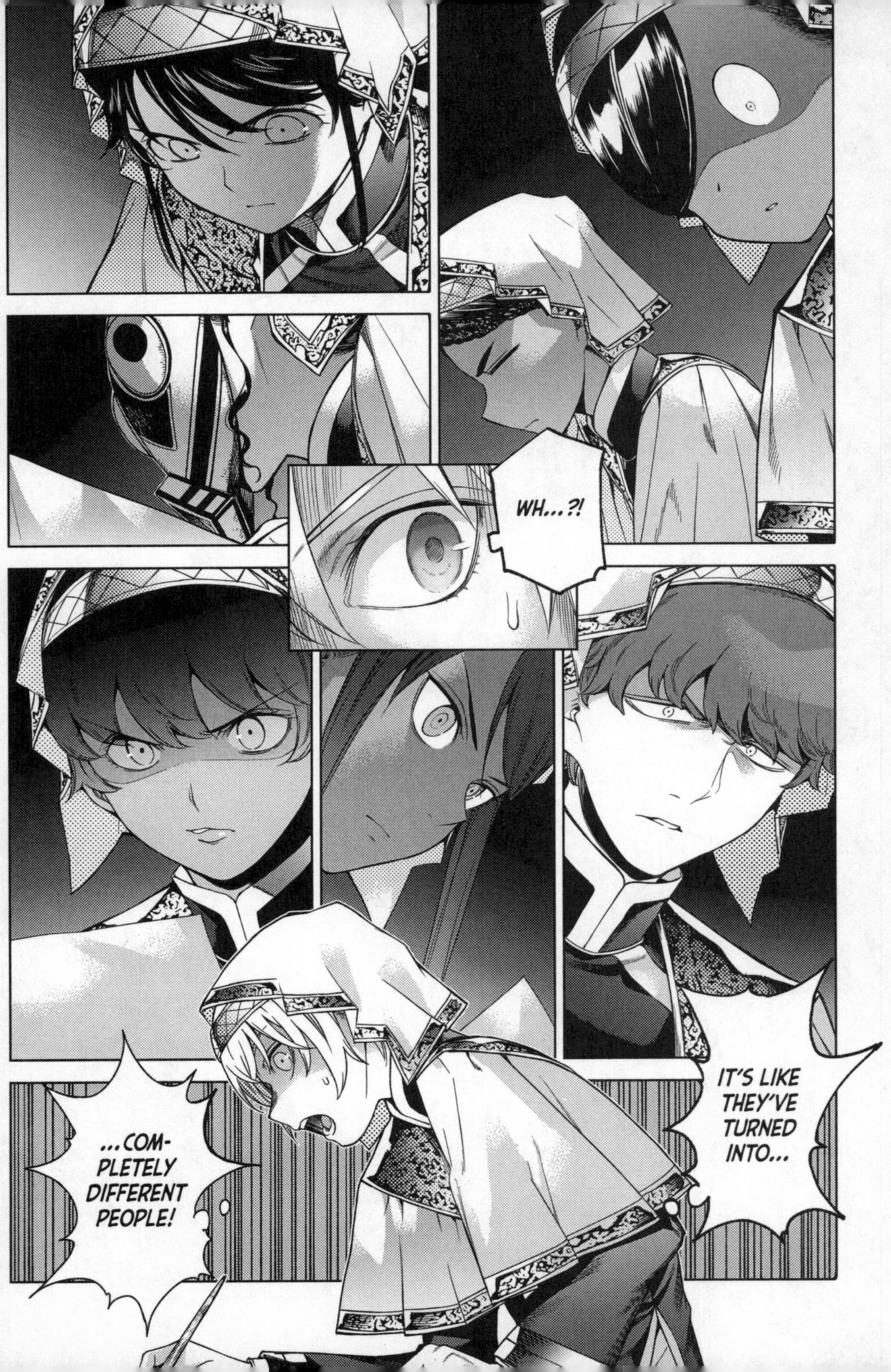
WH...?!
IT'S LIKE THEY'VE TURNED INTO...
...COM-PLETELY DIFFERENT PEOPLE!

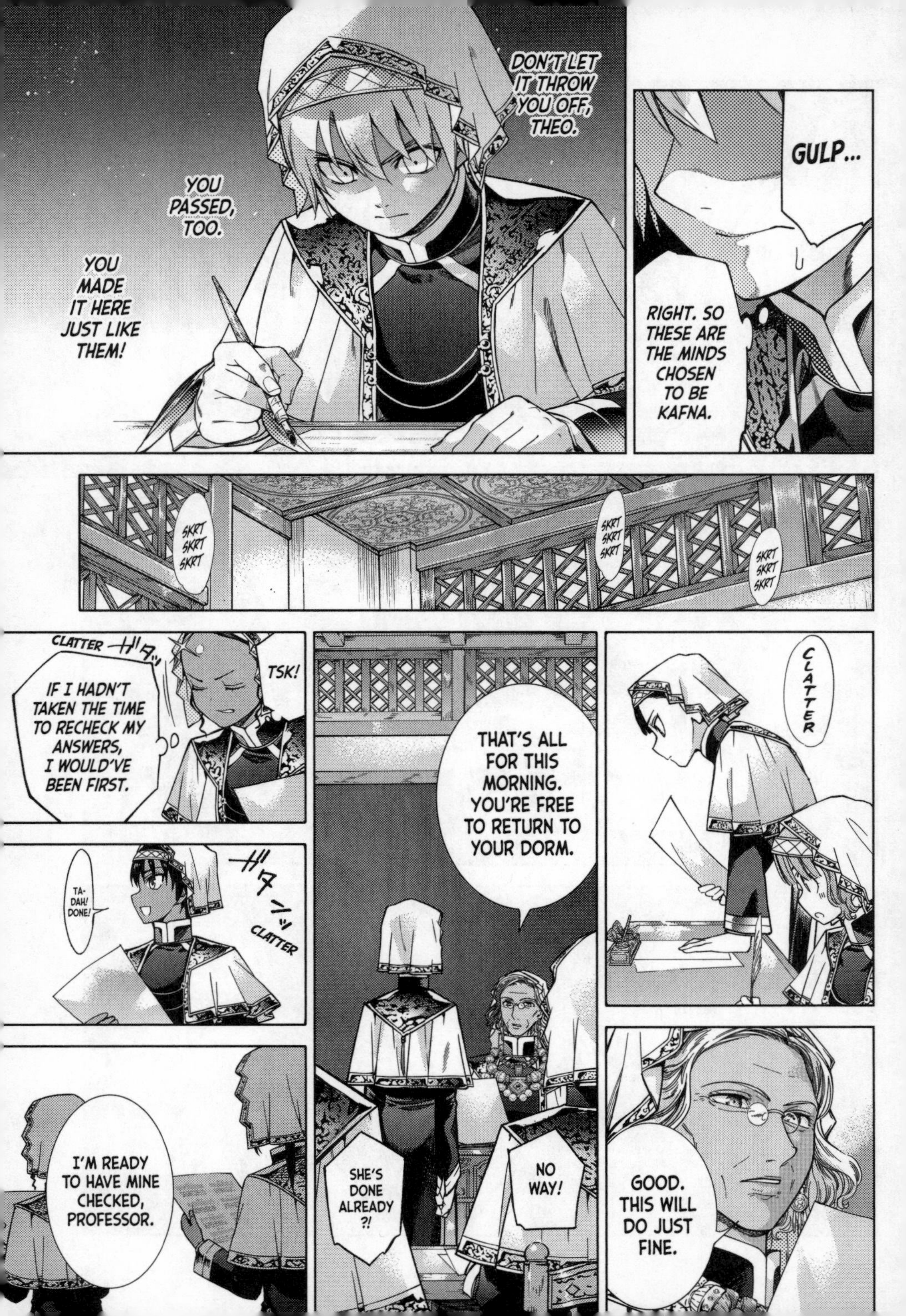
GULP...
RIGHT. SO THESE ARE THE MINDS CHOSEN TO BE KAFNA.
DON'T LET IT THROW YOU OFF, THEO.
YOU PASSED, TOO.
YOU MADE IT HERE JUST LIKE THEM!
SKRT SKRT SKRT
SKRT SKRT SKRT
SKRT SKRT SKRT
CLATTER
GOOD. THIS WILL DO JUST FINE.
THAT'S ALL FOR THIS MORNING. YOU'RE FREE TO RETURN TO YOUR DORM.
NO WAY!
SHE'S DONE ALREADY?!
CLATTER ガタッ
TSK!
IF I HADN'T TAKEN THE TIME TO RECHECK MY ANSWERS, I WOULD'VE BEEN FIRST.
ガタンッ
TA-DAH! DONE!
CLATTER
I'M READY TO HAVE MINE CHECKED, PROFESSOR.

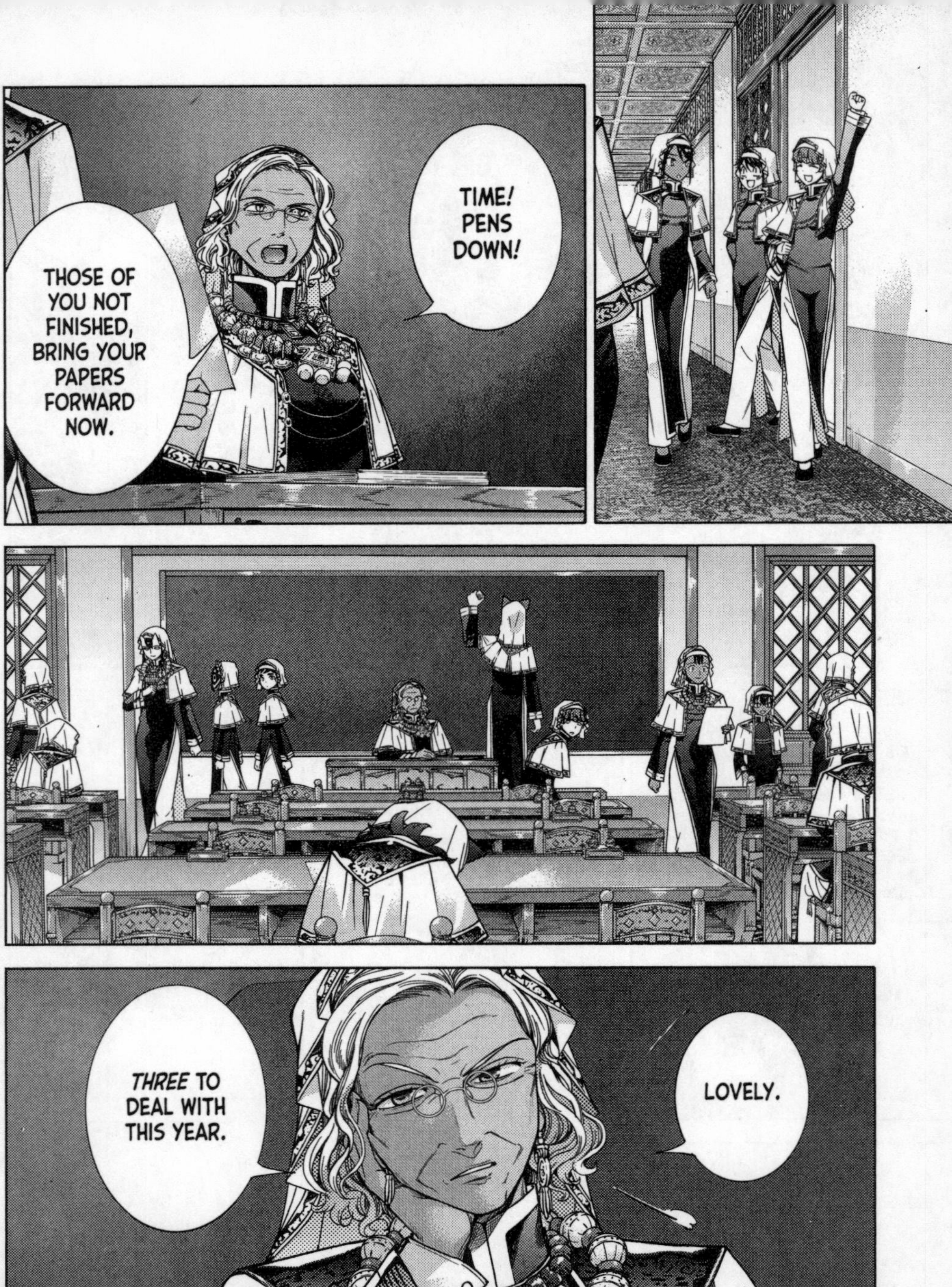
TIME! PENS DOWN!
THOSE OF YOU NOT FINISHED, BRING YOUR PAPERS FORWARD NOW.
LOVELY.
THREE TO DEAL WITH THIS YEAR.

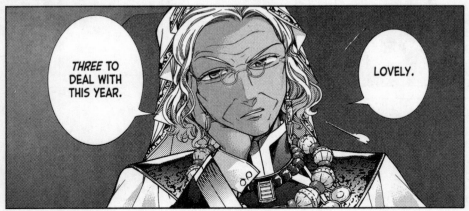

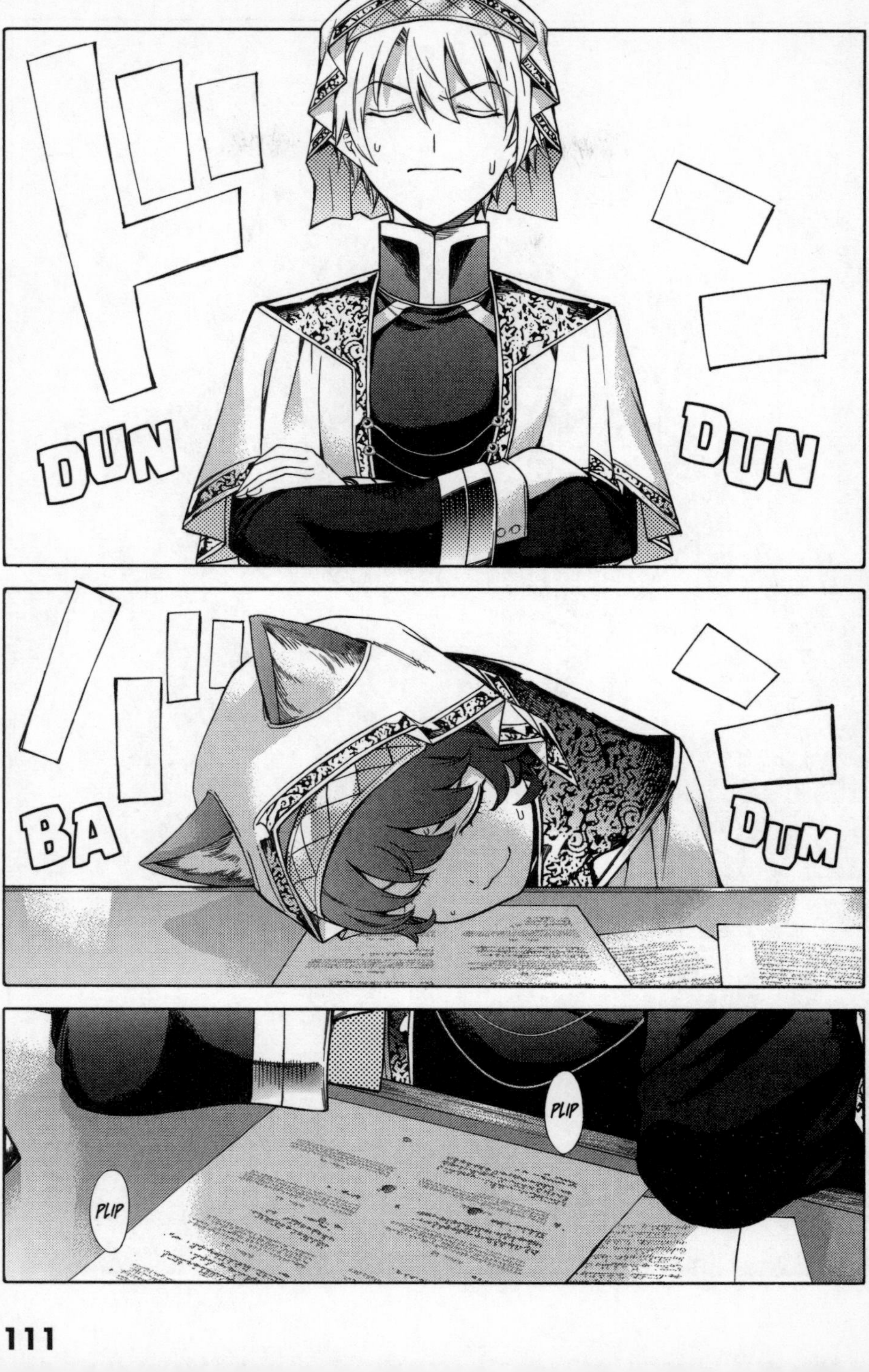
DUN
DUN
BA
DUM
PLIP
PLIP

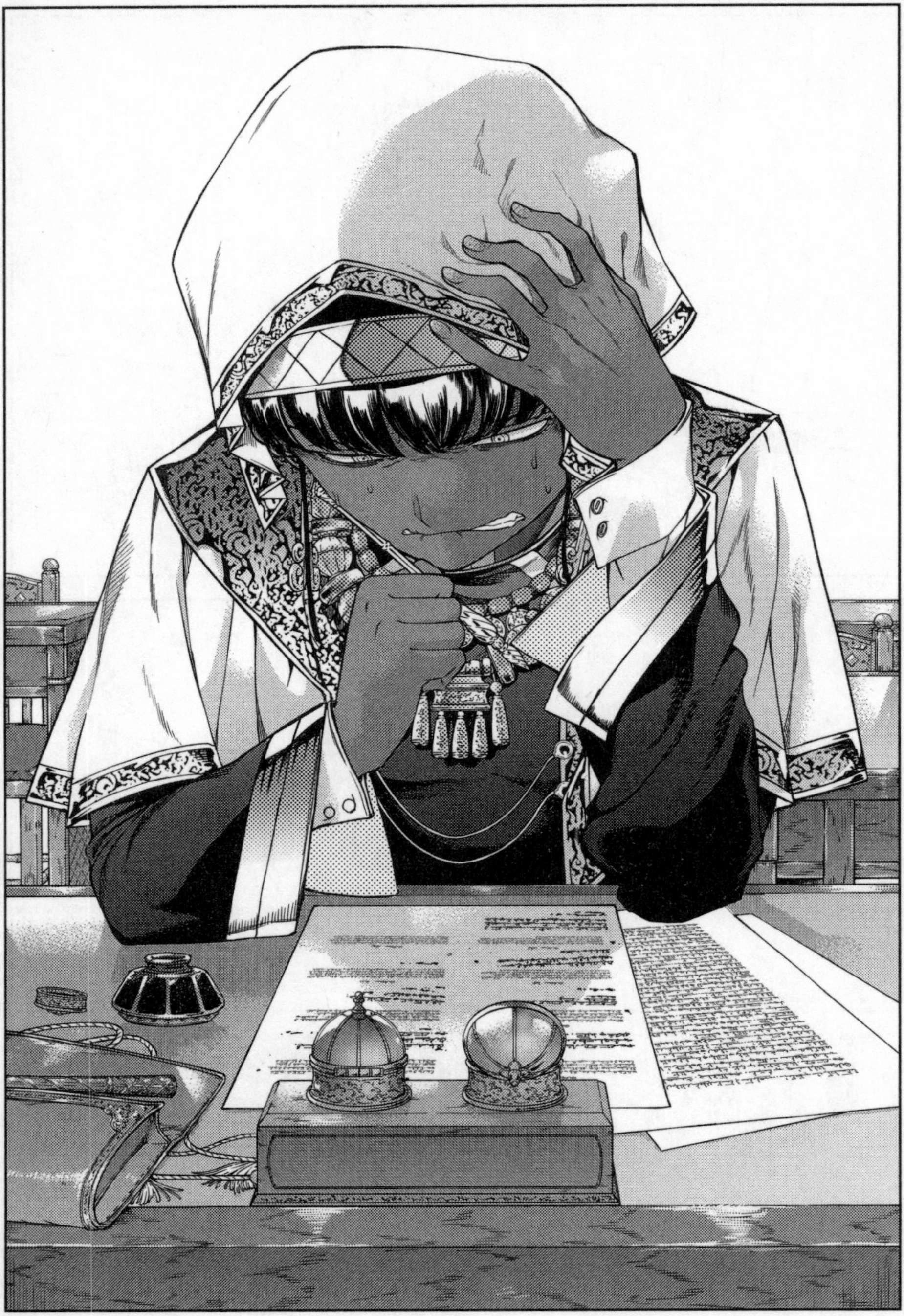

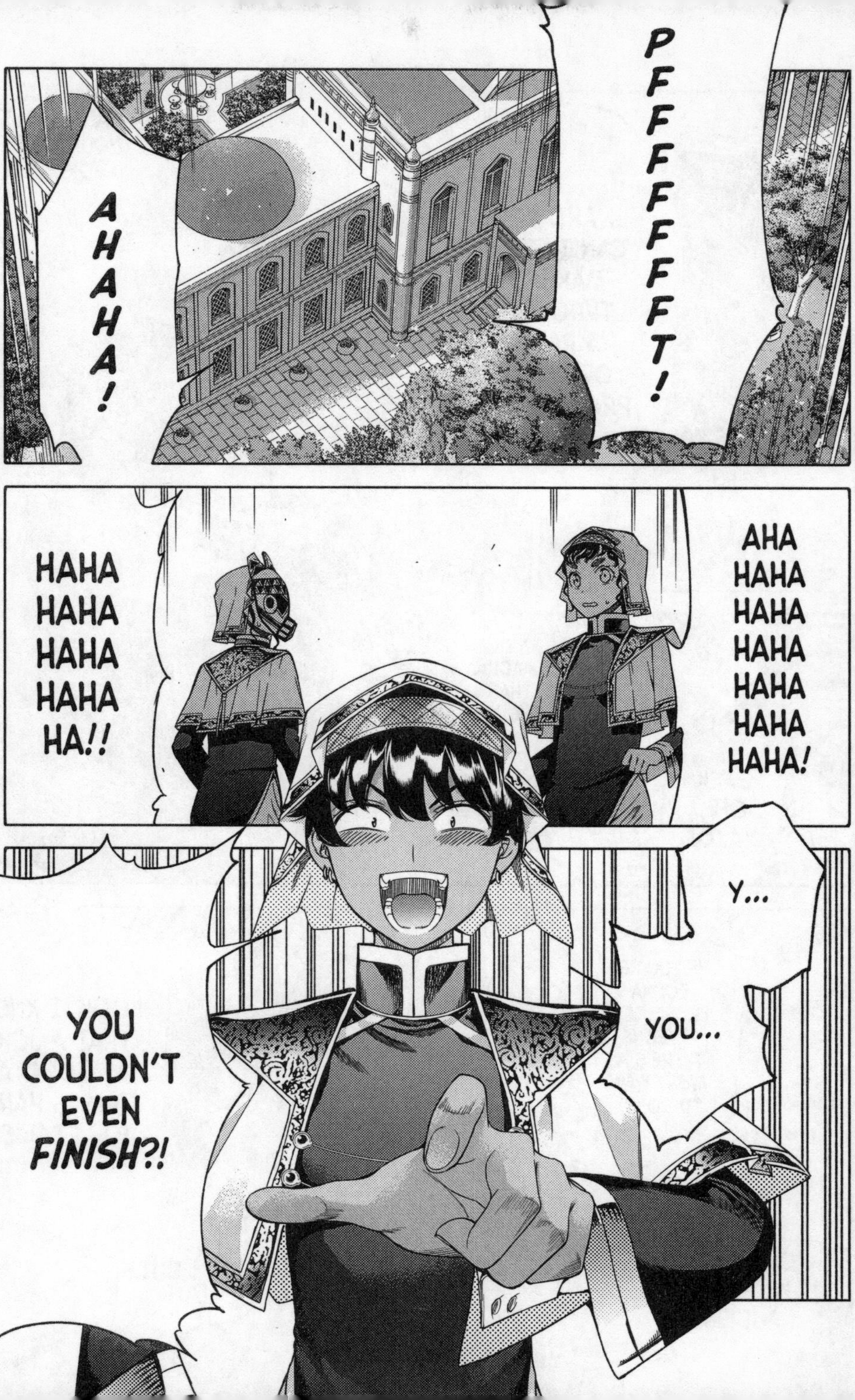
PFFFFFFFT!
AHAHAHA!
AHA HAHA HAHA HAHA HAHA HAHA HAHA!
HAHA HAHA HAHA HAHA HA!!
Y...
YOU...
YOU COULDN'T EVEN FINISH?!

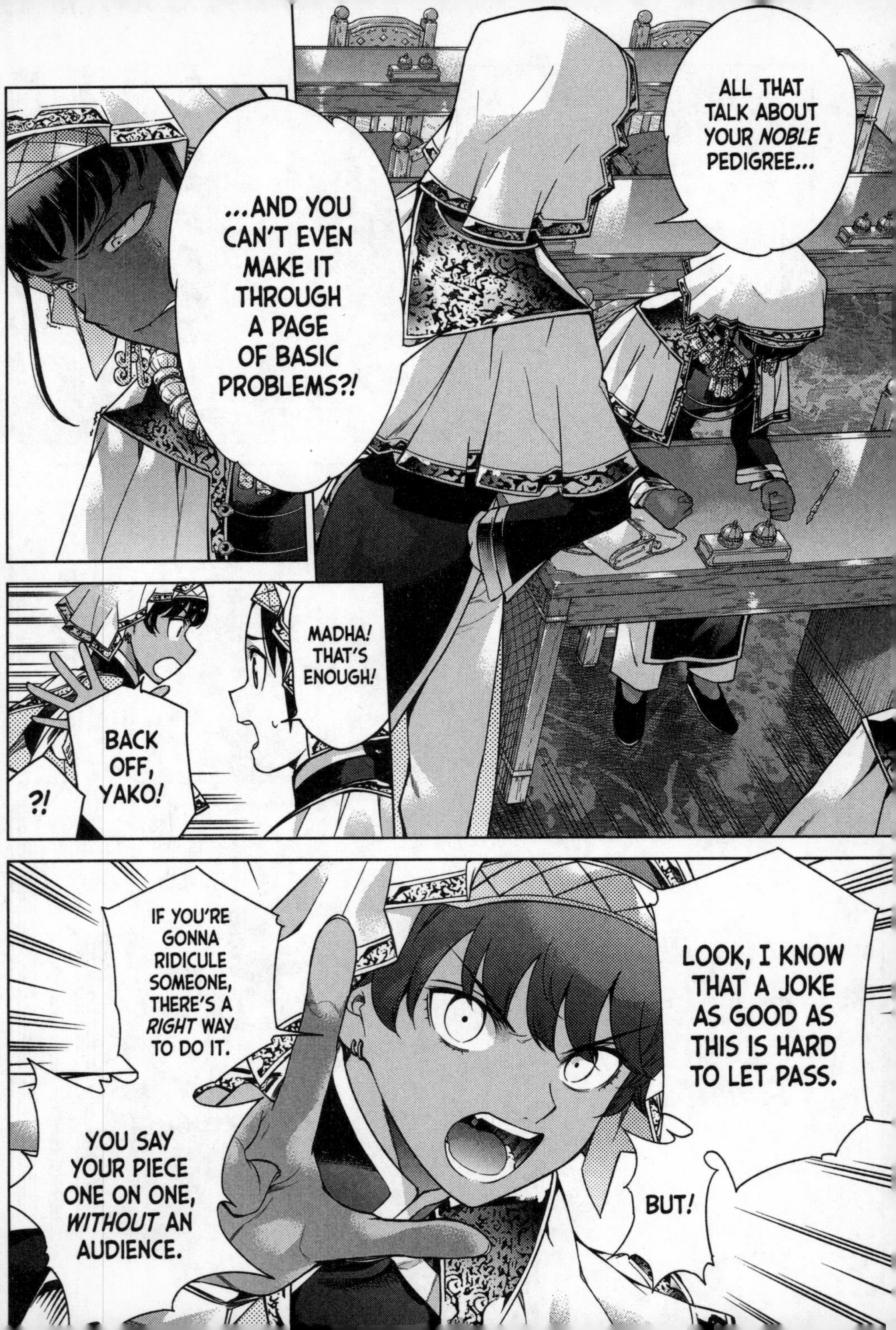
ALL THAT TALK ABOUT YOUR *NOBLE* PEDIGREE...
...AND YOU CAN'T EVEN MAKE IT THROUGH A PAGE OF BASIC PROBLEMS?!
MADHA! THAT'S ENOUGH!
BACK OFF, YAKO!
?!
LOOK, I KNOW THAT A JOKE AS GOOD AS THIS IS HARD TO LET PASS.
BUT!
IF YOU'RE GONNA RIDICULE SOMEONE, THERE'S A *RIGHT* WAY TO DO IT.
YOU SAY YOUR PIECE ONE ON ONE, *WITHOUT* AN AUDIENCE.

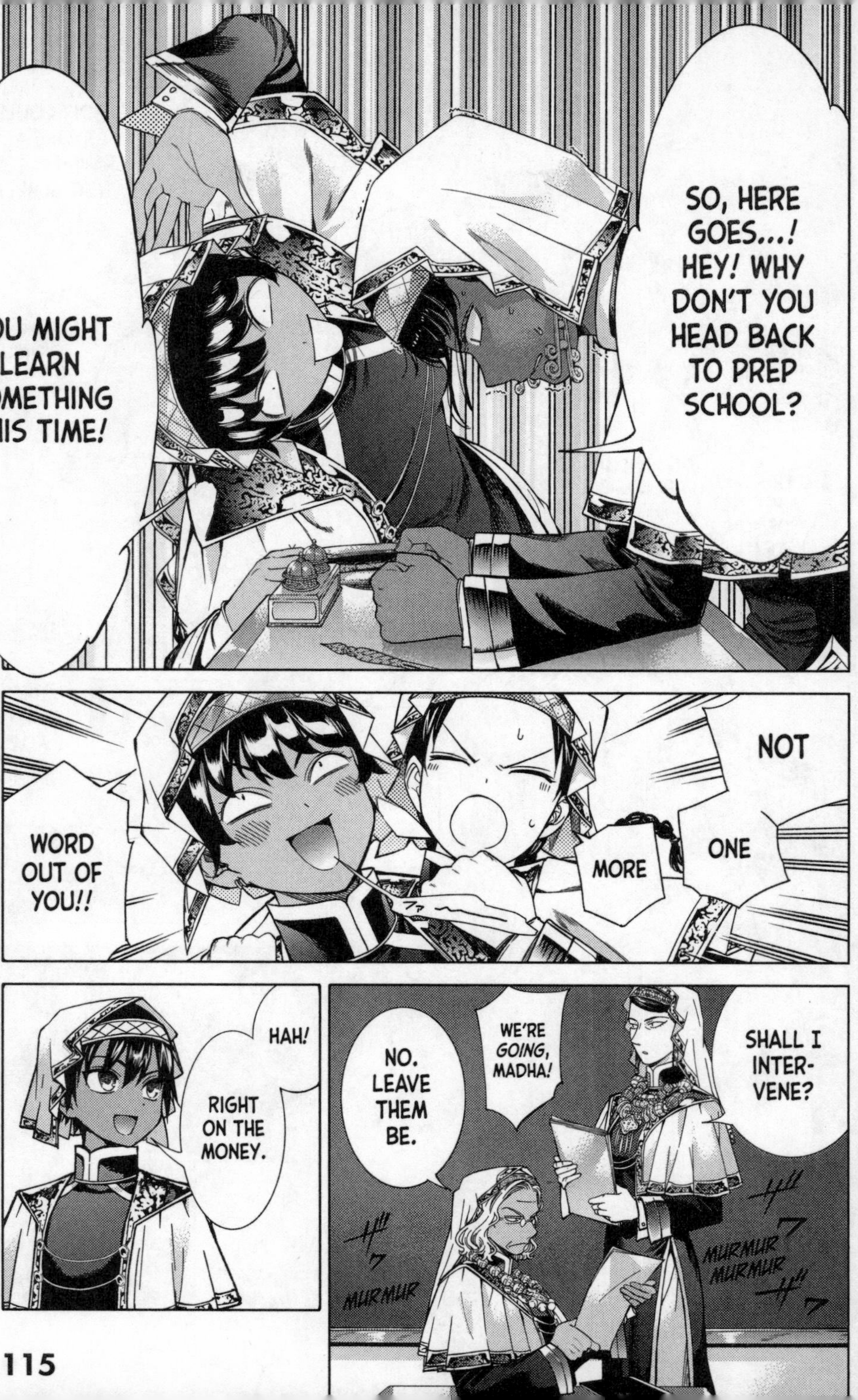
SO, HERE GOES...! HEY! WHY DON'T YOU HEAD BACK TO PREP SCHOOL?
YOU MIGHT LEARN SOMETHING THIS TIME!
NOT
ONE
MORE
WORD OUT OF YOU!!
SHALL I INTER-VENE?
WE'RE GOING, MADHA!
NO. LEAVE THEM BE.
MURMUR MURMUR
MURMUR
HAH!
RIGHT ON THE MONEY.

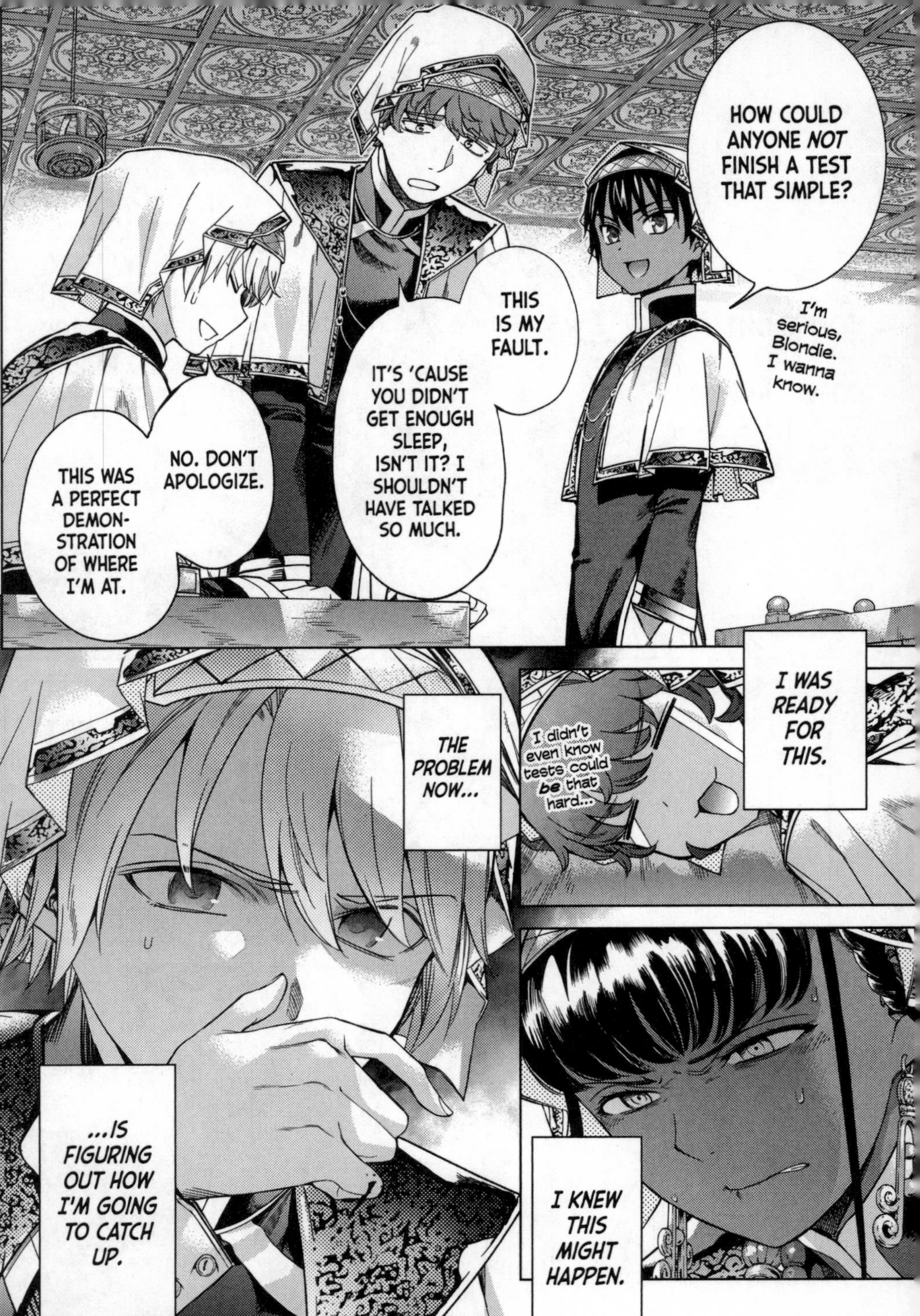
HOW COULD ANYONE *NOT* FINISH A TEST THAT SIMPLE?
I'm serious, Blondie. I wanna know.
THIS IS MY FAULT.
IT'S 'CAUSE YOU DIDN'T GET ENOUGH SLEEP, ISN'T IT? I SHOULDN'T HAVE TALKED SO MUCH.
NO. DON'T APOLOGIZE.
THIS WAS A PERFECT DEMON-STRATION OF WHERE I'M AT.
I WAS READY FOR THIS.
I didn't even know tests could **be** that hard...
I KNEW THIS MIGHT HAPPEN.
THE PROBLEM NOW...
...IS FIGURING OUT HOW I'M GOING TO CATCH UP.

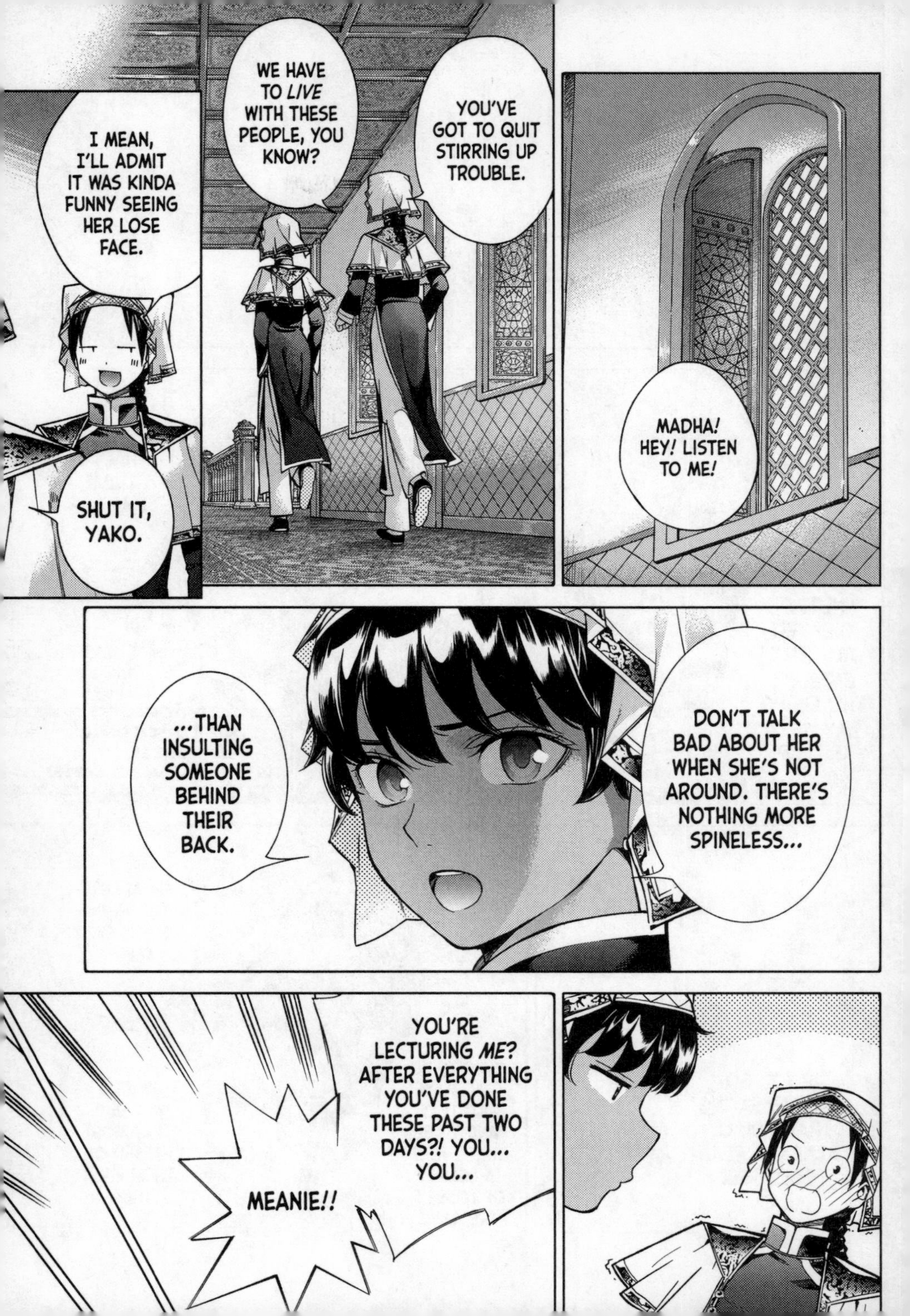
MADHA! HEY! LISTEN TO ME!
YOU'VE GOT TO QUIT STIRRING UP TROUBLE.
WE HAVE TO *LIVE* WITH THESE PEOPLE, YOU KNOW?
I MEAN, I'LL ADMIT IT WAS KINDA FUNNY SEEING HER LOSE FACE.
SHUT IT, YAKO.
DON'T TALK BAD ABOUT HER WHEN SHE'S NOT AROUND. THERE'S NOTHING MORE SPINELESS...
...THAN INSULTING SOMEONE BEHIND THEIR BACK.
YOU'RE LECTURING *ME*? AFTER EVERYTHING YOU'VE DONE THESE PAST TWO DAYS?! YOU... YOU...
MEANIE!!

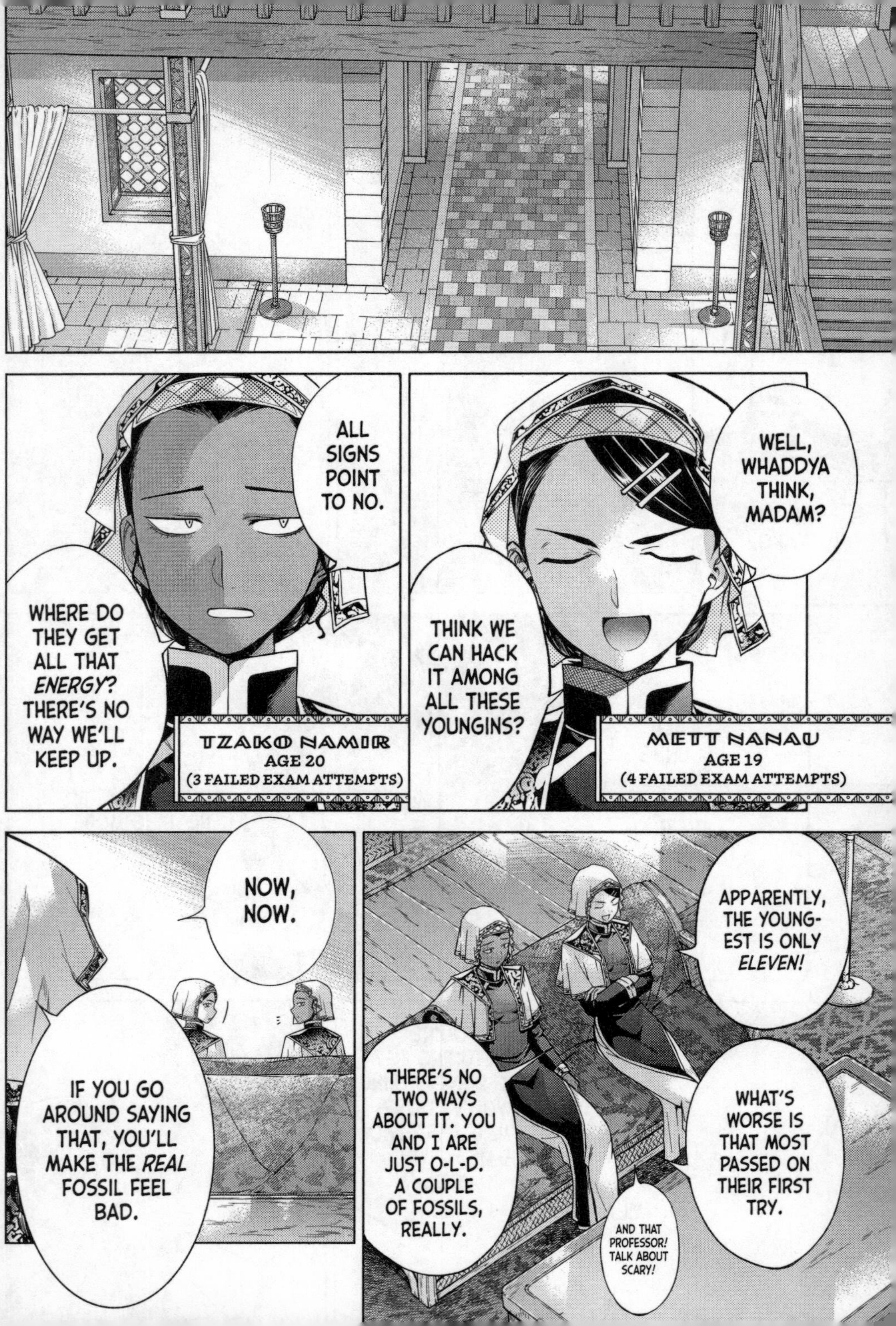
WELL, WHADDYA THINK, MADAM?
THINK WE CAN HACK IT AMONG ALL THESE YOUNGINS?
METT NANAU
AGE 19
(4 FAILED EXAM ATTEMPTS)
ALL SIGNS POINT TO NO.
WHERE DO THEY GET ALL THAT *ENERGY*? THERE'S NO WAY WE'LL KEEP UP.
TZAKO NAMIR
AGE 20
(3 FAILED EXAM ATTEMPTS)
APPARENTLY, THE YOUNG-EST IS ONLY *ELEVEN!*
WHAT'S WORSE IS THAT MOST PASSED ON THEIR FIRST TRY.
THERE'S NO TWO WAYS ABOUT IT. YOU AND I ARE JUST O-L-D. A COUPLE OF FOSSILS, REALLY.
AND THAT PROFESSOR! TALK ABOUT SCARY!
NOW, NOW.
IF YOU GO AROUND SAYING THAT, YOU'LL MAKE THE *REAL* FOSSIL FEEL BAD.

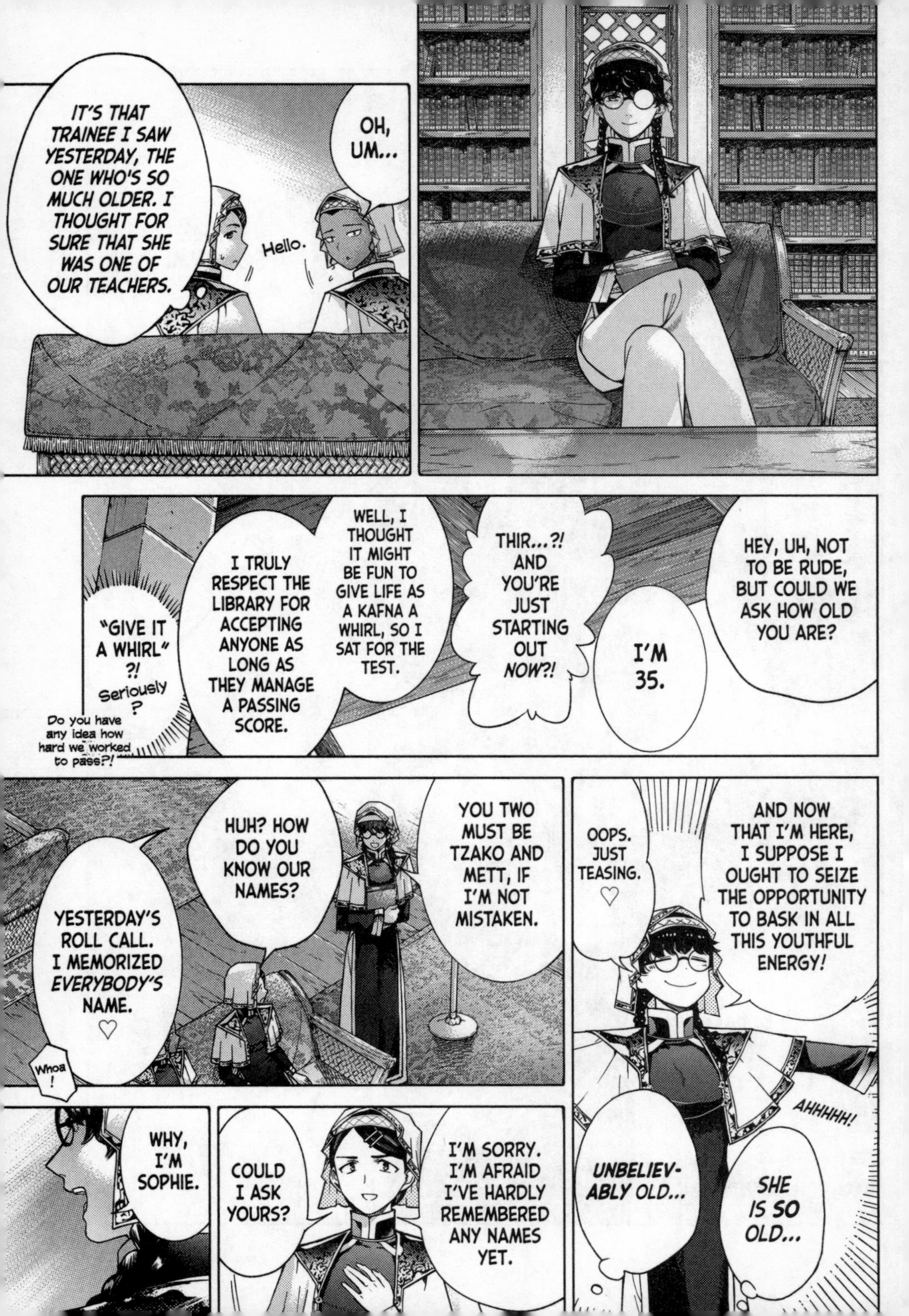
OH, UM...
IT'S THAT TRAINEE I SAW YESTERDAY, THE ONE WHO'S SO MUCH OLDER. I THOUGHT FOR SURE THAT SHE WAS ONE OF OUR TEACHERS.
Hello.
HEY, UH, NOT TO BE RUDE, BUT COULD WE ASK HOW OLD YOU ARE?
I'M 35.
THIR...?! AND YOU'RE JUST STARTING OUT *NOW?!*
WELL, I THOUGHT IT MIGHT BE FUN TO GIVE LIFE AS A KAFNA A WHIRL, SO I SAT FOR THE TEST.
I TRULY RESPECT THE LIBRARY FOR ACCEPTING ANYONE AS LONG AS THEY MANAGE A PASSING SCORE.
"GIVE IT A WHIRL" ?!
Seriously?
Do you have any idea how hard we worked to pass?!
AND NOW THAT I'M HERE, I SUPPOSE I OUGHT TO SEIZE THE OPPORTUNITY TO BASK IN ALL THIS YOUTHFUL ENERGY!
OOPS. JUST TEASING. ♡
AHHHHH!
SHE IS SO OLD...
UNBELIEV-ABLY OLD...
YOU TWO MUST BE TZAKO AND METT, IF I'M NOT MISTAKEN.
HUH? HOW DO YOU KNOW OUR NAMES?
YESTERDAY'S ROLL CALL. I MEMORIZED *EVERYBODY'S* NAME. ♡
Whoa!
I'M SORRY. I'M AFRAID I'VE HARDLY REMEMBERED ANY NAMES YET.
COULD I ASK YOURS?
WHY, I'M SOPHIE.

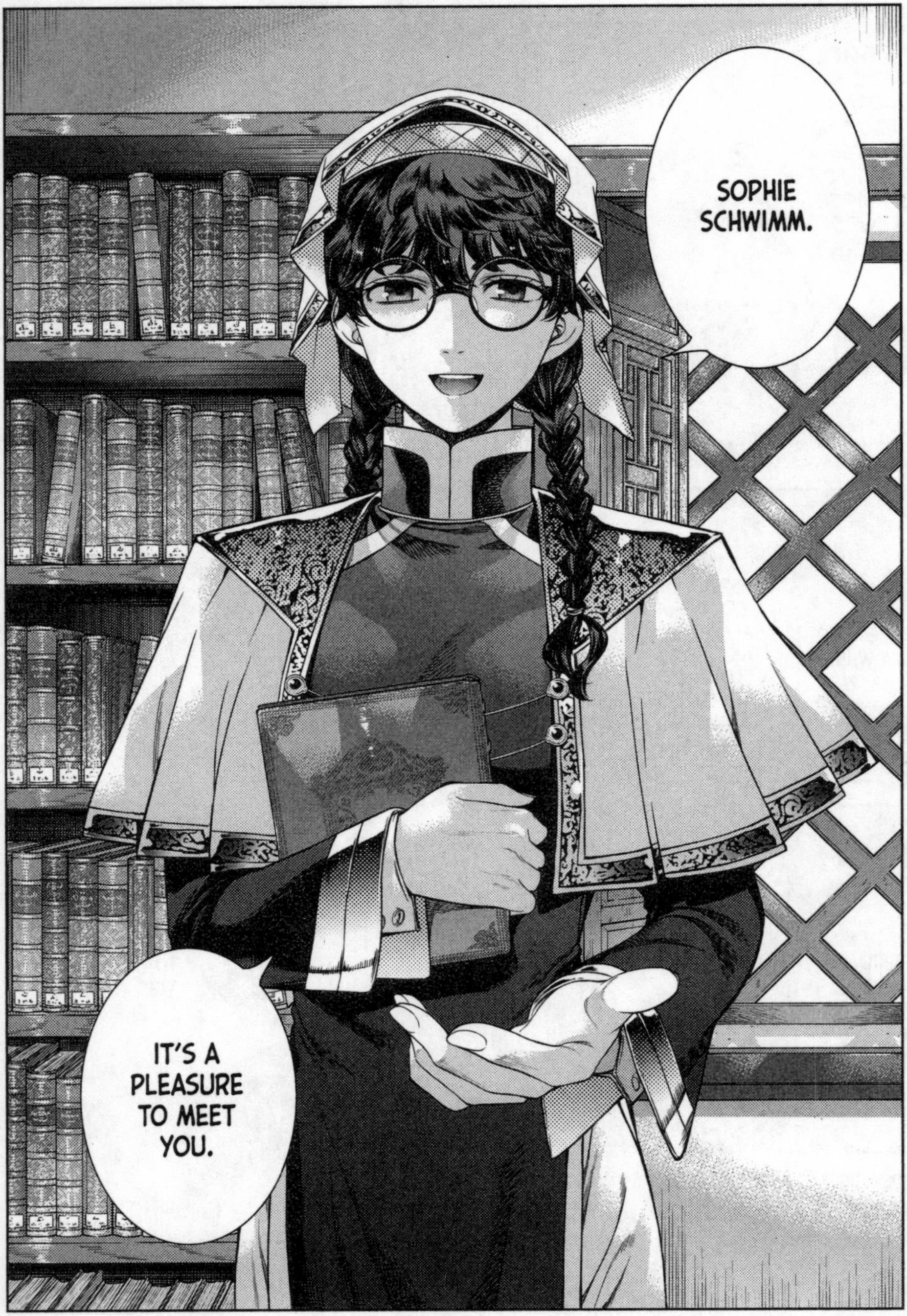
SOPHIE SCHWIMM.
IT'S A PLEASURE TO MEET YOU.

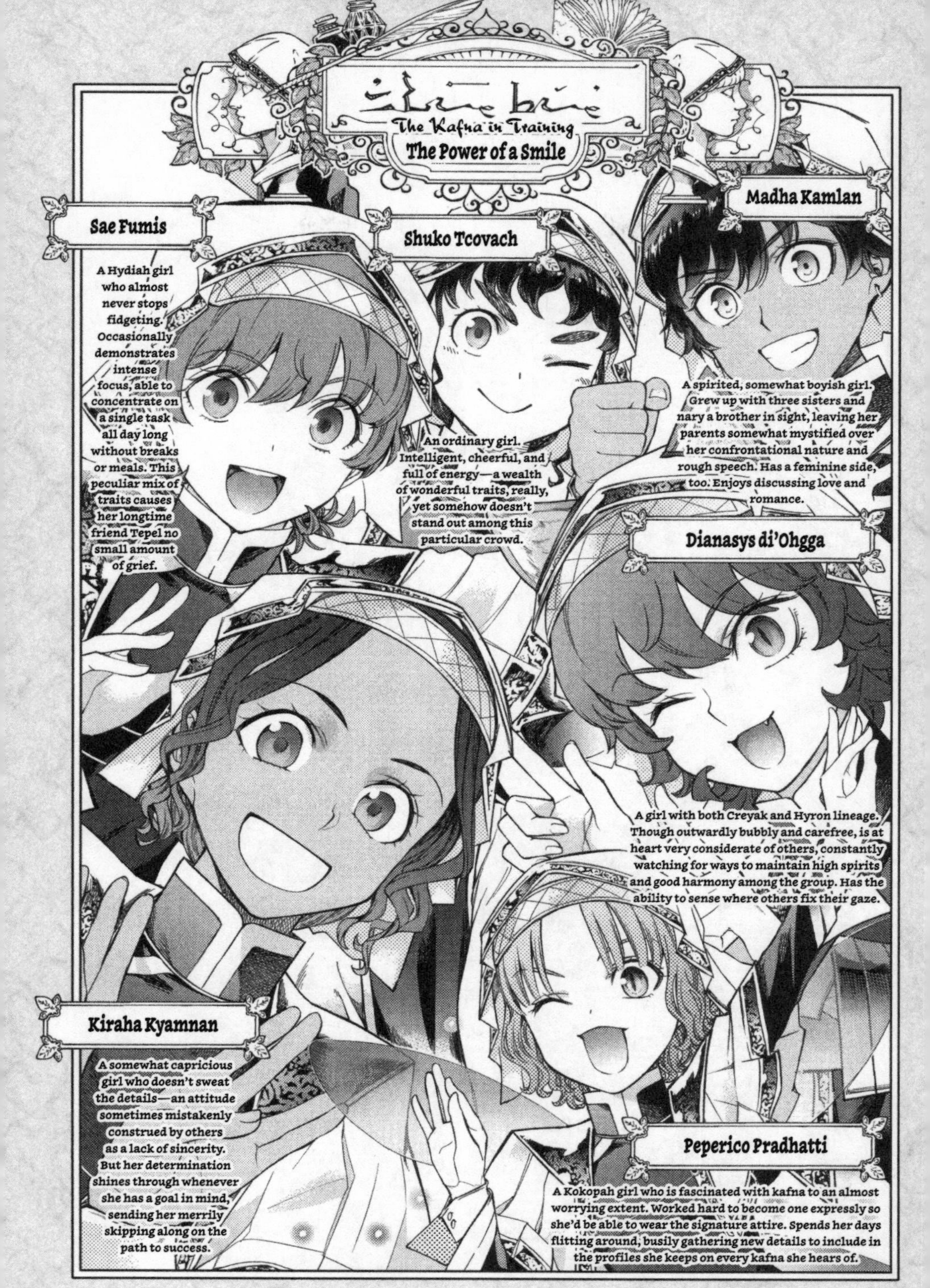
The Kafna in Training
The Power of a Smile
Madha Kamlan
A spirited, somewhat boyish girl. Grew up with three sisters and nary a brother in sight, leaving her parents somewhat mystified over her confrontational nature and rough speech. Has a feminine side, too. Enjoys discussing love and romance.
Shuko Tcovach
An ordinary girl. Intelligent, cheerful, and full of energy—a wealth of wonderful traits, really, yet somehow doesn't stand out among this particular crowd.
Sae Fumis
A Hydiah girl who almost never stops fidgeting. Occasionally demonstrates intense focus, able to concentrate on a single task all day long without breaks or meals. This peculiar mix of traits causes her longtime friend Tepel no small amount of grief.
Dianasys di'Ohgga
A girl with both Creyak and Hyron lineage. Though outwardly bubbly and carefree, is at heart very considerate of others, constantly watching for ways to maintain high spirits and good harmony among the group. Has the ability to sense where others fix their gaze.
Peperico Pradhatti
A Kokopah girl who is fascinated with kafna to an almost worrying extent. Worked hard to become one expressly so she'd be able to wear the signature attire. Spends her days flitting around, busily gathering new details to include in the profiles she keeps on every kafna she hears of.
Kiraha Kyamnan
A somewhat capricious girl who doesn't sweat the details—an attitude sometimes mistakenly construed by others as a lack of sincerity. But her determination shines through whenever she has a goal in mind, sending her merrily skipping along on the path to success.

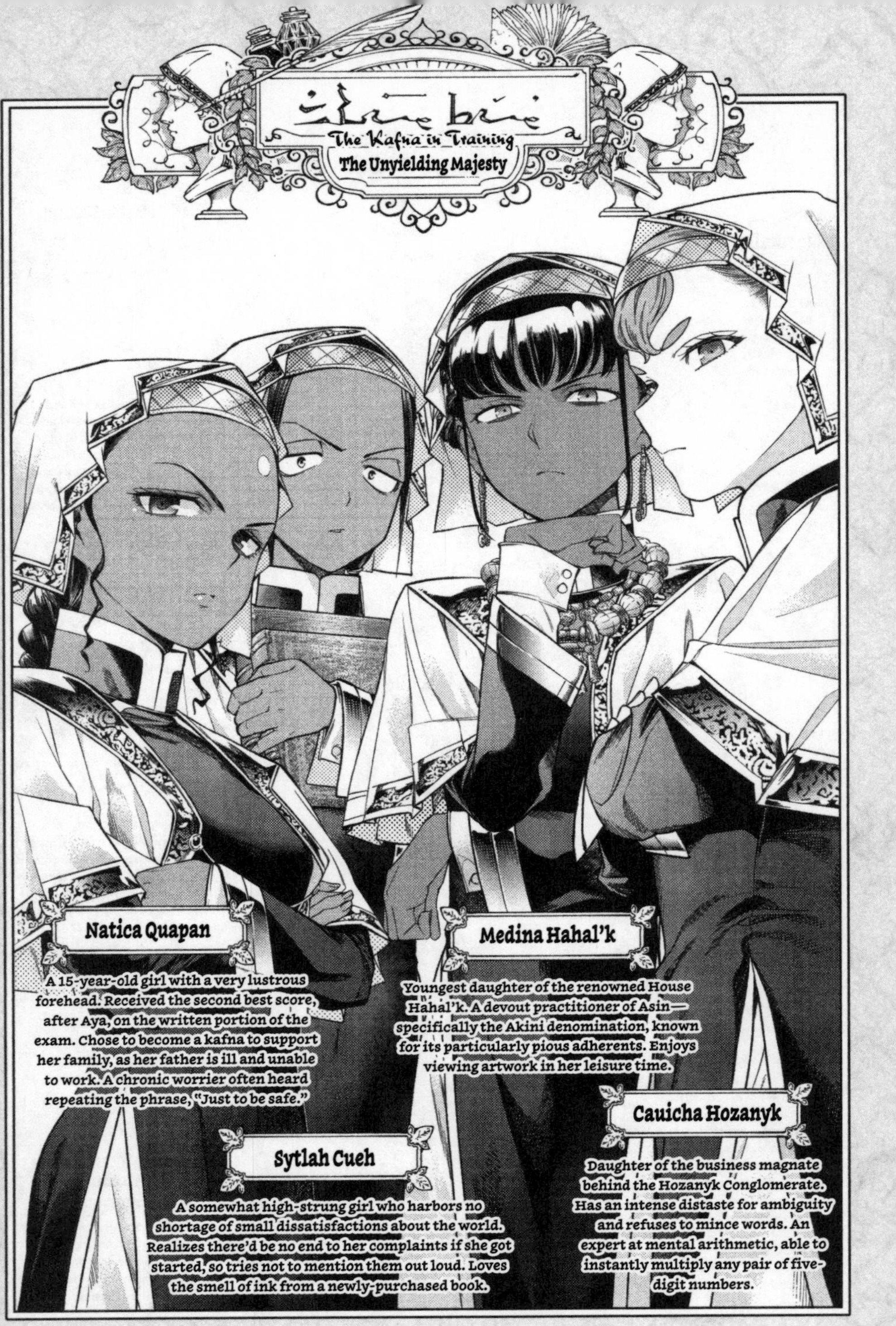
The Kafna in Training
The Unyielding Majesty
Medina Hahal'k
Youngest daughter of the renowned House Hahal'k. A devout practitioner of Asin—specifically the Akini denomination, known for its particularly pious adherents. Enjoys viewing artwork in her leisure time.
Natica Quapan
A 15-year-old girl with a very lustrous forehead. Received the second best score, after Aya, on the written portion of the exam. Chose to become a kafna to support her family, as her father is ill and unable to work. A chronic worrier often heard repeating the phrase, "Just to be safe."
Cauicha Hozanyk
Daughter of the business magnate behind the Hozanyk Conglomerate. Has an intense distaste for ambiguity and refuses to mince words. An expert at mental arithmetic, able to instantly multiply any pair of five-digit numbers.
Sytlah Cueh
A somewhat high-strung girl who harbors no shortage of small dissatisfactions about the world. Realizes there'd be no end to her complaints if she got started, so tries not to mention them out loud. Loves the smell of ink from a newly-purchased book.

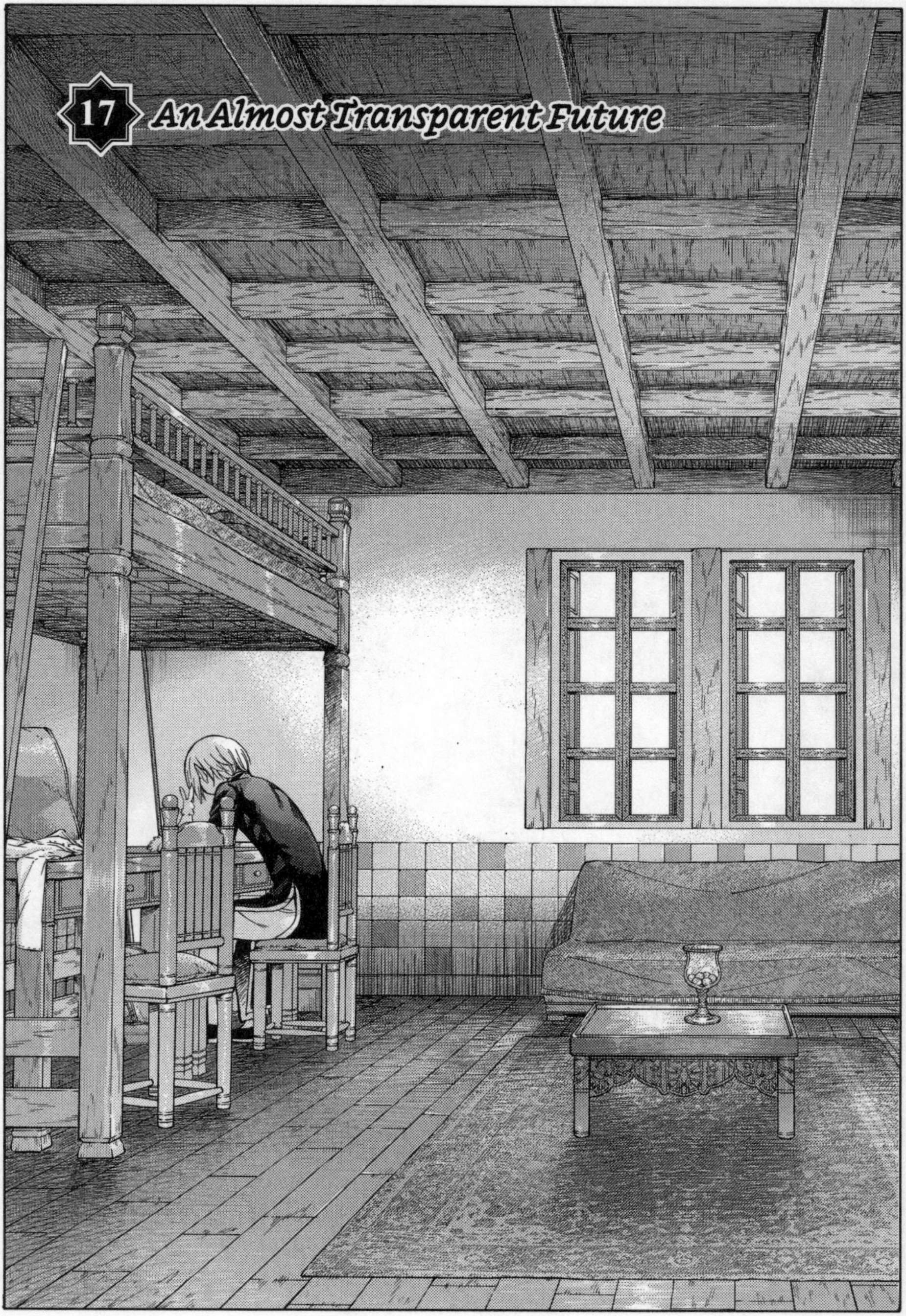
17
An Almost Transparent Future

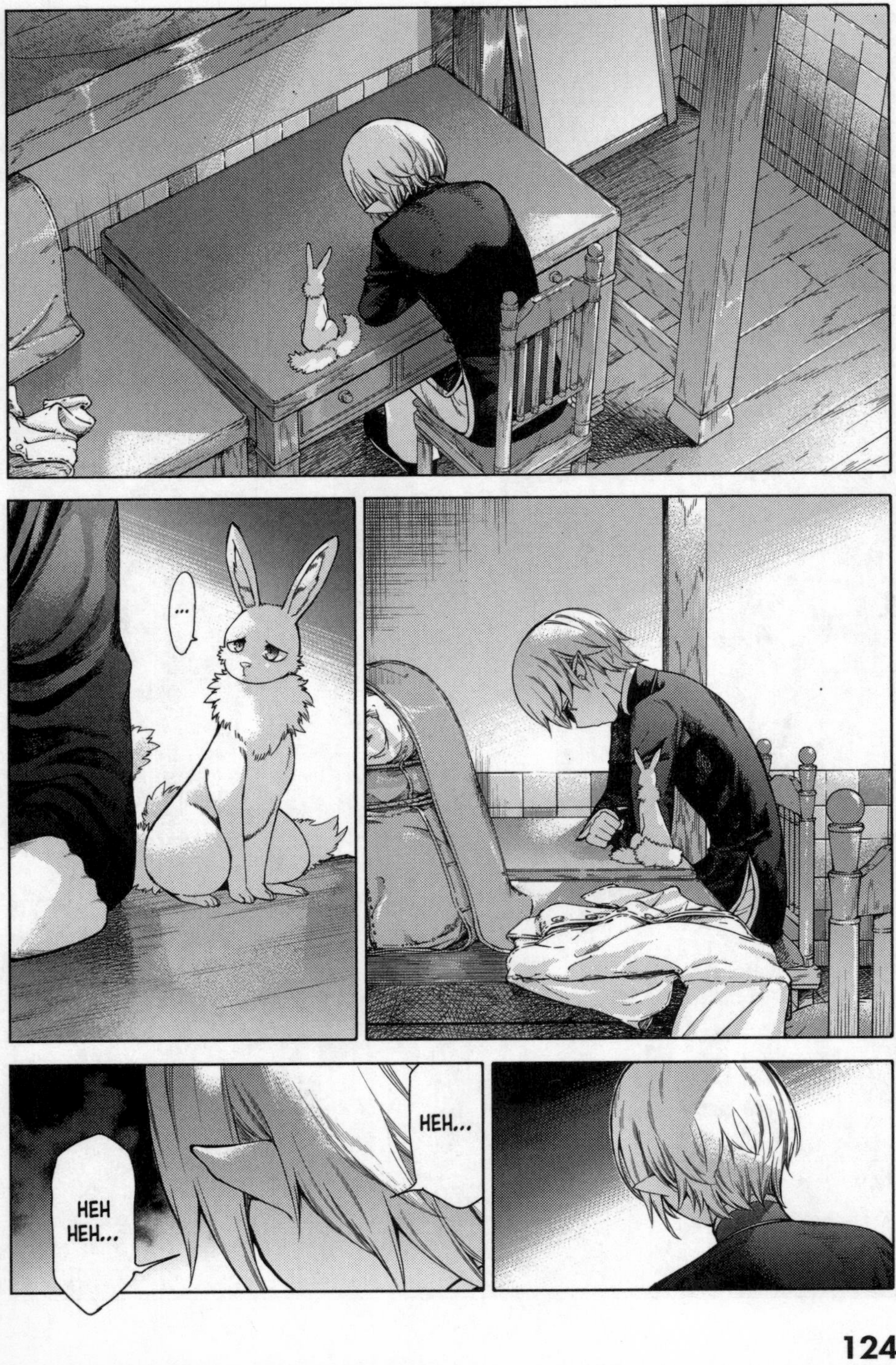
...
HEH...
HEH HEH...

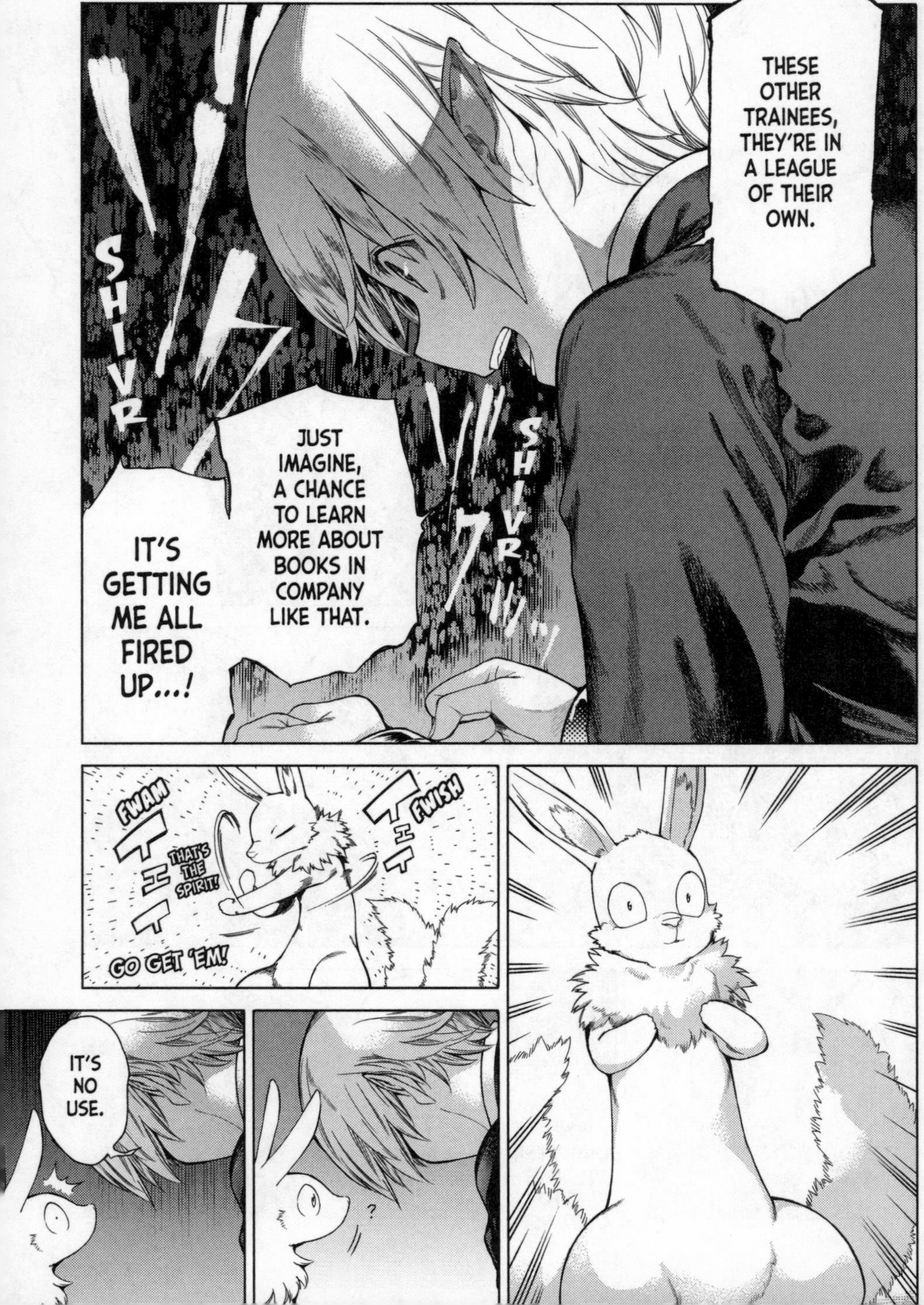
THESE OTHER TRAINEES, THEY'RE IN A LEAGUE OF THEIR OWN.
SHIVR
JUST IMAGINE, A CHANCE TO LEARN MORE ABOUT BOOKS IN COMPANY LIKE THAT.
SHIVR
IT'S GETTING ME ALL FIRED UP...!
FWISH
THAT'S THE SPIRIT!
FWAM
GO GET 'EM!
?
IT'S NO USE.

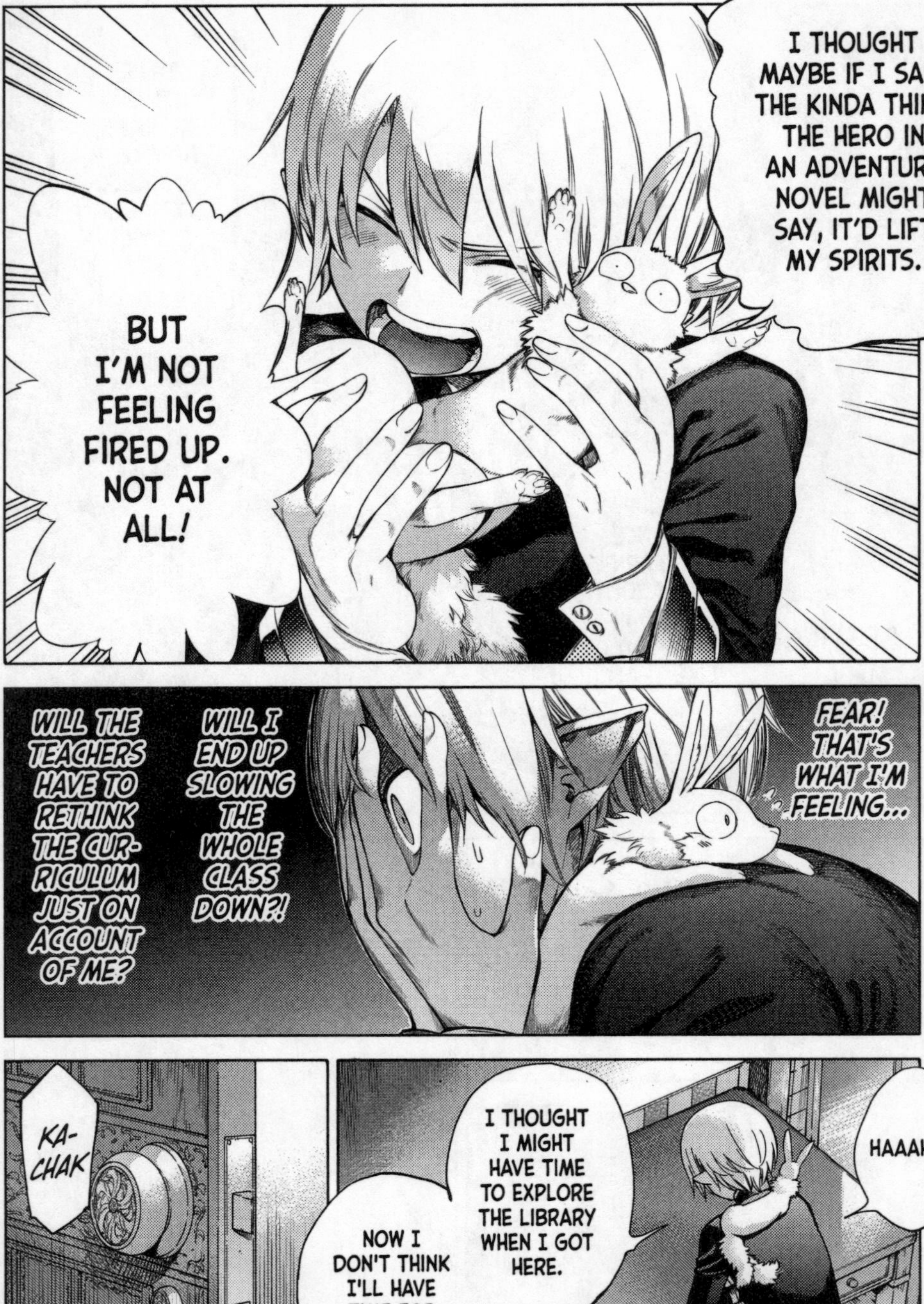
I THOUGHT MAYBE IF I SAID THE KINDA THING THE HERO IN AN ADVENTURE NOVEL MIGHT SAY, IT'D LIFT MY SPIRITS.
BUT I'M NOT FEELING FIRED UP. NOT AT ALL!
FEAR! THAT'S WHAT I'M FEELING...
WILL I END UP SLOWING THE WHOLE CLASS DOWN?!
WILL THE TEACHERS HAVE TO RETHINK THE CUR-RICULUM JUST ON ACCOUNT OF ME?
HAAAH...
I THOUGHT I MIGHT HAVE TIME TO EXPLORE THE LIBRARY WHEN I GOT HERE.
NOW I DON'T THINK I'LL HAVE TIME FOR *ANYTHING!*
KA-CHAK

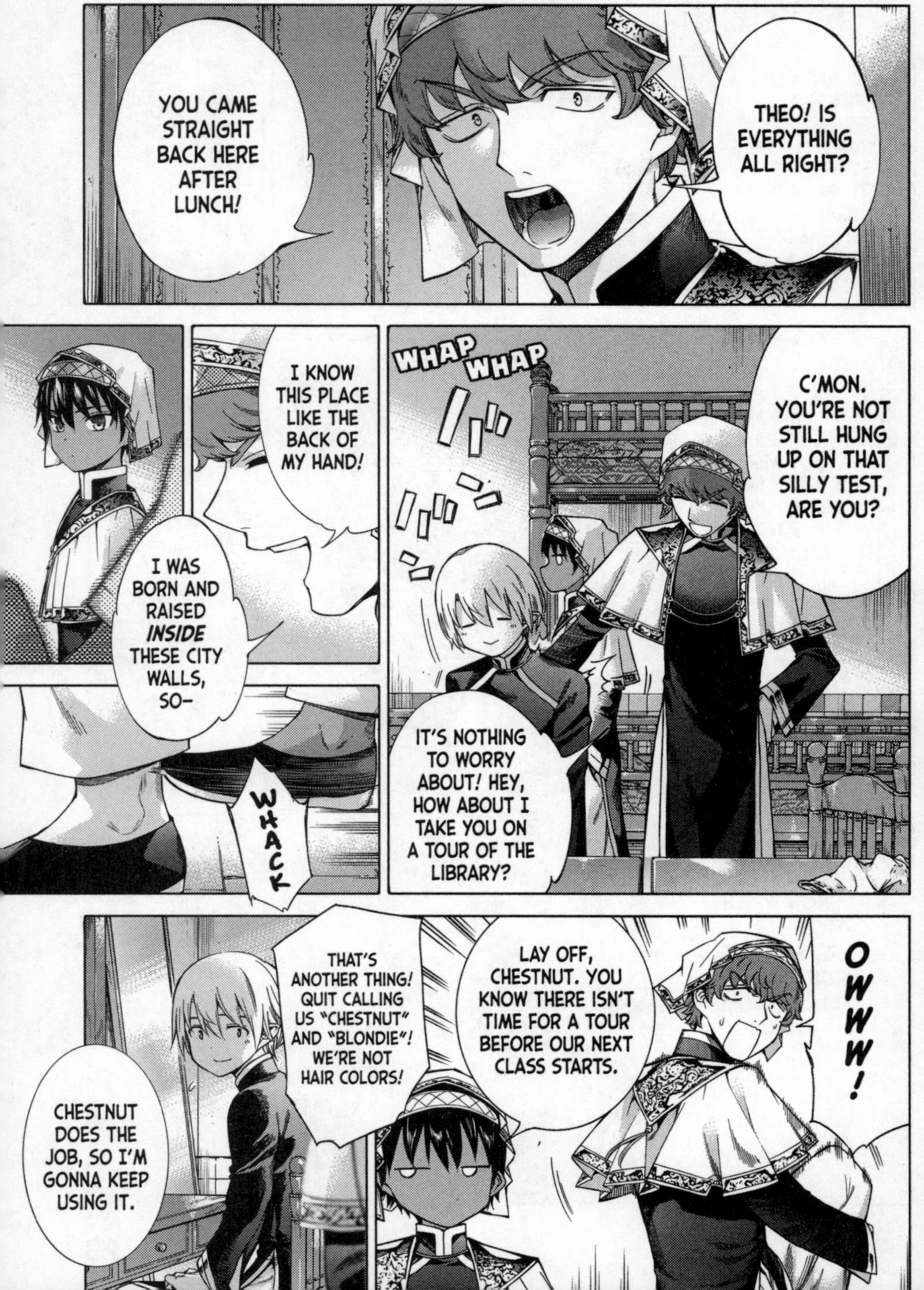
THEO! IS EVERYTHING ALL RIGHT?
YOU CAME STRAIGHT BACK HERE AFTER LUNCH!
C'MON. YOU'RE NOT STILL HUNG UP ON THAT SILLY TEST, ARE YOU?
WHAP WHAP
IT'S NOTHING TO WORRY ABOUT! HEY, HOW ABOUT I TAKE YOU ON A TOUR OF THE LIBRARY?
I KNOW THIS PLACE LIKE THE BACK OF MY HAND!
I WAS BORN AND RAISED *INSIDE* THESE CITY WALLS, SO–
WHACK
OWWW!
LAY OFF, CHESTNUT. YOU KNOW THERE ISN'T TIME FOR A TOUR BEFORE OUR NEXT CLASS STARTS.
THAT'S ANOTHER THING! QUIT CALLING US "CHESTNUT" AND "BLONDIE"! WE'RE NOT HAIR COLORS!
CHESTNUT DOES THE JOB, SO I'M GONNA KEEP USING IT.

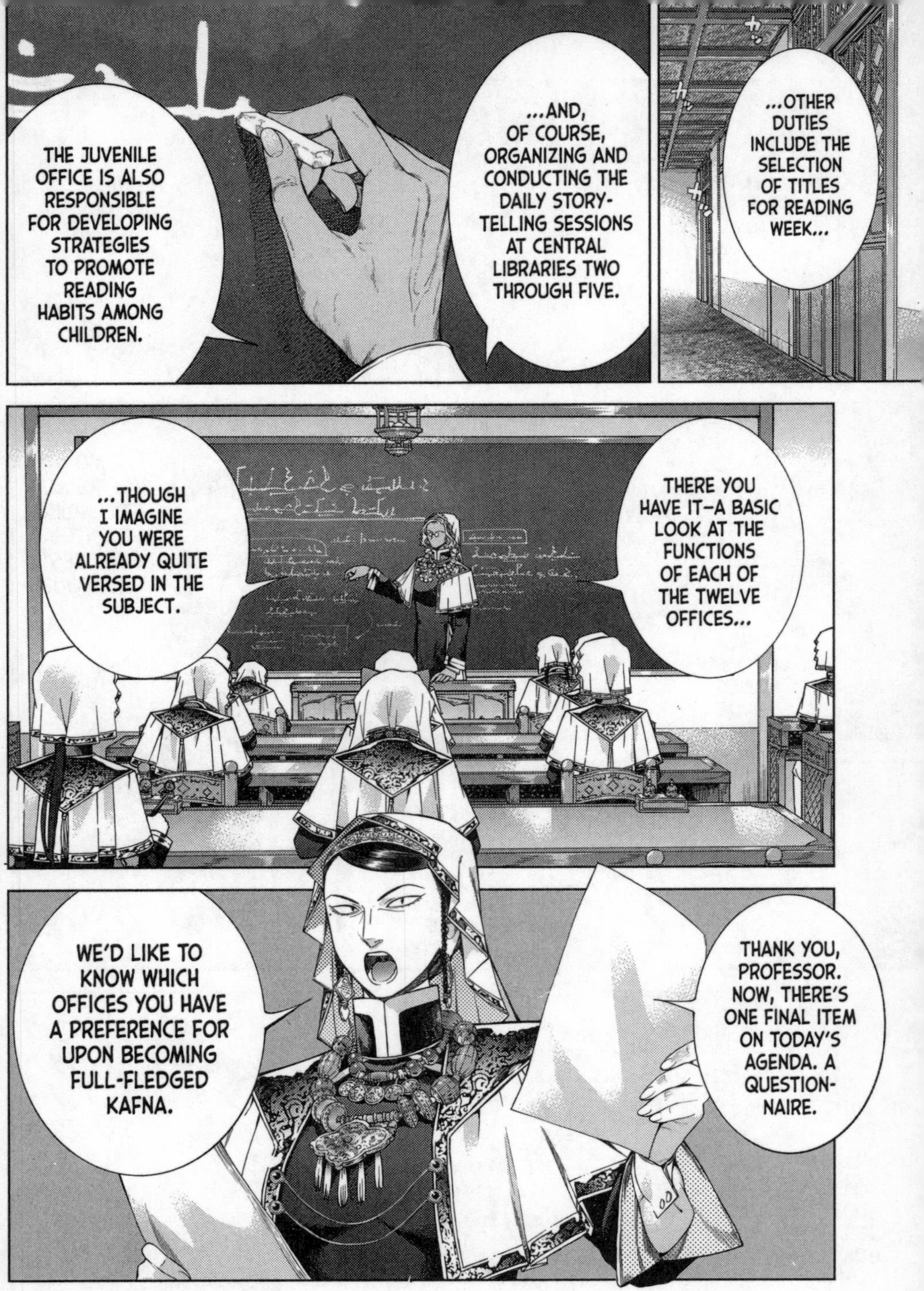
...OTHER DUTIES INCLUDE THE SELECTION OF TITLES FOR READING WEEK...
...AND, OF COURSE, ORGANIZING AND CONDUCTING THE DAILY STORY-TELLING SESSIONS AT CENTRAL LIBRARIES TWO THROUGH FIVE.
THE JUVENILE OFFICE IS ALSO RESPONSIBLE FOR DEVELOPING STRATEGIES TO PROMOTE READING HABITS AMONG CHILDREN.
THERE YOU HAVE IT—A BASIC LOOK AT THE FUNCTIONS OF EACH OF THE TWELVE OFFICES...
...THOUGH I IMAGINE YOU WERE ALREADY QUITE VERSED IN THE SUBJECT.
THANK YOU, PROFESSOR. NOW, THERE'S ONE FINAL ITEM ON TODAY'S AGENDA. A QUESTION-NAIRE.
WE'D LIKE TO KNOW WHICH OFFICES YOU HAVE A PREFERENCE FOR UPON BECOMING FULL-FLEDGED KAFNA.

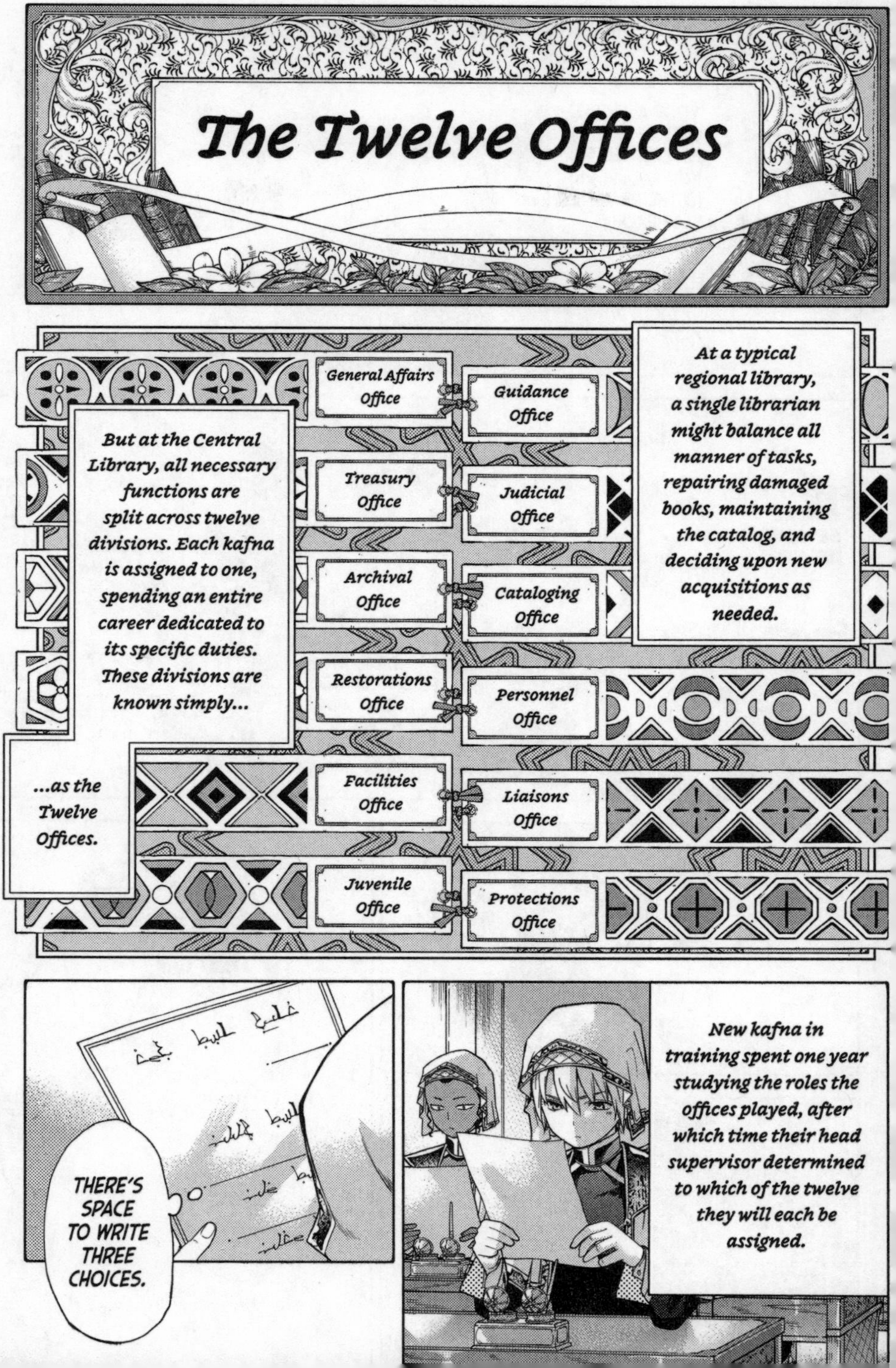
The Twelve Offices
At a typical regional library, a single librarian might balance all manner of tasks, repairing damaged books, maintaining the catalog, and deciding upon new acquisitions as needed.
But at the Central Library, all necessary functions are split across twelve divisions. Each kafna is assigned to one, spending an entire career dedicated to its specific duties. These divisions are known simply...
Guidance Office
General Affairs Office
Judicial Office
Treasury Office
Cataloging Office
Archival Office
Personnel Office
Restorations Office
Liaisons Office
Facilities Office
Protections Office
Juvenile Office
...as the Twelve Offices.
New kafna in training spent one year studying the roles the offices played, after which time their head supervisor determined to which of the twelve they will each be assigned.
THERE'S SPACE TO WRITE THREE CHOICES.

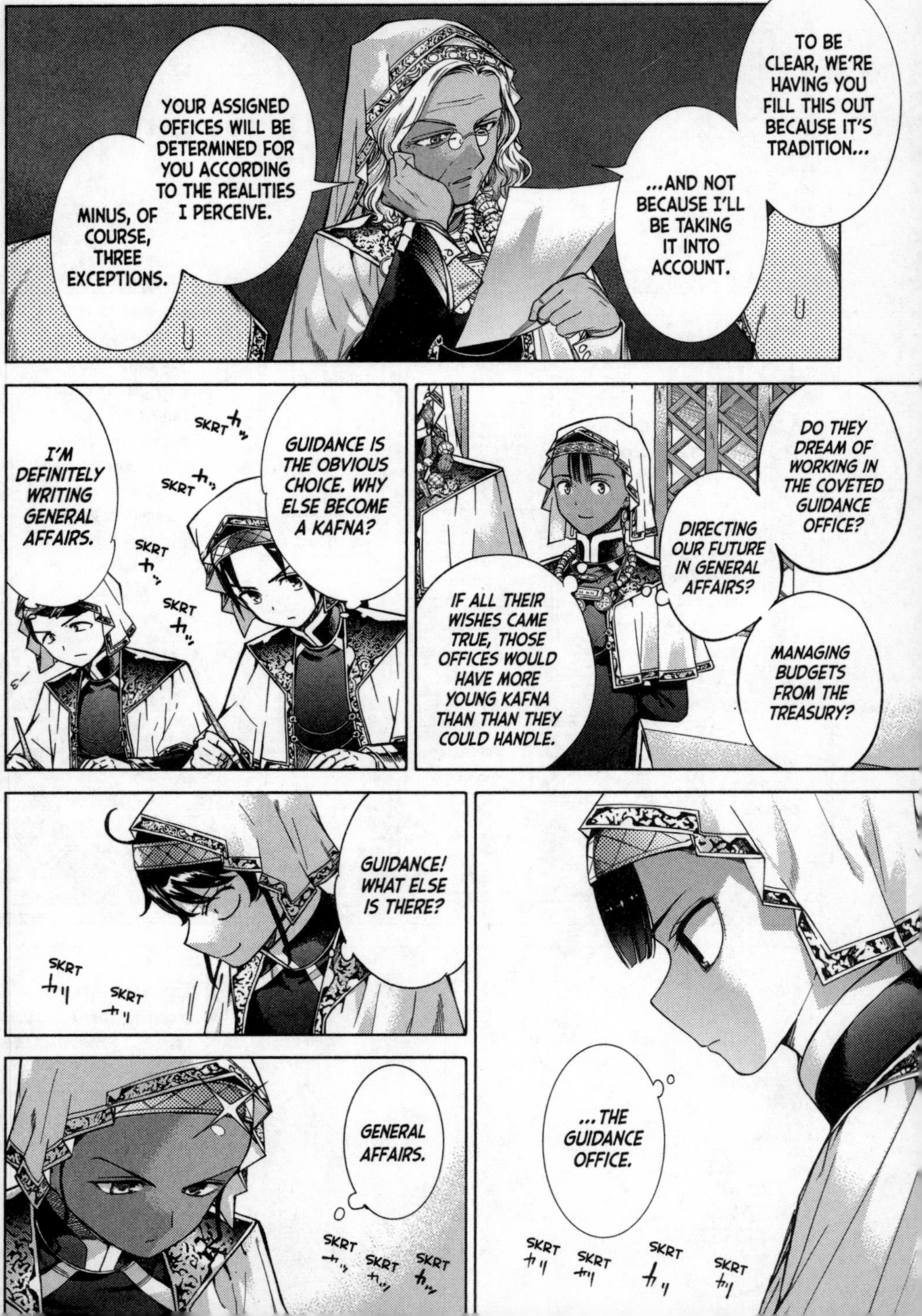
TO BE CLEAR, WE'RE HAVING YOU FILL THIS OUT BECAUSE IT'S TRADITION...
...AND NOT BECAUSE I'LL BE TAKING IT INTO ACCOUNT.
YOUR ASSIGNED OFFICES WILL BE DETERMINED FOR YOU ACCORDING TO THE REALITIES I PERCEIVE.
MINUS, OF COURSE, THREE EXCEPTIONS.
DO THEY DREAM OF WORKING IN THE COVETED GUIDANCE OFFICE?
DIRECTING OUR FUTURE IN GENERAL AFFAIRS?
MANAGING BUDGETS FROM THE TREASURY?
IF ALL THEIR WISHES CAME TRUE, THOSE OFFICES WOULD HAVE MORE YOUNG KAFNA THAN THAN THEY COULD HANDLE.
SKRT
GUIDANCE IS THE OBVIOUS CHOICE. WHY ELSE BECOME A KAFNA?
SKRT
I'M DEFINITELY WRITING GENERAL AFFAIRS.
SKRT
SKRT
...THE GUIDANCE OFFICE.
SKRT
SKRT
SKRT
SKRT
GUIDANCE! WHAT ELSE IS THERE?
SKRT
SKRT
GENERAL AFFAIRS.
SKRT
SKRT
SKRT

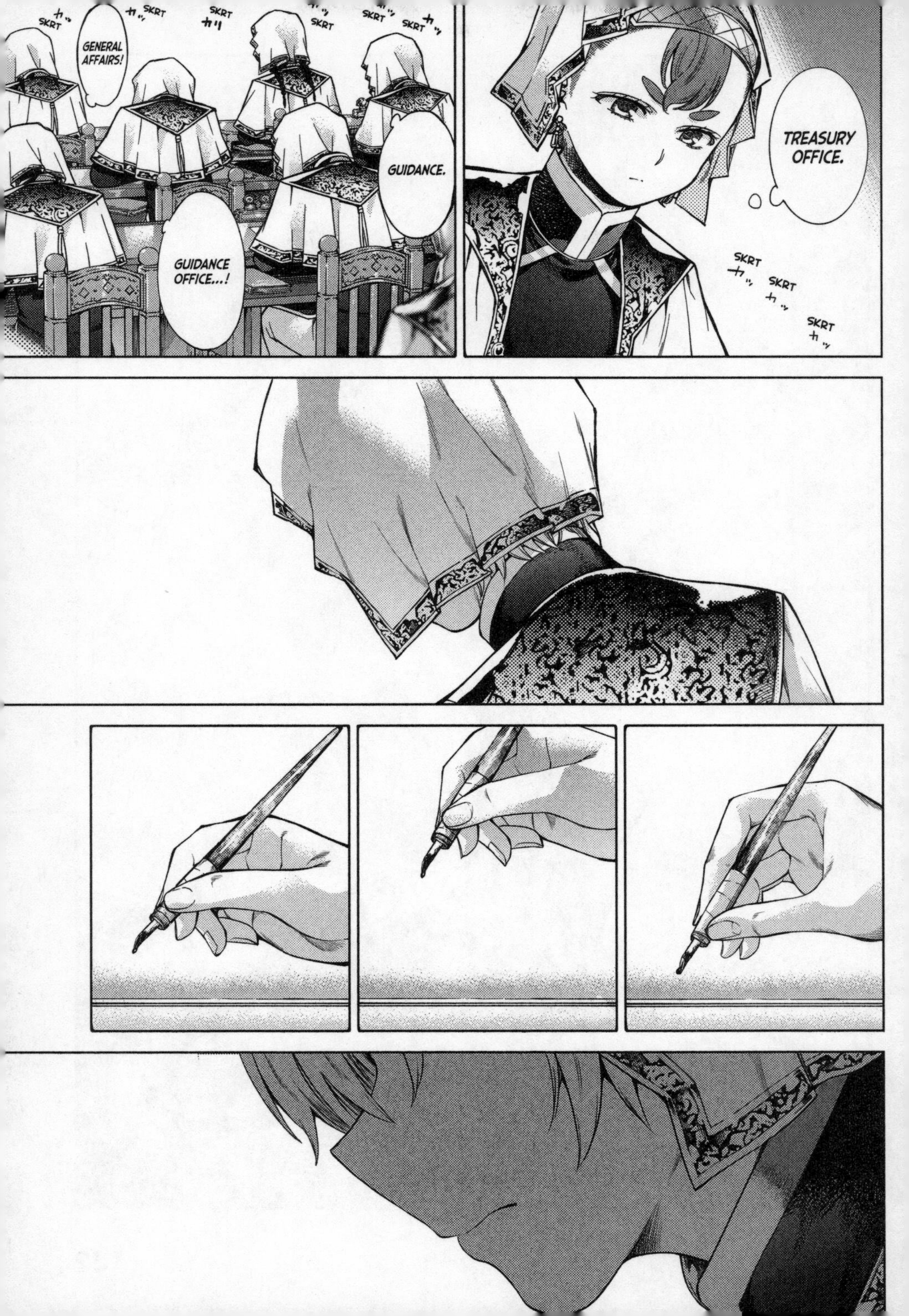
TREASURY OFFICE.
SKRT
SKRT
SKRT
SKRT
SKRT
SKRT
SKRT
SKRT
GENERAL AFFAIRS!
GUIDANCE.
GUIDANCE OFFICE...!

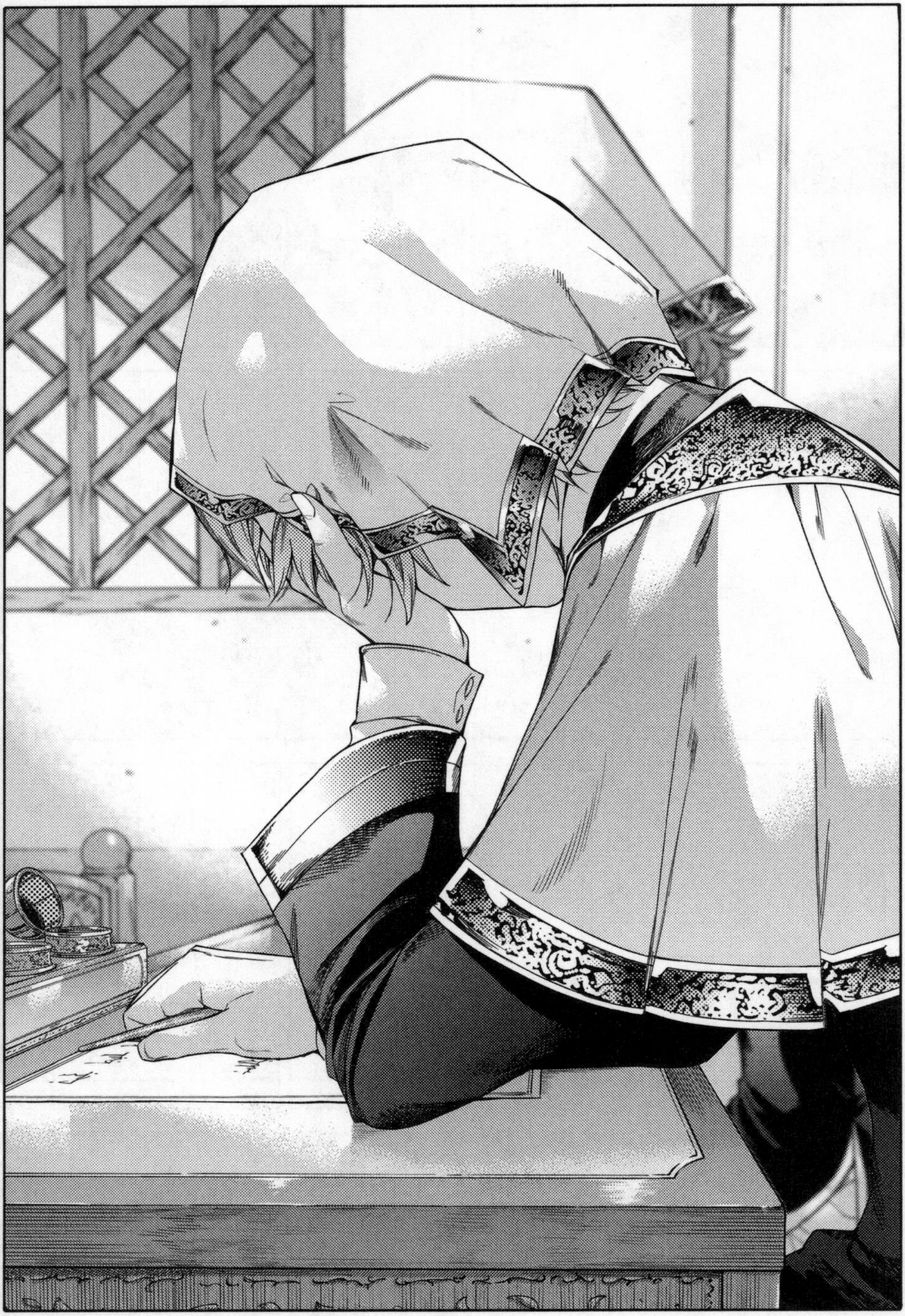

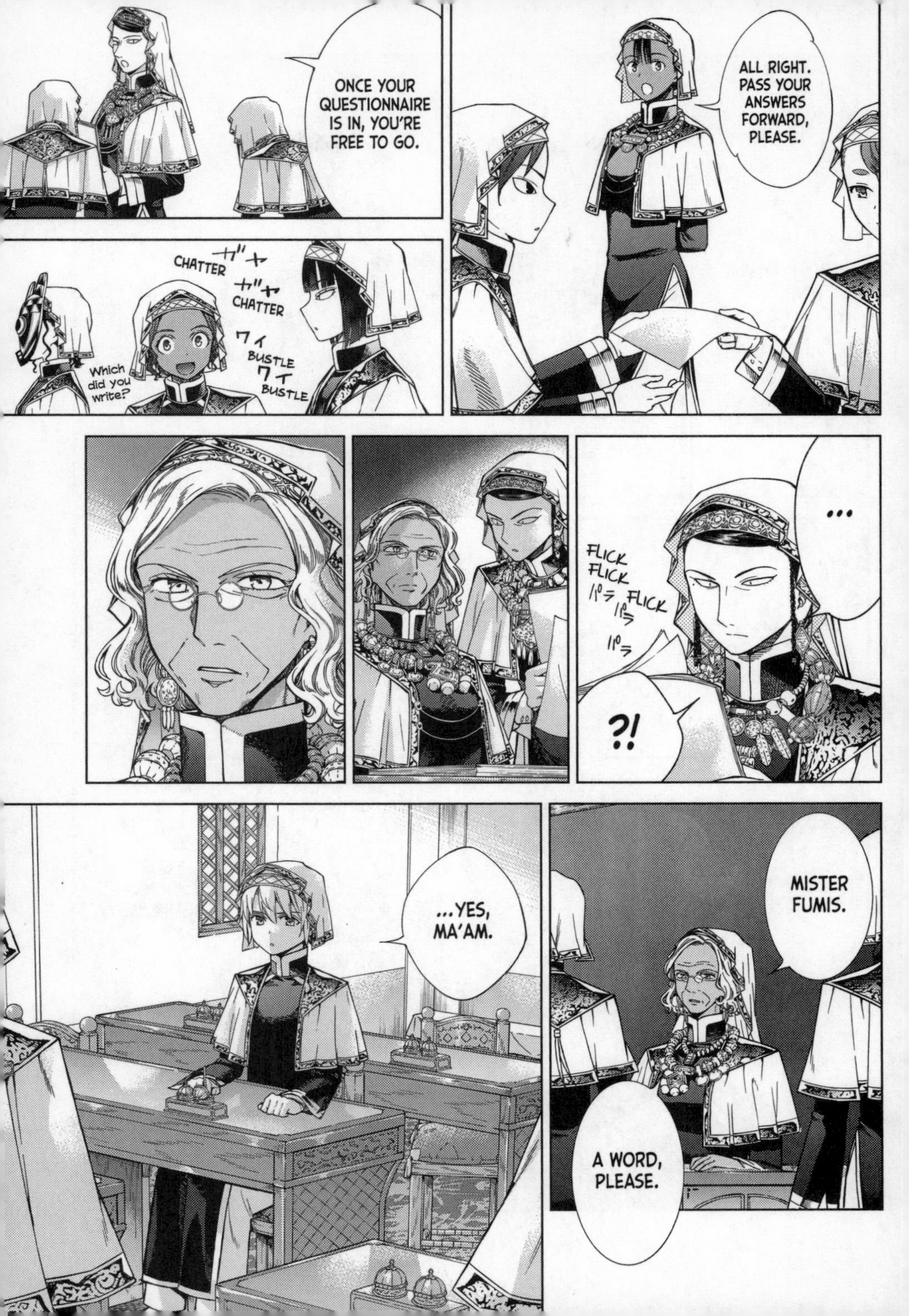
ALL RIGHT. PASS YOUR ANSWERS FORWARD, PLEASE.
ONCE YOUR QUESTIONNAIRE IS IN, YOU'RE FREE TO GO.
ガヤ CHATTER
ガヤ CHATTER
ワイ BUSTLE
ワイ BUSTLE
Which did you write?
...
FLICK FLICK
パラ FLICK
パラ
パラ
?!
MISTER FUMIS.
A WORD, PLEASE.
...YES, MA'AM.

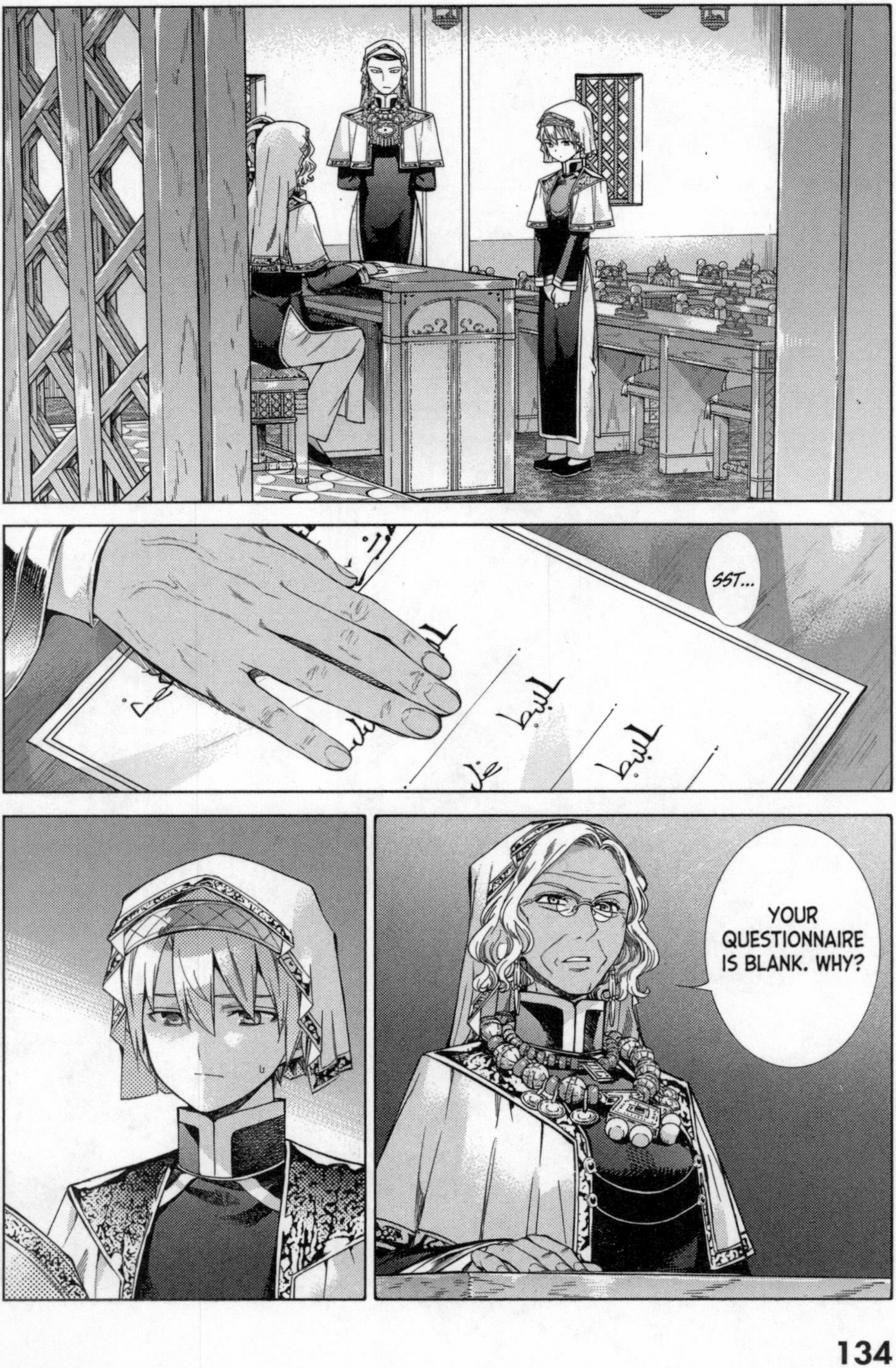
SST...
YOUR QUESTIONNAIRE IS BLANK. WHY?

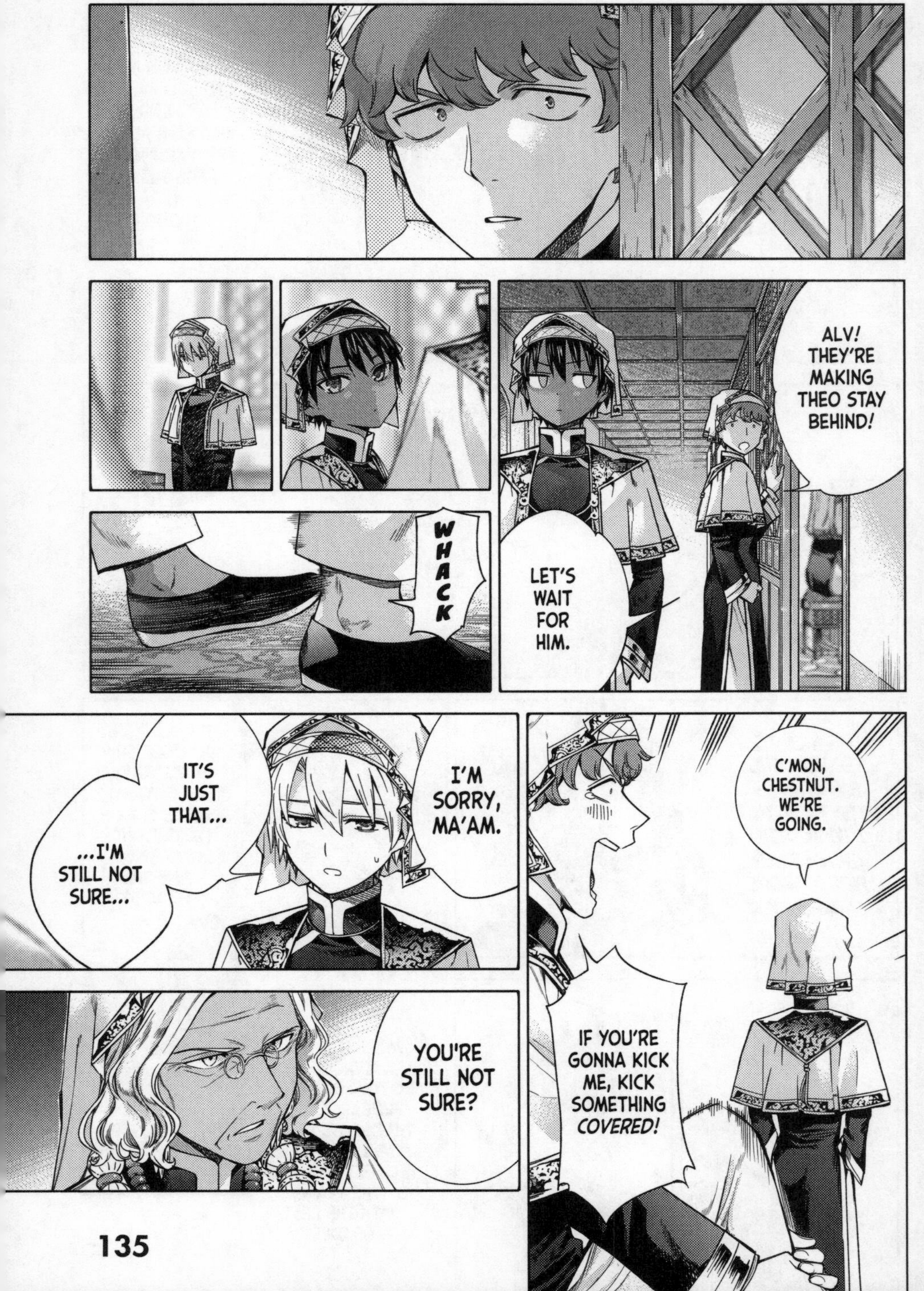
ALV! THEY'RE MAKING THEO STAY BEHIND!
LET'S WAIT FOR HIM.
WHACK
C'MON, CHESTNUT. WE'RE GOING.
IF YOU'RE GONNA KICK ME, KICK SOMETHING *COVERED!*
I'M SORRY, MA'AM.
IT'S JUST THAT...
...I'M STILL NOT SURE...
YOU'RE STILL NOT SURE?

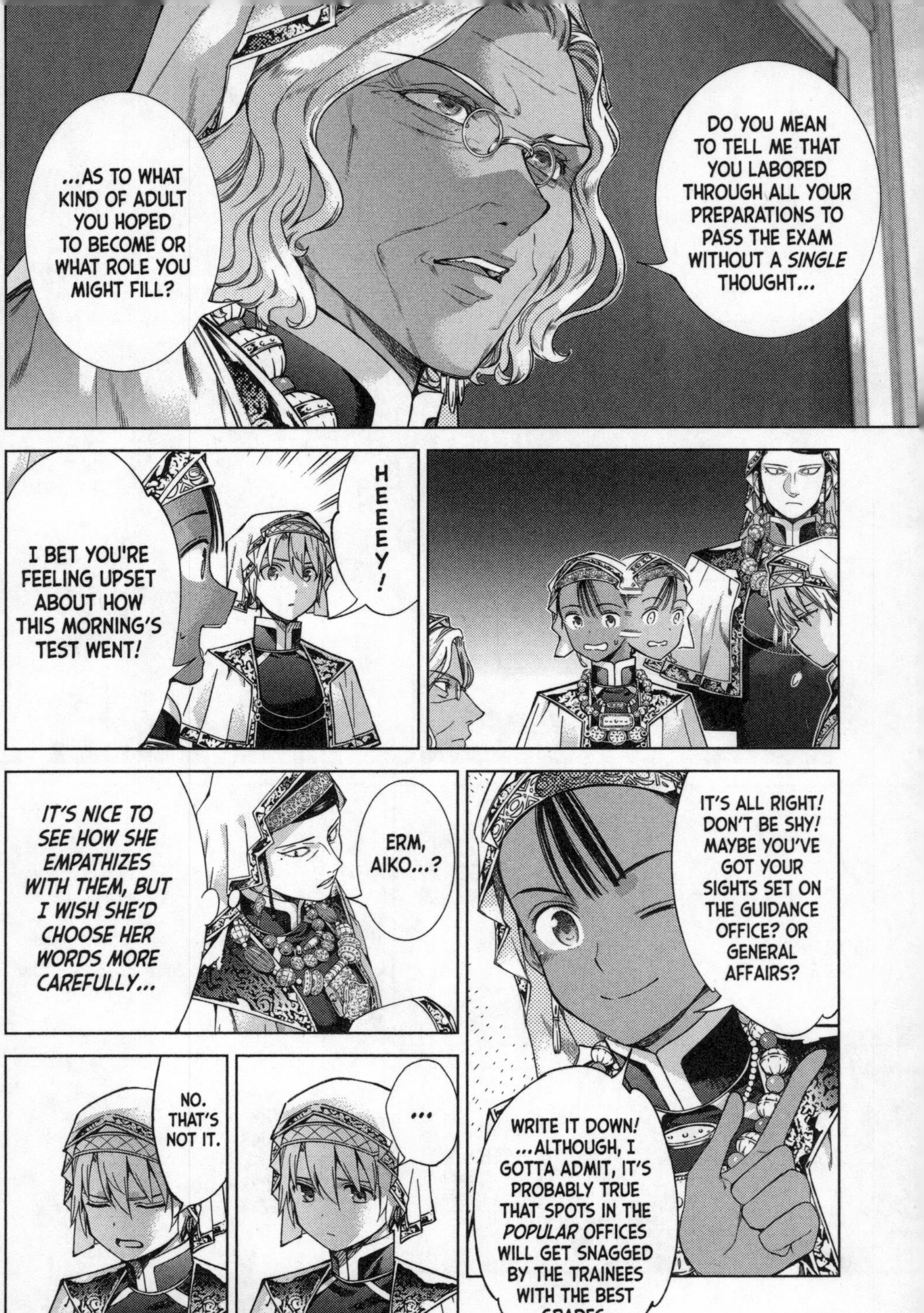
DO YOU MEAN TO TELL ME THAT YOU LABORED THROUGH ALL YOUR PREPARATIONS TO PASS THE EXAM WITHOUT A *SINGLE* THOUGHT...
...AS TO WHAT KIND OF ADULT YOU HOPED TO BECOME OR WHAT ROLE YOU MIGHT FILL?
HEEEY!
I BET YOU'RE FEELING UPSET ABOUT HOW THIS MORNING'S TEST WENT!
IT'S ALL RIGHT! DON'T BE SHY! MAYBE YOU'VE GOT YOUR SIGHTS SET ON THE GUIDANCE OFFICE? OR GENERAL AFFAIRS?
WRITE IT DOWN! ...ALTHOUGH, I GOTTA ADMIT, IT'S PROBABLY TRUE THAT SPOTS IN THE *POPULAR* OFFICES WILL GET SNAGGED BY THE TRAINEES WITH THE BEST GRADES.
ERM, AIKO...?
IT'S NICE TO SEE HOW SHE EMPATHIZES WITH THEM, BUT I WISH SHE'D CHOOSE HER WORDS MORE CAREFULLY...
...
NO. THAT'S NOT IT.

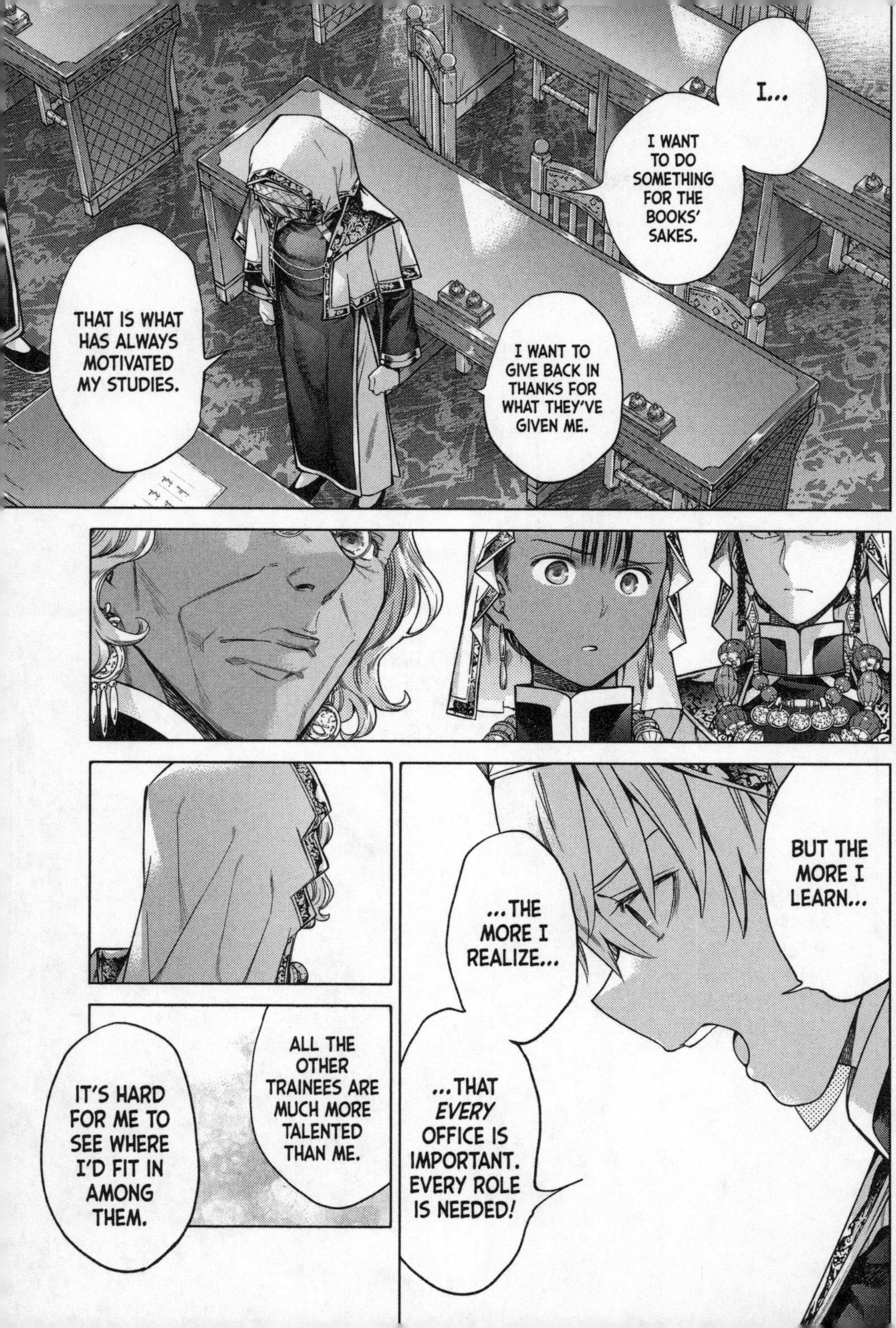
I...
I WANT TO DO SOMETHING FOR THE BOOKS' SAKES.
I WANT TO GIVE BACK IN THANKS FOR WHAT THEY'VE GIVEN ME.
THAT IS WHAT HAS ALWAYS MOTIVATED MY STUDIES.
BUT THE MORE I LEARN...
...THE MORE I REALIZE...
...THAT *EVERY* OFFICE IS IMPORTANT. EVERY ROLE IS NEEDED!
ALL THE OTHER TRAINEES ARE MUCH MORE TALENTED THAN ME.
IT'S HARD FOR ME TO SEE WHERE I'D FIT IN AMONG THEM.

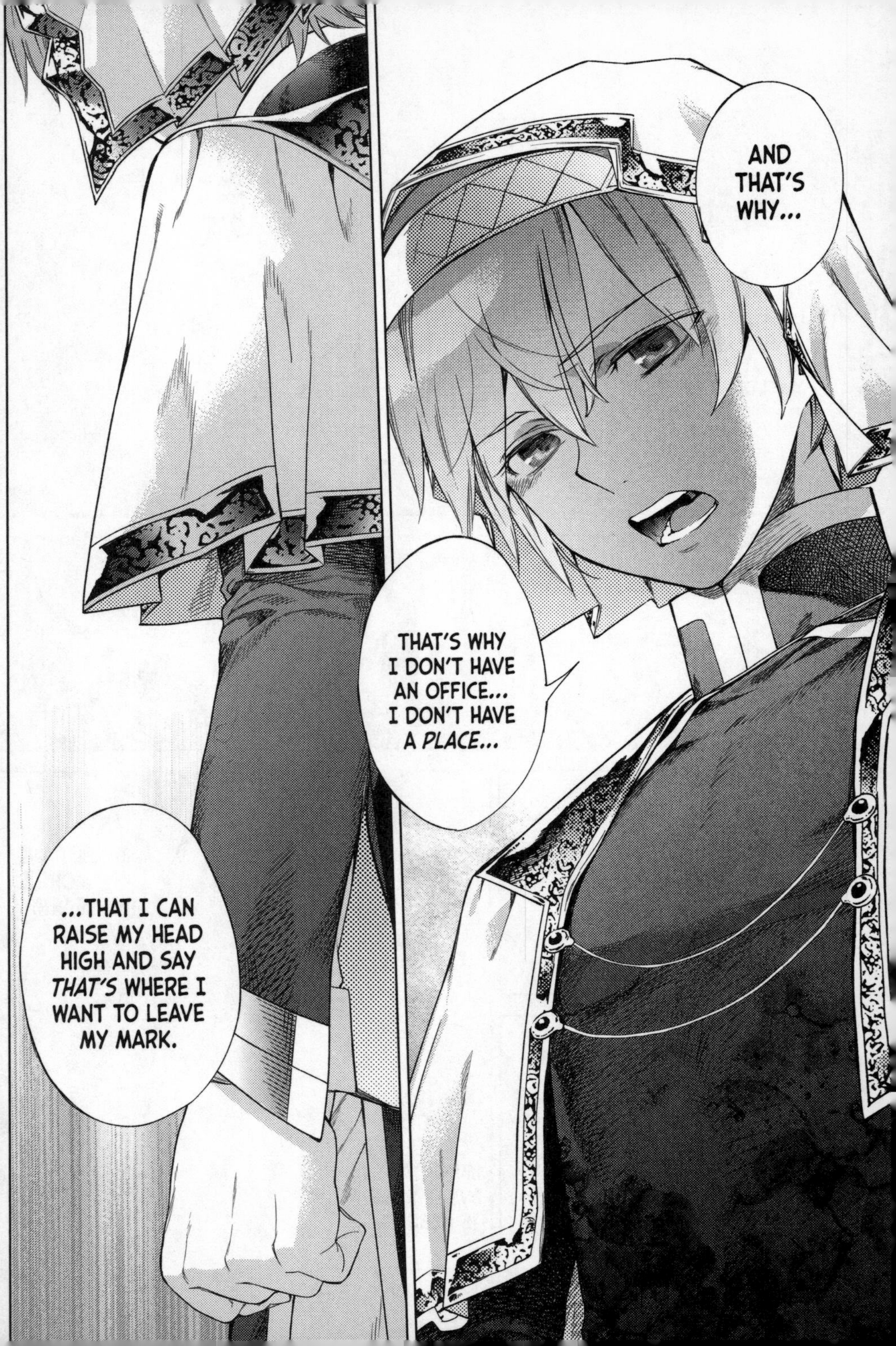
AND THAT'S WHY...
THAT'S WHY I DON'T HAVE AN OFFICE... I DON'T HAVE A *PLACE*...
...THAT I CAN RAISE MY HEAD HIGH AND SAY *THAT'S* WHERE I WANT TO LEAVE MY MARK.

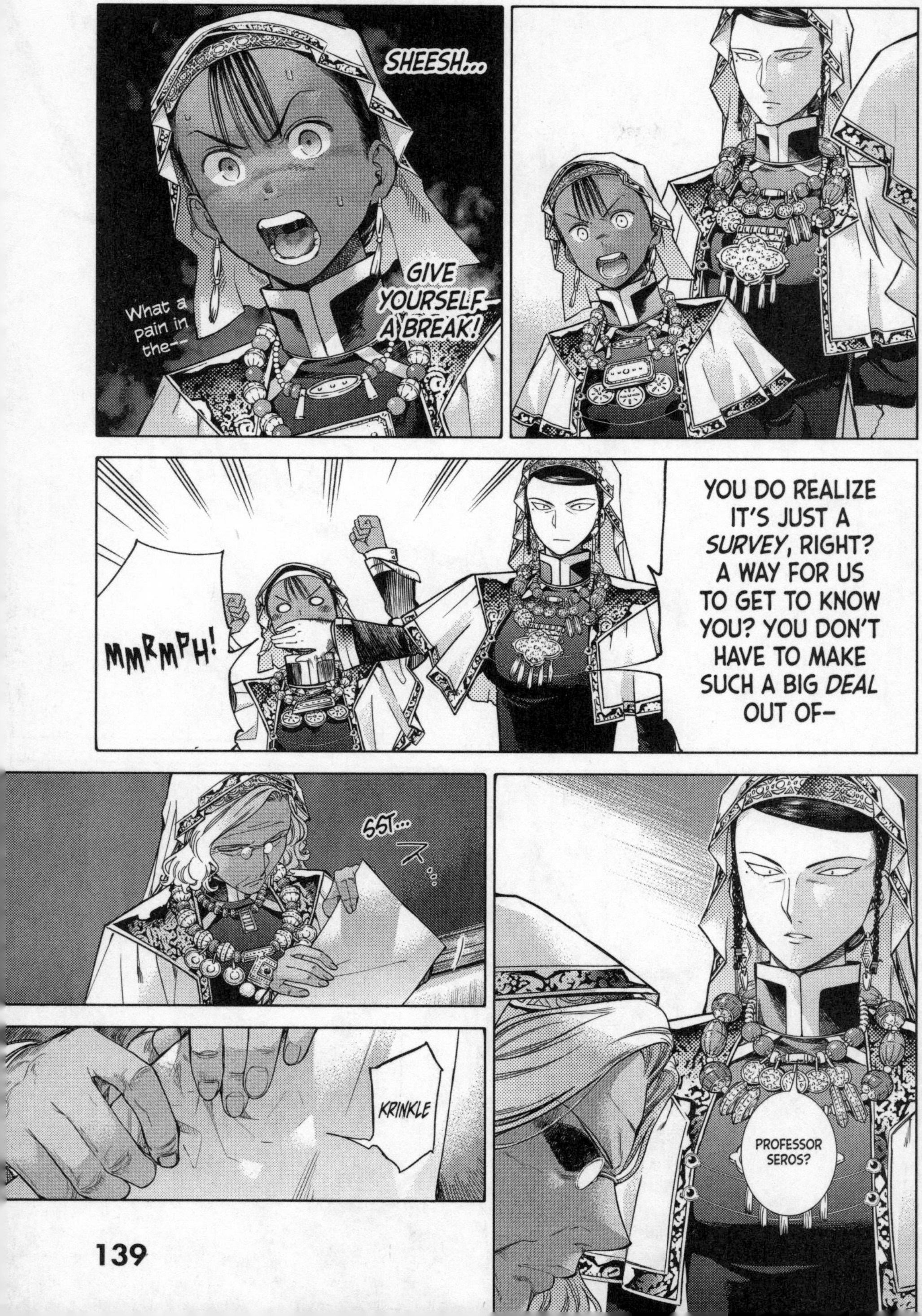
SHEESH...
GIVE YOURSELF A BREAK!
What a pain in the--
YOU DO REALIZE IT'S JUST A *SURVEY*, RIGHT? A WAY FOR US TO GET TO KNOW YOU? YOU DON'T HAVE TO MAKE SUCH A BIG *DEAL* OUT OF-
MMRMPH!
PROFESSOR SEROS?
SST...
ス...
KRINKLE

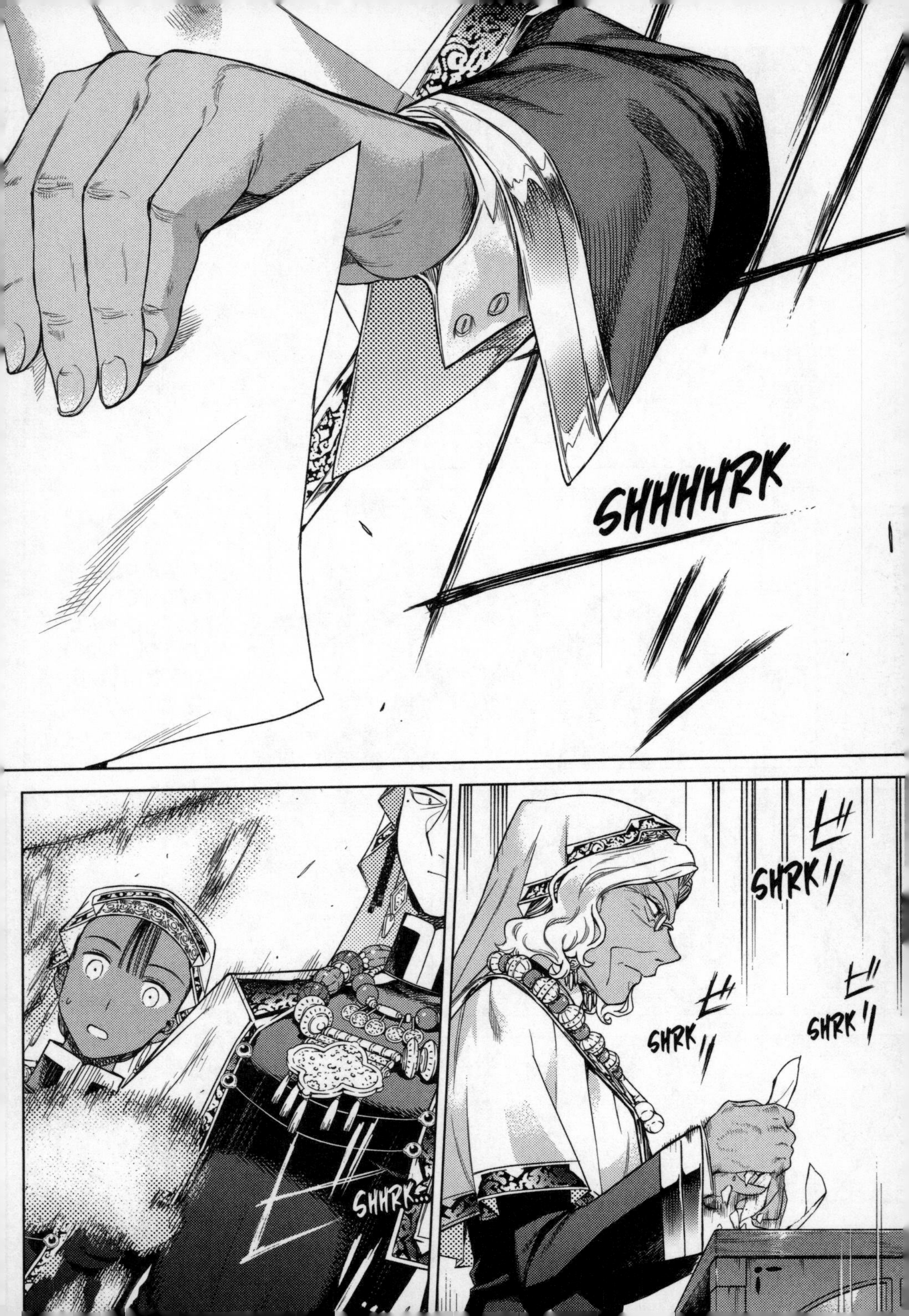
SHHHHRK
ビ
SHRK
ビ
SHRK
ビ
SHRK
SHHRK...

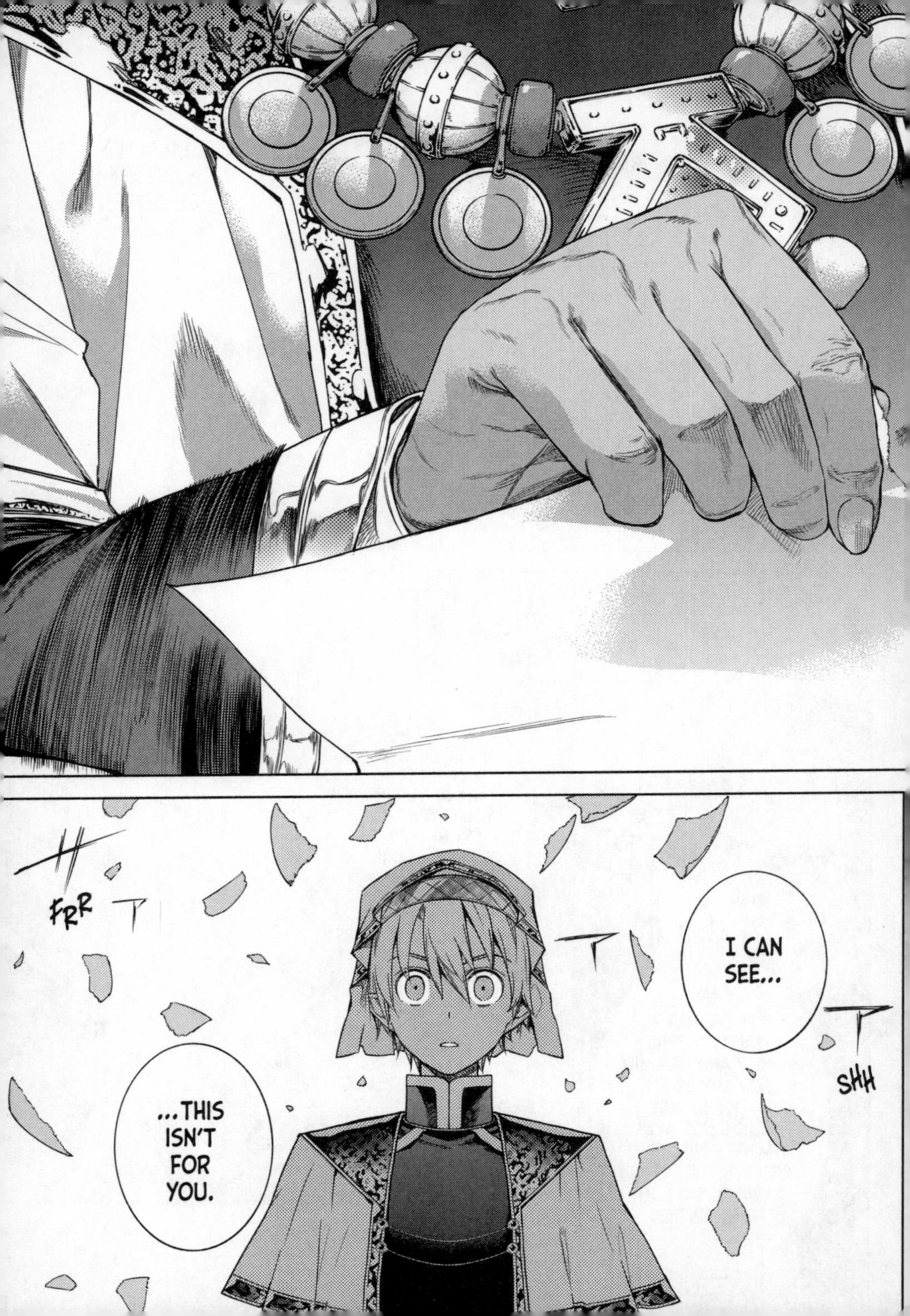
I CAN SEE...
SHH
FRR
...THIS ISN'T FOR YOU.

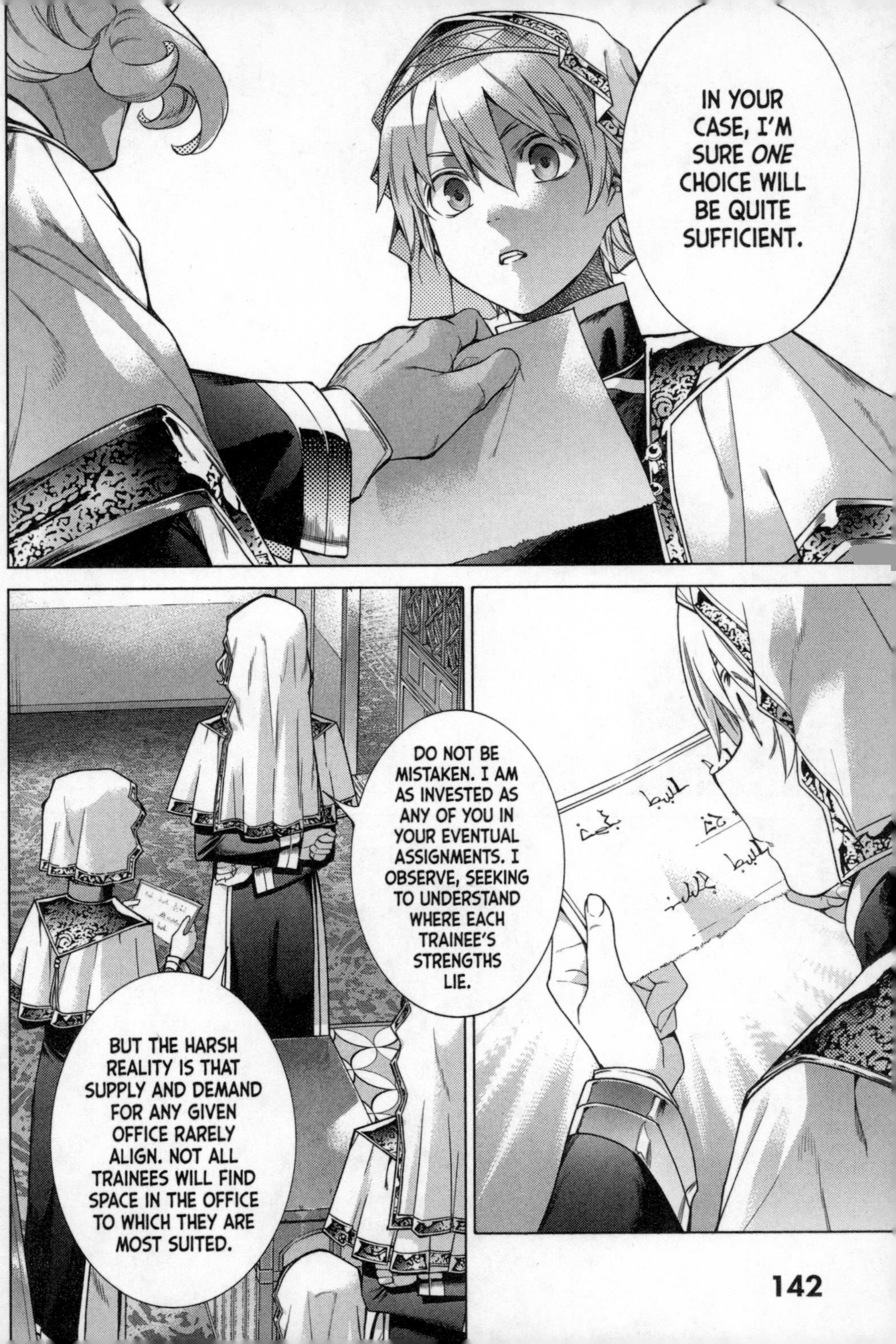
IN YOUR CASE, I'M SURE *ONE* CHOICE WILL BE QUITE SUFFICIENT.
DO NOT BE MISTAKEN. I AM AS INVESTED AS ANY OF YOU IN YOUR EVENTUAL ASSIGNMENTS. I OBSERVE, SEEKING TO UNDERSTAND WHERE EACH TRAINEE'S STRENGTHS LIE.
BUT THE HARSH REALITY IS THAT SUPPLY AND DEMAND FOR ANY GIVEN OFFICE RARELY ALIGN. NOT ALL TRAINEES WILL FIND SPACE IN THE OFFICE TO WHICH THEY ARE MOST SUITED.

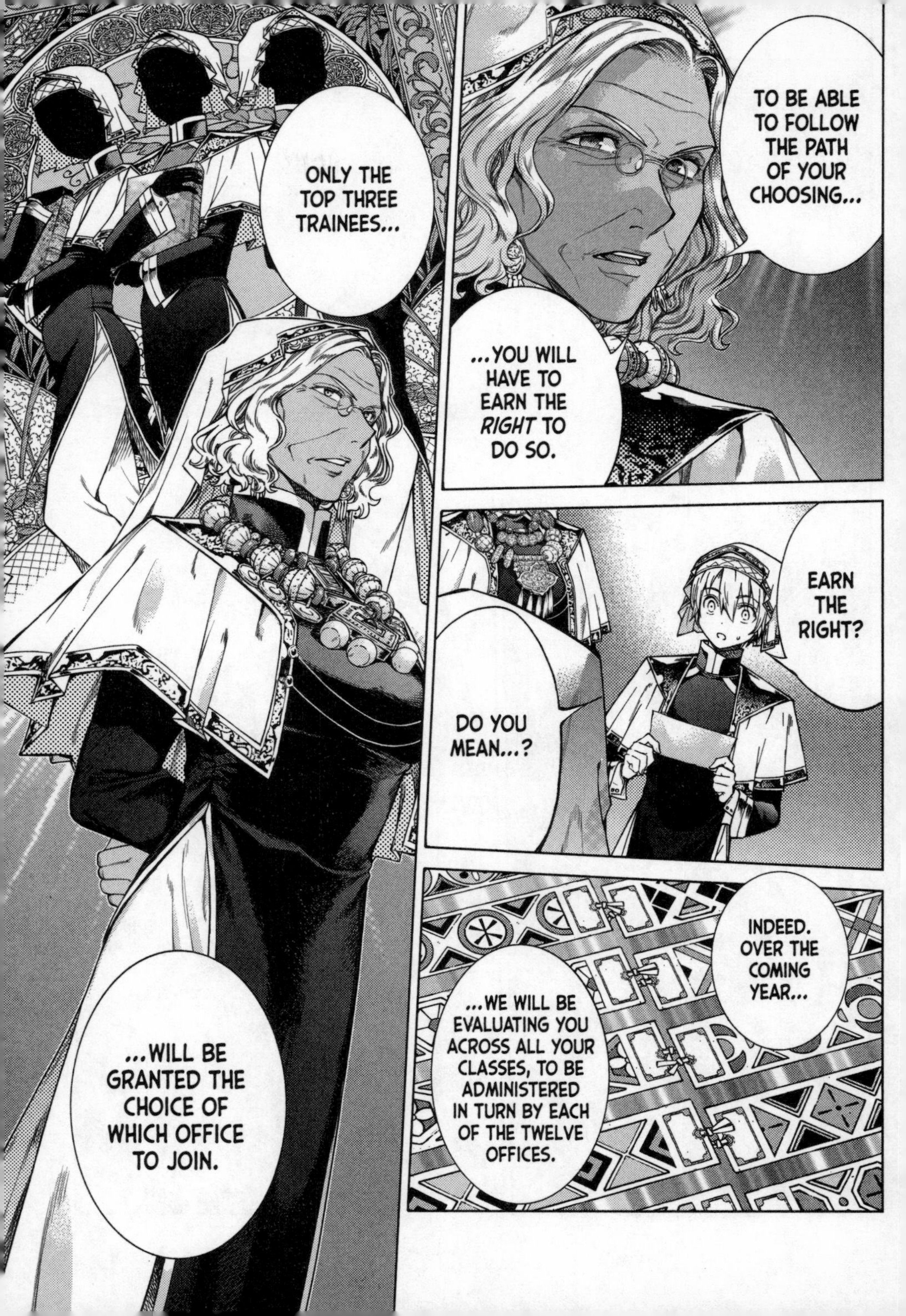
TO BE ABLE TO FOLLOW THE PATH OF YOUR CHOOSING...
...YOU WILL HAVE TO EARN THE *RIGHT* TO DO SO.
EARN THE RIGHT?
DO YOU MEAN...?
INDEED. OVER THE COMING YEAR...
...WE WILL BE EVALUATING YOU ACROSS ALL YOUR CLASSES, TO BE ADMINISTERED IN TURN BY EACH OF THE TWELVE OFFICES.
ONLY THE TOP THREE TRAINEES...
...WILL BE GRANTED THE CHOICE OF WHICH OFFICE TO JOIN.

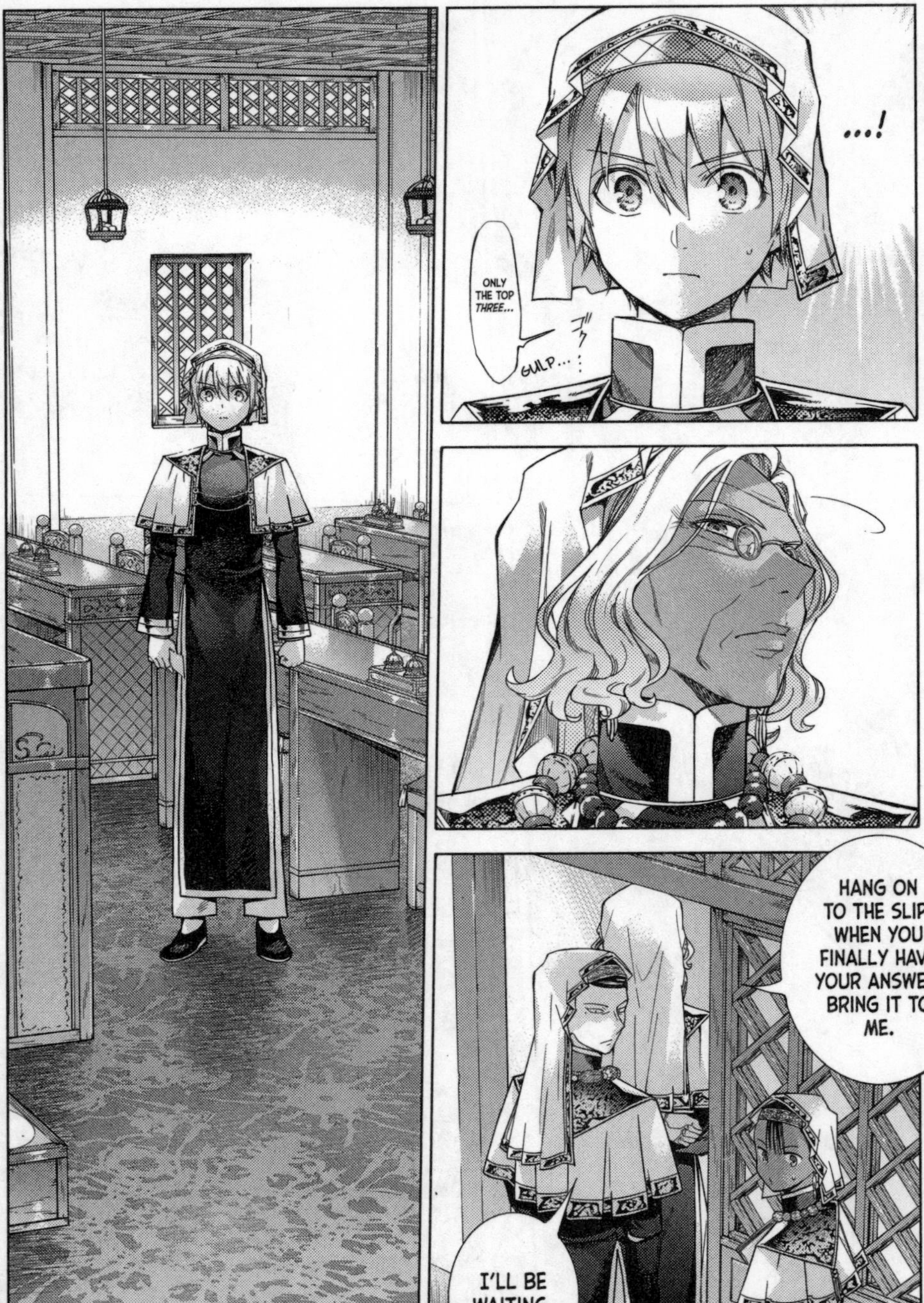
...!
ONLY THE TOP THREE...
GULP...
HANG ON TO THE SLIP. WHEN YOU FINALLY HAVE YOUR ANSWER, BRING IT TO ME.
I'LL BE WAITING.

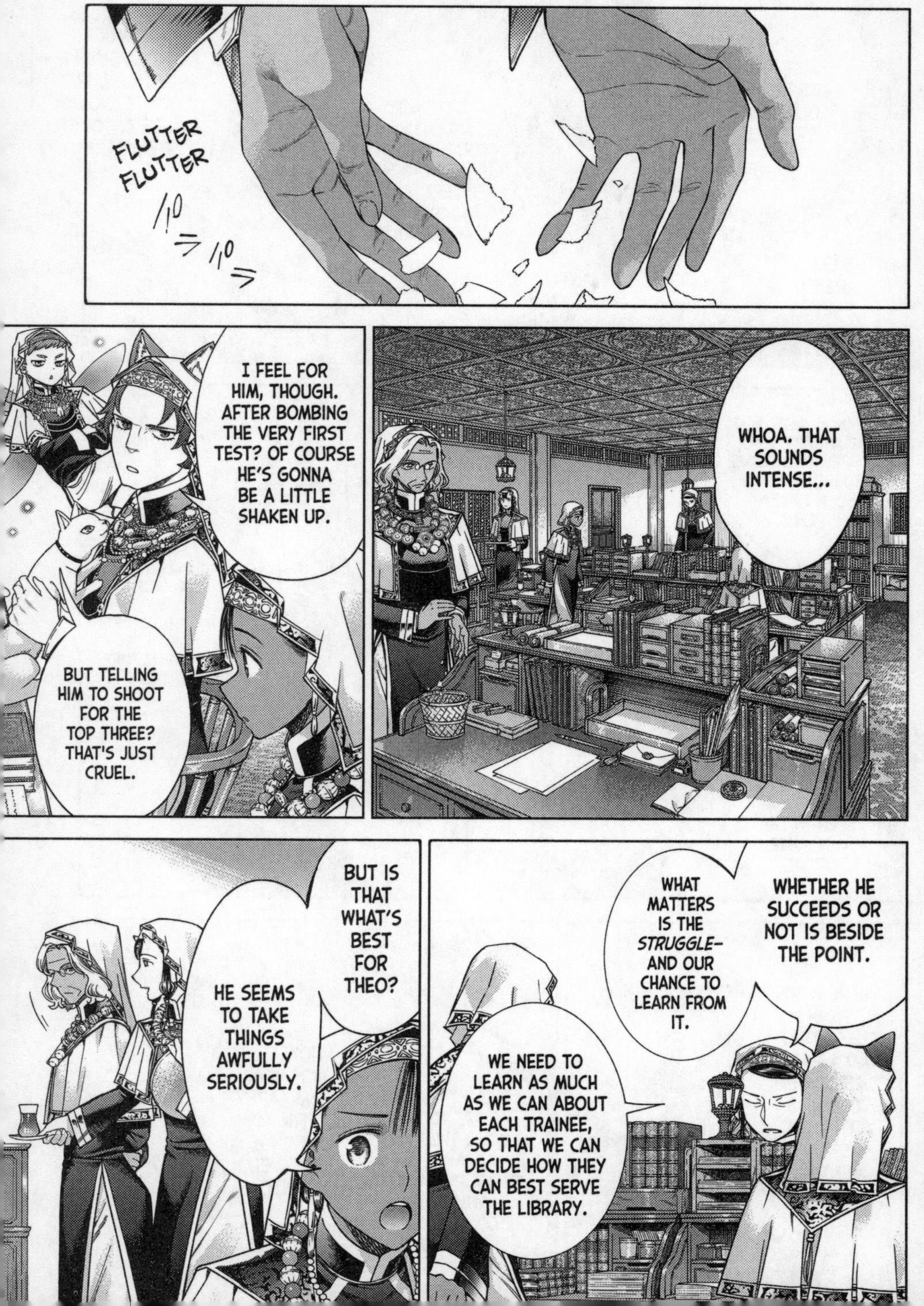
FLUTTER FLUTTER
WHOA. THAT SOUNDS INTENSE...
I FEEL FOR HIM, THOUGH. AFTER BOMBING THE VERY FIRST TEST? OF COURSE HE'S GONNA BE A LITTLE SHAKEN UP.
BUT TELLING HIM TO SHOOT FOR THE TOP THREE? THAT'S JUST CRUEL.
WHETHER HE SUCCEEDS OR NOT IS BESIDE THE POINT.
WHAT MATTERS IS THE *STRUGGLE*—AND OUR CHANCE TO LEARN FROM IT.
WE NEED TO LEARN AS MUCH AS WE CAN ABOUT EACH TRAINEE, SO THAT WE CAN DECIDE HOW THEY CAN BEST SERVE THE LIBRARY.
BUT IS THAT WHAT'S BEST FOR THEO?
HE SEEMS TO TAKE THINGS AWFULLY SERIOUSLY.

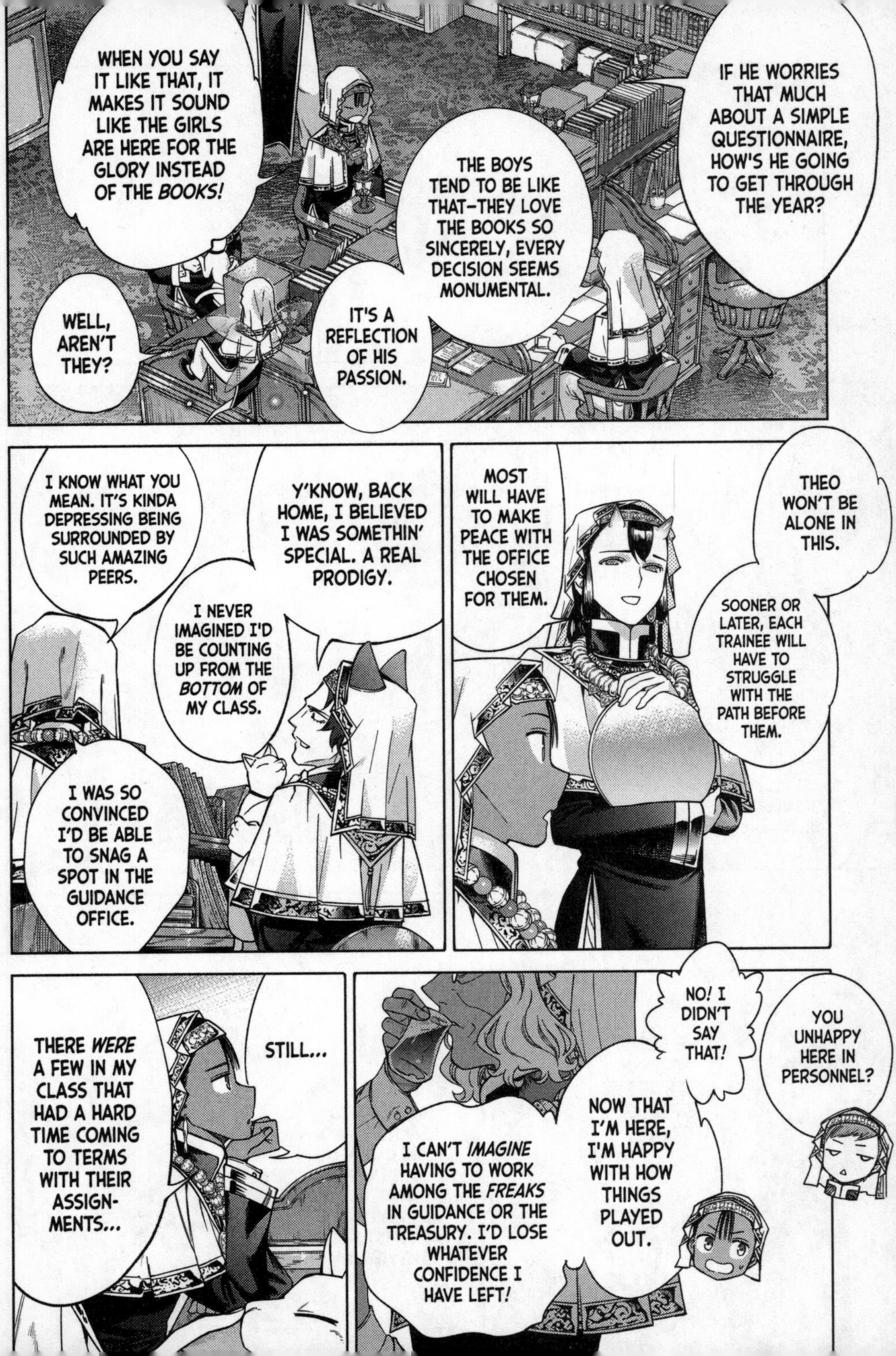
IF HE WORRIES THAT MUCH ABOUT A SIMPLE QUESTIONNAIRE, HOW'S HE GOING TO GET THROUGH THE YEAR?
IT'S A REFLECTION OF HIS PASSION.
THE BOYS TEND TO BE LIKE THAT–THEY LOVE THE BOOKS SO SINCERELY, EVERY DECISION SEEMS MONUMENTAL.
WHEN YOU SAY IT LIKE THAT, IT MAKES IT SOUND LIKE THE GIRLS ARE HERE FOR THE GLORY INSTEAD OF THE *BOOKS!*
WELL, AREN'T THEY?
THEO WON'T BE ALONE IN THIS.
SOONER OR LATER, EACH TRAINEE WILL HAVE TO STRUGGLE WITH THE PATH BEFORE THEM.
MOST WILL HAVE TO MAKE PEACE WITH THE OFFICE CHOSEN FOR THEM.
Y'KNOW, BACK HOME, I BELIEVED I WAS SOMETHIN' SPECIAL. A REAL PRODIGY.
I KNOW WHAT YOU MEAN. IT'S KINDA DEPRESSING BEING SURROUNDED BY SUCH AMAZING PEERS.
I NEVER IMAGINED I'D BE COUNTING UP FROM THE *BOTTOM* OF MY CLASS.
I WAS SO CONVINCED I'D BE ABLE TO SNAG A SPOT IN THE GUIDANCE OFFICE.
YOU UNHAPPY HERE IN PERSONNEL?
NO*!* I DIDN'T SAY THAT*!*
NOW THAT I'M HERE, I'M HAPPY WITH HOW THINGS PLAYED OUT.
I CAN'T *IMAGINE* HAVING TO WORK AMONG THE *FREAKS* IN GUIDANCE OR THE TREASURY. I'D LOSE WHATEVER CONFIDENCE I HAVE LEFT*!*
STILL...
THERE *WERE* A FEW IN MY CLASS THAT HAD A HARD TIME COMING TO TERMS WITH THEIR ASSIGN-MENTS...

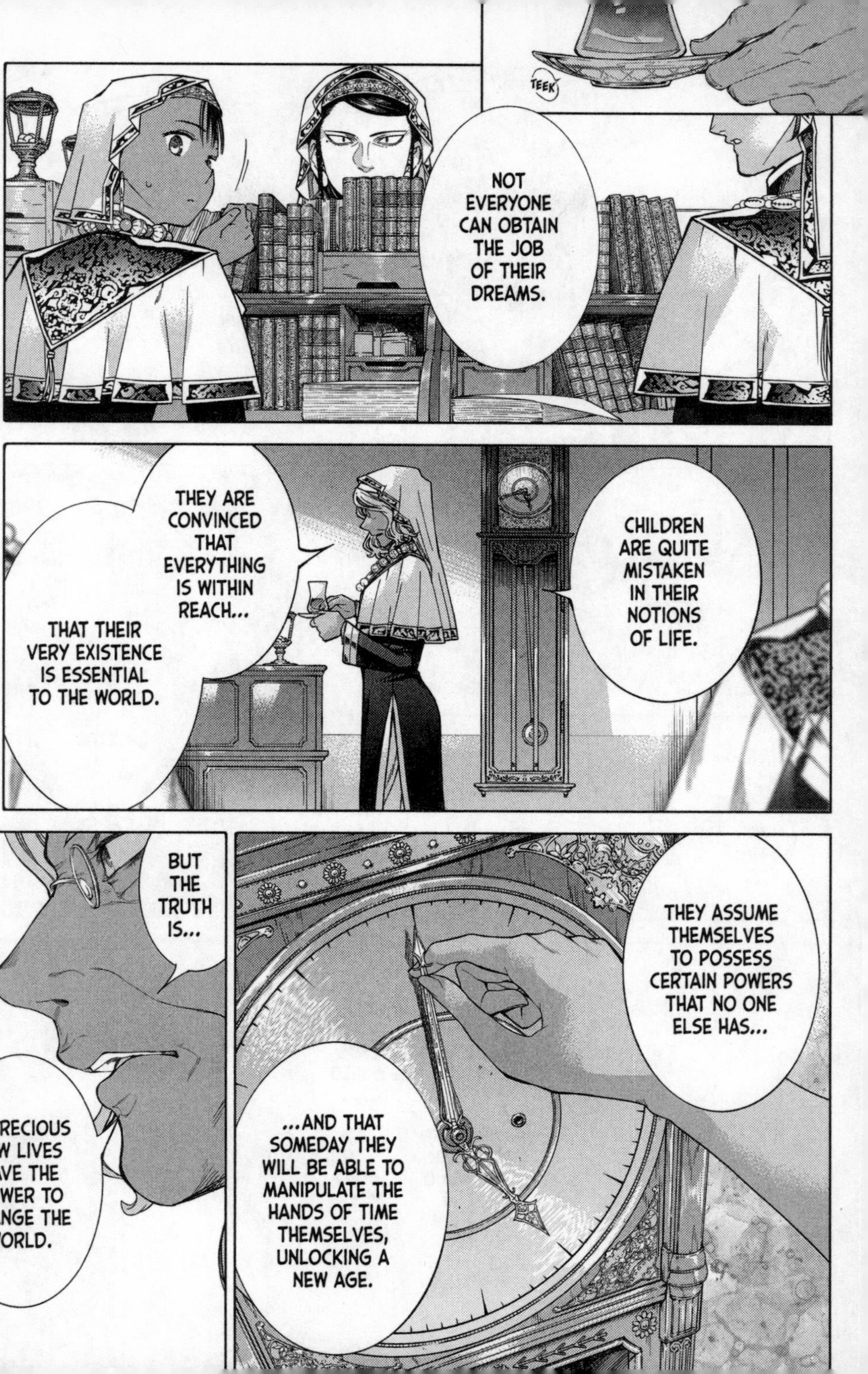
TEEK
NOT EVERYONE CAN OBTAIN THE JOB OF THEIR DREAMS.
CHILDREN ARE QUITE MISTAKEN IN THEIR NOTIONS OF LIFE.
THEY ARE CONVINCED THAT EVERYTHING IS WITHIN REACH...
THAT THEIR VERY EXISTENCE IS ESSENTIAL TO THE WORLD.
THEY ASSUME THEMSELVES TO POSSESS CERTAIN POWERS THAT NO ONE ELSE HAS...
...AND THAT SOMEDAY THEY WILL BE ABLE TO MANIPULATE THE HANDS OF TIME THEMSELVES, UNLOCKING A NEW AGE.
BUT THE TRUTH IS...
...PRECIOUS FEW LIVES HAVE THE POWER TO CHANGE THE WORLD.

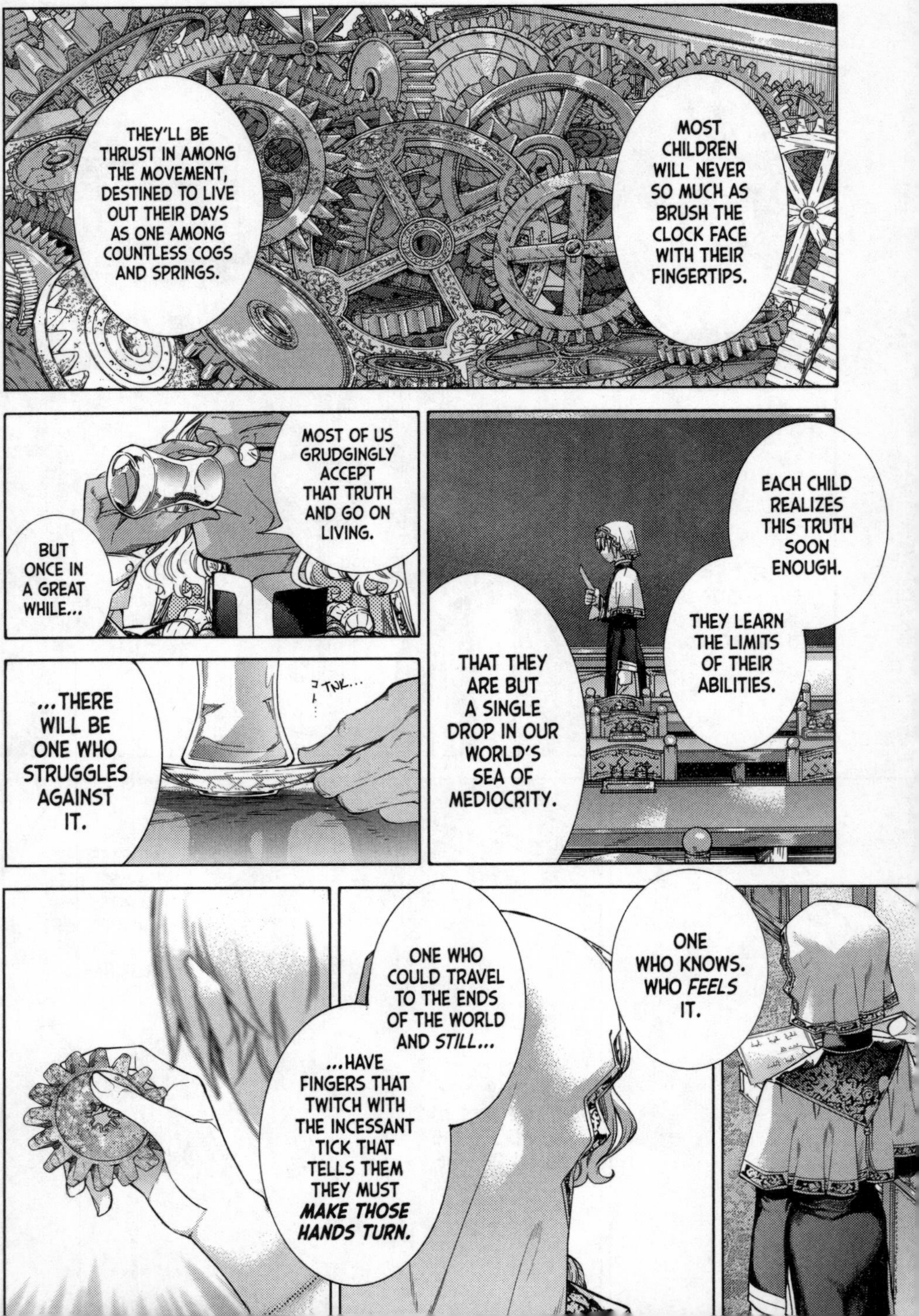
MOST CHILDREN WILL NEVER SO MUCH AS BRUSH THE CLOCK FACE WITH THEIR FINGERTIPS.
THEY'LL BE THRUST IN AMONG THE MOVEMENT, DESTINED TO LIVE OUT THEIR DAYS AS ONE AMONG COUNTLESS COGS AND SPRINGS.
EACH CHILD REALIZES THIS TRUTH SOON ENOUGH.
THEY LEARN THE LIMITS OF THEIR ABILITIES.
THAT THEY ARE BUT A SINGLE DROP IN OUR WORLD'S SEA OF MEDIOCRITY.
MOST OF US GRUDGINGLY ACCEPT THAT TRUTH AND GO ON LIVING.
BUT ONCE IN A GREAT WHILE...
...THERE WILL BE ONE WHO STRUGGLES AGAINST IT.
TNK...
ONE WHO KNOWS. WHO *FEELS* IT.
ONE WHO COULD TRAVEL TO THE ENDS OF THE WORLD AND *STILL*...
...HAVE FINGERS THAT TWITCH WITH THE INCESSANT TICK THAT TELLS THEM THEY MUST ***MAKE THOSE HANDS TURN.***

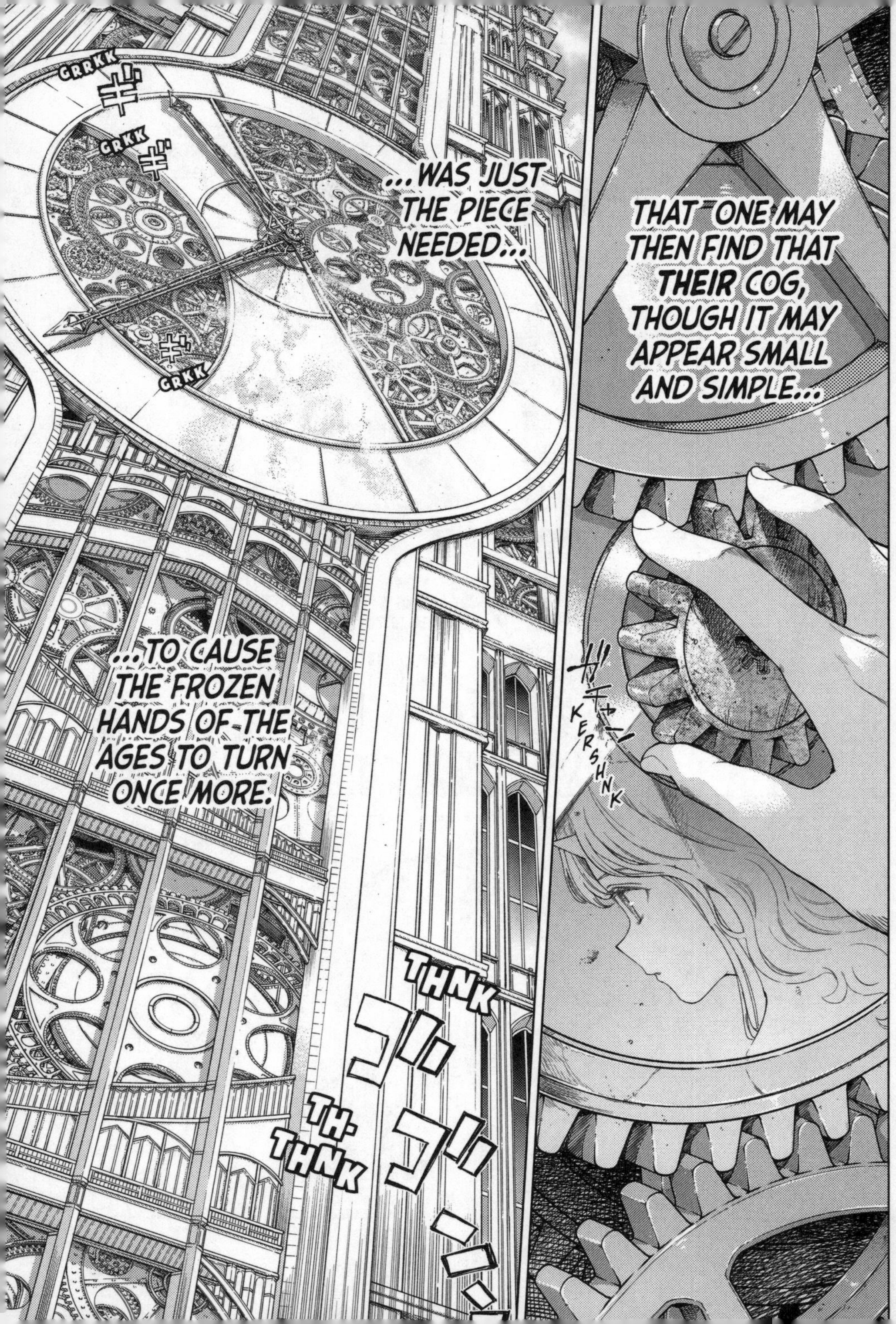
THAT ONE MAY THEN FIND THAT THEIR COG, THOUGH IT MAY APPEAR SMALL AND SIMPLE...
KERSHNK
GRRKK
GRKK
GRKK
...WAS JUST THE PIECE NEEDED...
...TO CAUSE THE FROZEN HANDS OF THE AGES TO TURN ONCE MORE.
THNK
TH-THNK

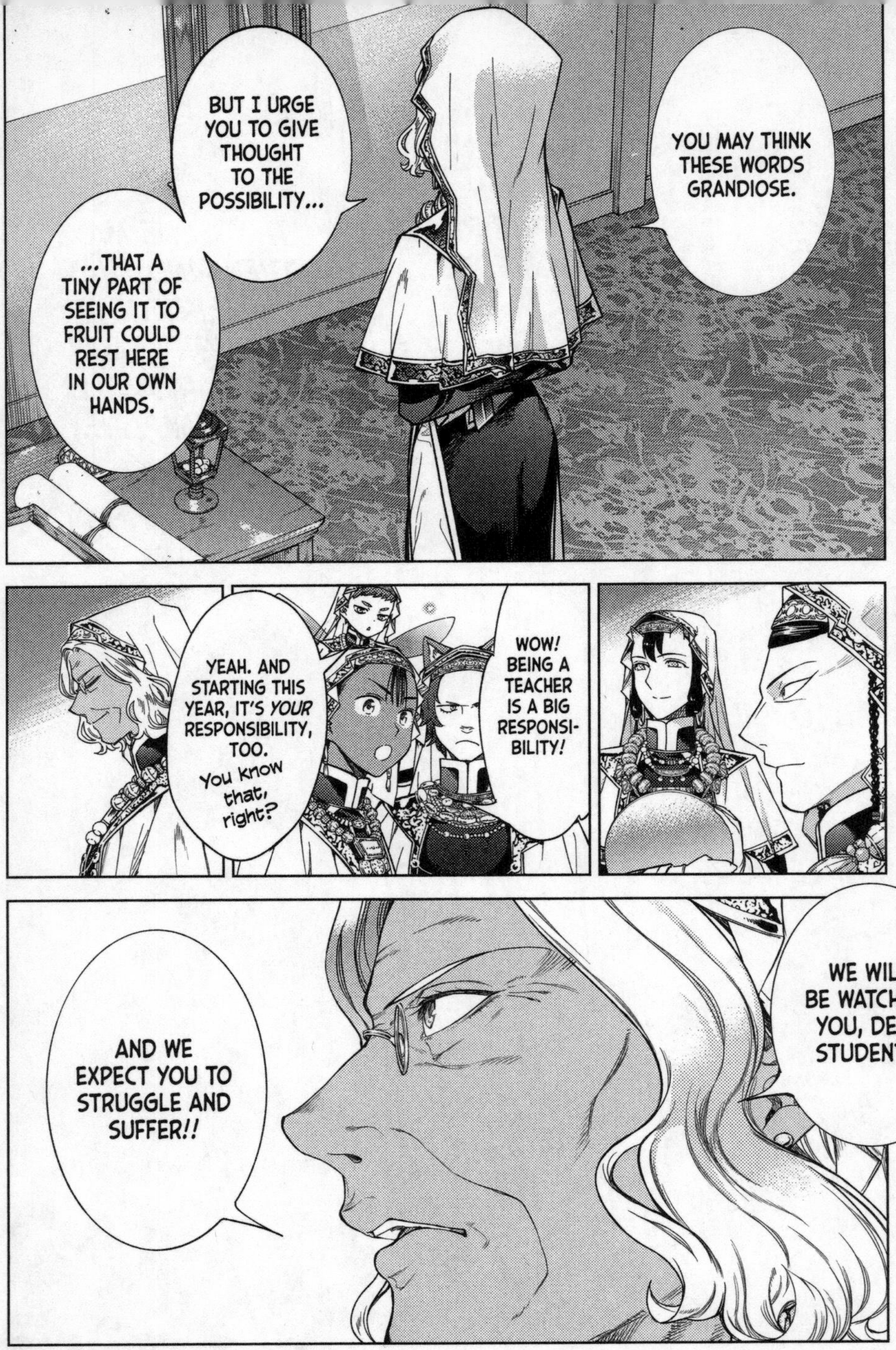
YOU MAY THINK THESE WORDS GRANDIOSE.
BUT I URGE YOU TO GIVE THOUGHT TO THE POSSIBILITY...
...THAT A TINY PART OF SEEING IT TO FRUIT COULD REST HERE IN OUR OWN HANDS.
WOW! BEING A TEACHER IS A BIG RESPONSIBILITY!
YEAH. AND STARTING THIS YEAR, IT'S *YOUR* RESPONSIBILITY, TOO. You know that, right?
WE WILL BE WATCHING YOU, DEAR STUDENTS.
AND WE EXPECT YOU TO STRUGGLE AND SUFFER!!

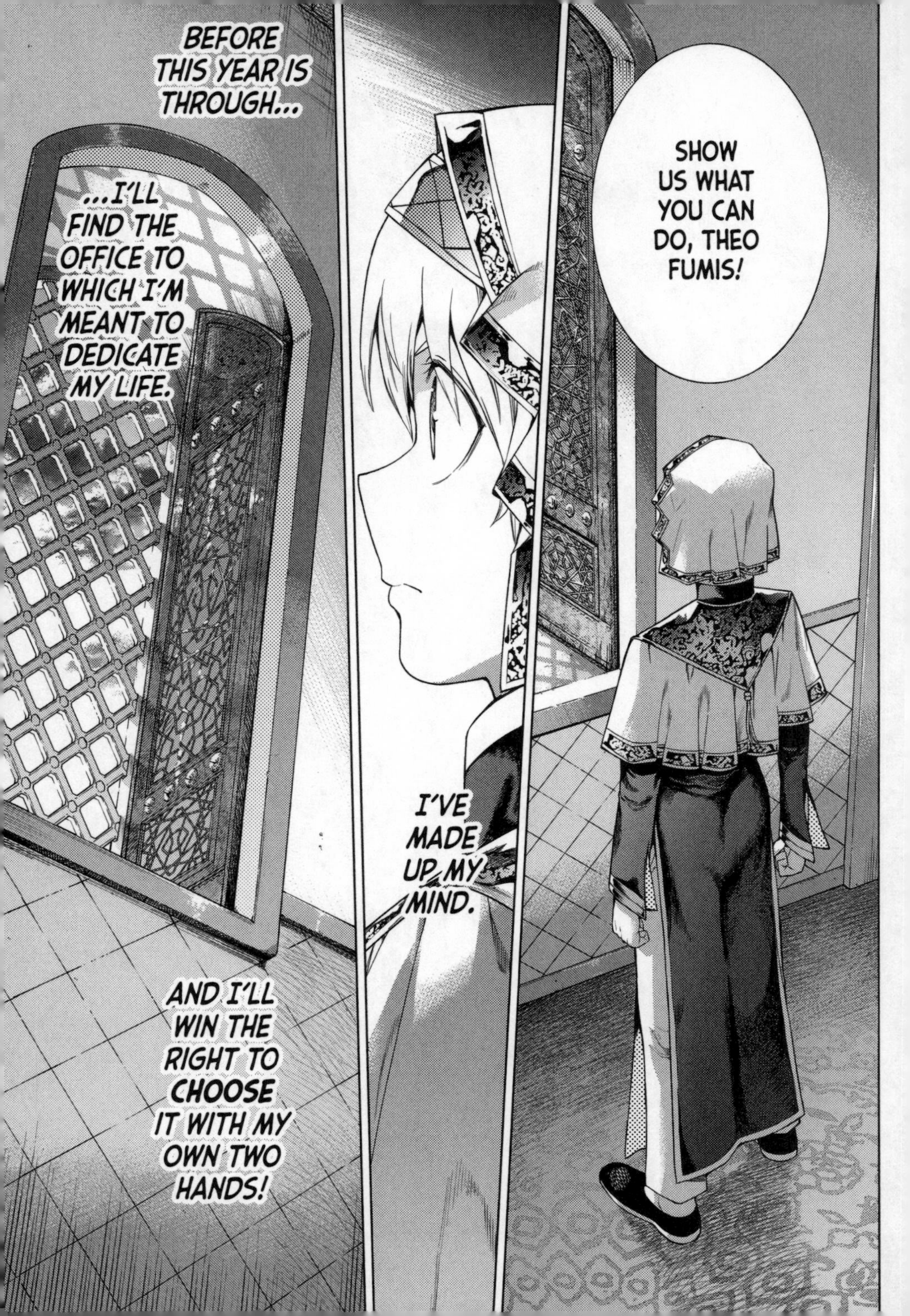
SHOW US WHAT YOU CAN DO, THEO FUMIS!
I'VE MADE UP MY MIND.
BEFORE THIS YEAR IS THROUGH...
...I'LL FIND THE OFFICE TO WHICH I'M MEANT TO DEDICATE MY LIFE.
AND I'LL WIN THE RIGHT TO CHOOSE IT WITH MY OWN TWO HANDS!

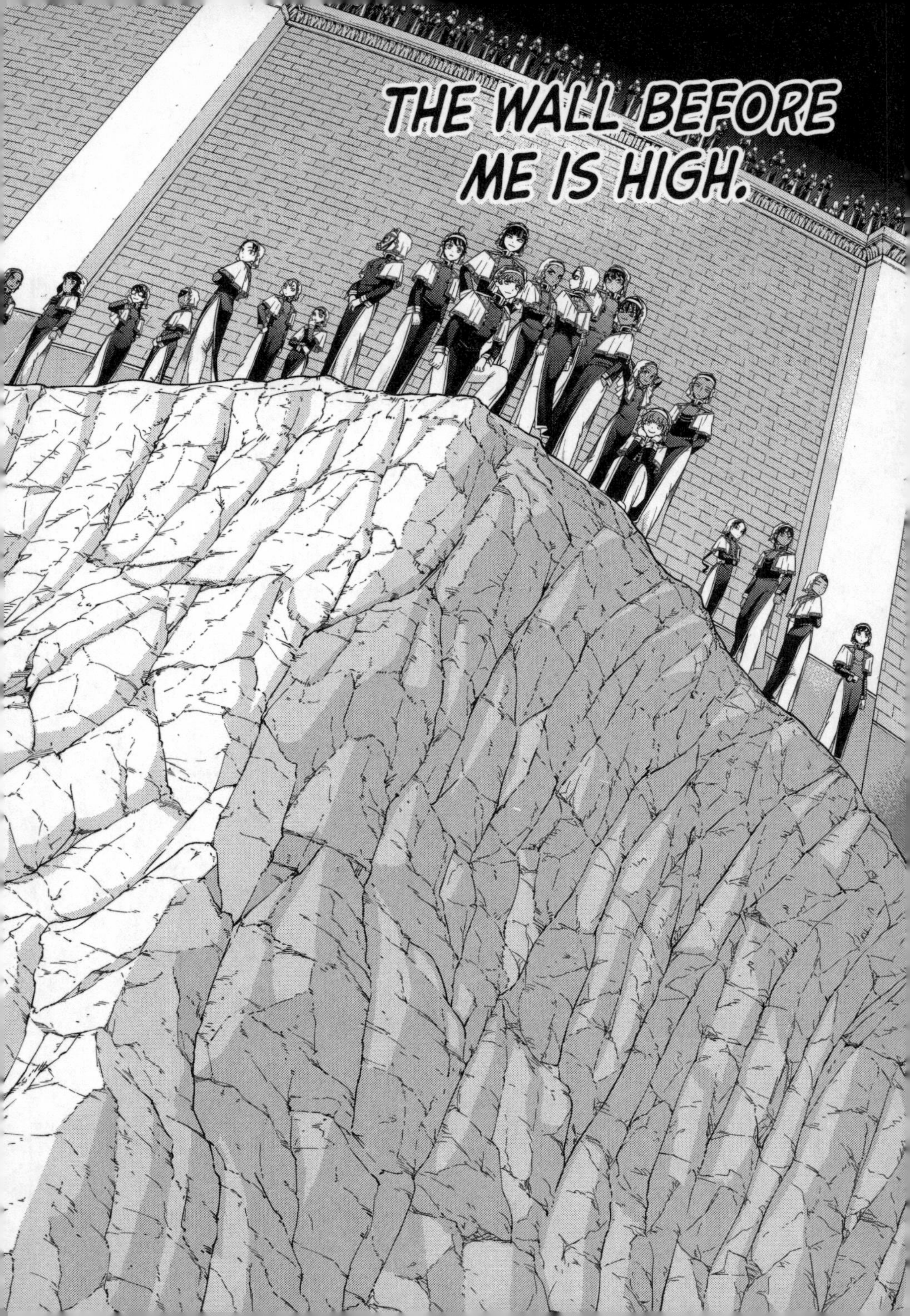
THE WALL BEFORE ME IS HIGH.

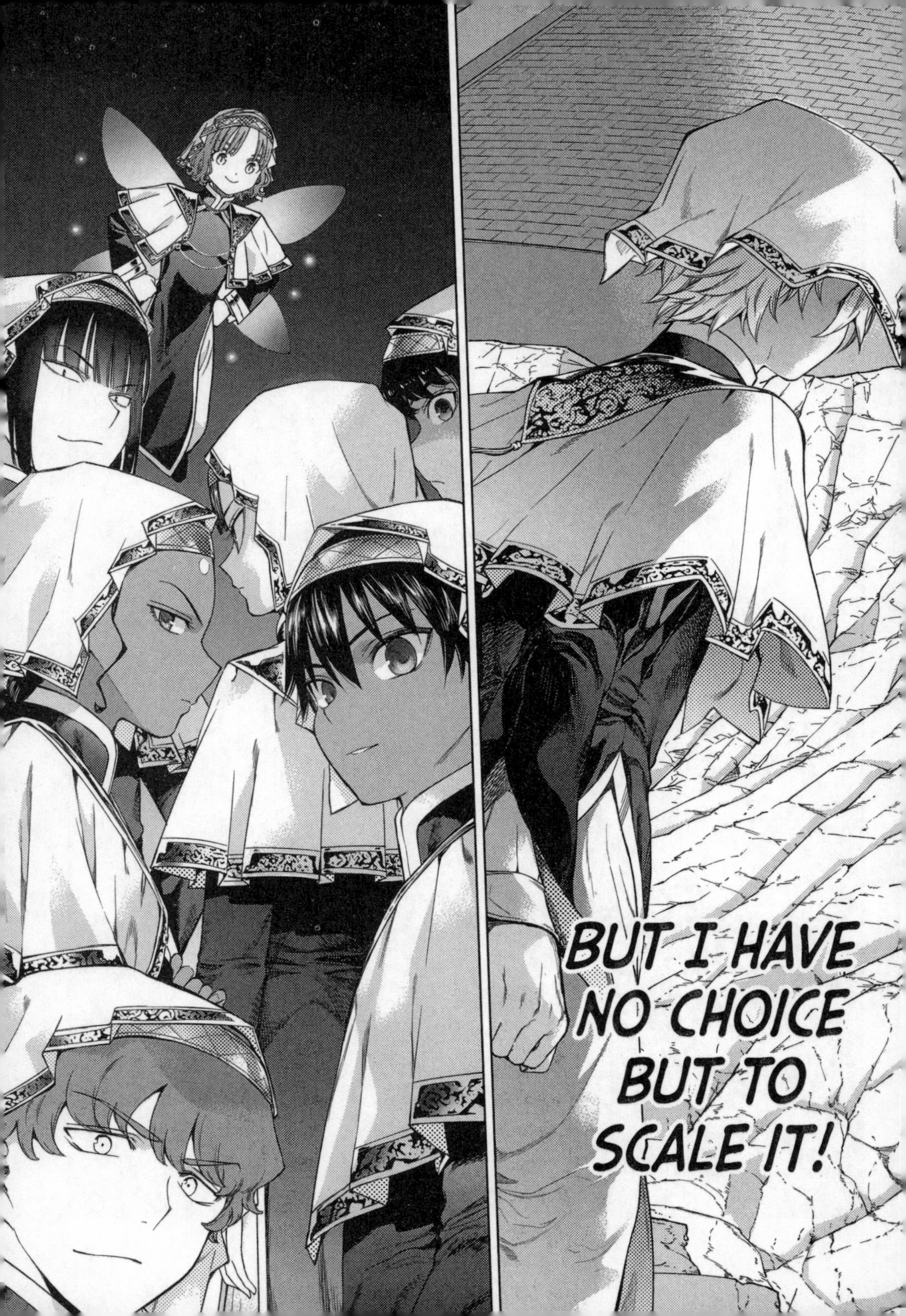
BUT I HAVE NO CHOICE BUT TO SCALE IT!

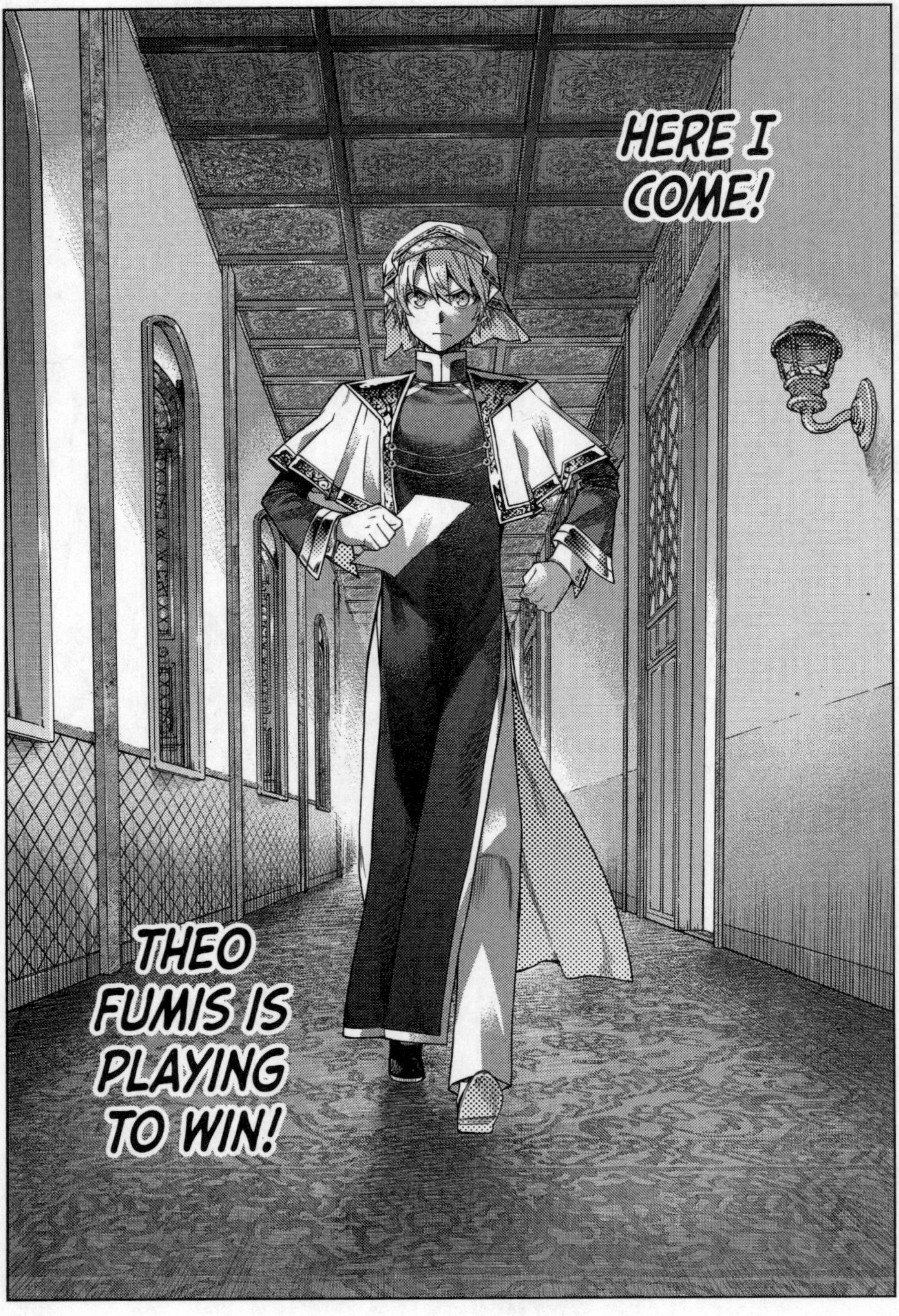
HERE I COME!
THEO FUMIS IS PLAYING TO WIN!

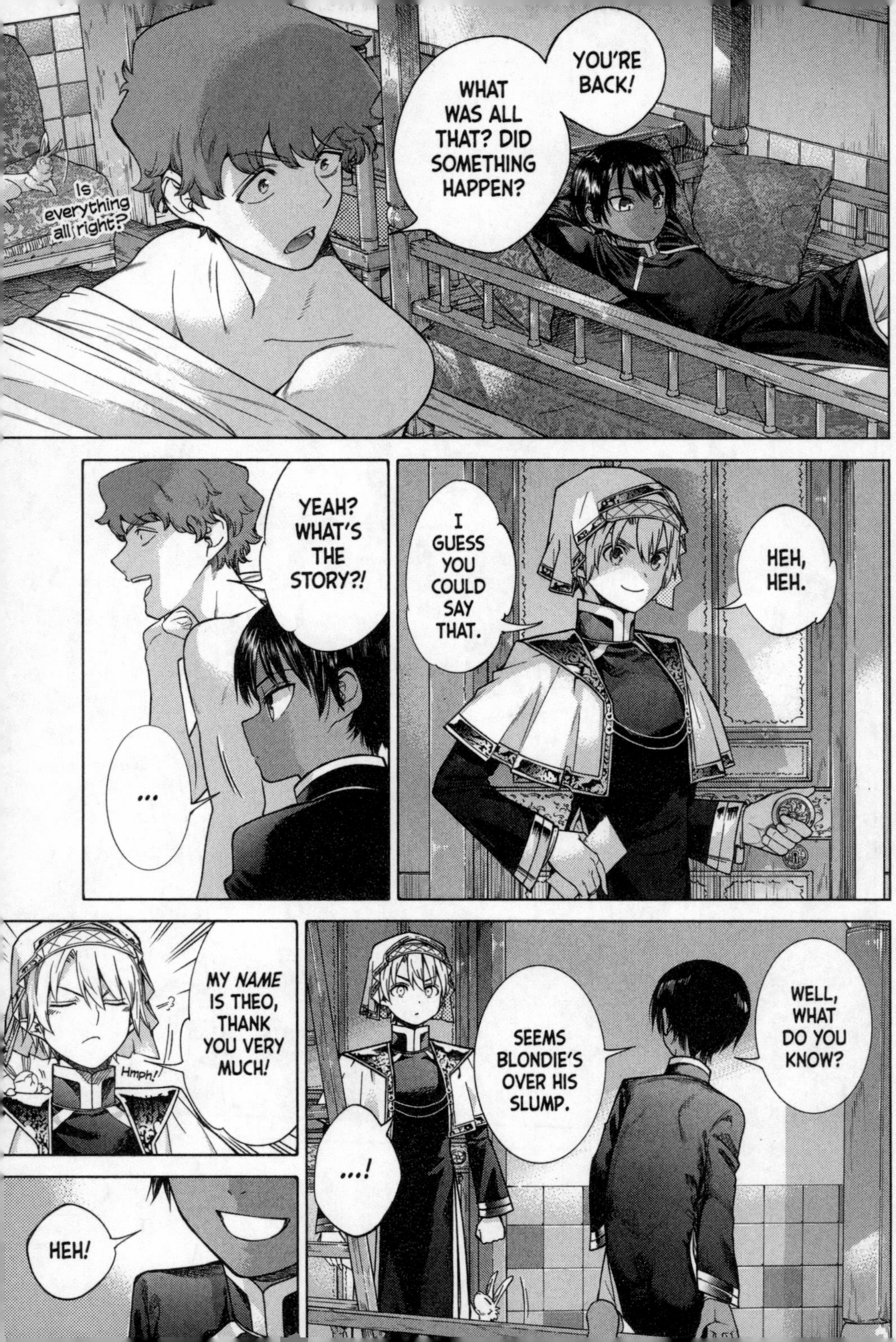
YOU'RE BACK!
WHAT WAS ALL THAT? DID SOMETHING HAPPEN?
Is everything all right?
HEH, HEH.
I GUESS YOU COULD SAY THAT.
YEAH? WHAT'S THE STORY?!
...
WELL, WHAT DO YOU KNOW?
SEEMS BLONDIE'S OVER HIS SLUMP.
...!
MY *NAME* IS THEO, THANK YOU VERY MUCH!
Hmph!
HEH!

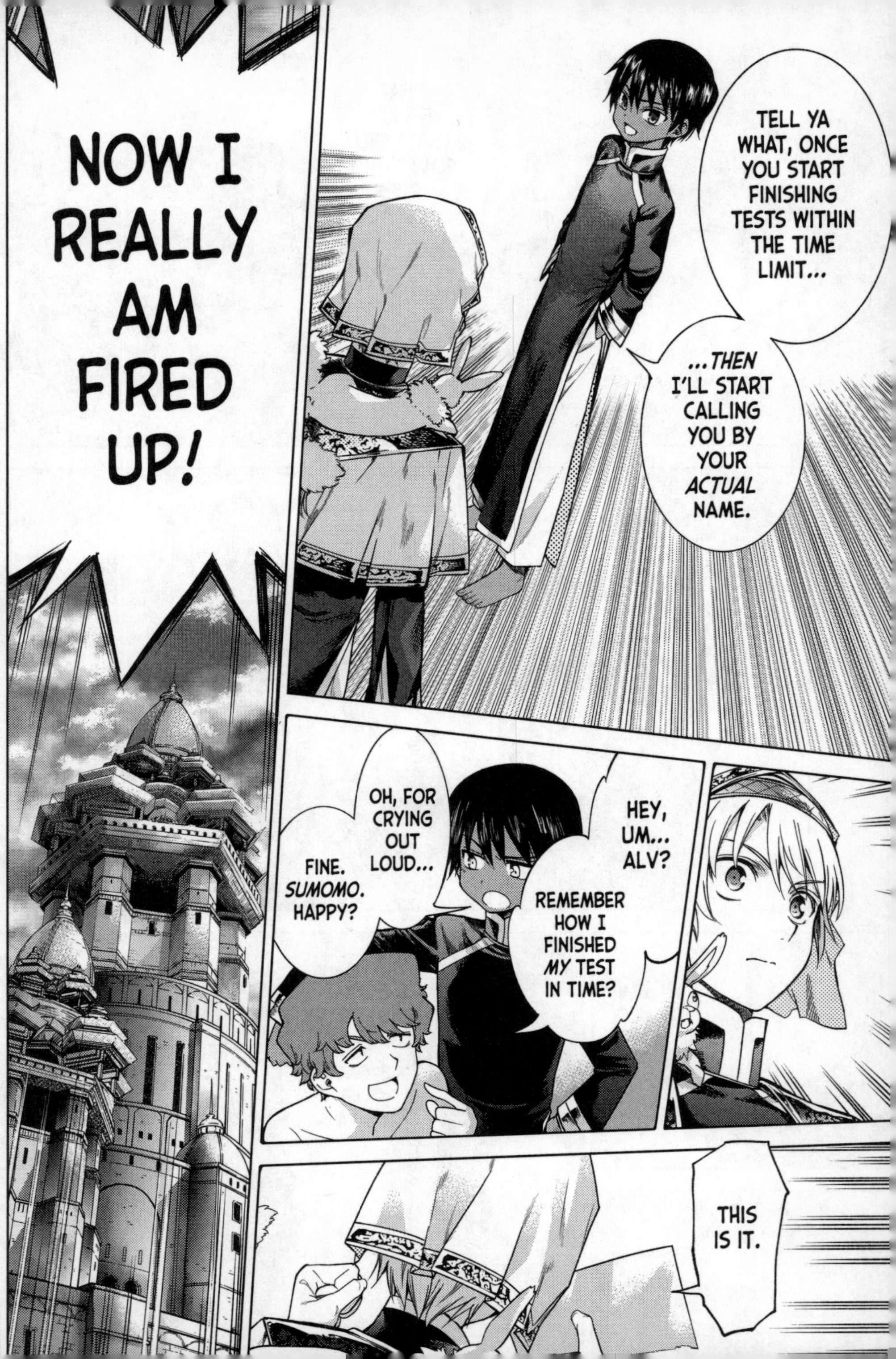
TELL YA WHAT, ONCE YOU START FINISHING TESTS WITHIN THE TIME LIMIT...
...THEN I'LL START CALLING YOU BY YOUR ACTUAL NAME.
HEY, UM... ALV?
REMEMBER HOW I FINISHED MY TEST IN TIME?
OH, FOR CRYING OUT LOUD...
FINE. SUMOMO. HAPPY?
THIS IS IT.
NOW I REALLY AM FIRED UP!

The Kafna in Training

The Harried Handlers

Mihona Qoahau

A girl who just can't seem to nail the critical moments. Easily swayed by whatever novel she's currently reading, and endlessly dreams of playing the suave, sophisticated heroine—a dream that never quite works out. Tends to choke, so her results don't reflect her true talent. Feels more harried than ever looking after herself as a kafna in training.

Yako Musuf

A girl who has it all together and is very sensitive to others' feelings. Dislikes any hint of turbulence among the group. At prep school, was the one to mend relations whenever her seatmate Madha—a neverending source of turbulence—stirred up trouble. Feels more harried than ever looking after Madha as a kafna in training.

Tepel Huracaan

A girl who has it all together but is quick to chide others for their shortcomings. At school, was the one to drag her longtime friend Sae back to her seat whenever the latter began wandering the room during class. Feels more harried than ever looking after Sae as a kafna in training.

The Kafna in Training

The Ends of the Spectrum

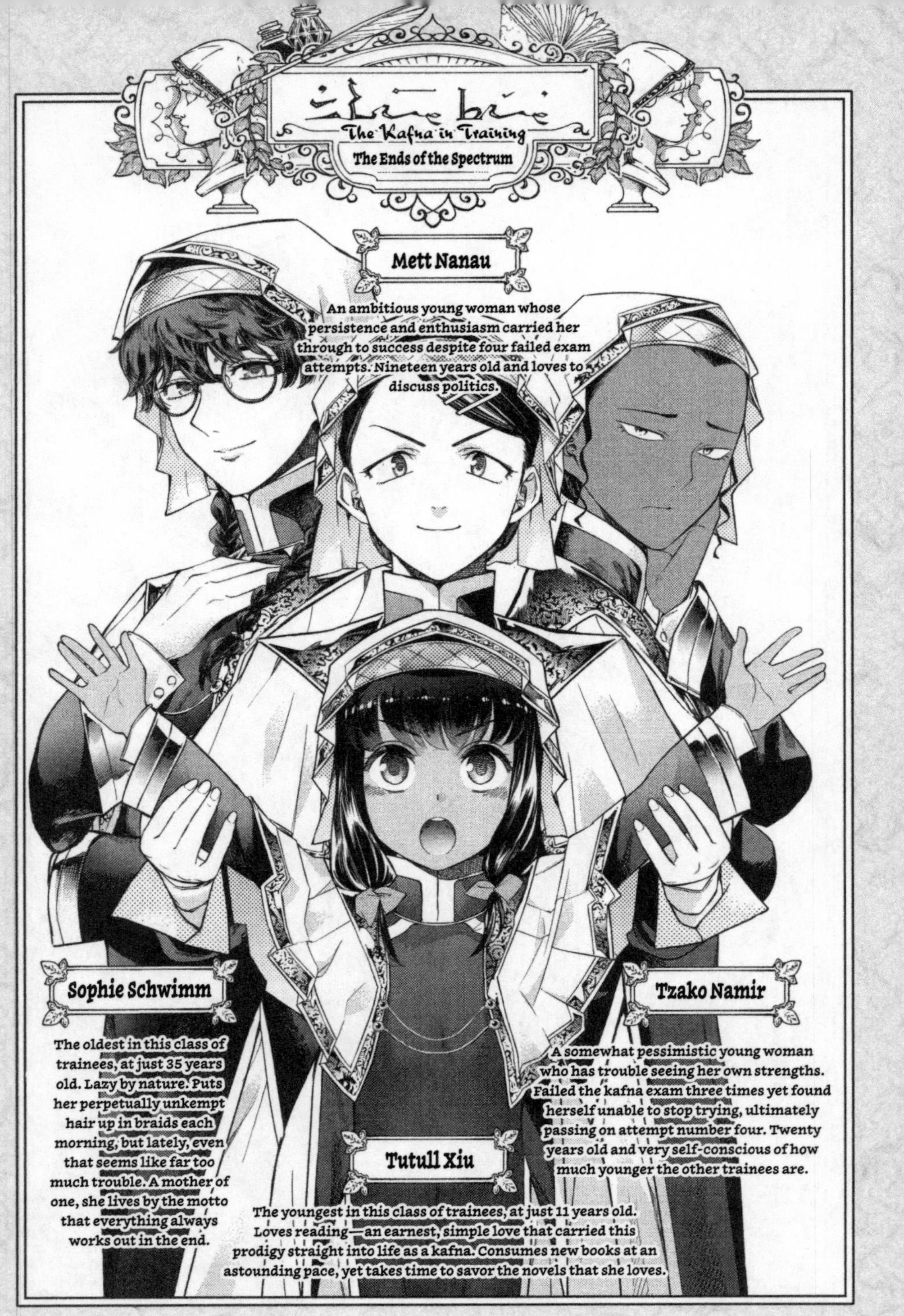

Mett Nanau

An ambitious young woman whose persistence and enthusiasm carried her through to success despite four failed exam attempts. Nineteen years old and loves to discuss politics.

Sophie Schwimm

The oldest in this class of trainees, at just 35 years old. Lazy by nature. Puts her perpetually unkempt hair up in braids each morning, but lately, even that seems like far too much trouble. A mother of one, she lives by the motto that everything always works out in the end.

Tzako Namir

A somewhat pessimistic young woman who has trouble seeing her own strengths. Failed the kafna exam three times yet found herself unable to stop trying, ultimately passing on attempt number four. Twenty years old and very self-conscious of how much younger the other trainees are.

Tutull Xiu

The youngest in this class of trainees, at just 11 years old. Loves reading—an earnest, simple love that carried this prodigy straight into life as a kafna. Consumes new books at an astounding pace, yet takes time to savor the novels that she loves.

18 Acting the High and Mighty Regal Curatrix

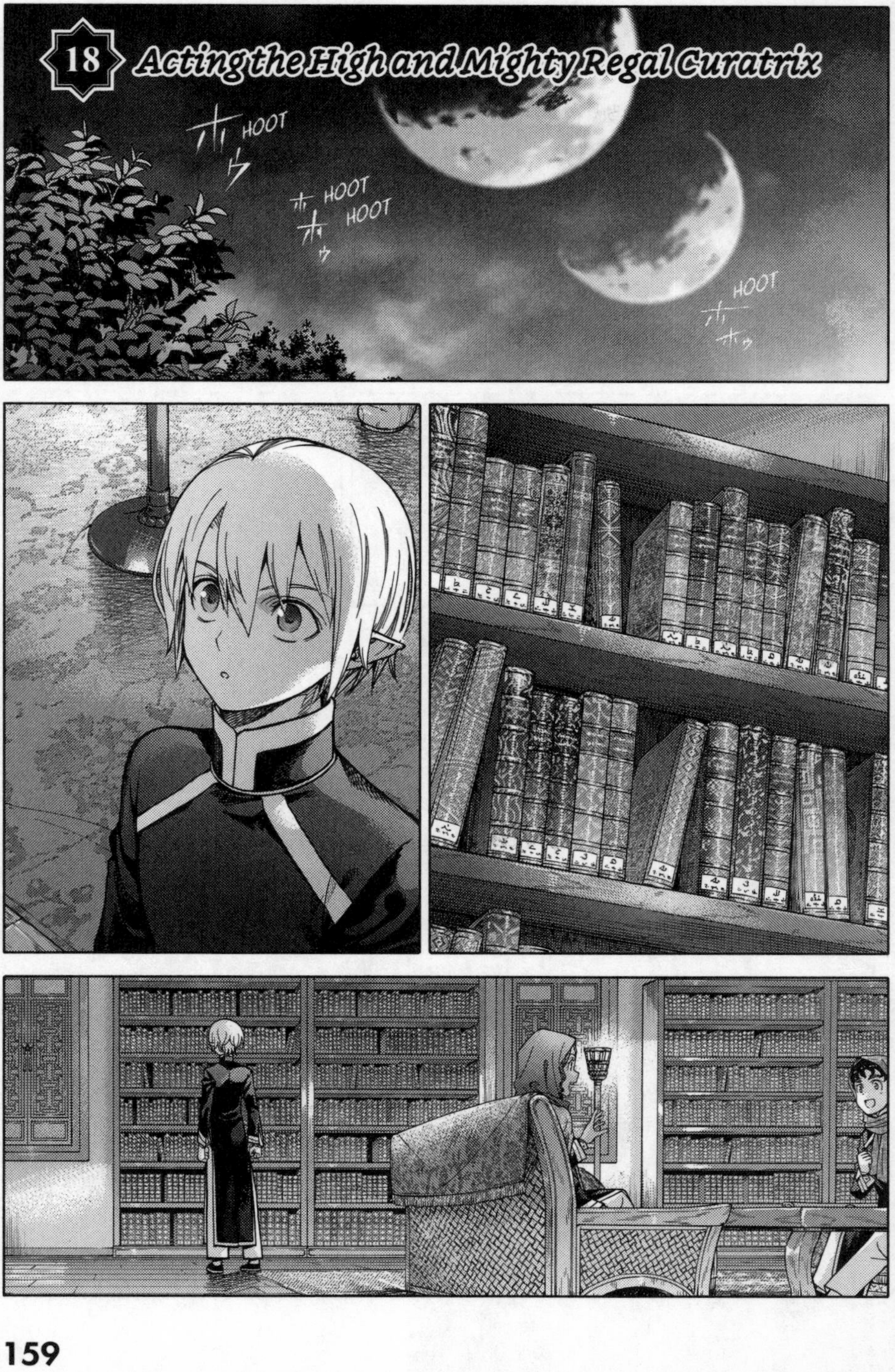
HOOT
HOOT
HOOT
HOOT

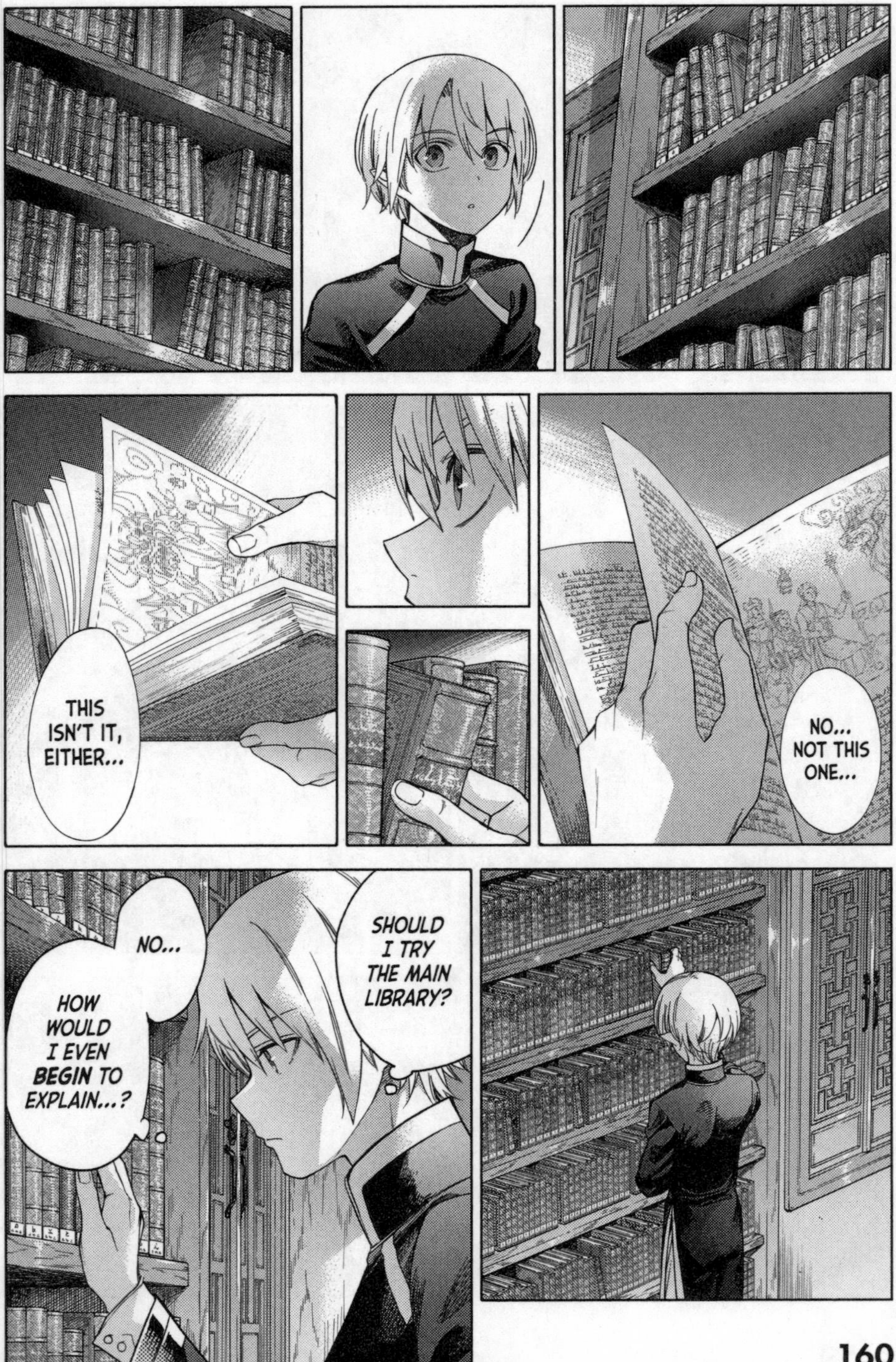
NO... NOT THIS ONE...
THIS ISN'T IT, EITHER...
SHOULD I TRY THE MAIN LIBRARY?
NO...
HOW WOULD I EVEN BEGIN TO EXPLAIN...?

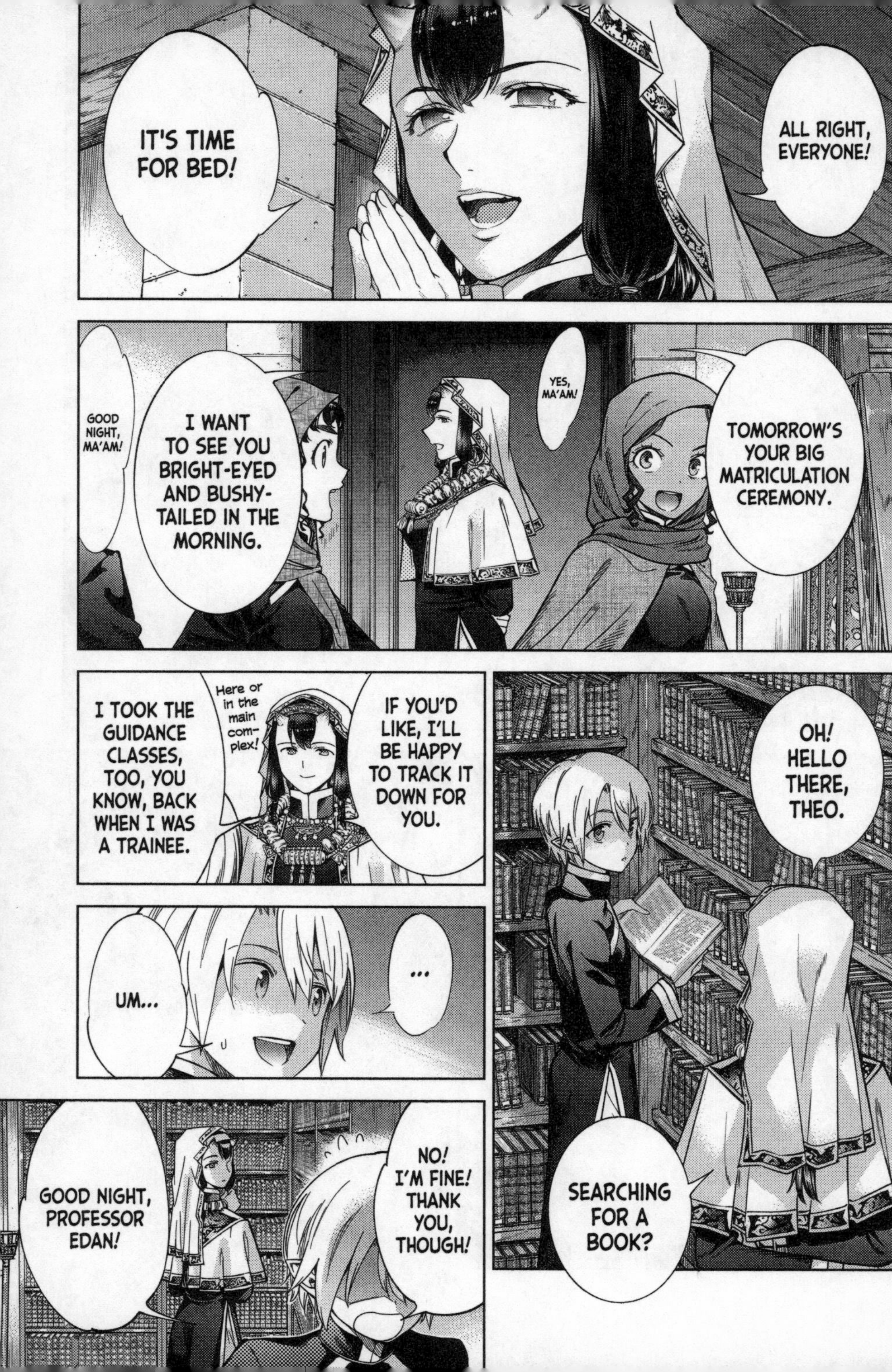
ALL RIGHT, EVERYONE!
IT'S TIME FOR BED!
TOMORROW'S YOUR BIG MATRICULATION CEREMONY.
YES, MA'AM!
I WANT TO SEE YOU BRIGHT-EYED AND BUSHY-TAILED IN THE MORNING.
GOOD NIGHT, MA'AM!
OH! HELLO THERE, THEO.
SEARCHING FOR A BOOK?
IF YOU'D LIKE, I'LL BE HAPPY TO TRACK IT DOWN FOR YOU.
Here or in the main complex!
I TOOK THE GUIDANCE CLASSES, TOO, YOU KNOW, BACK WHEN I WAS A TRAINEE.
...
UM...
NO! I'M FINE! THANK YOU, THOUGH!
GOOD NIGHT, PROFESSOR EDAN!

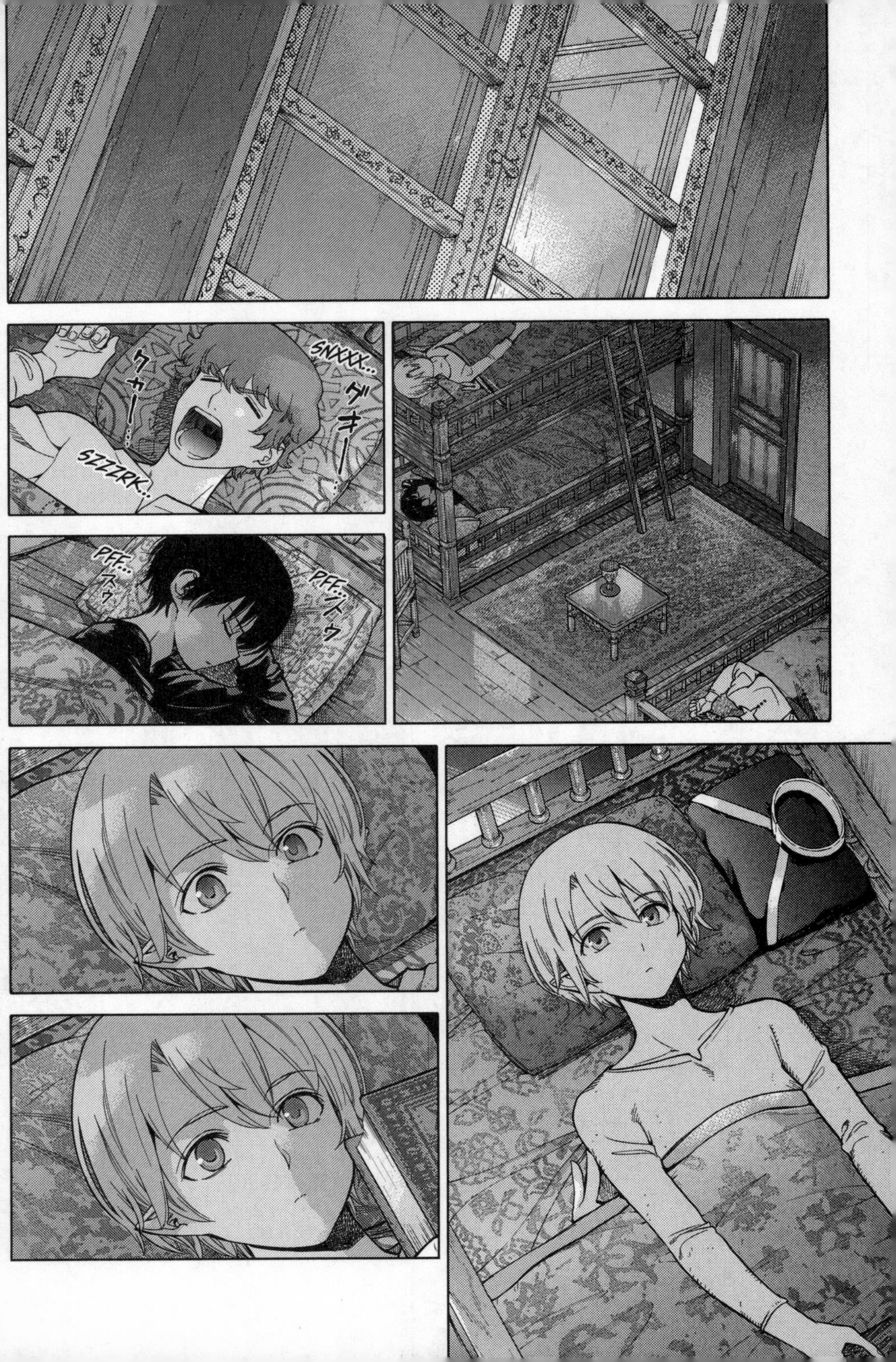
SNXXX...
ゲオー…
クカー…
SZZZRK...
PFF... スゥ
PFF... スゥ

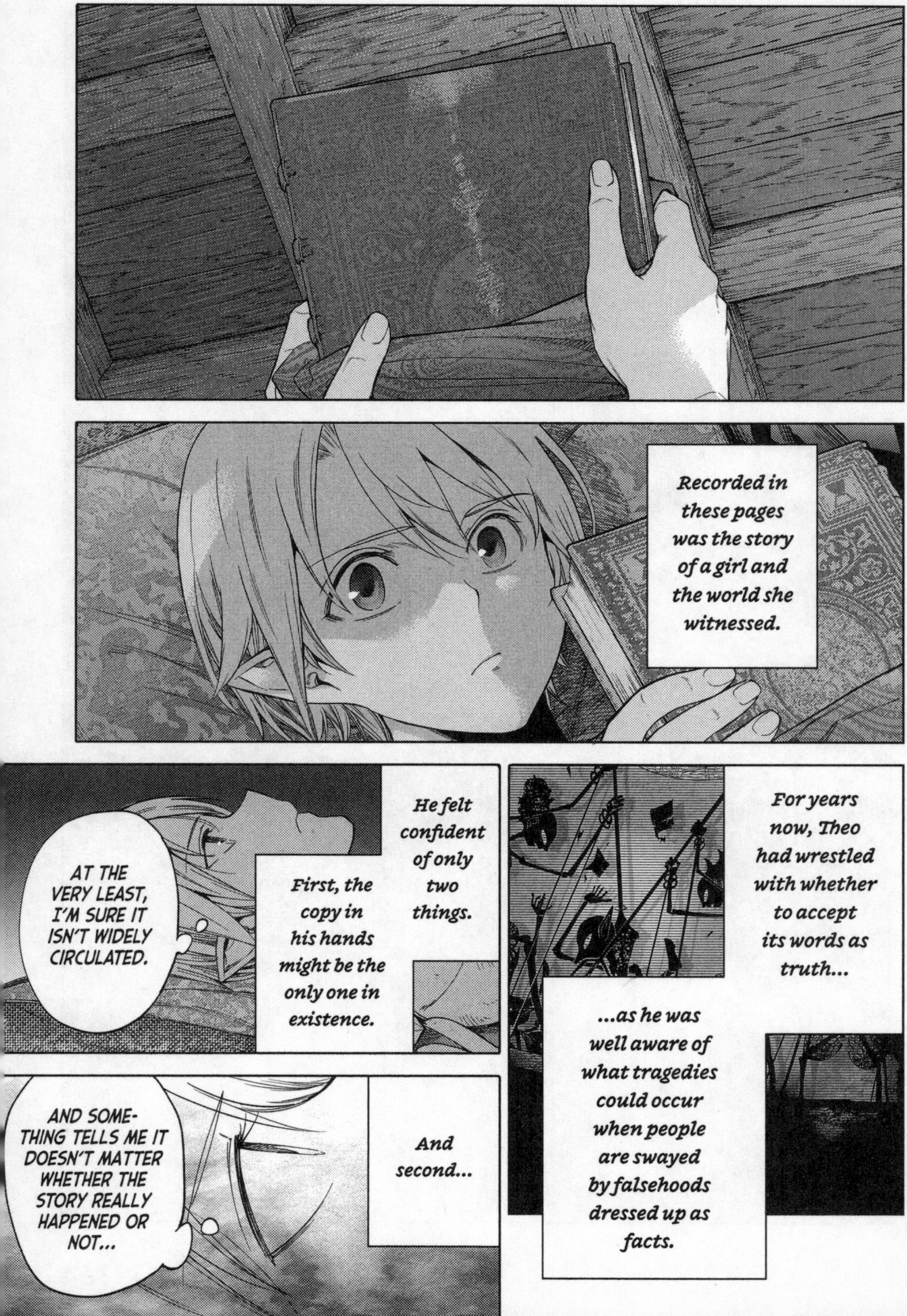
Recorded in these pages was the story of a girl and the world she witnessed.
For years now, Theo had wrestled with whether to accept its words as truth...
...as he was well aware of what tragedies could occur when people are swayed by falsehoods dressed up as facts.
He felt confident of only two things.
First, the copy in his hands might be the only one in existence.
AT THE VERY LEAST, I'M SURE IT ISN'T WIDELY CIRCULATED.
And second...
AND SOME-THING TELLS ME IT DOESN'T MATTER WHETHER THE STORY REALLY HAPPENED OR NOT...

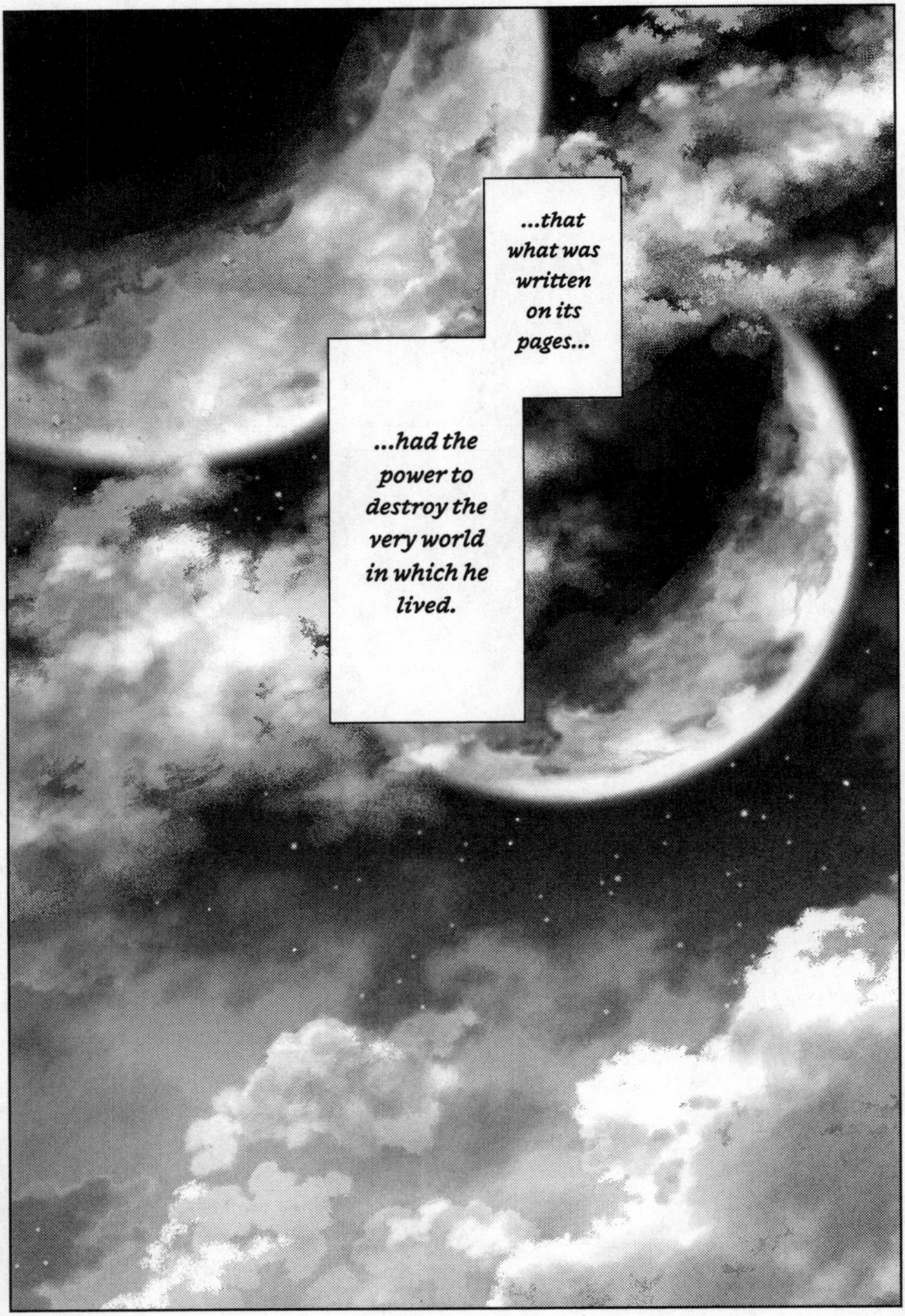
...that what was written on its pages...
...had the power to destroy the very world in which he lived.

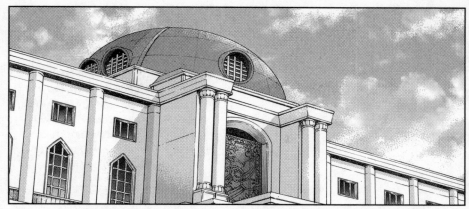

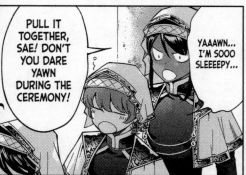

YAAAWN... I'M SOOO SLEEEEPY...
PULL IT TOGETHER, SAE! DON'T YOU DARE YAWN DURING THE CEREMONY!
GASP!!
In truth, the Central Library's three main structures...
AFTZAAK LIBRARY, MAIN COMPLEX
AFTZAAK MUSEUM OF ART
AFTZAAK MUSEUM OF HISTORY
...were its most recent additions. Many times had the grounds and facilities been expanded.
Just beyond the library's primary complex rested its "first" in another sense.

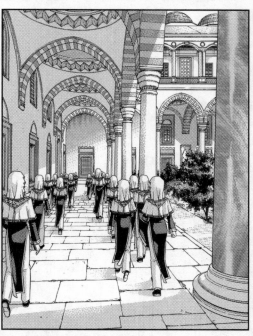

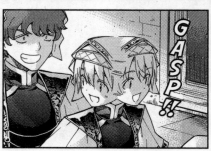

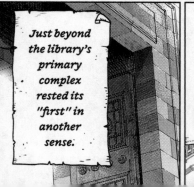

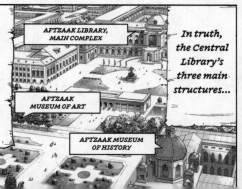

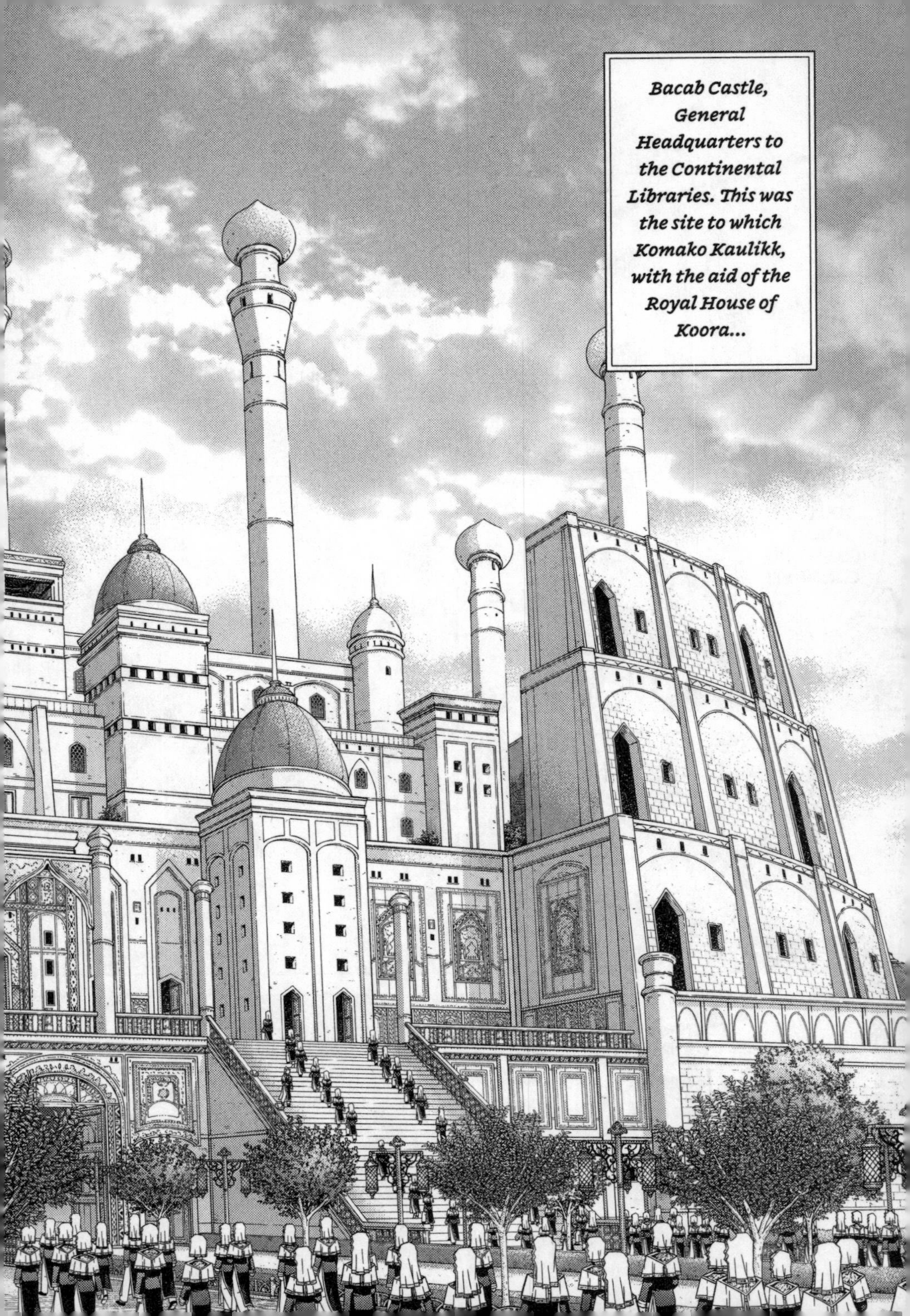
Bacab Castle, General Headquarters to the Continental Libraries. This was the site to which Komako Kaulikk, with the aid of the Royal House of Koora...

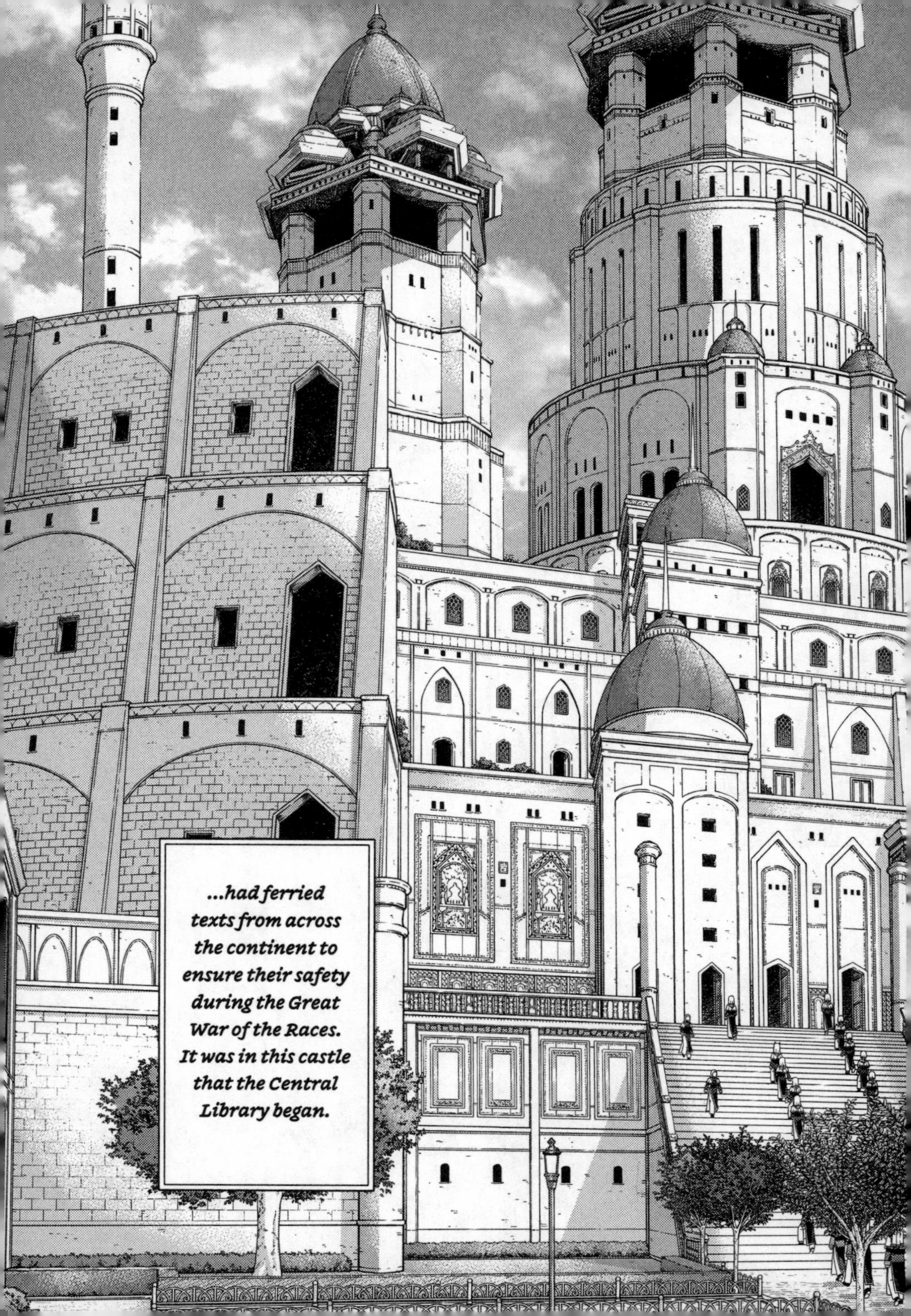
...had ferried texts from across the continent to ensure their safety during the Great War of the Races. It was in this castle that the Central Library began.

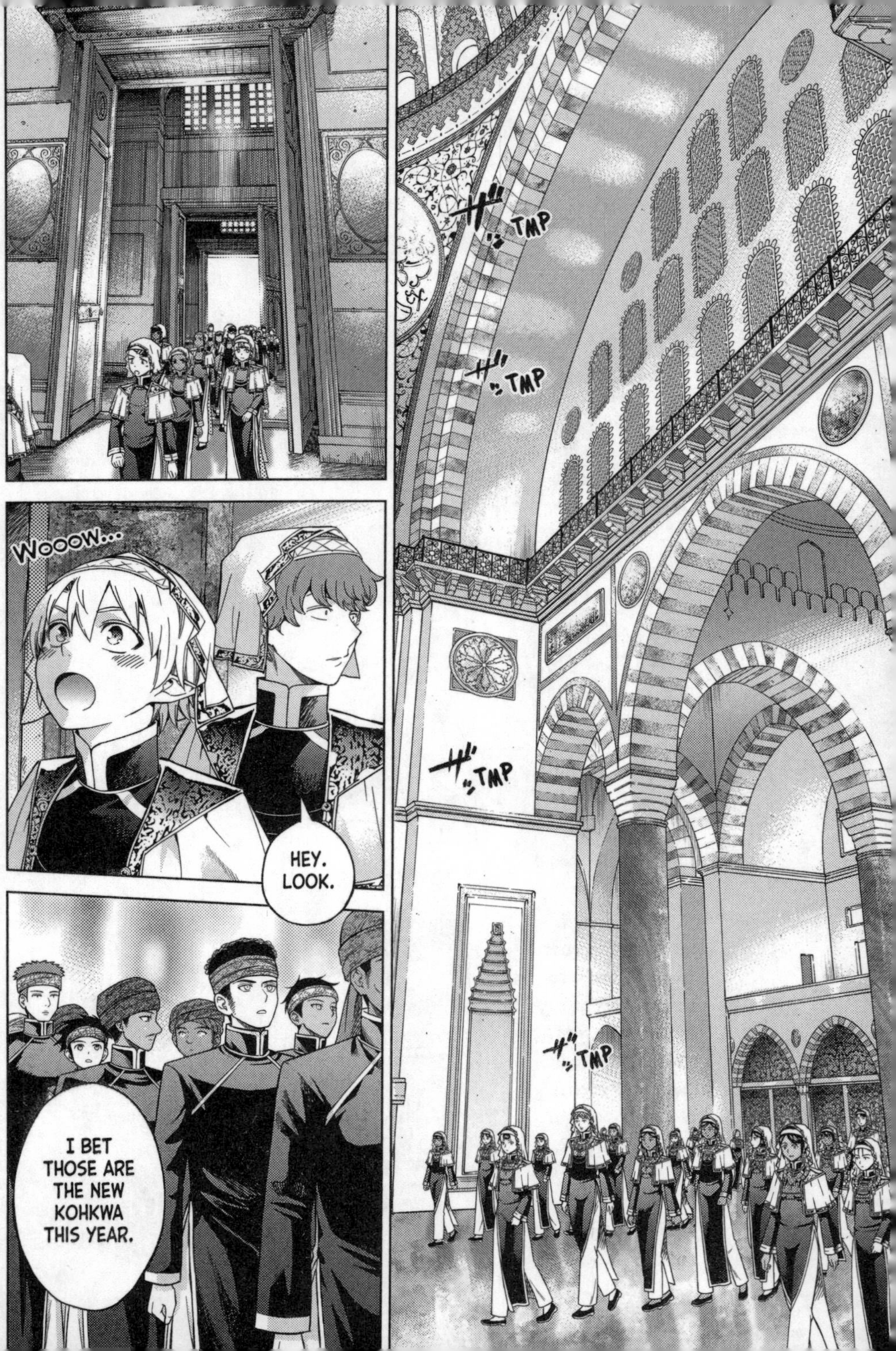
TMP
TMP
TMP
TMP
Wooow...
HEY. LOOK.
I BET THOSE ARE THE NEW KOHKWA THIS YEAR.

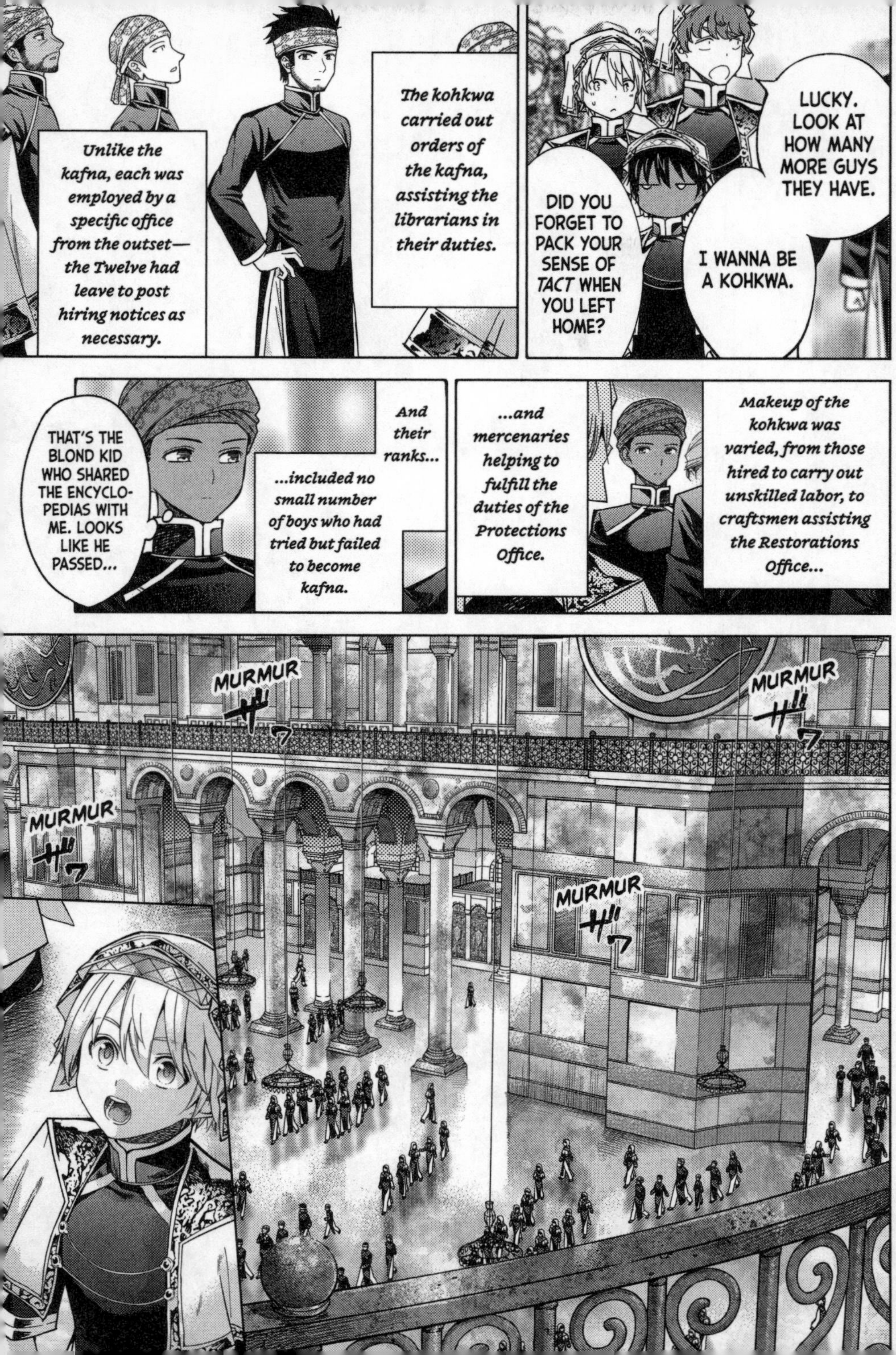
LUCKY. LOOK AT HOW MANY MORE GUYS THEY HAVE.
I WANNA BE A KOHKWA.
DID YOU FORGET TO PACK YOUR SENSE OF *TACT* WHEN YOU LEFT HOME?
The kohkwa carried out orders of the kafna, assisting the librarians in their duties.
Unlike the kafna, each was employed by a specific office from the outset—the Twelve had leave to post hiring notices as necessary.
Makeup of the kohkwa was varied, from those hired to carry out unskilled labor, to craftsmen assisting the Restorations Office...
...and mercenaries helping to fulfill the duties of the Protections Office.
And their ranks...
...included no small number of boys who had tried but failed to become kafna.
THAT'S THE BLOND KID WHO SHARED THE ENCYCLOPEDIAS WITH ME. LOOKS LIKE HE PASSED...
MURMUR
ザワ
MURMUR
ザワ
MURMUR
ザワ
MURMUR
ザワ

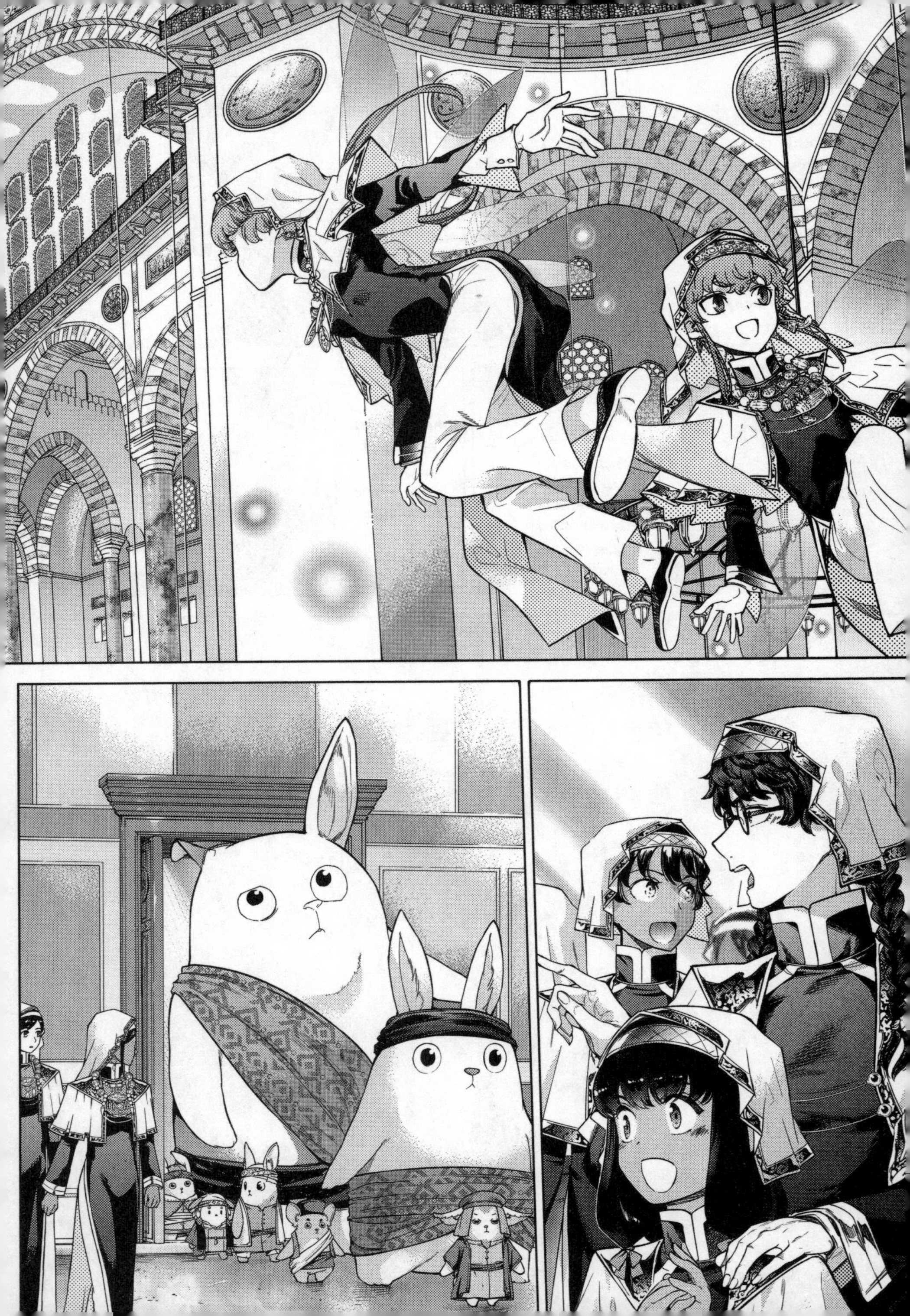

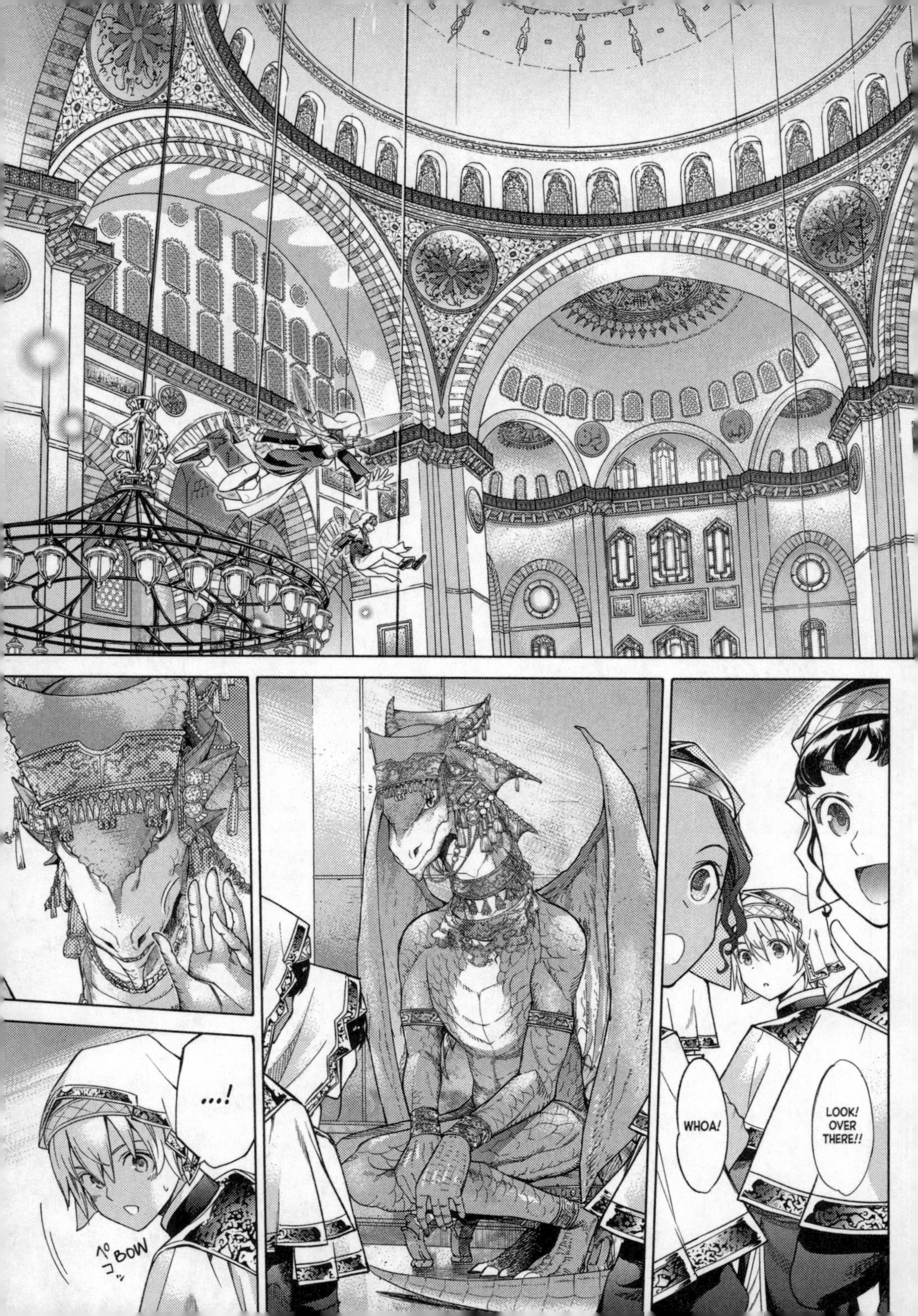

LOOK! OVER THERE!!
WHOA!
...!
ペコッ
BOW

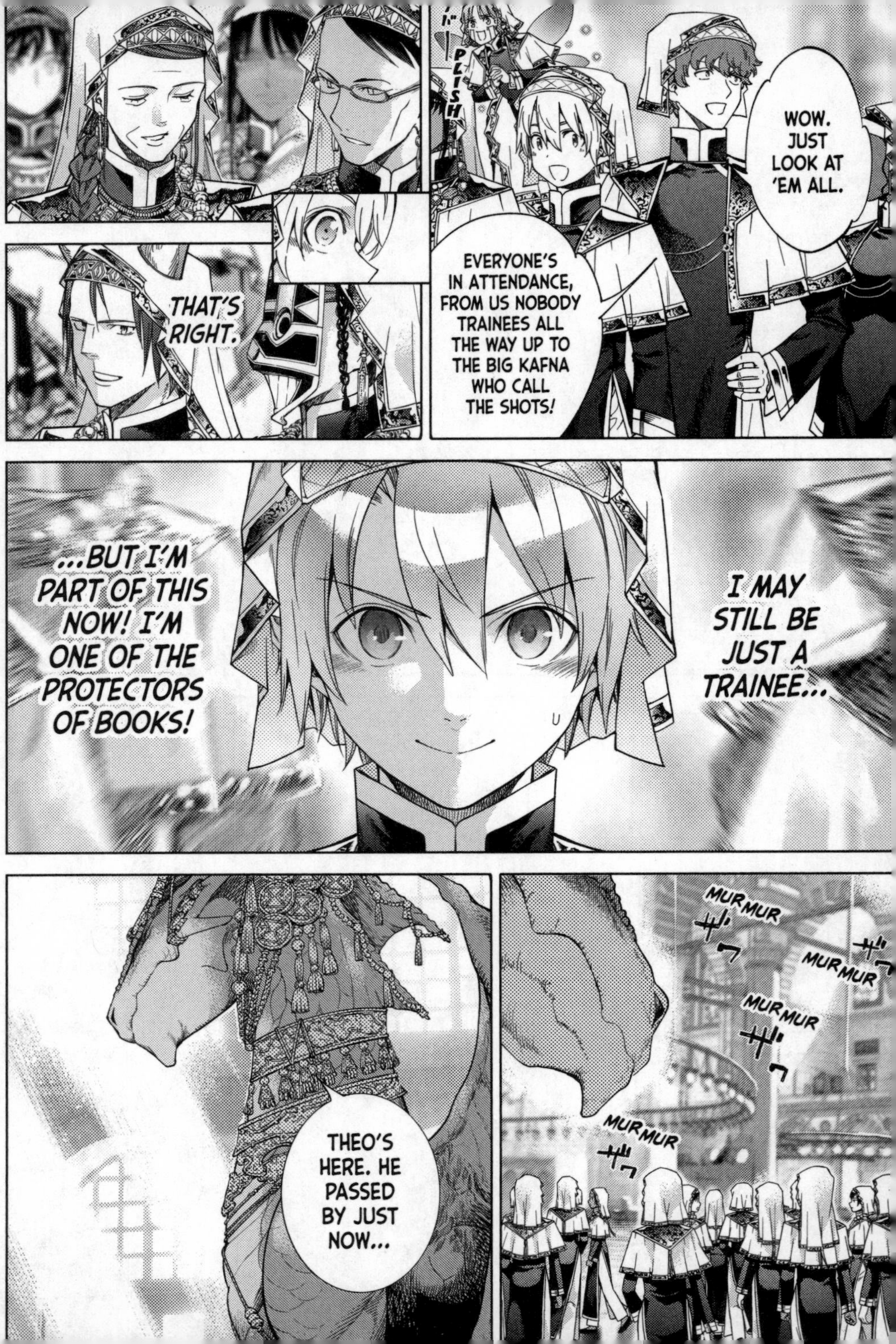
PLISH
WOW. JUST LOOK AT 'EM ALL.
EVERYONE'S IN ATTENDANCE, FROM US NOBODY TRAINEES ALL THE WAY UP TO THE BIG KAFNA WHO CALL THE SHOTS!
THAT'S RIGHT.
I MAY STILL BE JUST A TRAINEE...
...BUT I'M PART OF THIS NOW! I'M ONE OF THE PROTECTORS OF BOOKS!
MURMUR
MURMUR
MURMUR
MURMUR
THEO'S HERE. HE PASSED BY JUST NOW...

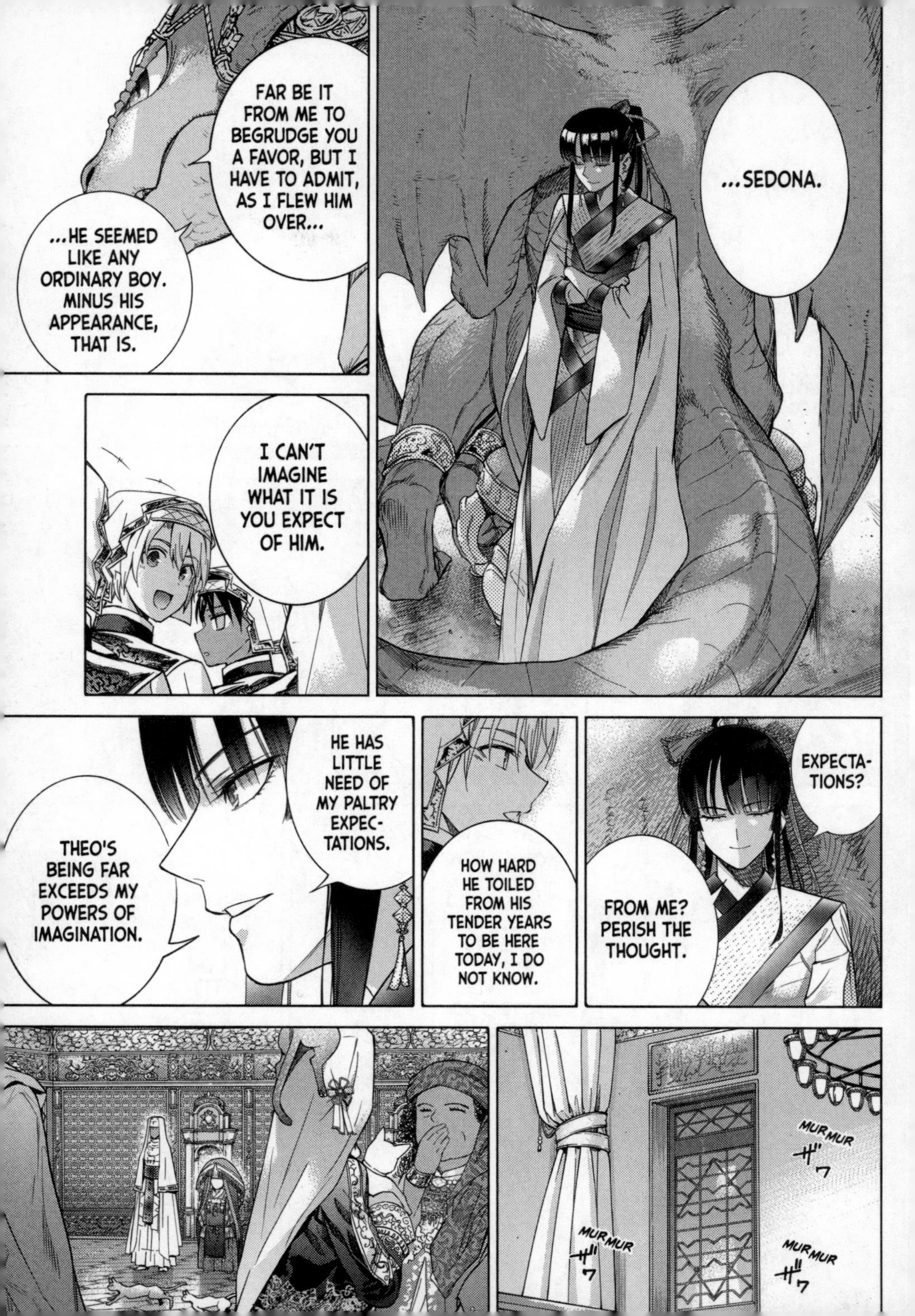
...SEDONA.
FAR BE IT FROM ME TO BEGRUDGE YOU A FAVOR, BUT I HAVE TO ADMIT, AS I FLEW HIM OVER...
...HE SEEMED LIKE ANY ORDINARY BOY. MINUS HIS APPEARANCE, THAT IS.
I CAN'T IMAGINE WHAT IT IS YOU EXPECT OF HIM.
EXPECTA-TIONS?
FROM ME? PERISH THE THOUGHT.
HOW HARD HE TOILED FROM HIS TENDER YEARS TO BE HERE TODAY, I DO NOT KNOW.
HE HAS LITTLE NEED OF MY PALTRY EXPEC-TATIONS.
THEO'S BEING FAR EXCEEDS MY POWERS OF IMAGINATION.
MURMUR
MURMUR
MURMUR

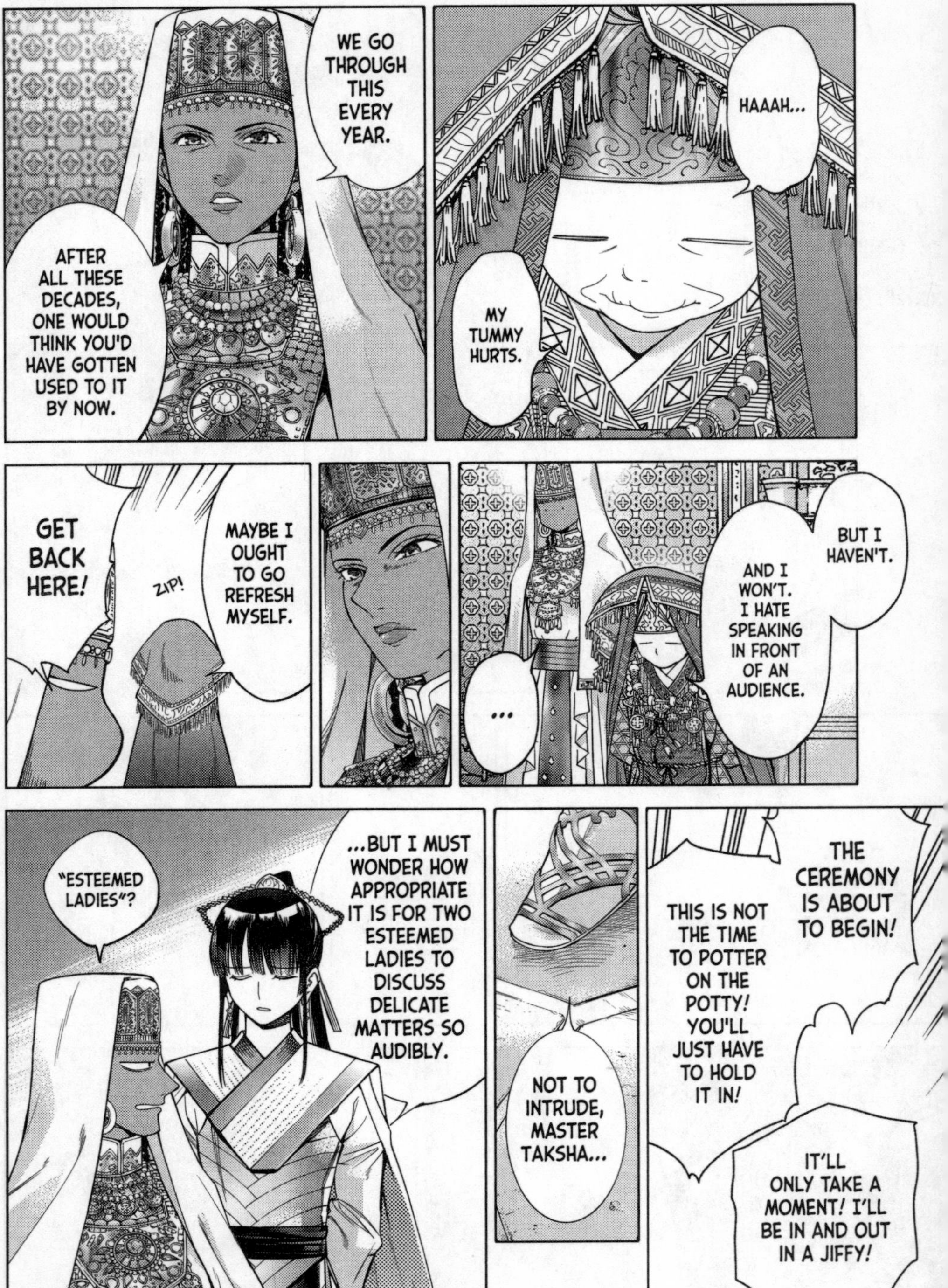
HAAAH...
MY TUMMY HURTS.
WE GO THROUGH THIS EVERY YEAR.
AFTER ALL THESE DECADES, ONE WOULD THINK YOU'D HAVE GOTTEN USED TO IT BY NOW.
BUT I HAVEN'T.
AND I WON'T. I HATE SPEAKING IN FRONT OF AN AUDIENCE.
...
MAYBE I OUGHT TO GO REFRESH MYSELF.
ZIP!
GET BACK HERE!
THE CEREMONY IS ABOUT TO BEGIN!
THIS IS NOT THE TIME TO POTTER ON THE POTTY! YOU'LL JUST HAVE TO HOLD IT IN!
IT'LL ONLY TAKE A MOMENT! I'LL BE IN AND OUT IN A JIFFY!
NOT TO INTRUDE, MASTER TAKSHA...
...BUT I MUST WONDER HOW APPROPRIATE IT IS FOR TWO ESTEEMED LADIES TO DISCUSS DELICATE MATTERS SO AUDIBLY.
"ESTEEMED LADIES"?

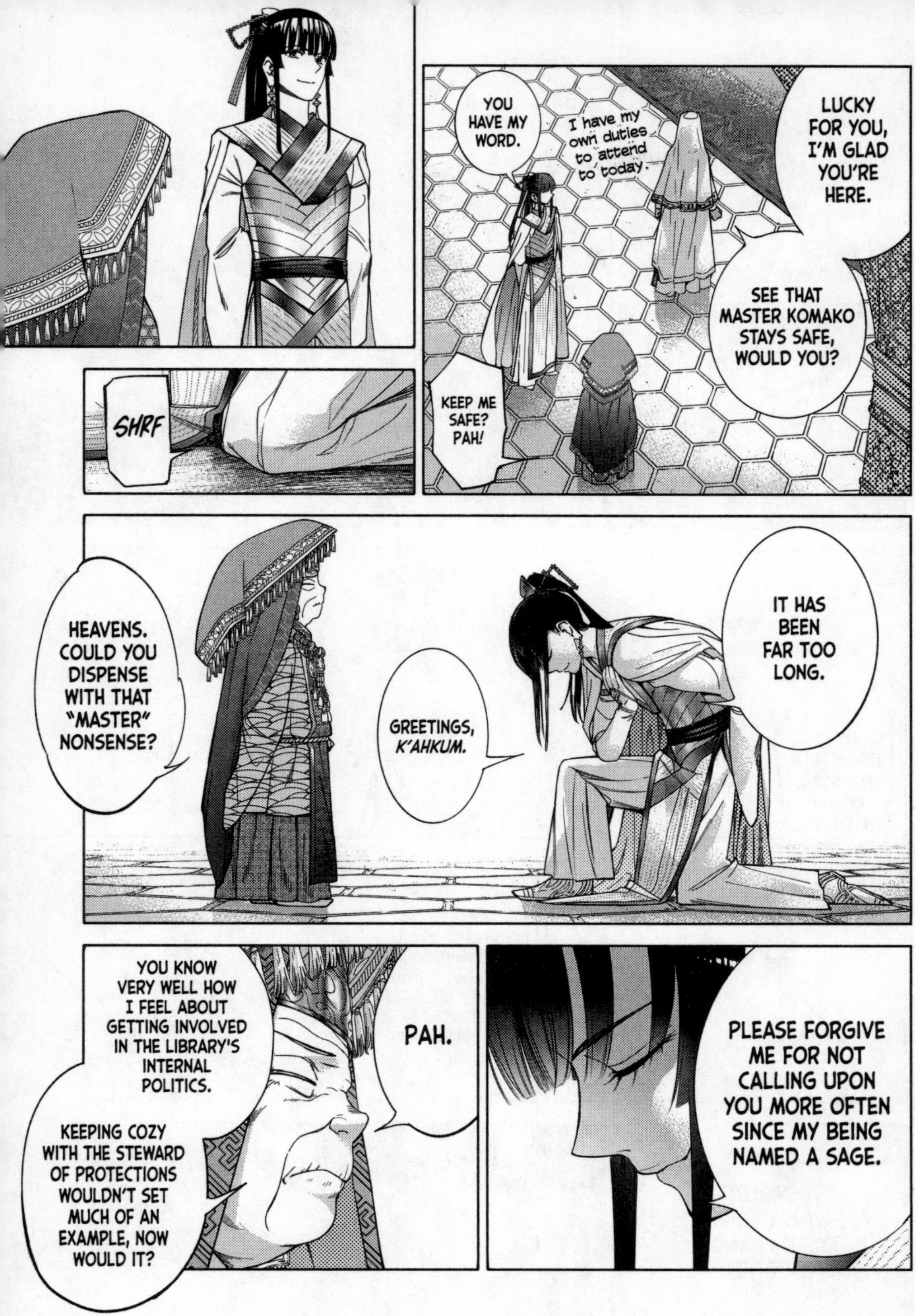
LUCKY FOR YOU, I'M GLAD YOU'RE HERE.
SEE THAT MASTER KOMAKO STAYS SAFE, WOULD YOU?
YOU HAVE MY WORD.
I have my own duties to attend to today.
KEEP ME SAFE? PAH!
SHRF
IT HAS BEEN FAR TOO LONG.
GREETINGS, *K'AHKUM.*
HEAVENS. COULD YOU DISPENSE WITH THAT "MASTER" NONSENSE?
PLEASE FORGIVE ME FOR NOT CALLING UPON YOU MORE OFTEN SINCE MY BEING NAMED A SAGE.
PAH.
YOU KNOW VERY WELL HOW I FEEL ABOUT GETTING INVOLVED IN THE LIBRARY'S INTERNAL POLITICS.
KEEPING COZY WITH THE STEWARD OF PROTECTIONS WOULDN'T SET MUCH OF AN EXAMPLE, NOW WOULD IT?

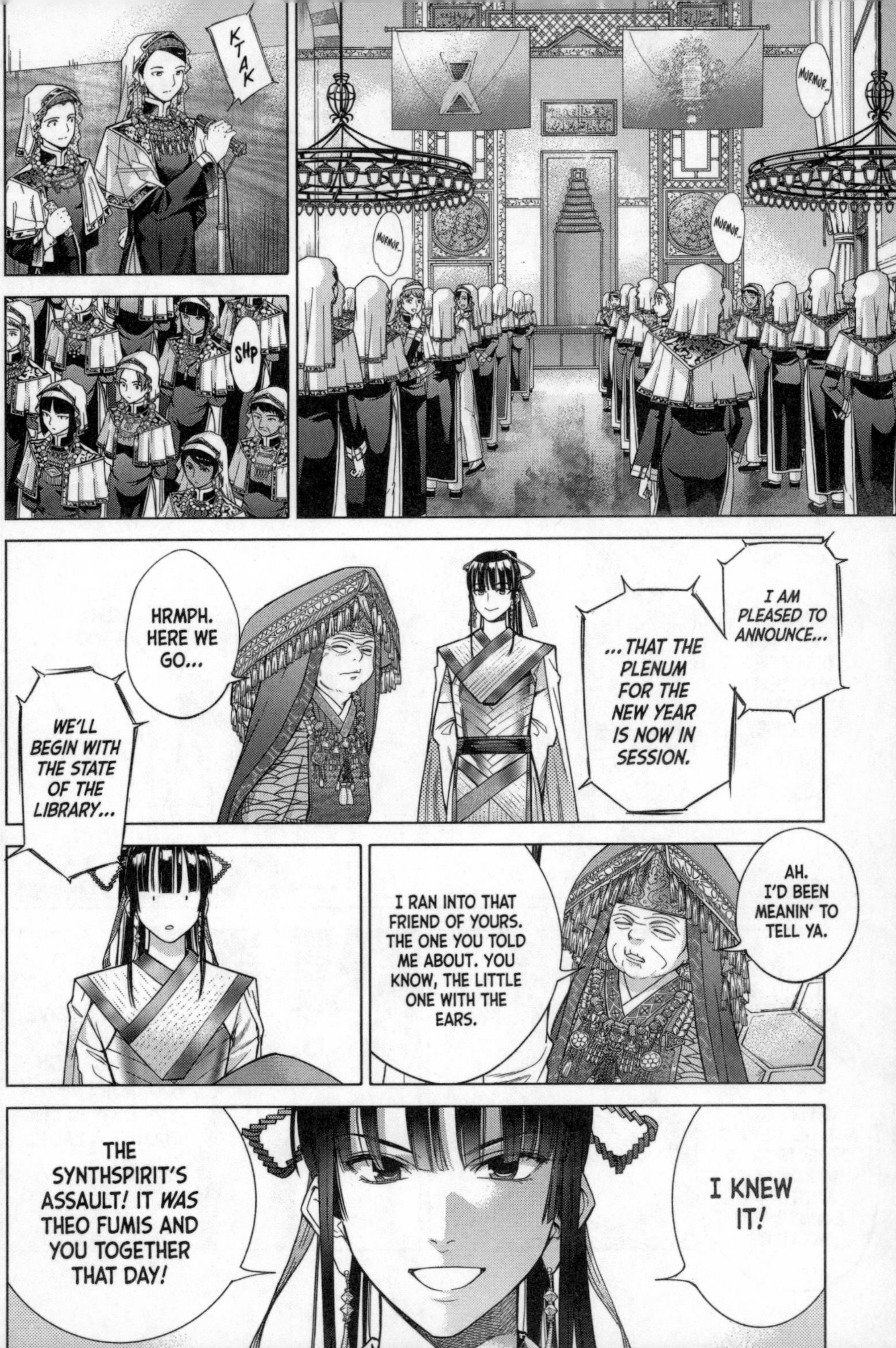
MURMUR...
MURMUR...
MURMUR...
KTAK
SHP
I AM PLEASED TO ANNOUNCE...
...THAT THE PLENUM FOR THE NEW YEAR IS NOW IN SESSION.
HRMPH. HERE WE GO...
WE'LL BEGIN WITH THE STATE OF THE LIBRARY...
AH. I'D BEEN MEANIN' TO TELL YA.
I RAN INTO THAT FRIEND OF YOURS. THE ONE YOU TOLD ME ABOUT. YOU KNOW, THE LITTLE ONE WITH THE EARS.
I KNEW IT!
THE SYNTHSPIRIT'S ASSAULT! IT *WAS* THEO FUMIS AND YOU TOGETHER THAT DAY!

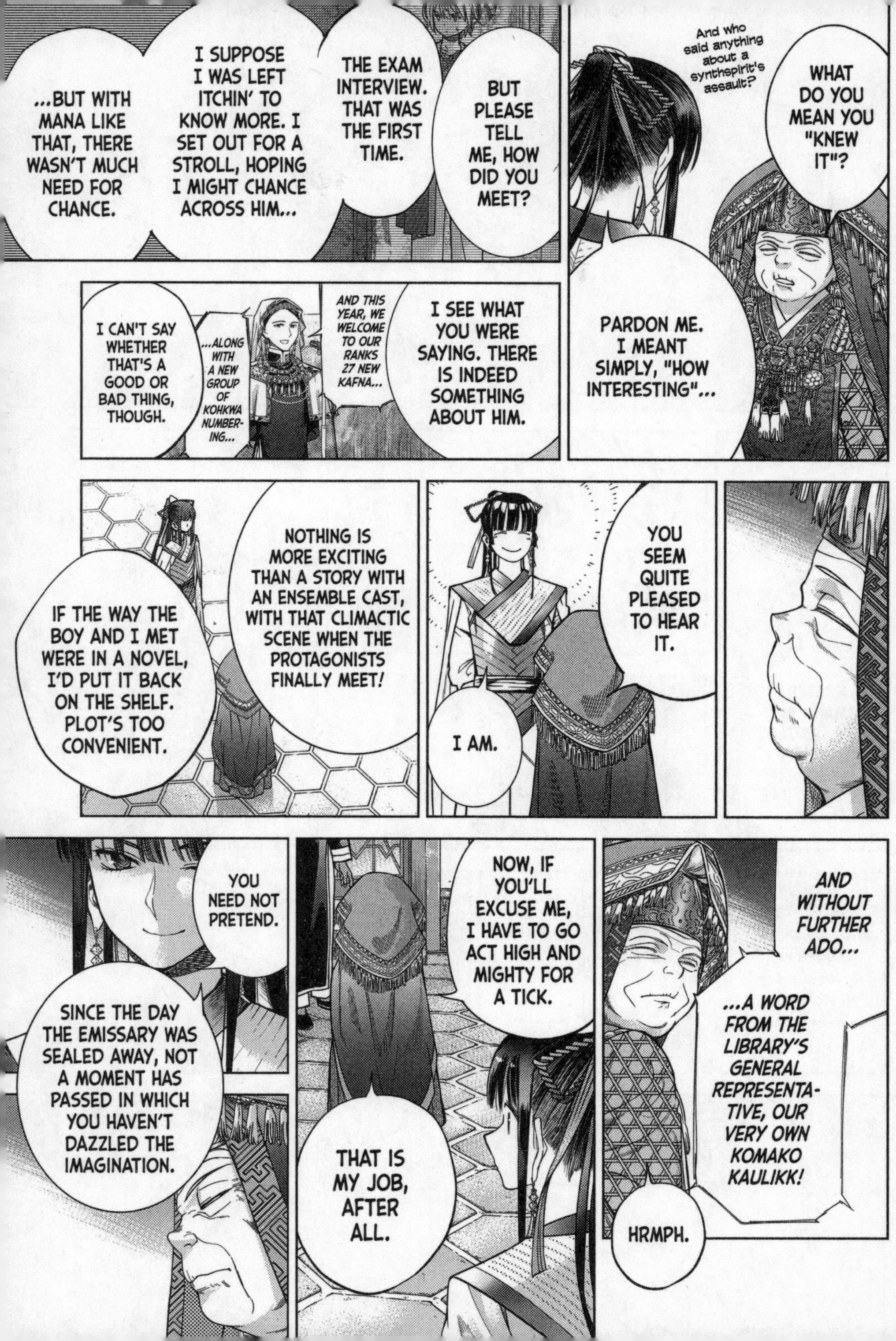
WHAT DO YOU MEAN YOU "KNEW IT"?
And who said anything about a synthspirit's assault?
PARDON ME. I MEANT SIMPLY, "HOW INTERESTING"...
BUT PLEASE TELL ME, HOW DID YOU MEET?
THE EXAM INTERVIEW. THAT WAS THE FIRST TIME.
I SUPPOSE I WAS LEFT ITCHIN' TO KNOW MORE. I SET OUT FOR A STROLL, HOPING I MIGHT CHANCE ACROSS HIM...
...BUT WITH MANA LIKE THAT, THERE WASN'T MUCH NEED FOR CHANCE.
I SEE WHAT YOU WERE SAYING. THERE IS INDEED SOMETHING ABOUT HIM.
AND THIS YEAR, WE WELCOME TO OUR RANKS 27 NEW KAFNA...
...ALONG WITH A NEW GROUP OF KOHKWA NUMBERING...
I CAN'T SAY WHETHER THAT'S A GOOD OR BAD THING, THOUGH.
YOU SEEM QUITE PLEASED TO HEAR IT.
I AM.
NOTHING IS MORE EXCITING THAN A STORY WITH AN ENSEMBLE CAST, WITH THAT CLIMACTIC SCENE WHEN THE PROTAGONISTS FINALLY MEET!
IF THE WAY THE BOY AND I MET WERE IN A NOVEL, I'D PUT IT BACK ON THE SHELF. PLOT'S TOO CONVENIENT.
AND WITHOUT FURTHER ADO...
...A WORD FROM THE LIBRARY'S GENERAL REPRESENTATIVE, OUR VERY OWN KOMAKO KAULIKK!
HRMPH.
NOW, IF YOU'LL EXCUSE ME, I HAVE TO GO ACT HIGH AND MIGHTY FOR A TICK.
THAT IS MY JOB, AFTER ALL.
YOU NEED NOT PRETEND.
SINCE THE DAY THE EMISSARY WAS SEALED AWAY, NOT A MOMENT HAS PASSED IN WHICH YOU HAVEN'T DAZZLED THE IMAGINATION.

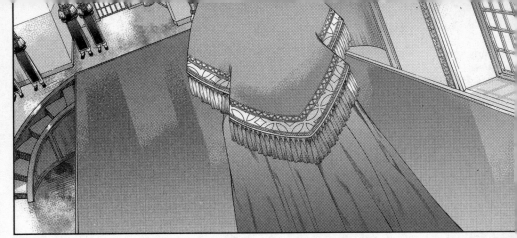

MRMR ...

WHSPR, WHSPR...

HAVE YOU HEARD?

SHRP

...!

MRMR ...

MRMR ...

MASTER KOMAKO WAS ONLY *THIRTEEN YEARS OLD* WHEN SHE DEFEATED THE CALAMITY!

SHP

...

An artifact able to carry a speaker's voice by amplifying its vibrations via sky mana.

A phono-staff—

...

MRMR ...

MRMR ...

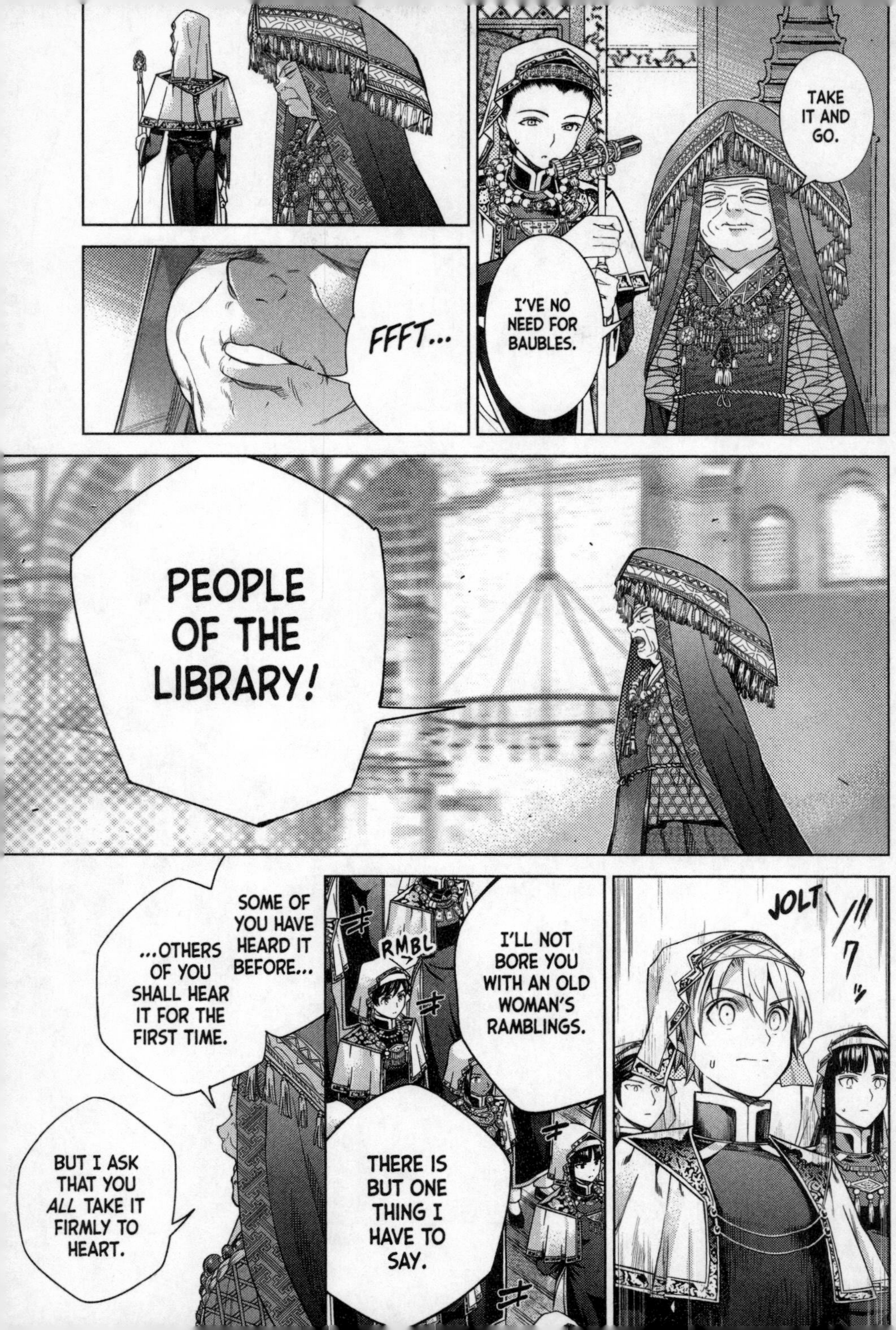
TAKE IT AND GO.
I'VE NO NEED FOR BAUBLES.
FFFT...
PEOPLE OF THE LIBRARY!
JOLT
I'LL NOT BORE YOU WITH AN OLD WOMAN'S RAMBLINGS.
RMBL
THERE IS BUT ONE THING I HAVE TO SAY.
SOME OF YOU HAVE HEARD IT BEFORE...
...OTHERS OF YOU SHALL HEAR IT FOR THE FIRST TIME.
BUT I ASK THAT YOU *ALL* TAKE IT FIRMLY TO HEART.

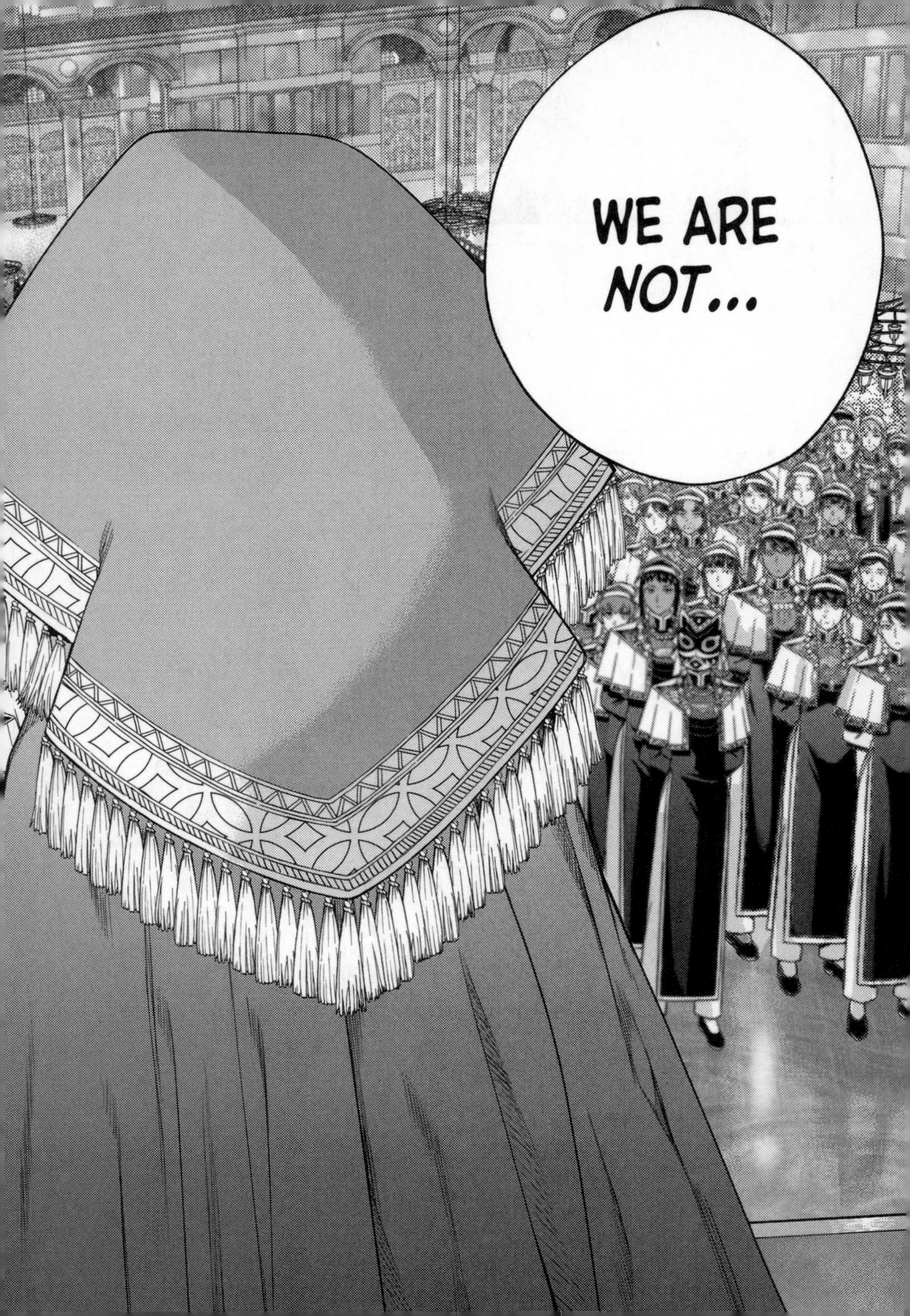
WE ARE NOT...

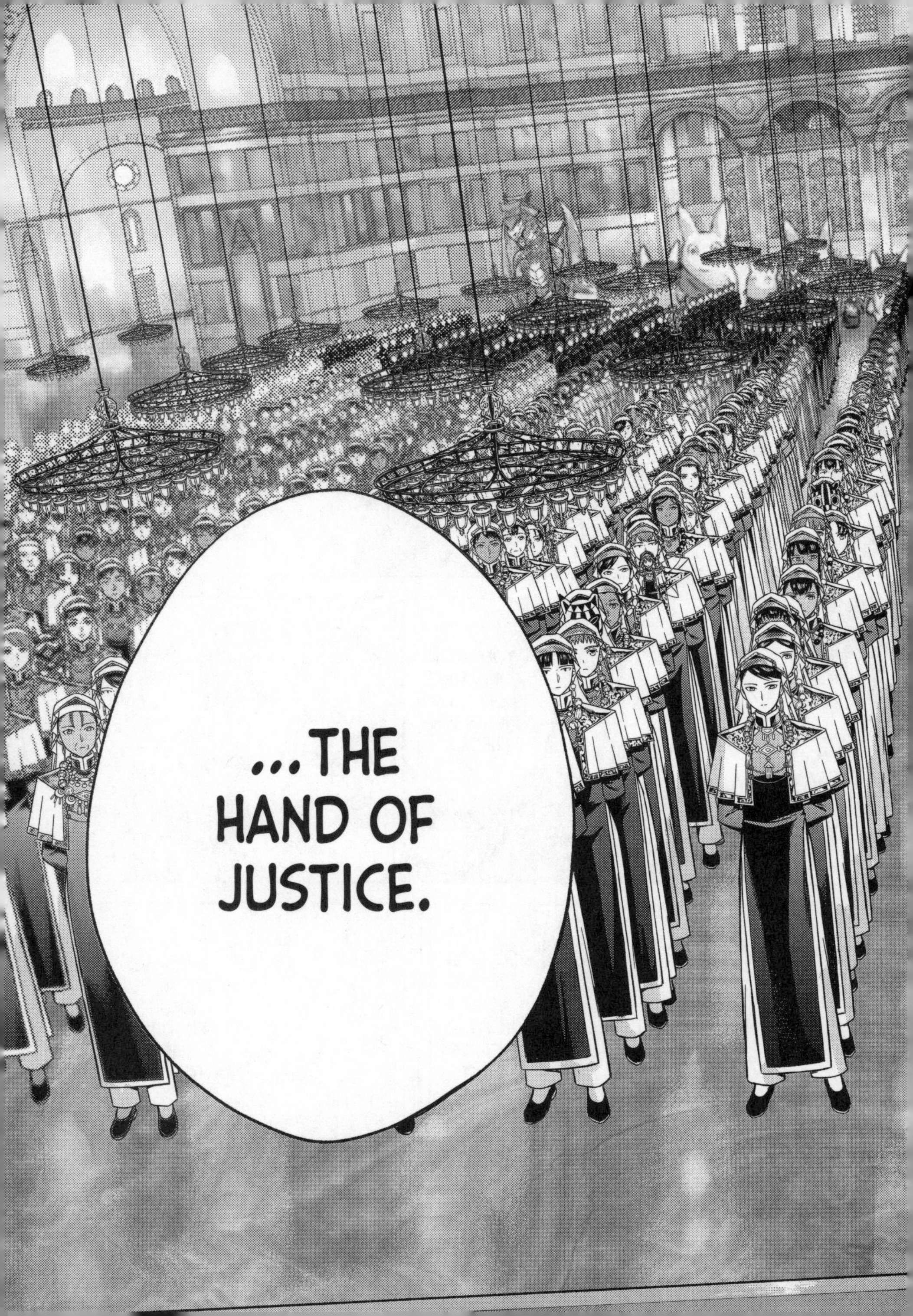
...THE HAND OF JUSTICE.

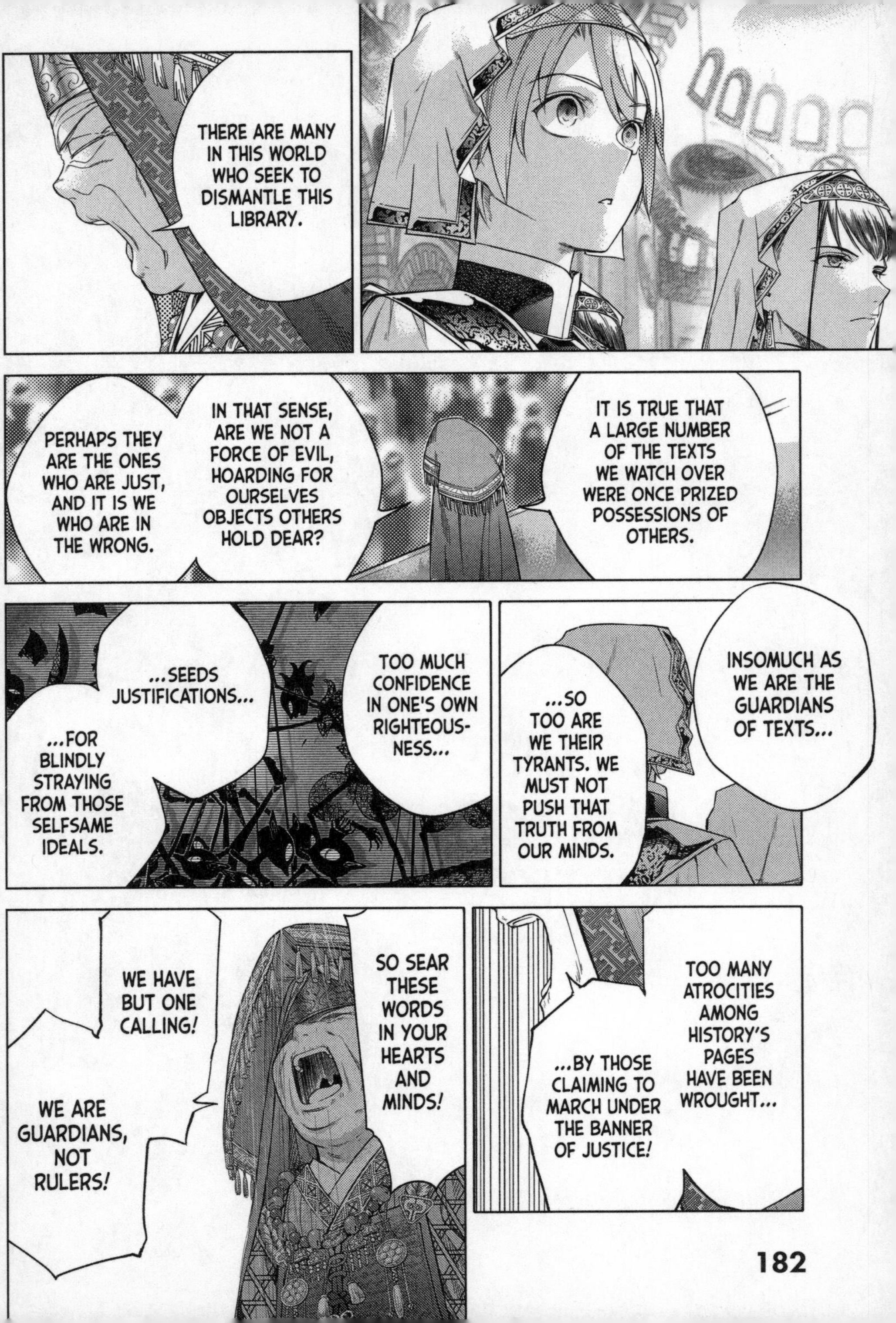
THERE ARE MANY IN THIS WORLD WHO SEEK TO DISMANTLE THIS LIBRARY.
IT IS TRUE THAT A LARGE NUMBER OF THE TEXTS WE WATCH OVER WERE ONCE PRIZED POSSESSIONS OF OTHERS.
IN THAT SENSE, ARE WE NOT A FORCE OF EVIL, HOARDING FOR OURSELVES OBJECTS OTHERS HOLD DEAR?
PERHAPS THEY ARE THE ONES WHO ARE JUST, AND IT IS WE WHO ARE IN THE WRONG.
INSOMUCH AS WE ARE THE GUARDIANS OF TEXTS...
...SO TOO ARE WE THEIR TYRANTS. WE MUST NOT PUSH THAT TRUTH FROM OUR MINDS.
TOO MUCH CONFIDENCE IN ONE'S OWN RIGHTEOUS-NESS...
...SEEDS JUSTIFICATIONS...
...FOR BLINDLY STRAYING FROM THOSE SELFSAME IDEALS.
TOO MANY ATROCITIES AMONG HISTORY'S PAGES HAVE BEEN WROUGHT...
...BY THOSE CLAIMING TO MARCH UNDER THE BANNER OF JUSTICE!
SO SEAR THESE WORDS IN YOUR HEARTS AND MINDS!
WE HAVE BUT ONE CALLING!
WE ARE GUARDIANS, NOT RULERS!

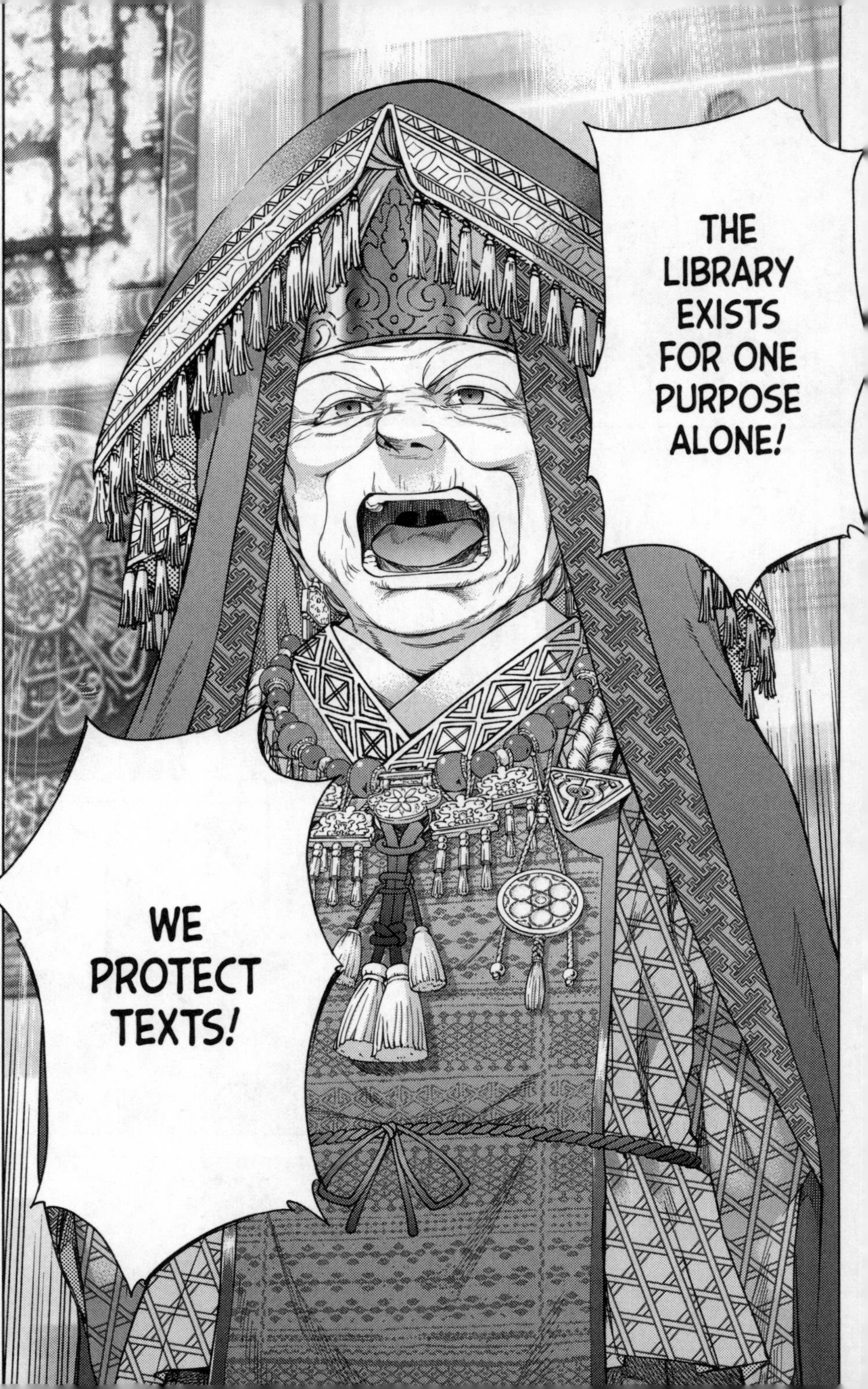
THE LIBRARY EXISTS FOR ONE PURPOSE ALONE!
WE PROTECT TEXTS!

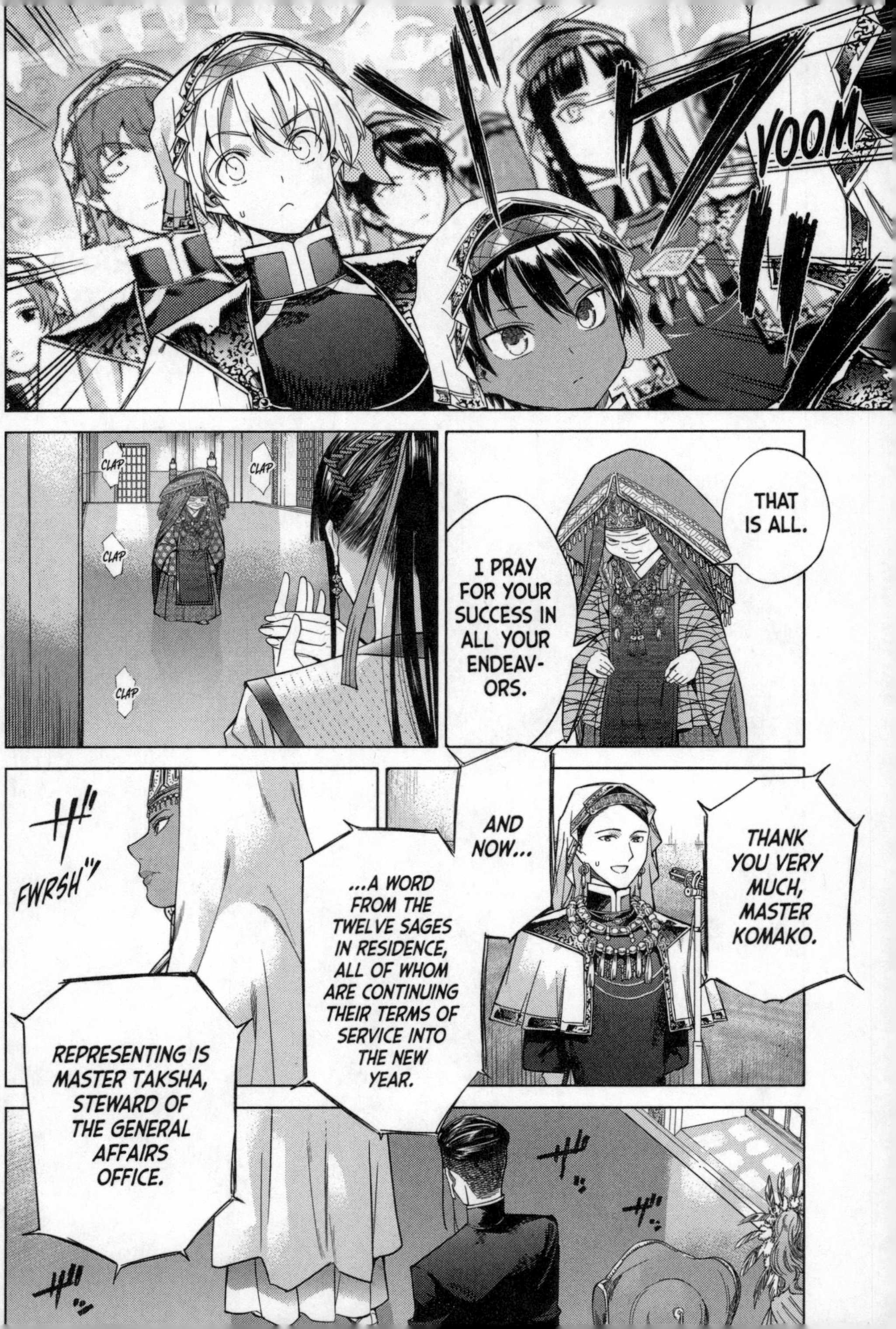
VOOM
THAT IS ALL.
I PRAY FOR YOUR SUCCESS IN ALL YOUR ENDEAV-ORS.
CLAP
CLAP
CLAP
CLAP
THANK YOU VERY MUCH, MASTER KOMAKO.
AND NOW...
...A WORD FROM THE TWELVE SAGES IN RESIDENCE, ALL OF WHOM ARE CONTINUING THEIR TERMS OF SERVICE INTO THE NEW YEAR.
FWRSH
REPRESENTING IS MASTER TAKSHA, STEWARD OF THE GENERAL AFFAIRS OFFICE.

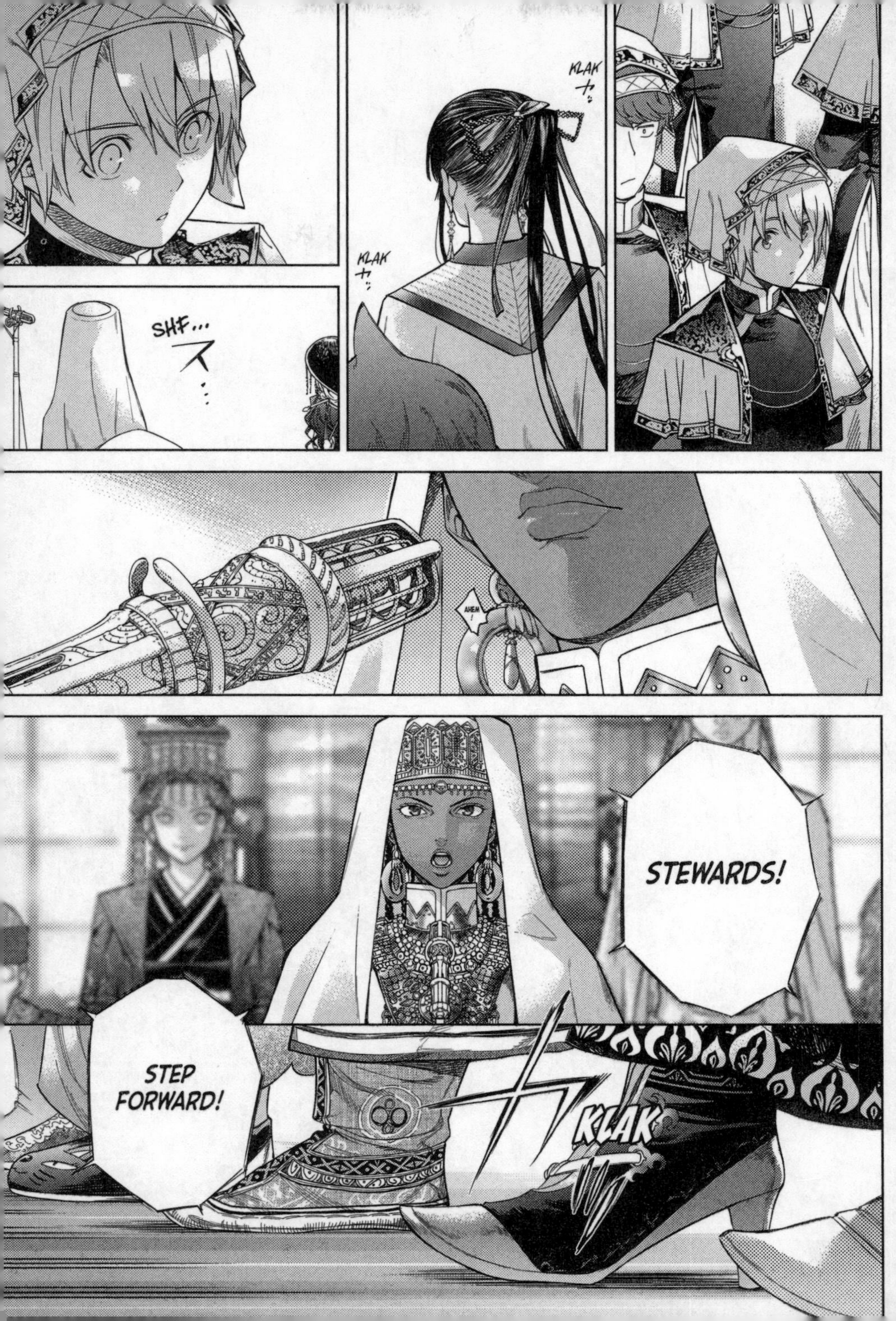
KLAK
KLAK
SHF...
AHEM!
STEWARDS!
STEP FORWARD!
KLAK

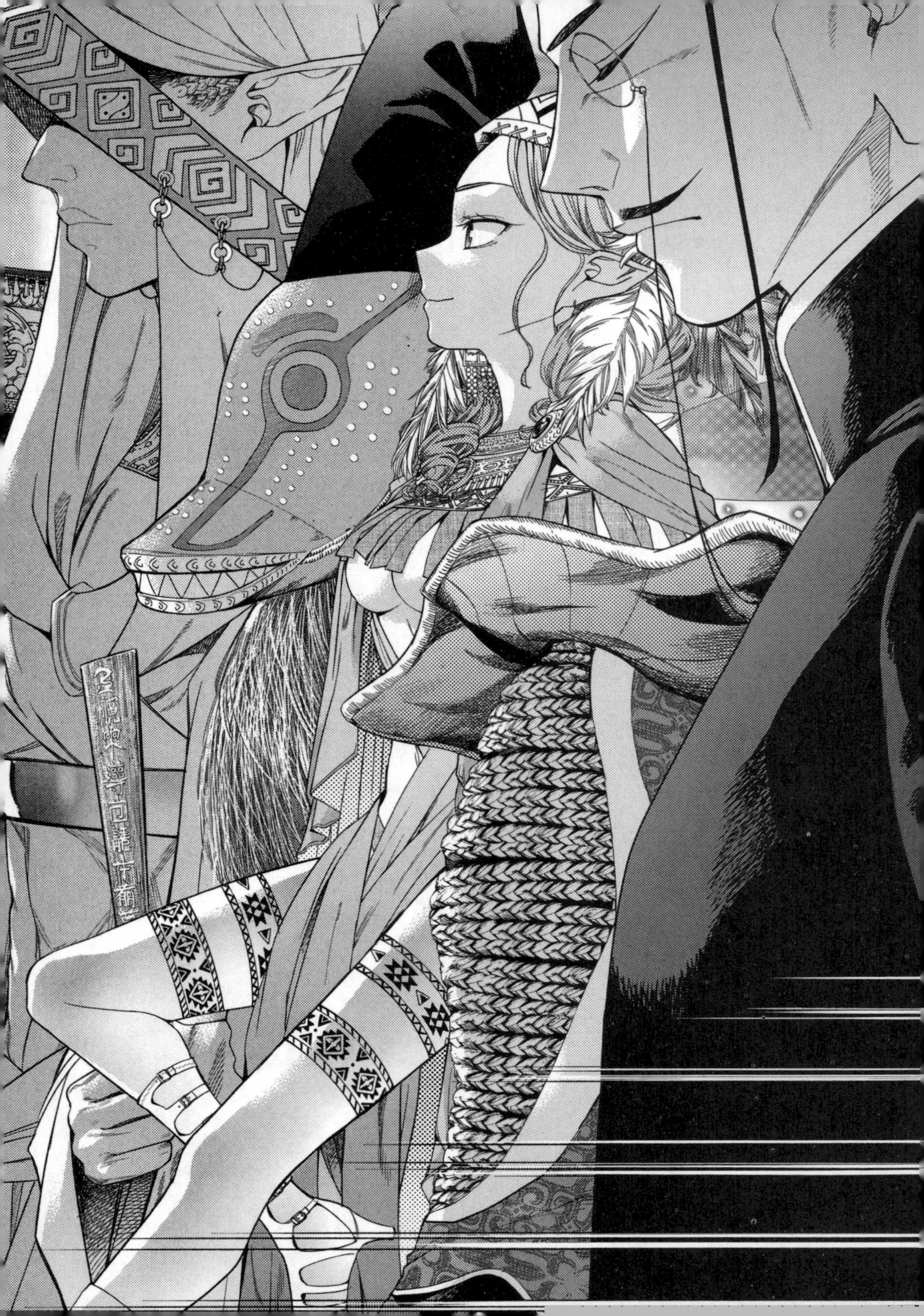

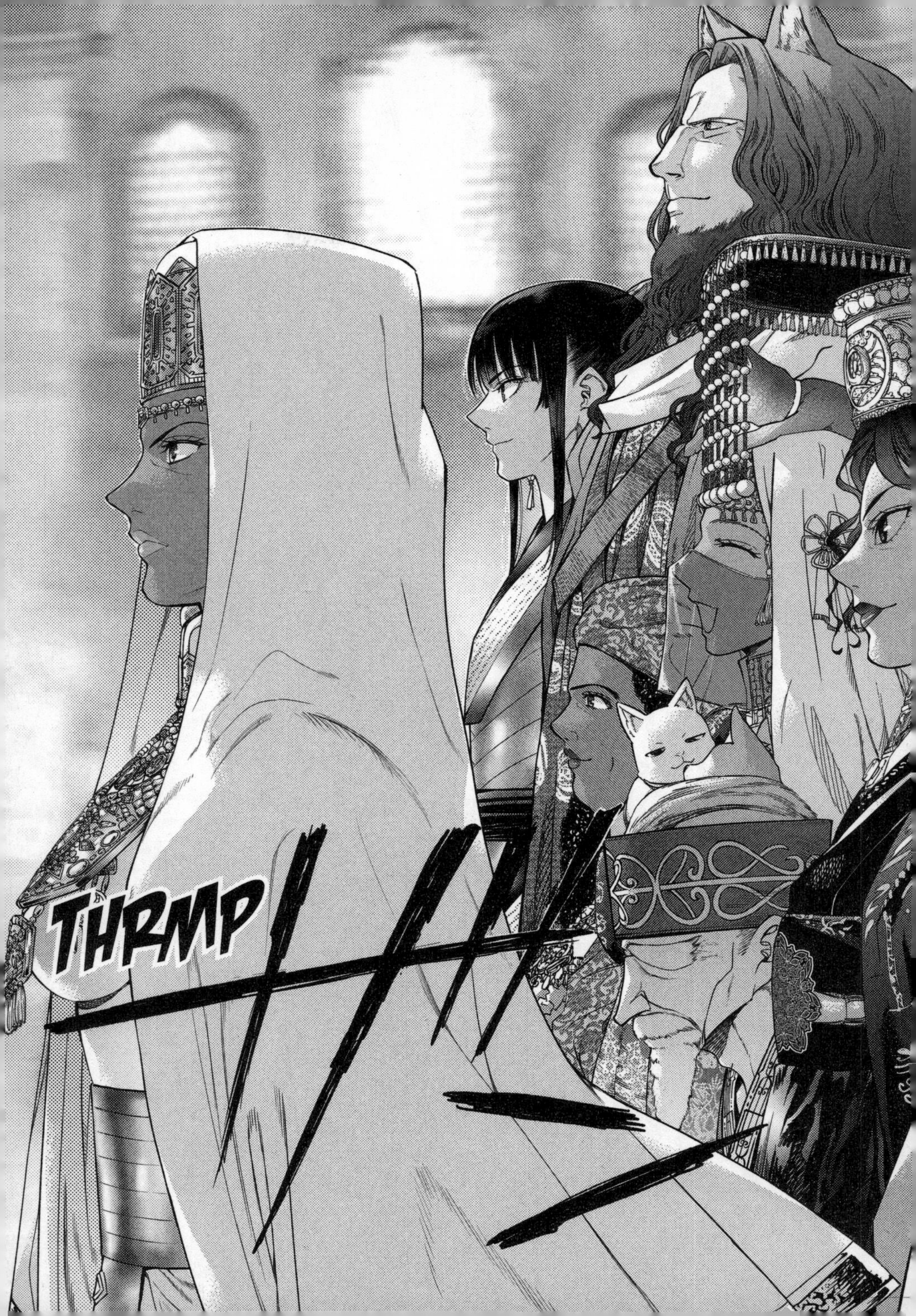
THRMP

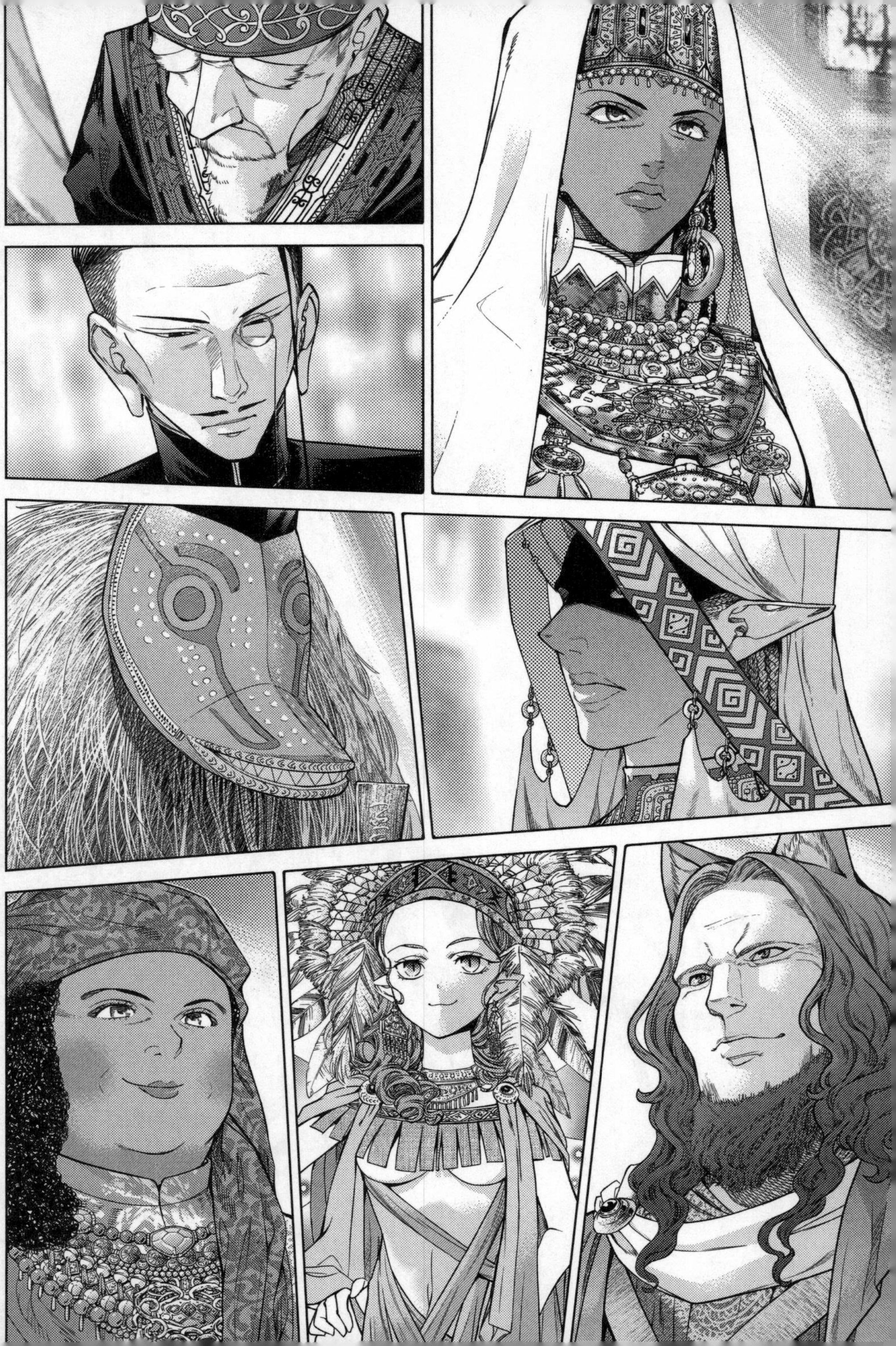

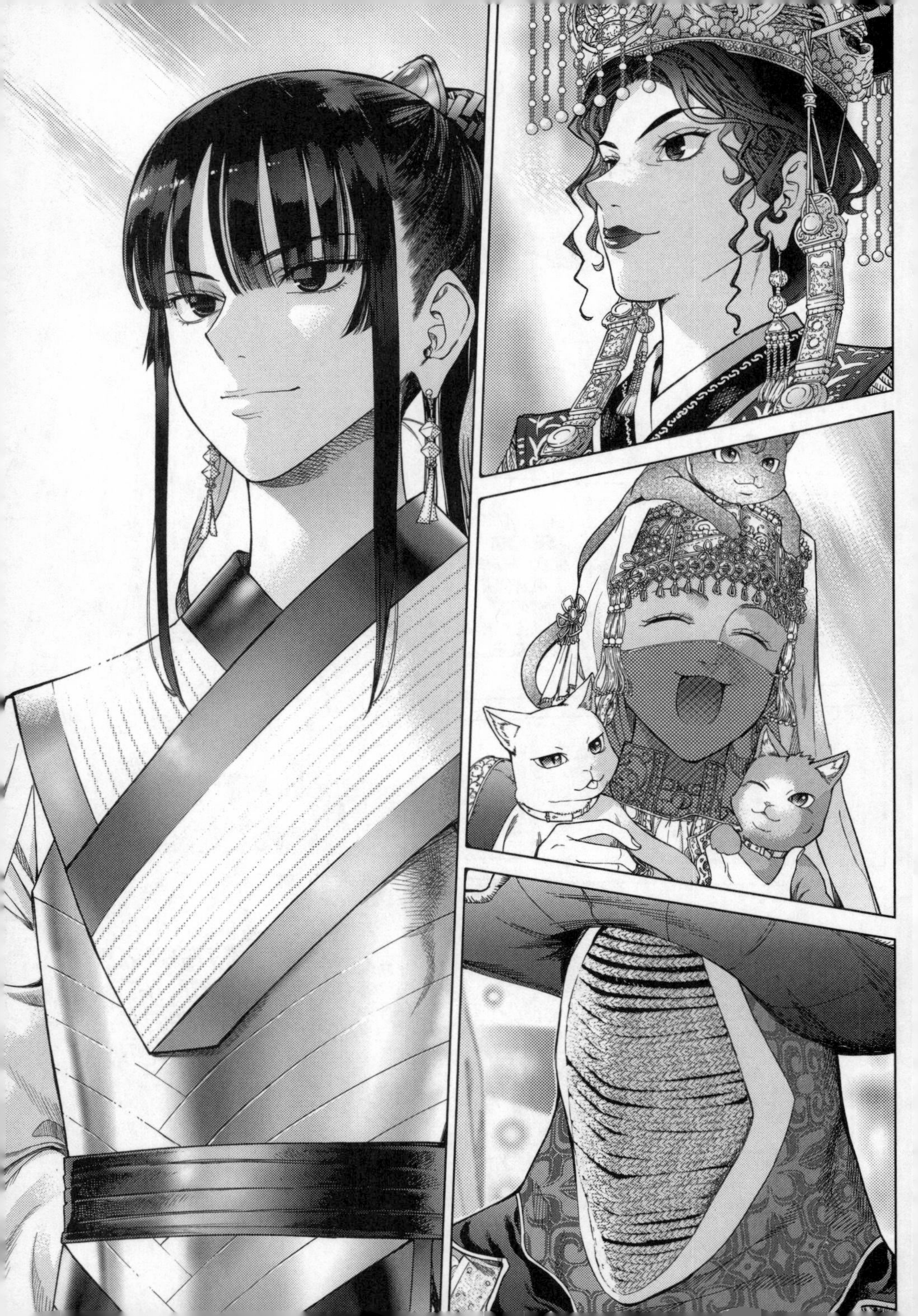

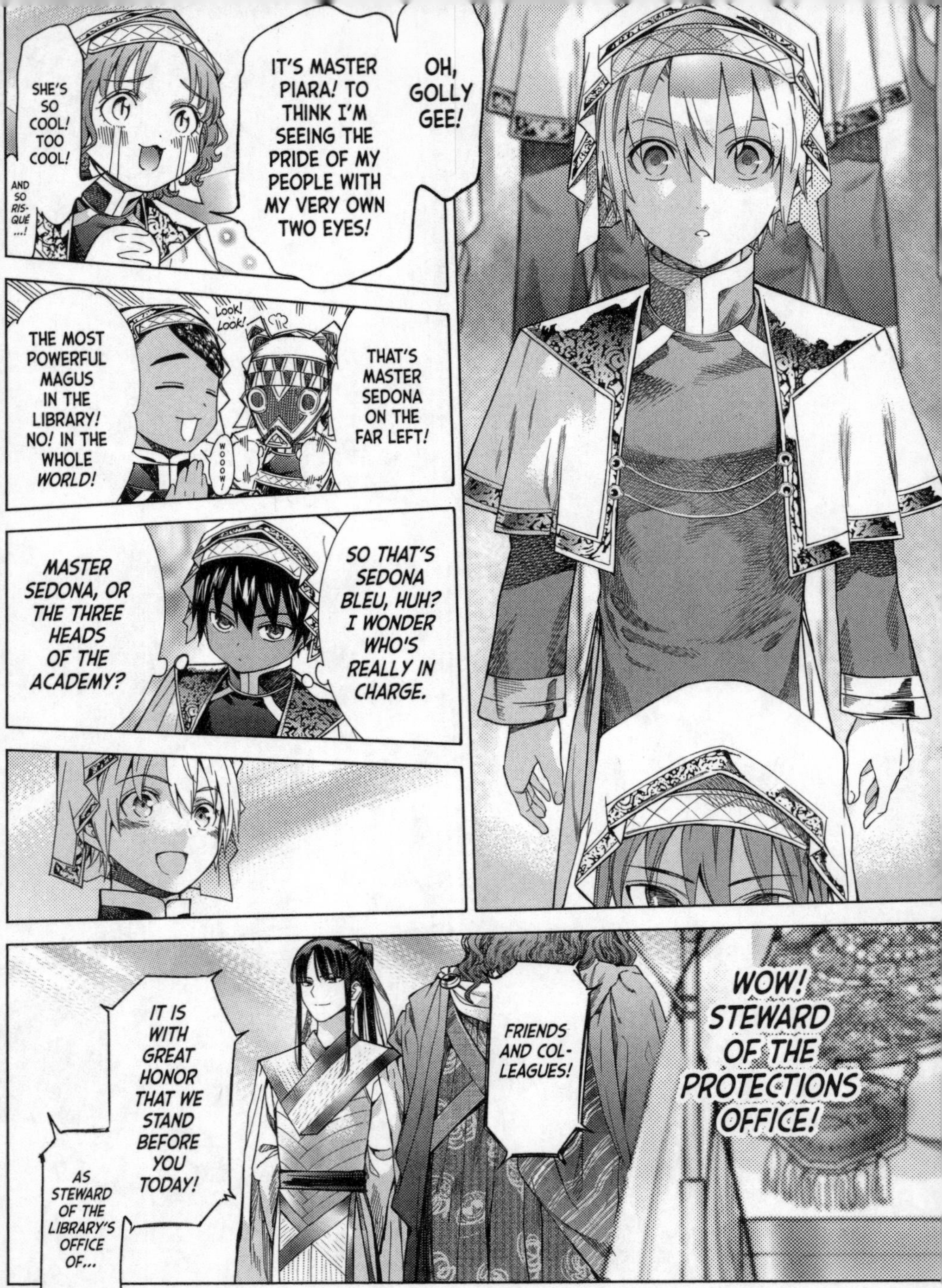
OH, GOLLY GEE!
IT'S MASTER PIARA! TO THINK I'M SEEING THE PRIDE OF MY PEOPLE WITH MY VERY OWN TWO EYES!
SHE'S SO COOL! TOO COOL!
AND SO RISQUÉ ...!
THAT'S MASTER SEDONA ON THE FAR LEFT!
LOOK! LOOK!
WOOOW!
THE MOST POWERFUL MAGUS IN THE LIBRARY! NO! IN THE WHOLE WORLD!
SO THAT'S SEDONA BLEU, HUH? I WONDER WHO'S REALLY IN CHARGE.
MASTER SEDONA, OR THE THREE HEADS OF THE ACADEMY?
WOW! STEWARD OF THE PROTECTIONS OFFICE!
FRIENDS AND COLLEAGUES!
IT IS WITH GREAT HONOR THAT WE STAND BEFORE YOU TODAY!
AS STEWARD OF THE LIBRARY'S OFFICE OF...

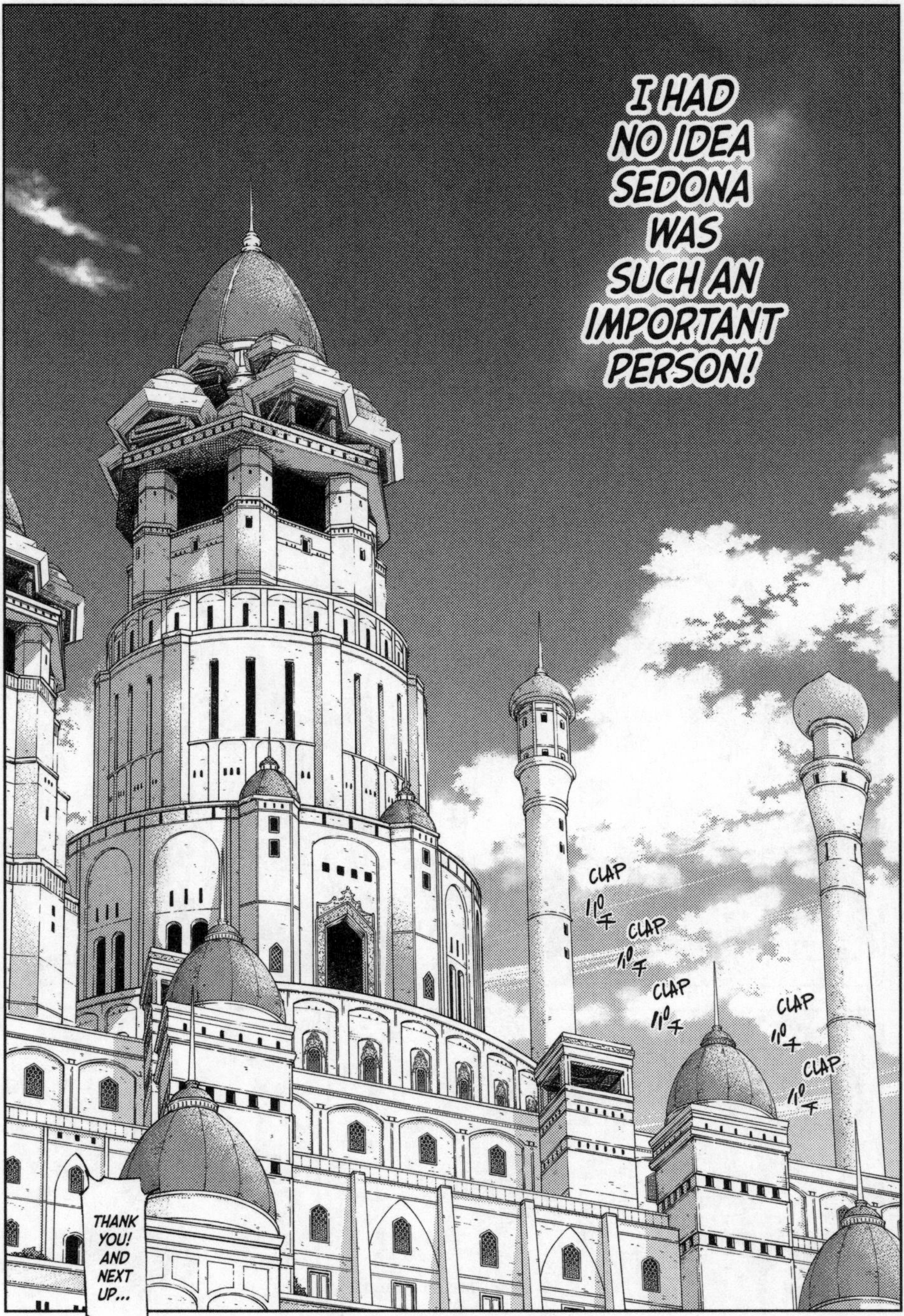
I HAD NO IDEA SEDONA WAS SUCH AN IMPORTANT PERSON!
CLAP
CLAP
CLAP
CLAP
CLAP
THANK YOU! AND NEXT UP...

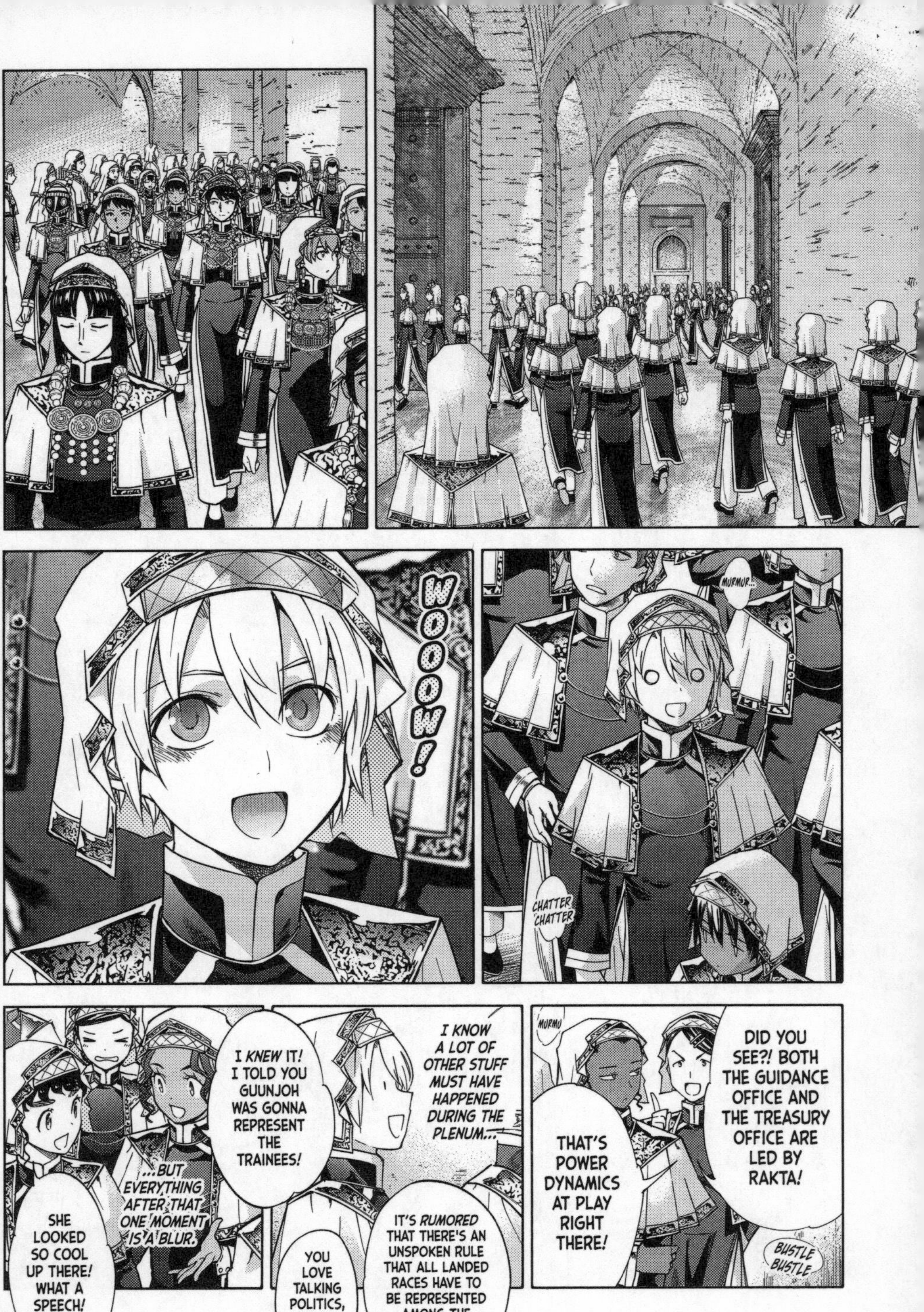
MURMUR...
CHATTER CHATTER
WOOOOW!
MURMU
DID YOU SEE?! BOTH THE GUIDANCE OFFICE AND THE TREASURY OFFICE ARE LED BY RAKTA!
THAT'S POWER DYNAMICS AT PLAY RIGHT THERE!
BUSTLE BUSTLE
I KNOW A LOT OF OTHER STUFF MUST HAVE HAPPENED DURING THE PLENUM...
IT'S RUMORED THAT THERE'S AN UNSPOKEN RULE THAT ALL LANDED RACES HAVE TO BE REPRESENTED AMONG THE SAGES, AND...
YOU LOVE TALKING POLITICS, DON'T YOU?
I KNEW IT! I TOLD YOU GUUNJOH WAS GONNA REPRESENT THE TRAINEES!
...BUT EVERYTHING AFTER THAT ONE MOMENT IS A BLUR.
SHE LOOKED SO COOL UP THERE! WHAT A SPEECH!

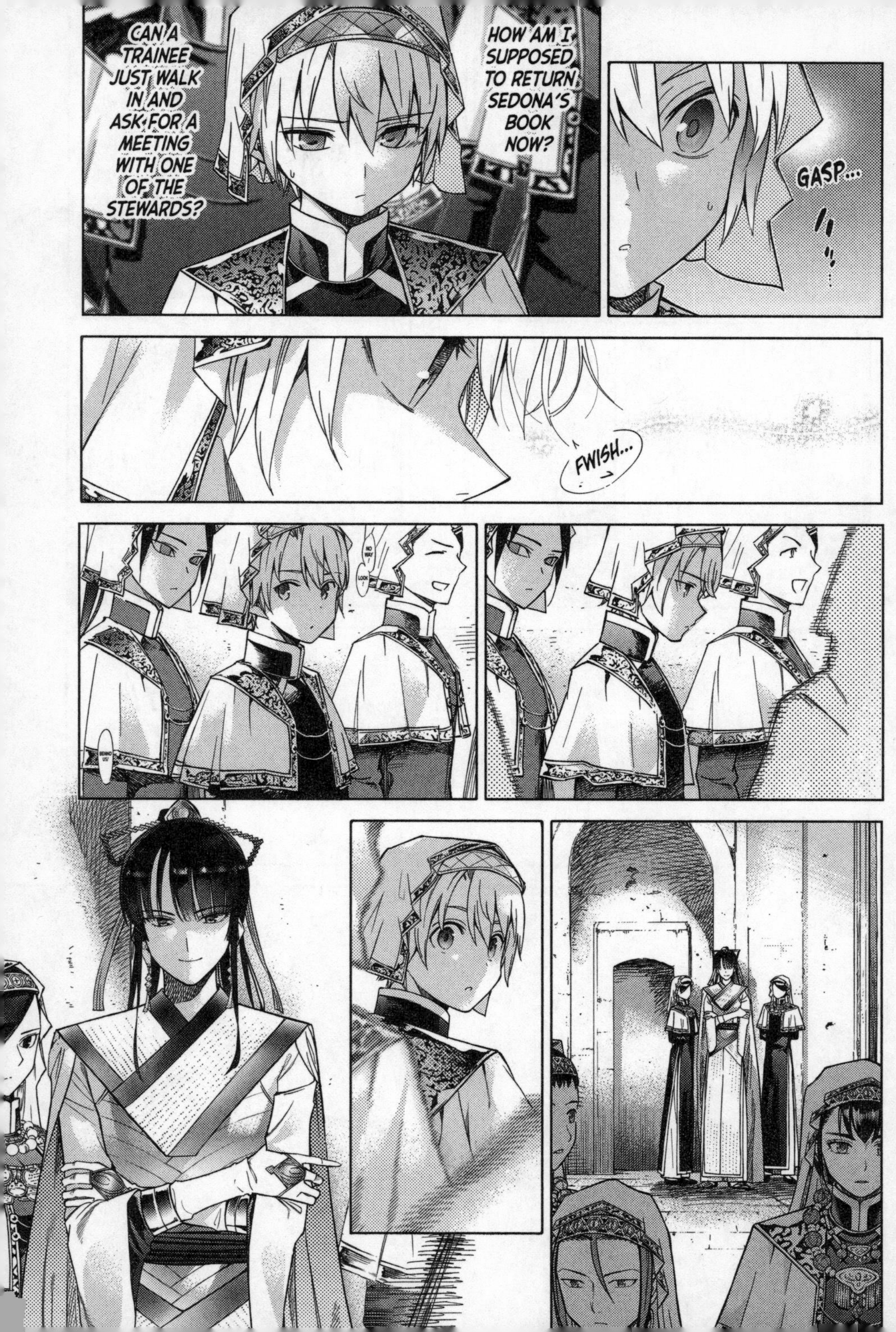
GASP...
HOW AM I SUPPOSED TO RETURN SEDONA'S BOOK NOW?
CAN A TRAINEE JUST WALK IN AND ASK FOR A MEETING WITH ONE OF THE STEWARDS?
FWISH...
NO WAY!
LOOK!
BEHIND US!

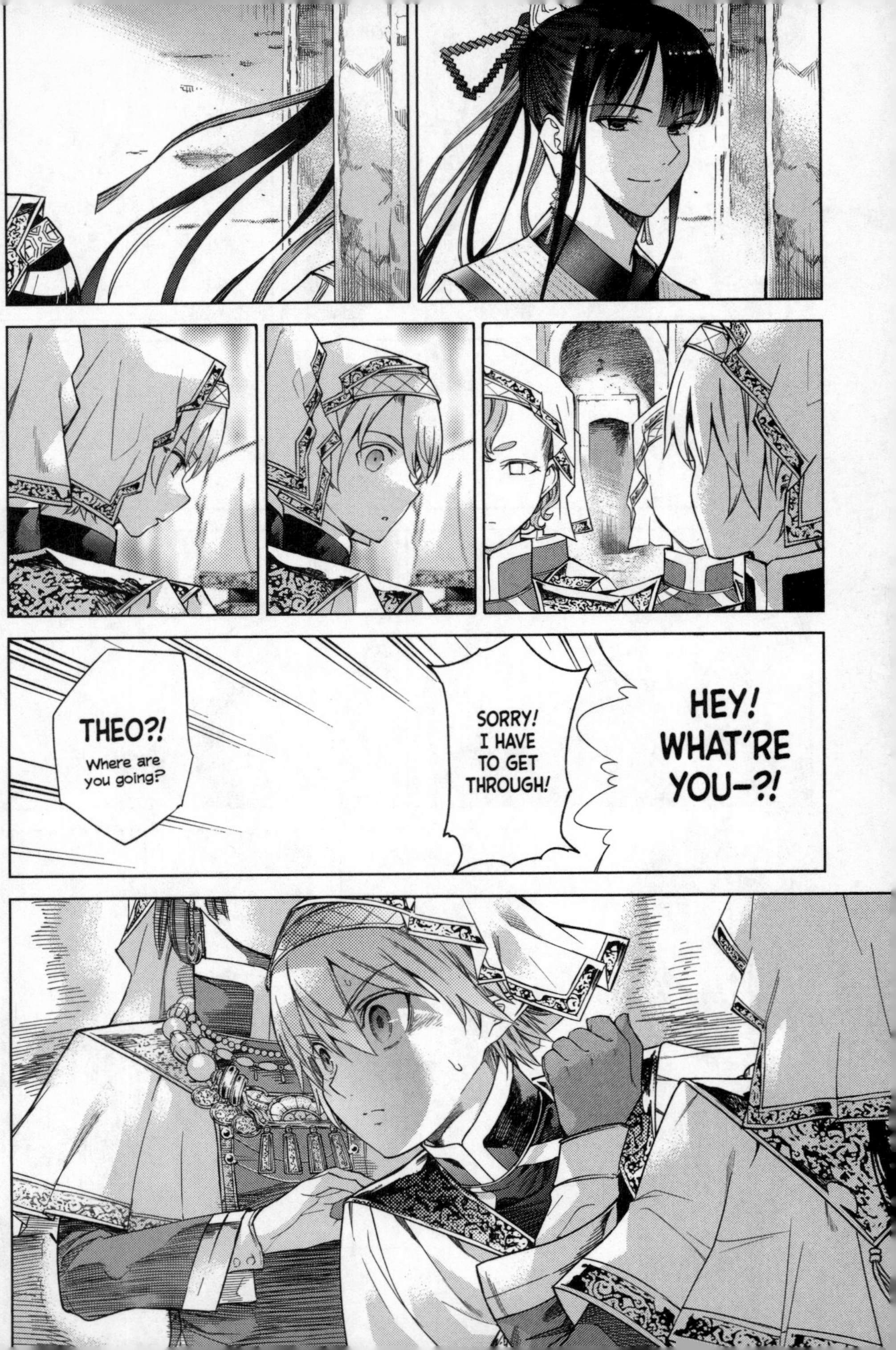
HEY! WHAT'RE YOU–?!
SORRY! I HAVE TO GET THROUGH!
THEO?! Where are you going?

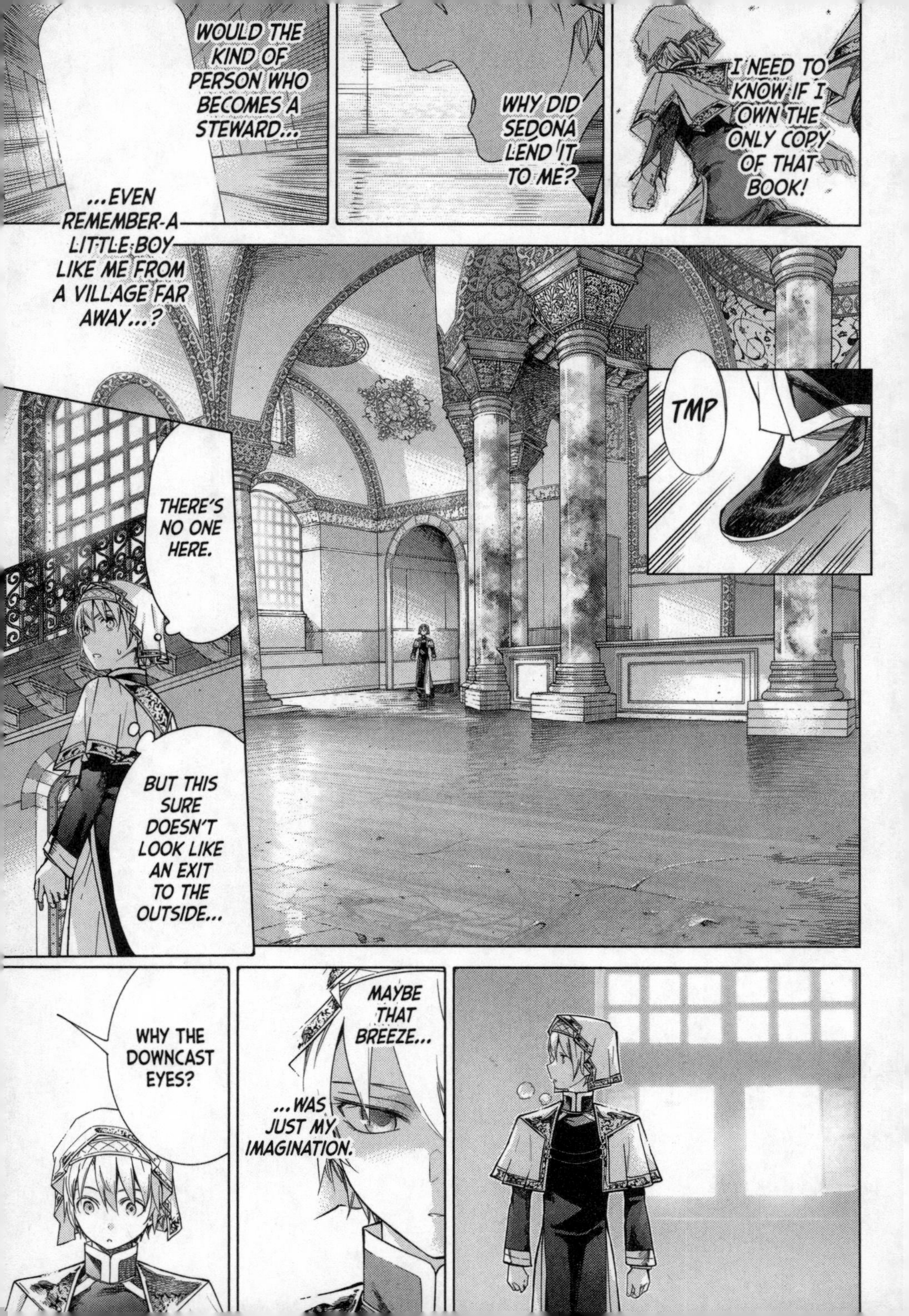
I NEED TO KNOW IF I OWN THE ONLY COPY OF THAT BOOK!
WHY DID SEDONA LEND IT TO ME?
WOULD THE KIND OF PERSON WHO BECOMES A STEWARD...
...EVEN REMEMBER A LITTLE BOY LIKE ME FROM A VILLAGE FAR AWAY...?
TMP
THERE'S NO ONE HERE.
BUT THIS SURE DOESN'T LOOK LIKE AN EXIT TO THE OUTSIDE...
MAYBE THAT BREEZE...
...WAS JUST MY IMAGINATION.
WHY THE DOWNCAST EYES?

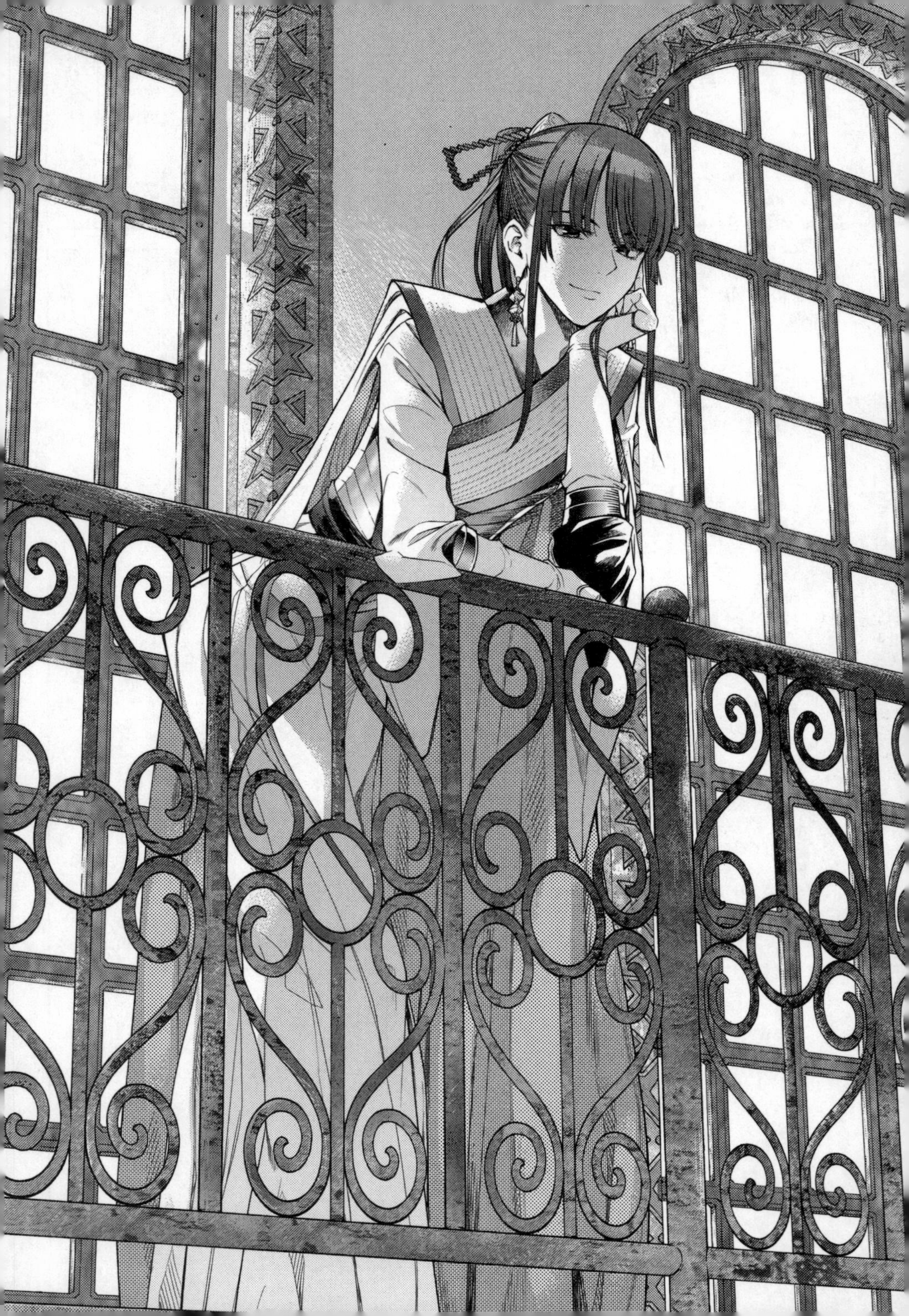

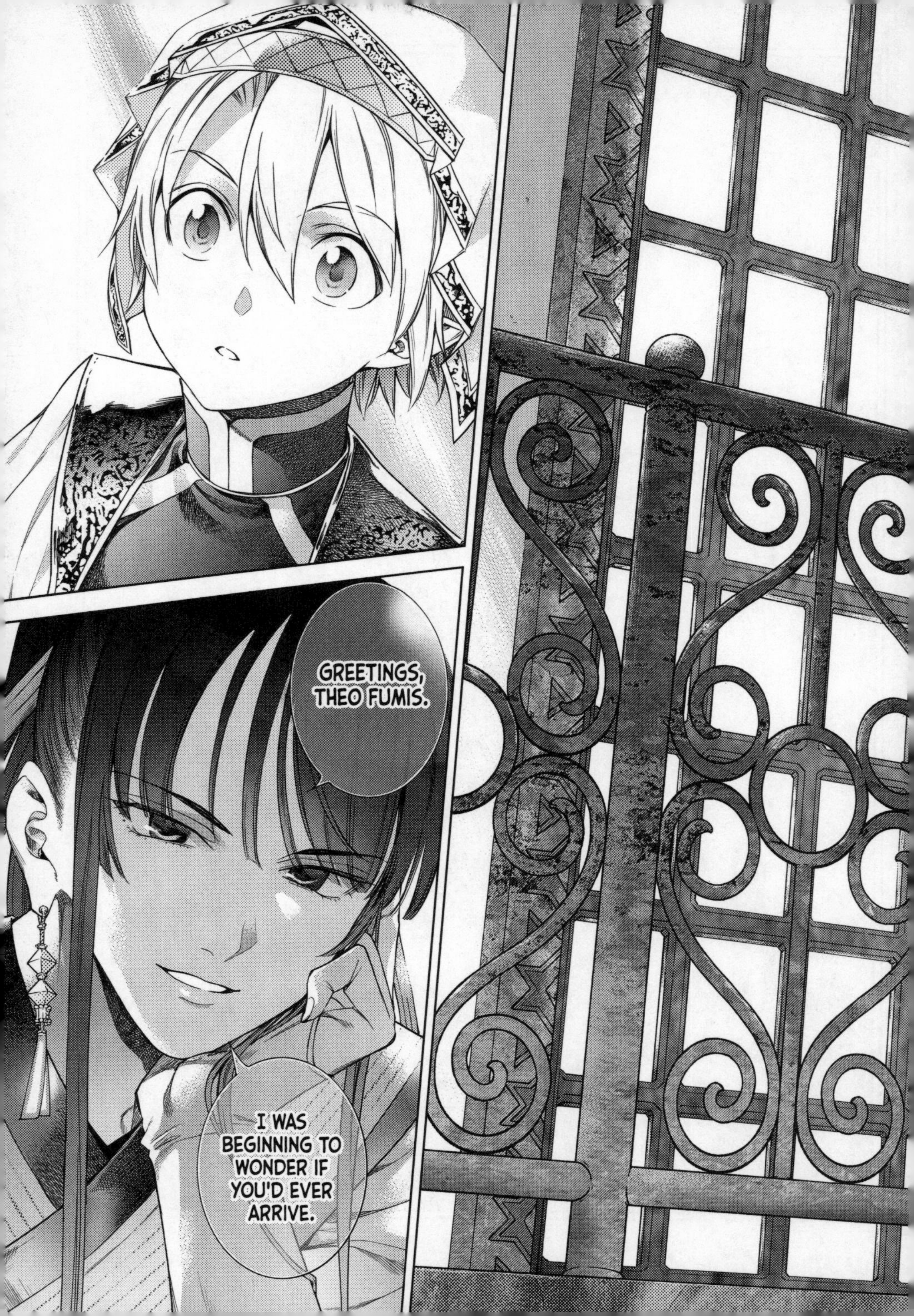
GREETINGS, THEO FUMIS.
I WAS BEGINNING TO WONDER IF YOU'D EVER ARRIVE.

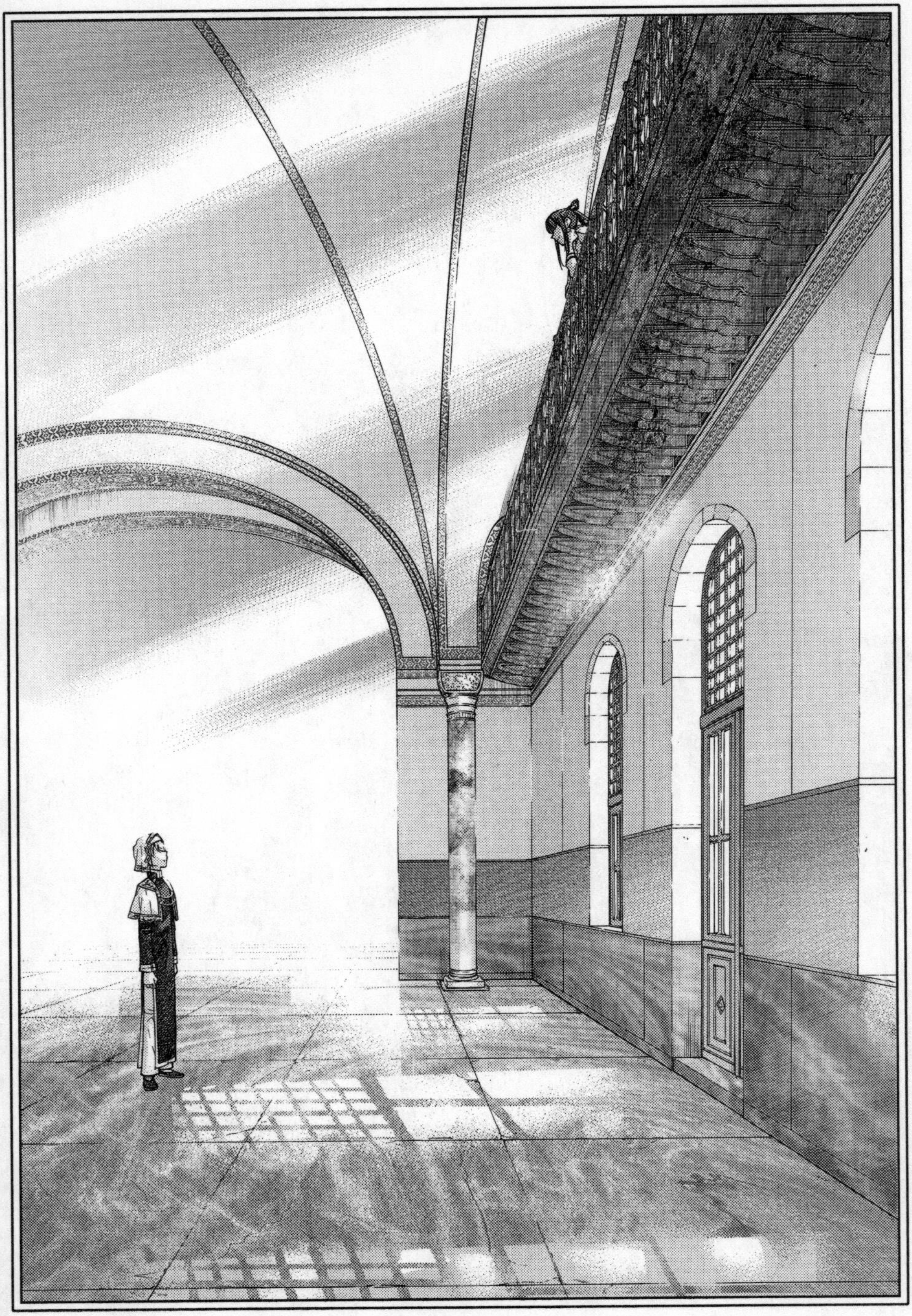

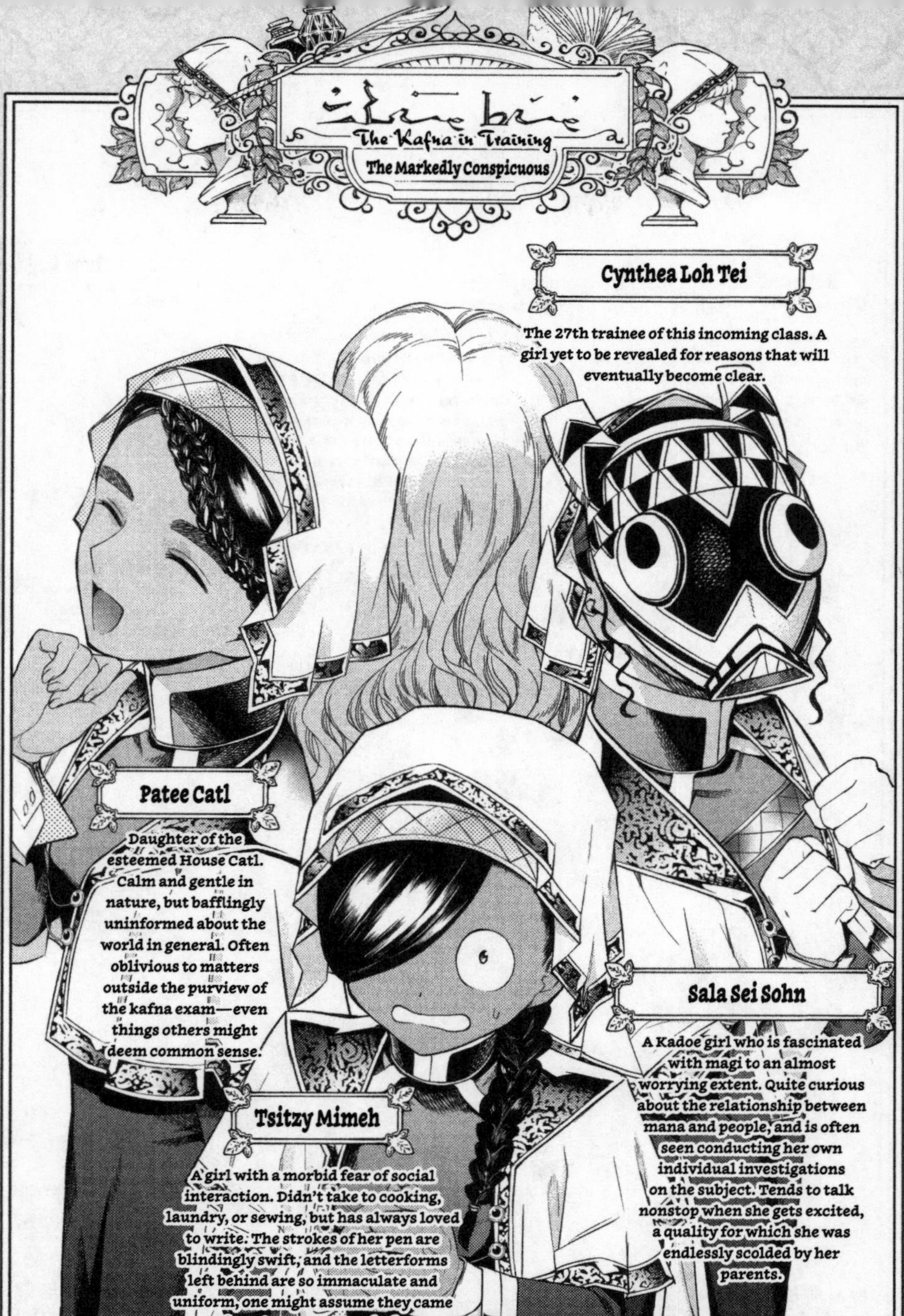
The Kafna in Training
The Markedly Conspicuous
Cynthea Loh Tei
The 27th trainee of this incoming class. A girl yet to be revealed for reasons that will eventually become clear.
Patee Catl
Daughter of the esteemed House Catl. Calm and gentle in nature, but bafflingly uninformed about the world in general. Often oblivious to matters outside the purview of the kafna exam—even things others might deem common sense.
Sala Sei Sohn
A Kadoe girl who is fascinated with magi to an almost worrying extent. Quite curious about the relationship between mana and people, and is often seen conducting her own individual investigations on the subject. Tends to talk nonstop when she gets excited, a quality for which she was endlessly scolded by her parents.
Tsitzy Mimeh
A girl with a morbid fear of social interaction. Didn't take to cooking, laundry, or sewing, but has always loved to write. The strokes of her pen are blindingly swift, and the letterforms left behind are so immaculate and uniform, one might assume they came from type on a press bed.

The Kafna in Training
The Guiding Hands

Rei Ana Edan

A 32-year-old Kadoe. Has two children of mixed heritage with her Hyron husband. Enjoys baking sweets in her free time.

Bustas d'Kayser

A 25-year-old Creyak who is in love with falling in love. Quickly develops crushes on kohkwa, but is slow to act, instead analyzing the potential relationship to pieces, after which she determines there's no common ground to be had and moves on to the next crush. Skilled at cooking and handicrafts.

Chise Redd

A 43-year-old Rakta woman and the deputy head supervisor for the current class of trainees. An expert swordfighter as well as a kafna, and qualified as an instructor at the swordfighting academy run by her family. Immensely strict with herself; with others, strict but fair.

Puputo Raputabbis

A 29-year-old Kokopah and the only male supervisor for the trainees this year. Perpetually bears a sullen expression, and is thus easily misconstrued as being in a sour mood—a fact that bothers him a little, as that's just how his face naturally rests!

Xtoh Seros

A 58-year-old Hyron and the head supervisor responsible for the education of the current batch of trainees. Feared by some for her reputation as the rulu owlai—the tremor that treads lightly. Silent and delicate at times; ferociously intimidating at others.

Aiko Joramis

A 17-year-old Hyron who easily gets along with anyone regardless of gender or age, but who is superbly unsubtle. Can't take a hint, and is the perpetrator of many an awkward silence. A source of grief for the other supervisors, as three days after being lectured, she's back to doing whatever warranted a lecture in the first place.

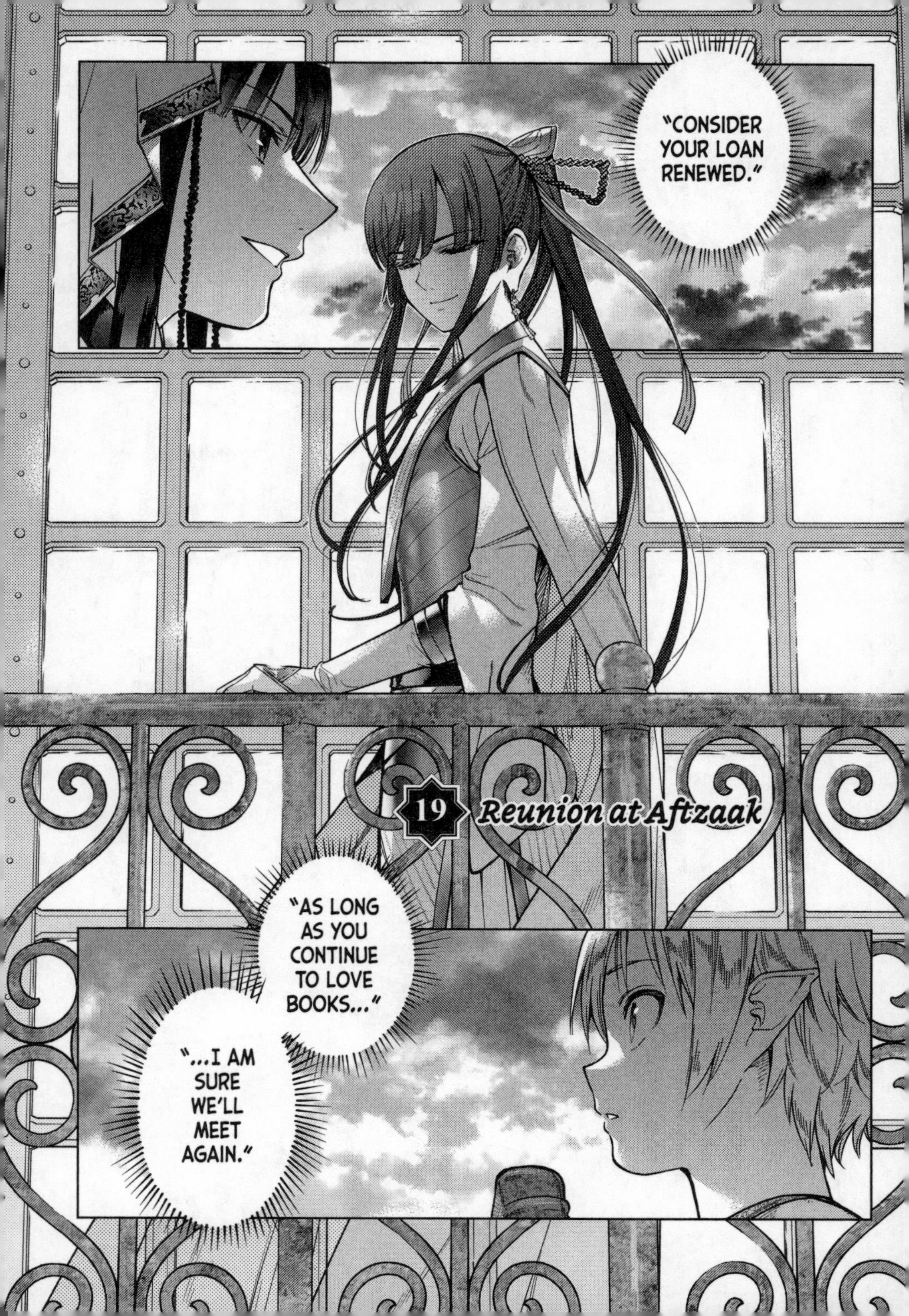
"CONSIDER YOUR LOAN RENEWED."
19 Reunion at Aftzaak
"AS LONG AS YOU CONTINUE TO LOVE BOOKS..."
"...I AM SURE WE'LL MEET AGAIN."

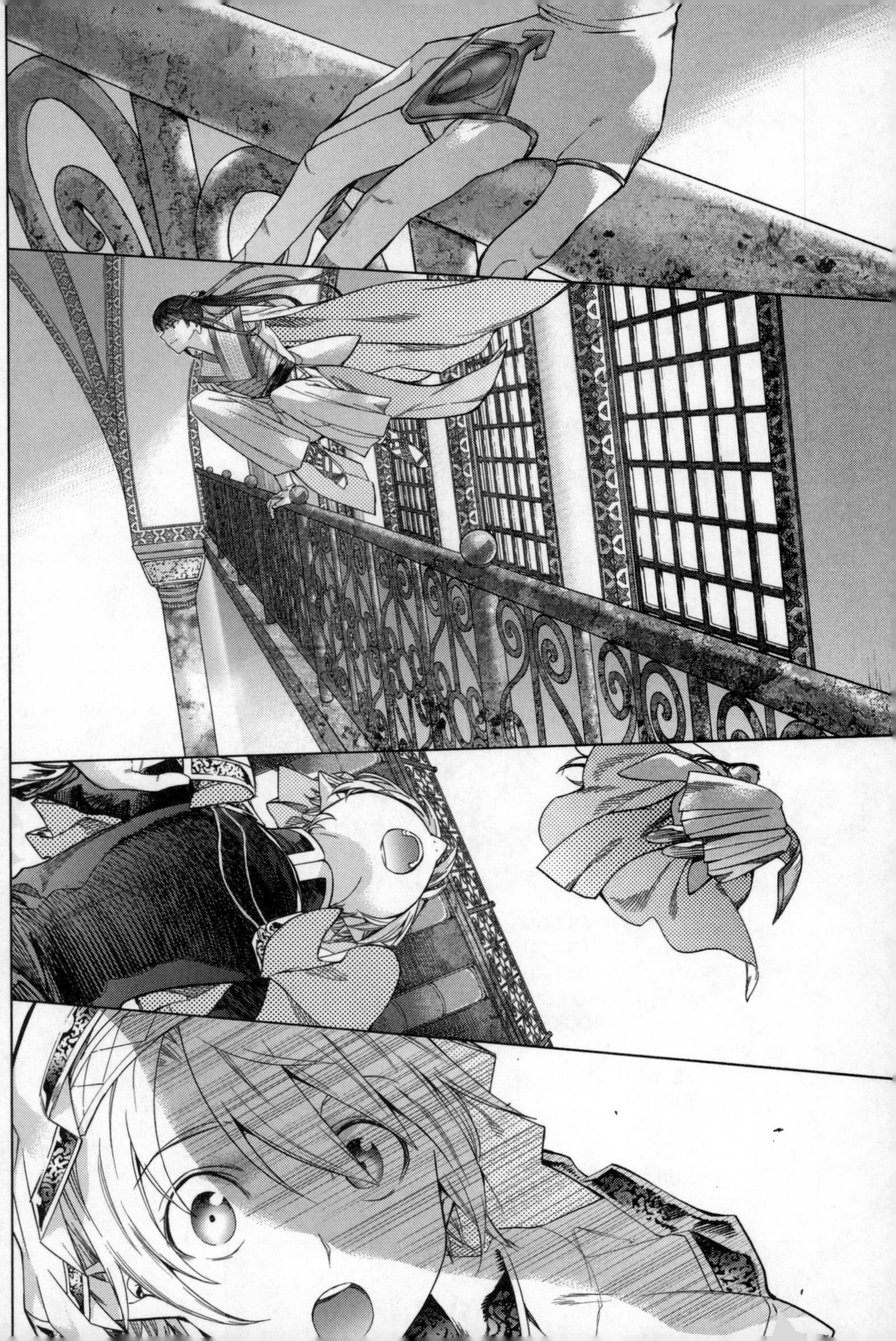

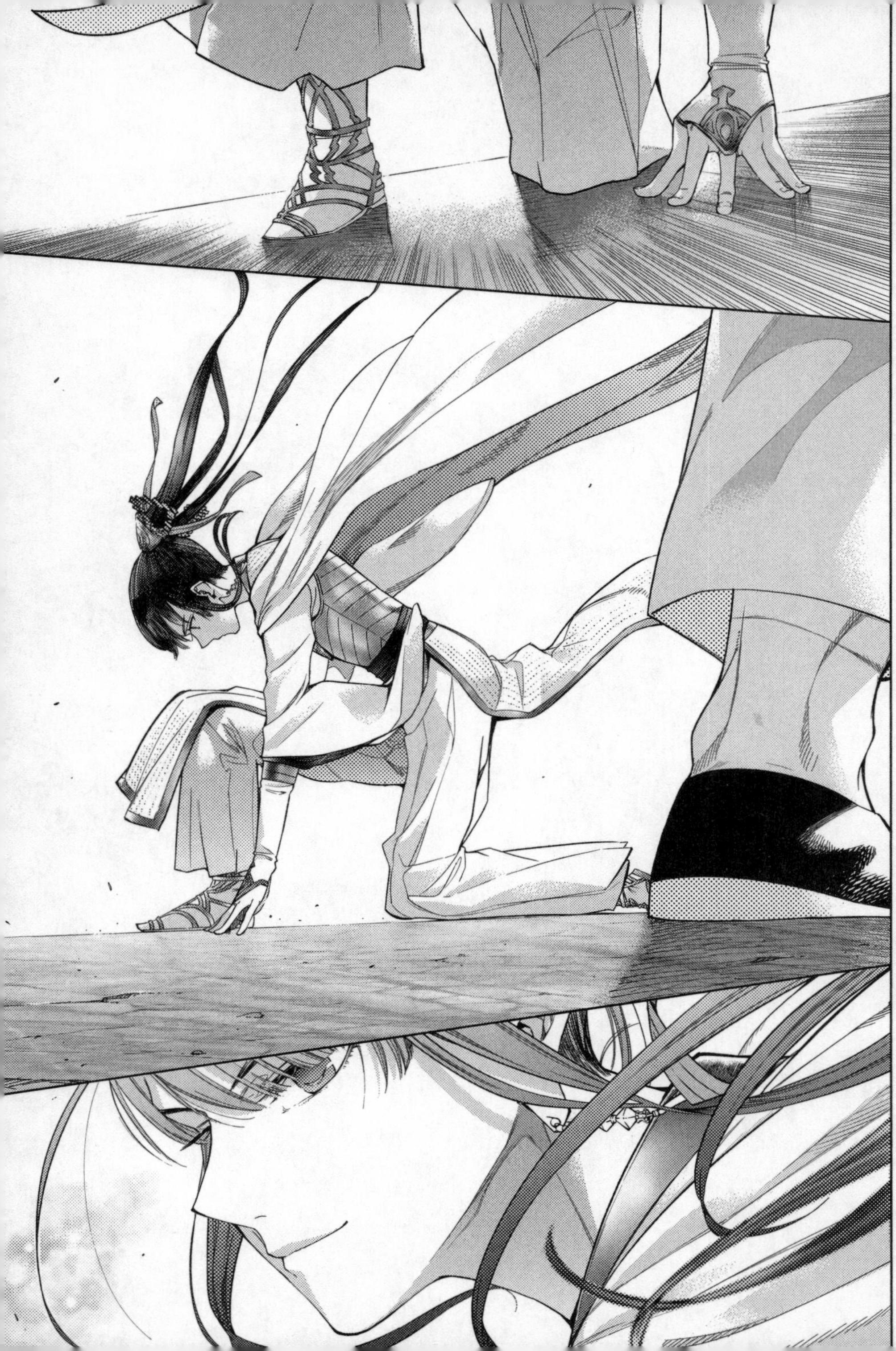

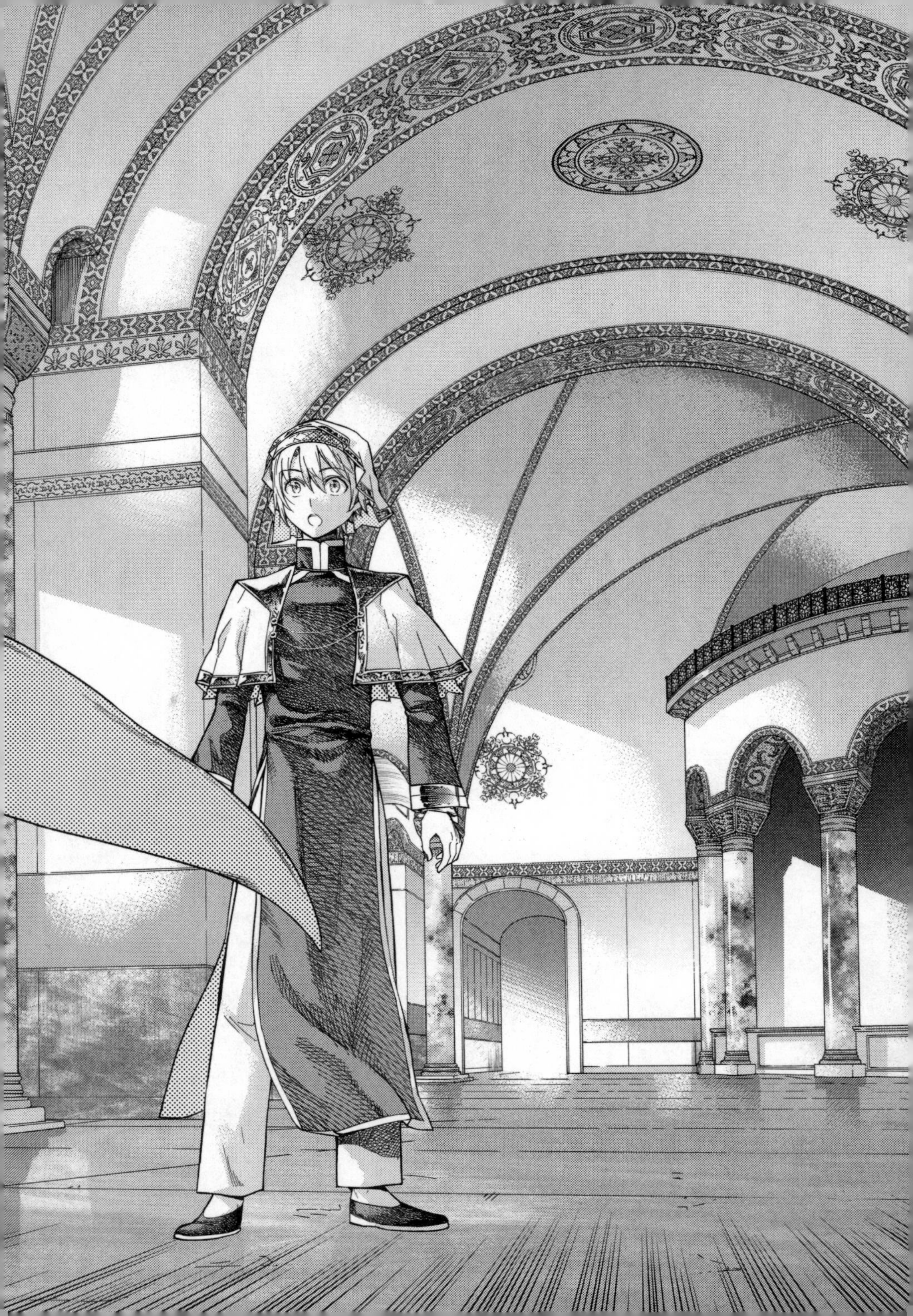

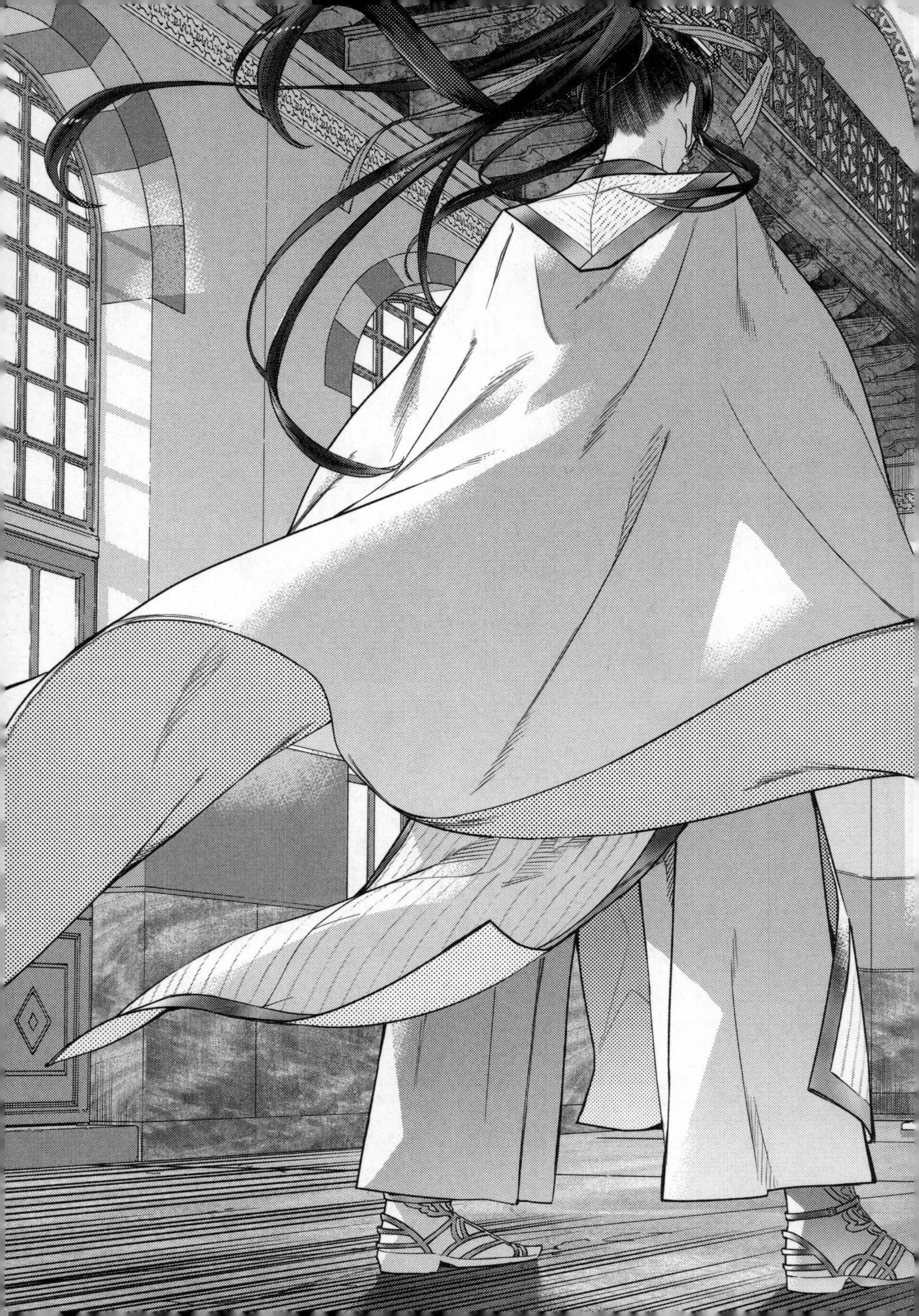

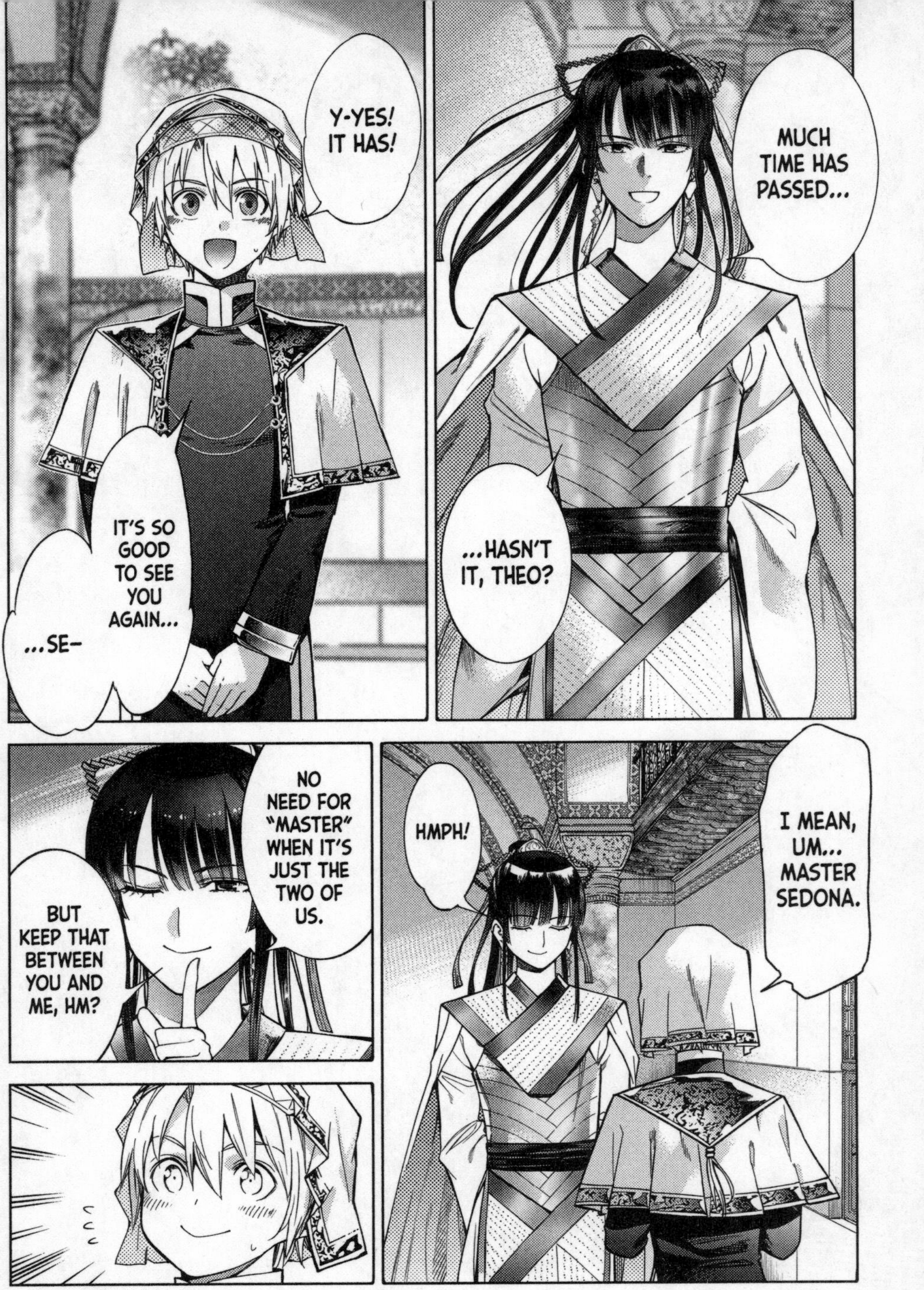
MUCH TIME HAS PASSED...
...HASN'T IT, THEO?
Y-YES! IT HAS!
IT'S SO GOOD TO SEE YOU AGAIN...
...SE-
I MEAN, UM... MASTER SEDONA.
HMPH!
NO NEED FOR "MASTER" WHEN IT'S JUST THE TWO OF US.
BUT KEEP THAT BETWEEN YOU AND ME, HM?

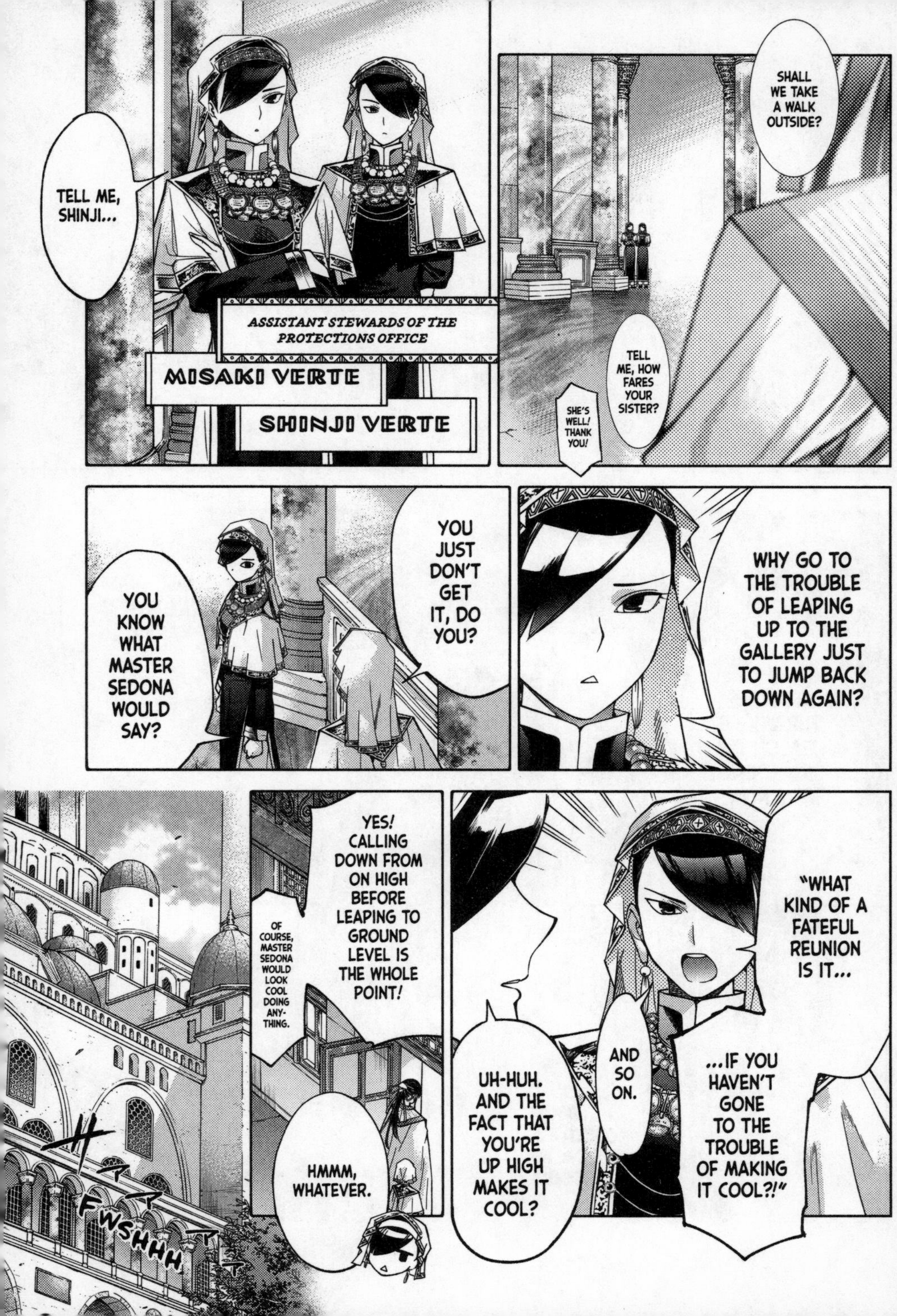
SHALL WE TAKE A WALK OUTSIDE?
TELL ME, HOW FARES YOUR SISTER?
SHE'S WELL! THANK YOU!
TELL ME, SHINJI...
ASSISTANT STEWARDS OF THE PROTECTIONS OFFICE
MISAKI VERTE
SHINJI VERTE
WHY GO TO THE TROUBLE OF LEAPING UP TO THE GALLERY JUST TO JUMP BACK DOWN AGAIN?
YOU JUST DON'T GET IT, DO YOU?
YOU KNOW WHAT MASTER SEDONA WOULD SAY?
"WHAT KIND OF A FATEFUL REUNION IS IT...
...IF YOU HAVEN'T GONE TO THE TROUBLE OF MAKING IT COOL?!"
AND SO ON.
UH-HUH. AND THE FACT THAT YOU'RE UP HIGH MAKES IT COOL?
YES! CALLING DOWN FROM ON HIGH BEFORE LEAPING TO GROUND LEVEL IS THE WHOLE POINT!
OF COURSE, MASTER SEDONA WOULD LOOK COOL DOING ANY-THING.
HMMM, WHATEVER.
FWSHHH

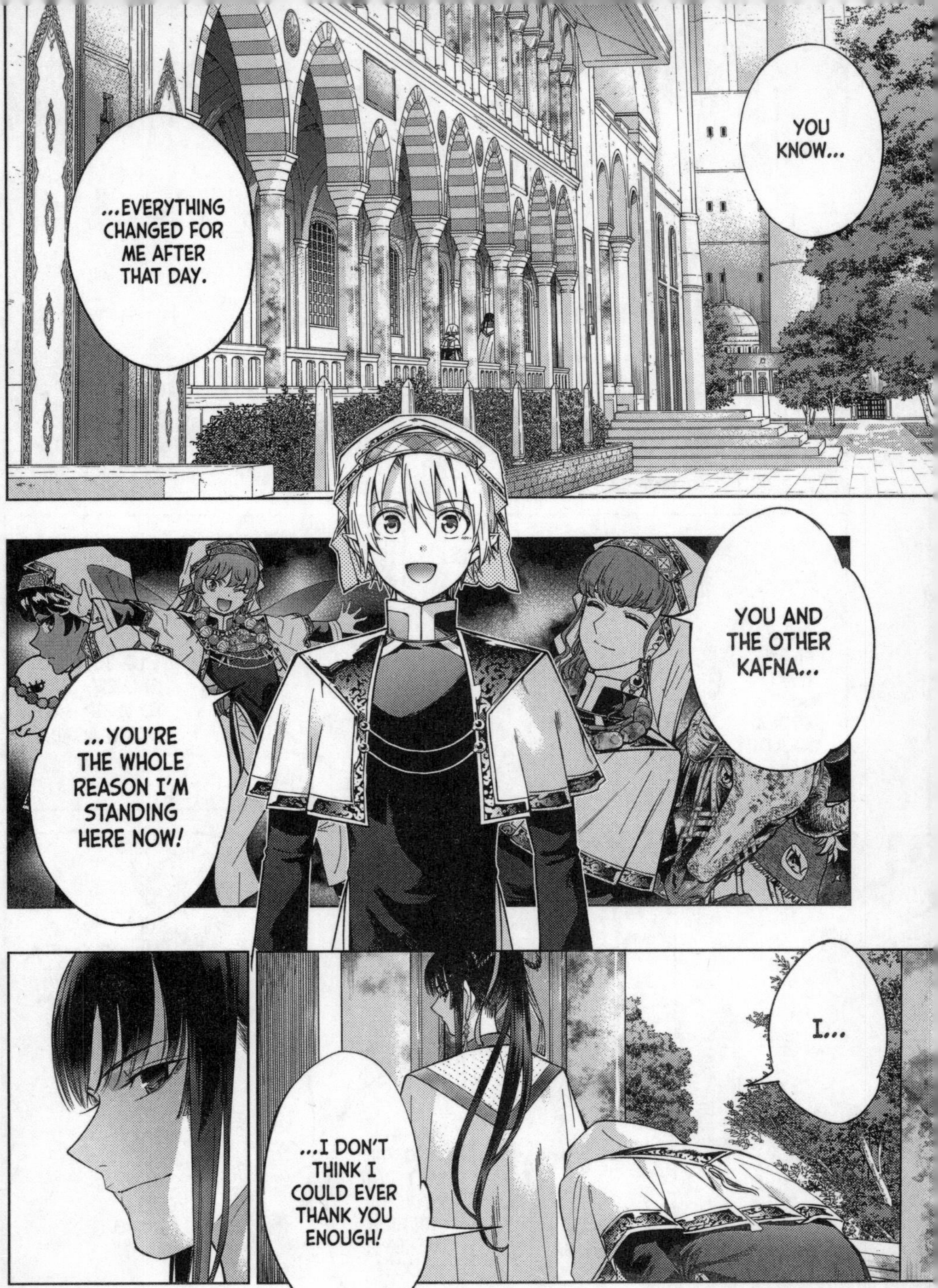
YOU KNOW...
...EVERYTHING CHANGED FOR ME AFTER THAT DAY.
YOU AND THE OTHER KAFNA...
...YOU'RE THE WHOLE REASON I'M STANDING HERE NOW!
I...
...I DON'T THINK I COULD EVER THANK YOU ENOUGH!

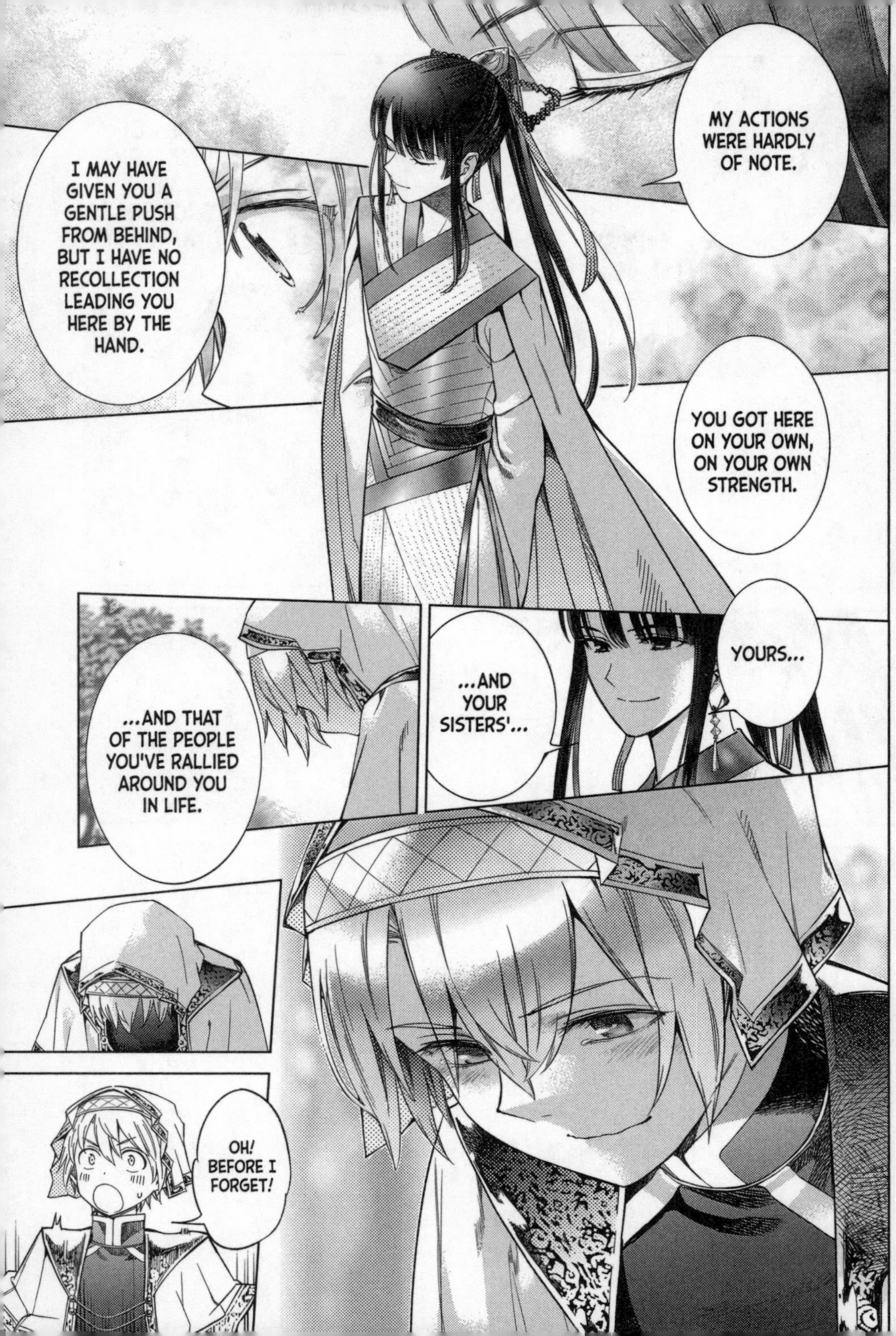
MY ACTIONS WERE HARDLY OF NOTE.
I MAY HAVE GIVEN YOU A GENTLE PUSH FROM BEHIND, BUT I HAVE NO RECOLLECTION LEADING YOU HERE BY THE HAND.
YOU GOT HERE ON YOUR OWN, ON YOUR OWN STRENGTH.
YOURS...
...AND YOUR SISTERS'...
...AND THAT OF THE PEOPLE YOU'VE RALLIED AROUND YOU IN LIFE.
OH! BEFORE I FORGET!

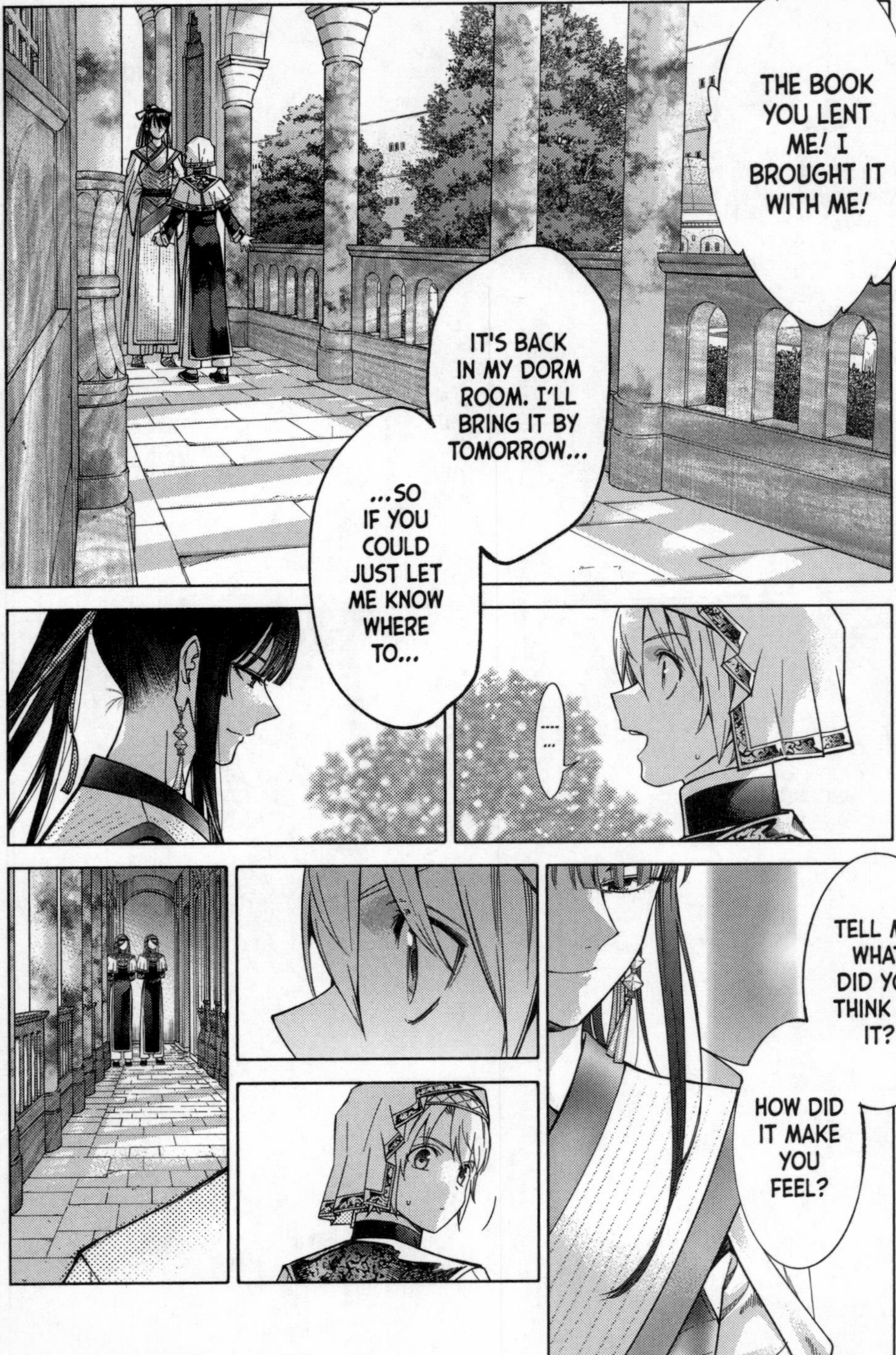
THE BOOK YOU LENT ME! I BROUGHT IT WITH ME!
IT'S BACK IN MY DORM ROOM. I'LL BRING IT BY TOMORROW...
...SO IF YOU COULD JUST LET ME KNOW WHERE TO...
......
TELL ME, WHAT DID YOU THINK OF IT?
HOW DID IT MAKE YOU FEEL?

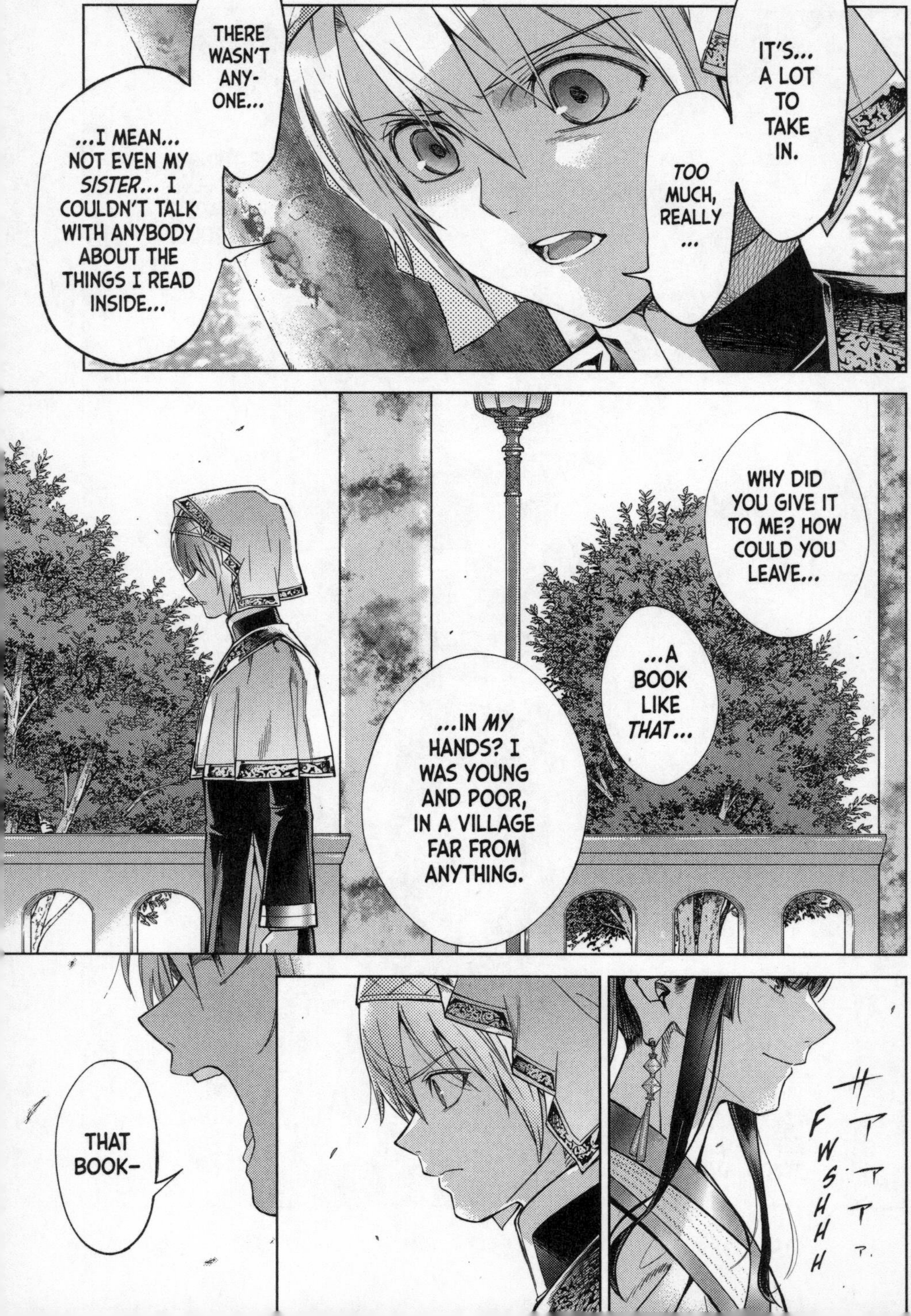
IT'S... A LOT TO TAKE IN.
TOO MUCH, REALLY...
THERE WASN'T ANYONE...
...I MEAN... NOT EVEN MY *SISTER*... I COULDN'T TALK WITH ANYBODY ABOUT THE THINGS I READ INSIDE...
WHY DID YOU GIVE IT TO ME? HOW COULD YOU LEAVE...
...A BOOK LIKE *THAT*...
...IN *MY* HANDS? I WAS YOUNG AND POOR, IN A VILLAGE FAR FROM ANYTHING.
FWSHHH
THAT BOOK—

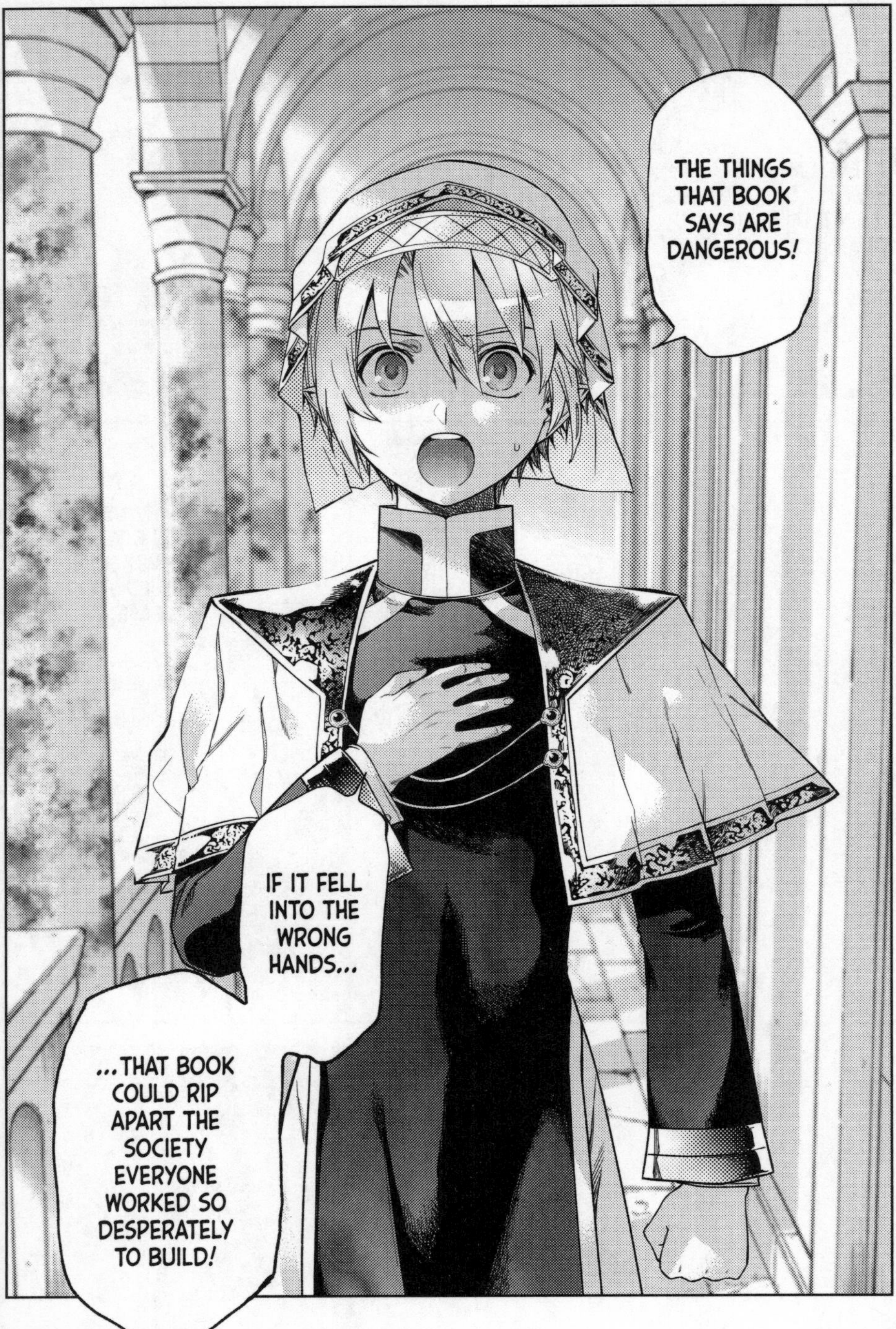
THE THINGS THAT BOOK SAYS ARE DANGEROUS!
IF IT FELL INTO THE WRONG HANDS...
...THAT BOOK COULD RIP APART THE SOCIETY EVERYONE WORKED SO DESPERATELY TO BUILD!

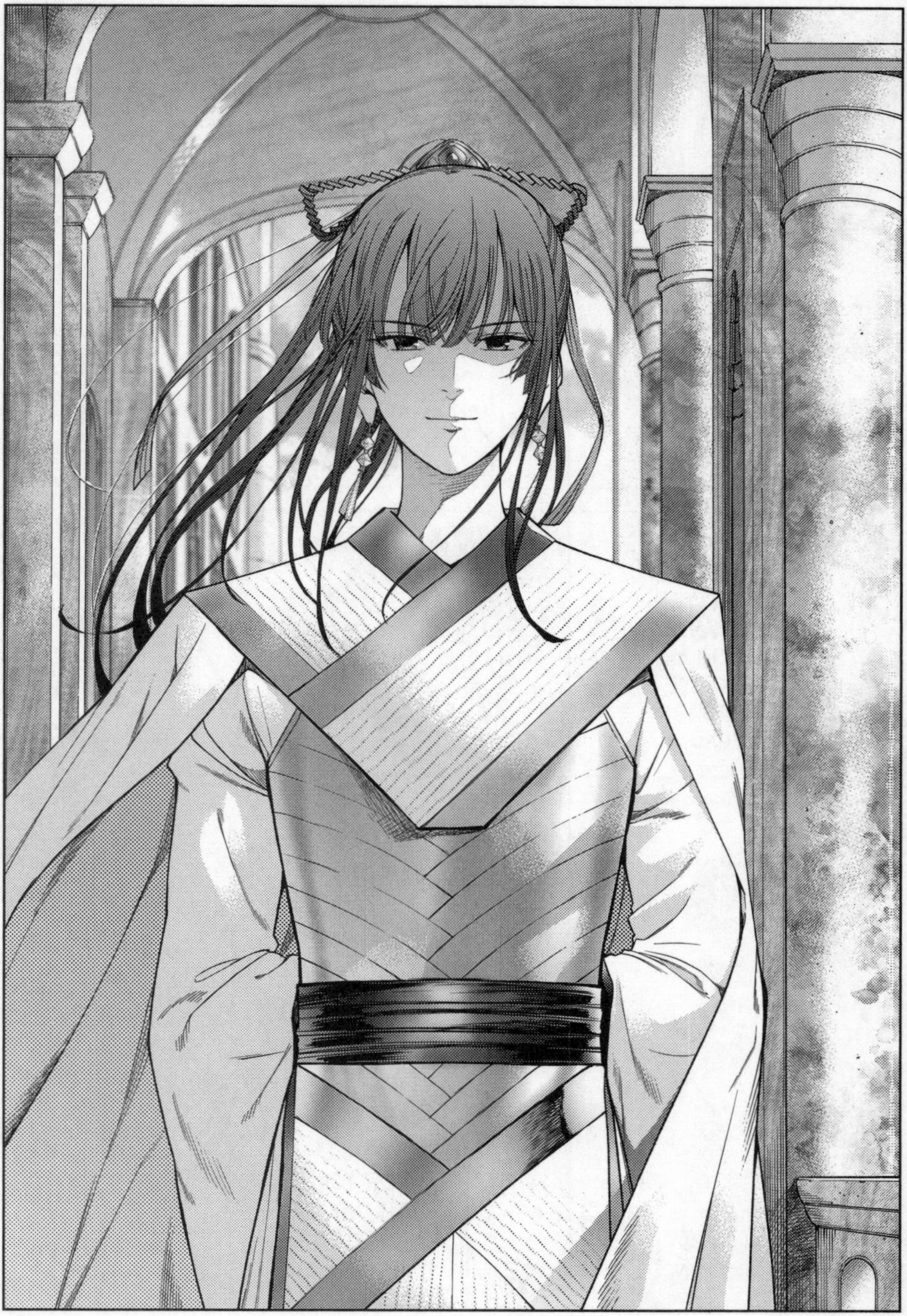

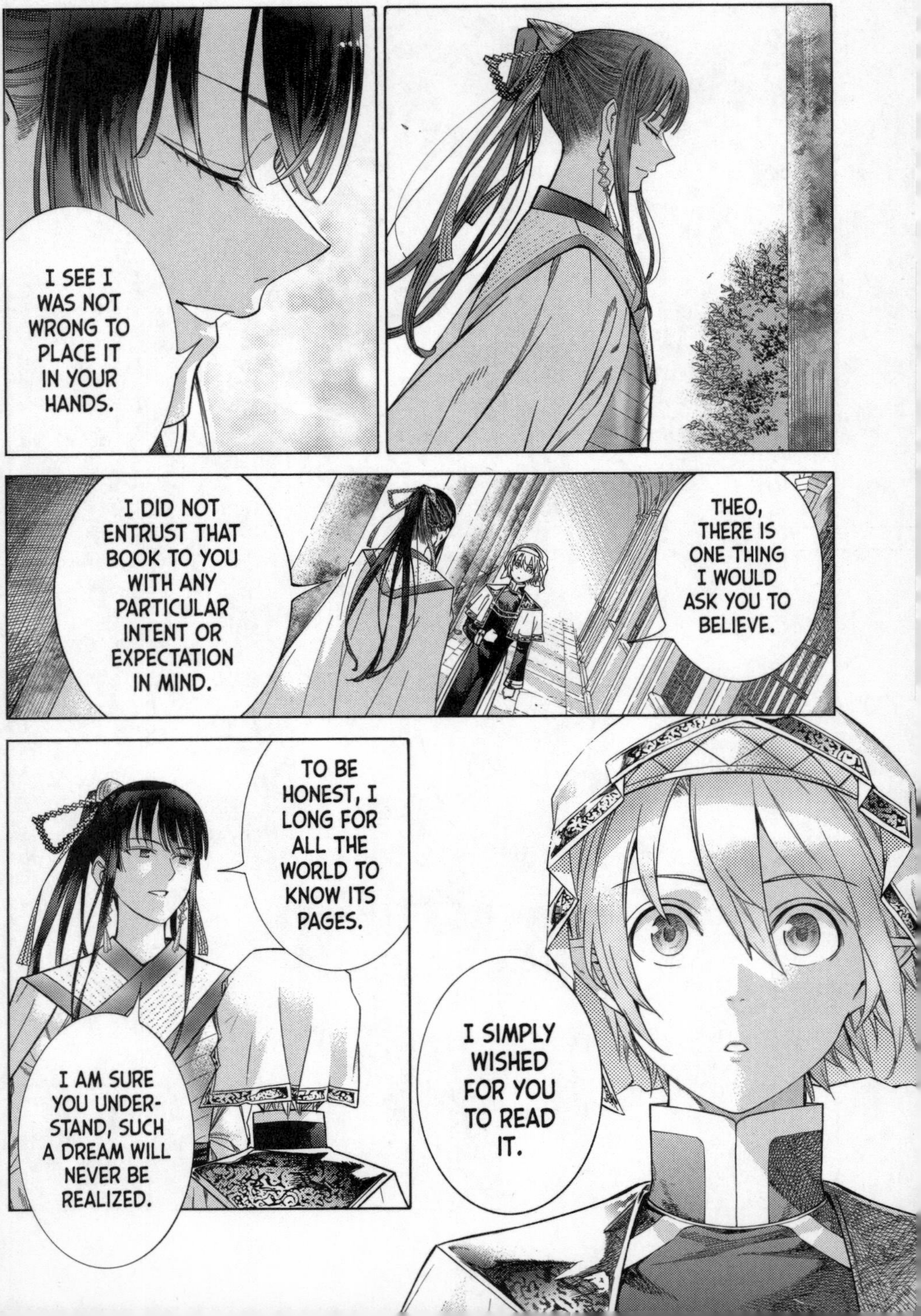
I SEE I WAS NOT WRONG TO PLACE IT IN YOUR HANDS.
THEO, THERE IS ONE THING I WOULD ASK YOU TO BELIEVE.
I DID NOT ENTRUST THAT BOOK TO YOU WITH ANY PARTICULAR INTENT OR EXPECTATION IN MIND.
I SIMPLY WISHED FOR YOU TO READ IT.
TO BE HONEST, I LONG FOR ALL THE WORLD TO KNOW ITS PAGES.
I AM SURE YOU UNDER-STAND, SUCH A DREAM WILL NEVER BE REALIZED.

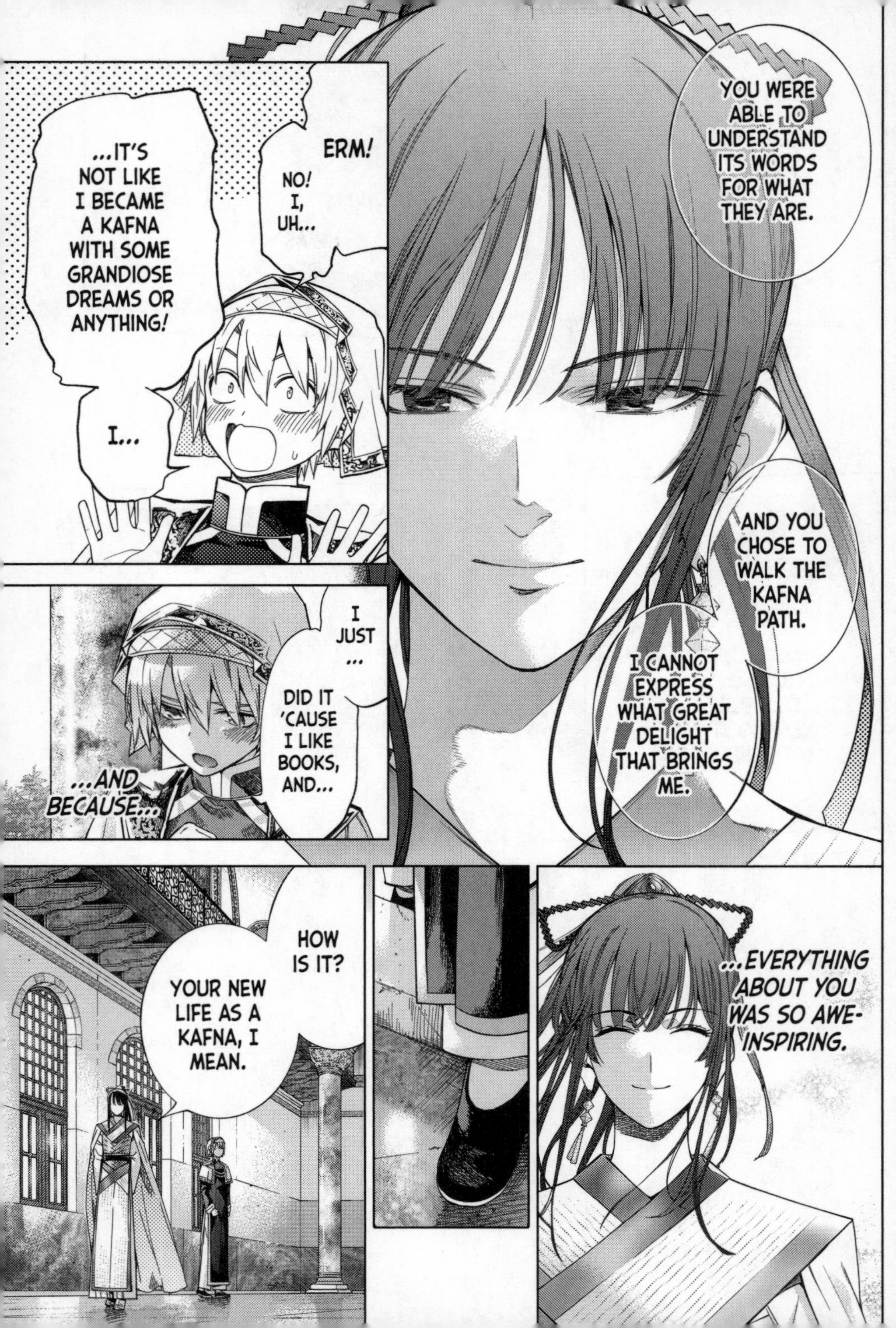
YOU WERE ABLE TO UNDERSTAND ITS WORDS FOR WHAT THEY ARE.
AND YOU CHOSE TO WALK THE KAFNA PATH.
I CANNOT EXPRESS WHAT GREAT DELIGHT THAT BRINGS ME.
ERM!
NO! I, UH...
...IT'S NOT LIKE I BECAME A KAFNA WITH SOME GRANDIOSE DREAMS OR ANYTHING!
I...
I JUST...
DID IT 'CAUSE I LIKE BOOKS, AND...
...AND BECAUSE...
...EVERYTHING ABOUT YOU WAS SO AWE-INSPIRING.
HOW IS IT?
YOUR NEW LIFE AS A KAFNA, I MEAN.

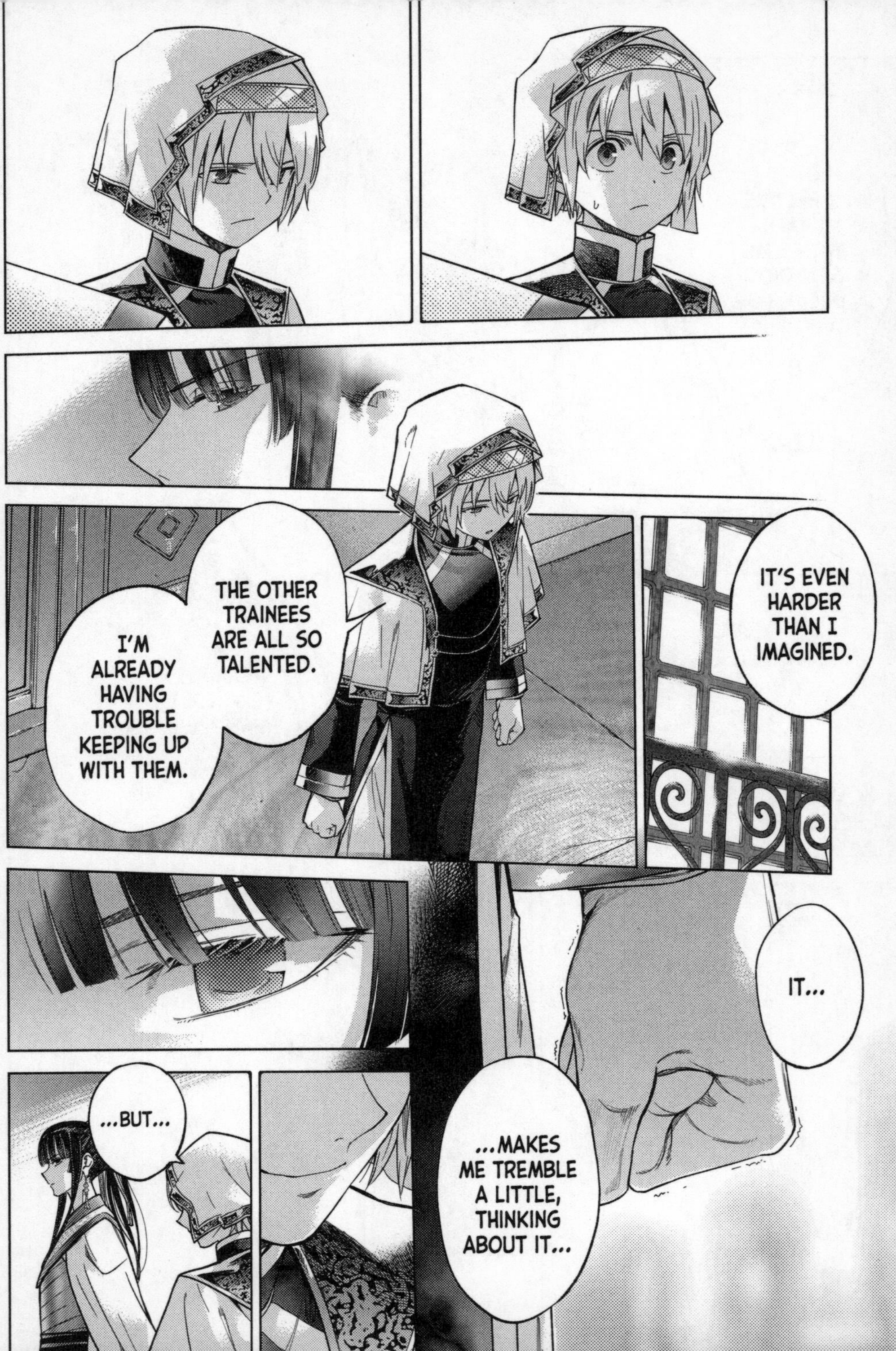
IT'S EVEN HARDER THAN I IMAGINED.
THE OTHER TRAINEES ARE ALL SO TALENTED.
I'M ALREADY HAVING TROUBLE KEEPING UP WITH THEM.
IT...
...MAKES ME TREMBLE A LITTLE, THINKING ABOUT IT...
...BUT...

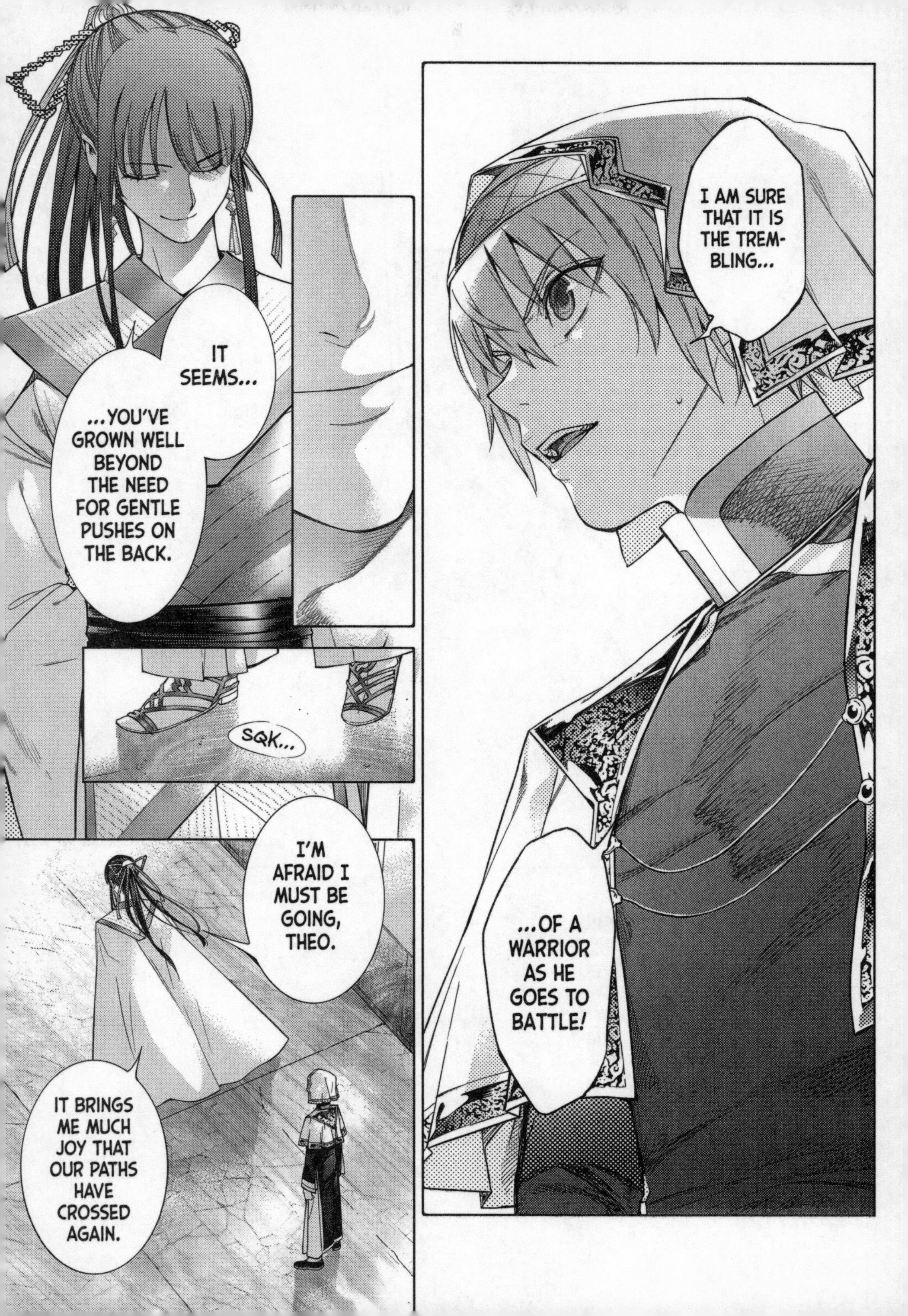
I AM SURE THAT IT IS THE TREM-BLING...
...OF A WARRIOR AS HE GOES TO BATTLE!
IT SEEMS...
...YOU'VE GROWN WELL BEYOND THE NEED FOR GENTLE PUSHES ON THE BACK.
SQK...
I'M AFRAID I MUST BE GOING, THEO.
IT BRINGS ME MUCH JOY THAT OUR PATHS HAVE CROSSED AGAIN.

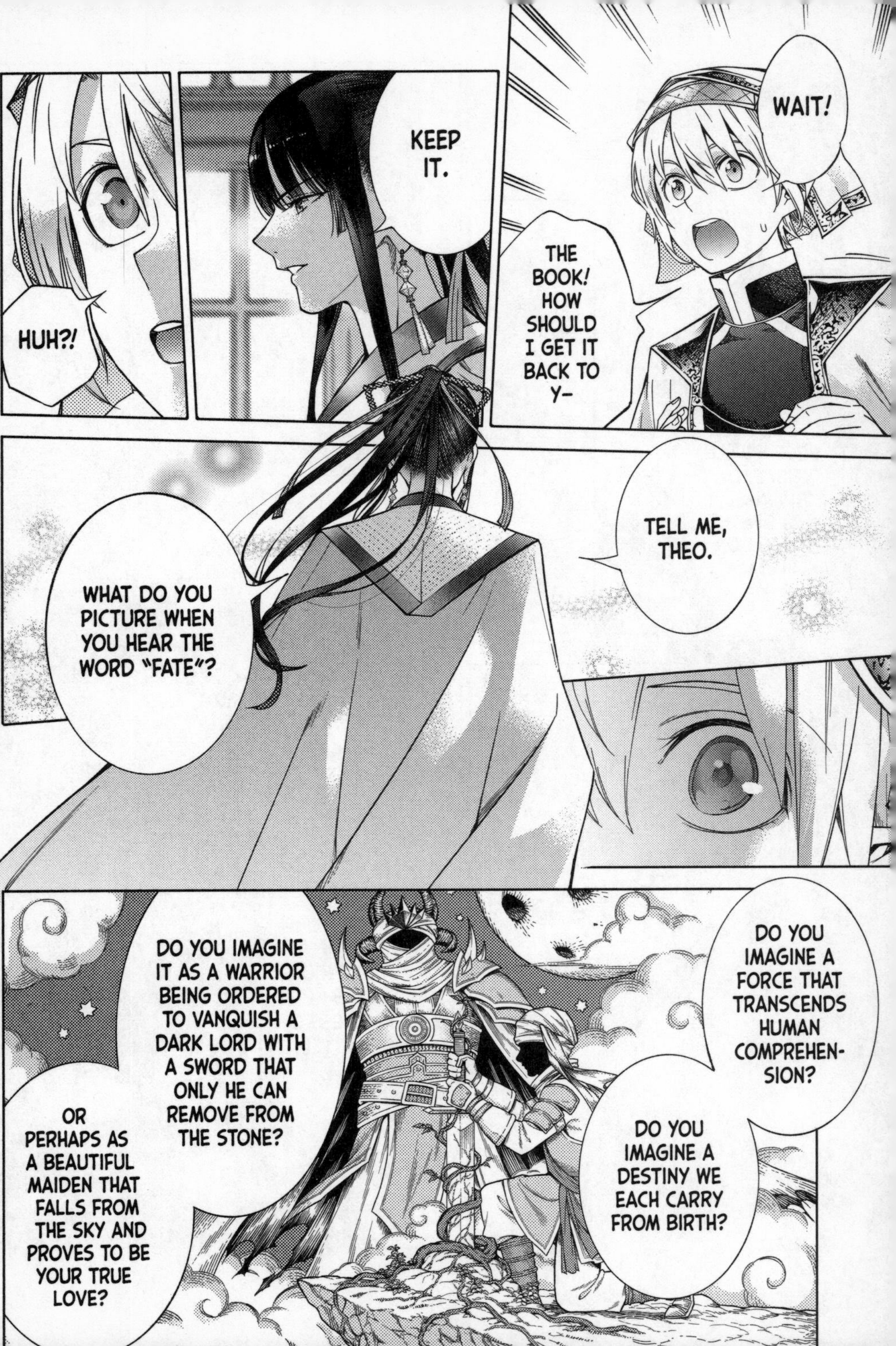
WAIT!
THE BOOK! HOW SHOULD I GET IT BACK TO Y–
KEEP IT.
HUH?!
TELL ME, THEO.
WHAT DO YOU PICTURE WHEN YOU HEAR THE WORD "FATE"?
DO YOU IMAGINE A FORCE THAT TRANSCENDS HUMAN COMPREHENSION?
DO YOU IMAGINE A DESTINY WE EACH CARRY FROM BIRTH?
DO YOU IMAGINE IT AS A WARRIOR BEING ORDERED TO VANQUISH A DARK LORD WITH A SWORD THAT ONLY HE CAN REMOVE FROM THE STONE?
OR PERHAPS AS A BEAUTIFUL MAIDEN THAT FALLS FROM THE SKY AND PROVES TO BE YOUR TRUE LOVE?

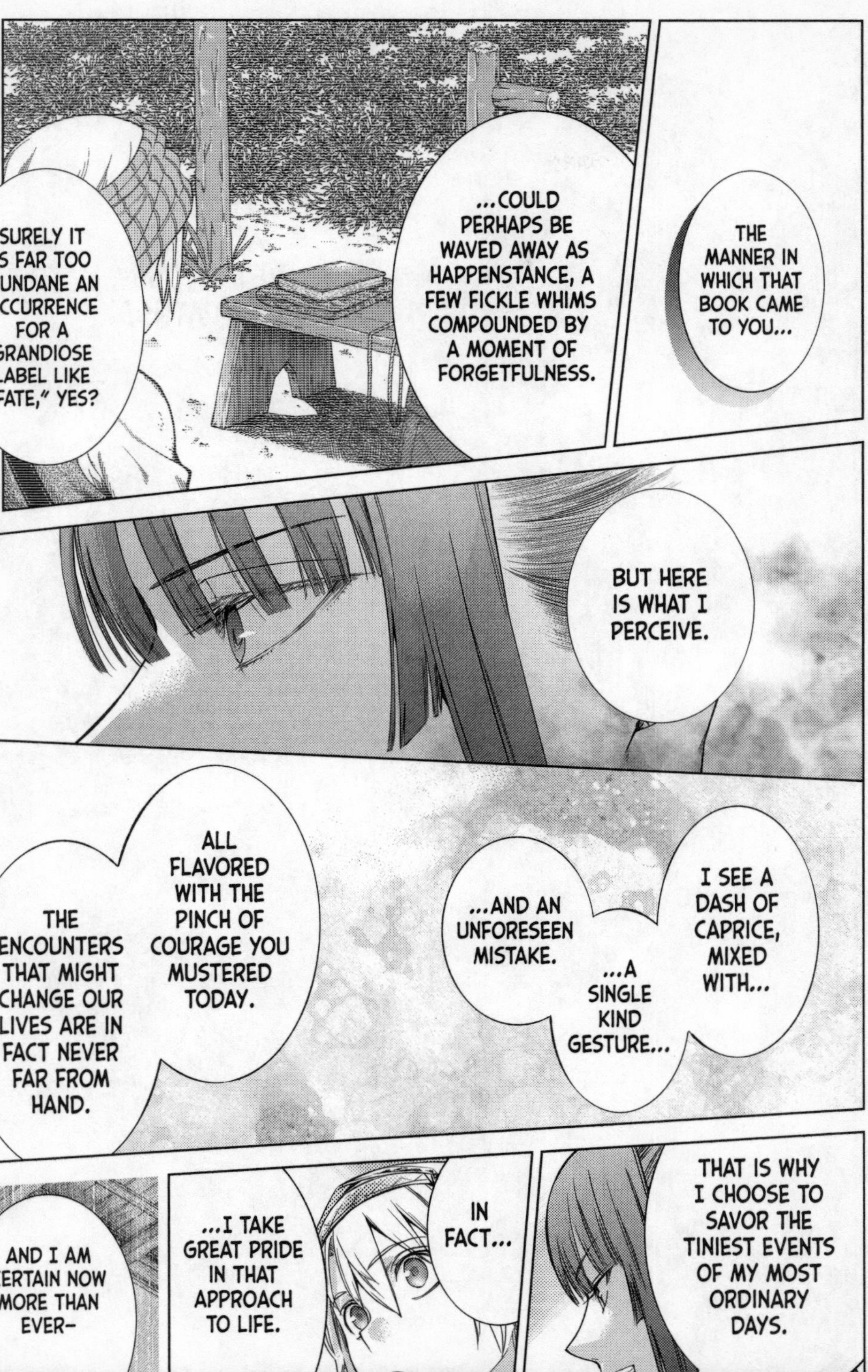
THE MANNER IN WHICH THAT BOOK CAME TO YOU...
...COULD PERHAPS BE WAVED AWAY AS HAPPENSTANCE, A FEW FICKLE WHIMS COMPOUNDED BY A MOMENT OF FORGETFULNESS.
SURELY IT IS FAR TOO MUNDANE AN OCCURRENCE FOR A GRANDIOSE LABEL LIKE "FATE," YES?
BUT HERE IS WHAT I PERCEIVE.
I SEE A DASH OF CAPRICE, MIXED WITH...
...A SINGLE KIND GESTURE...
...AND AN UNFORESEEN MISTAKE.
ALL FLAVORED WITH THE PINCH OF COURAGE YOU MUSTERED TODAY.
THE ENCOUNTERS THAT MIGHT CHANGE OUR LIVES ARE IN FACT NEVER FAR FROM HAND.
THAT IS WHY I CHOOSE TO SAVOR THE TINIEST EVENTS OF MY MOST ORDINARY DAYS.
IN FACT...
...I TAKE GREAT PRIDE IN THAT APPROACH TO LIFE.
AND I AM CERTAIN NOW MORE THAN EVER–

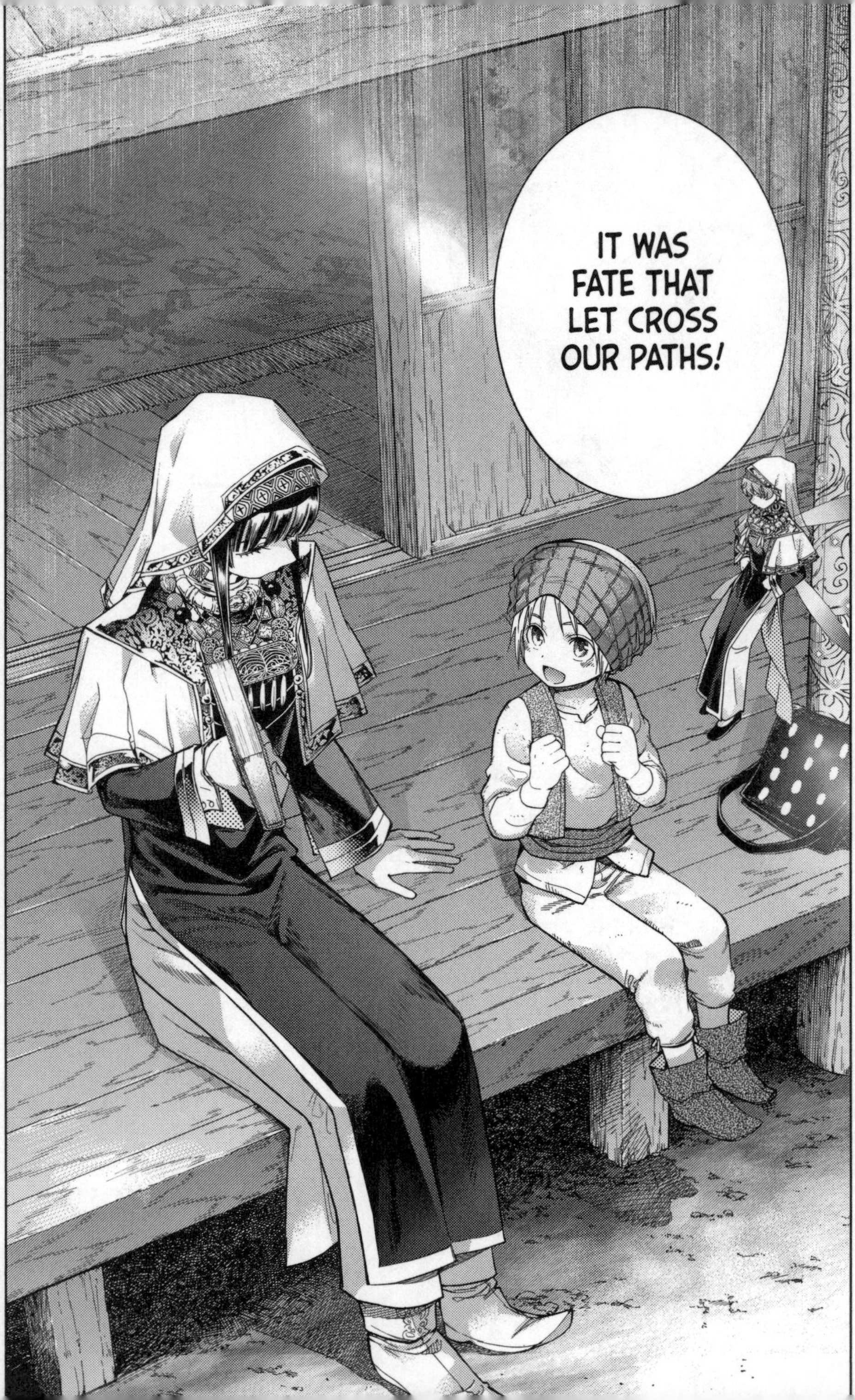
IT WAS FATE THAT LET CROSS OUR PATHS!

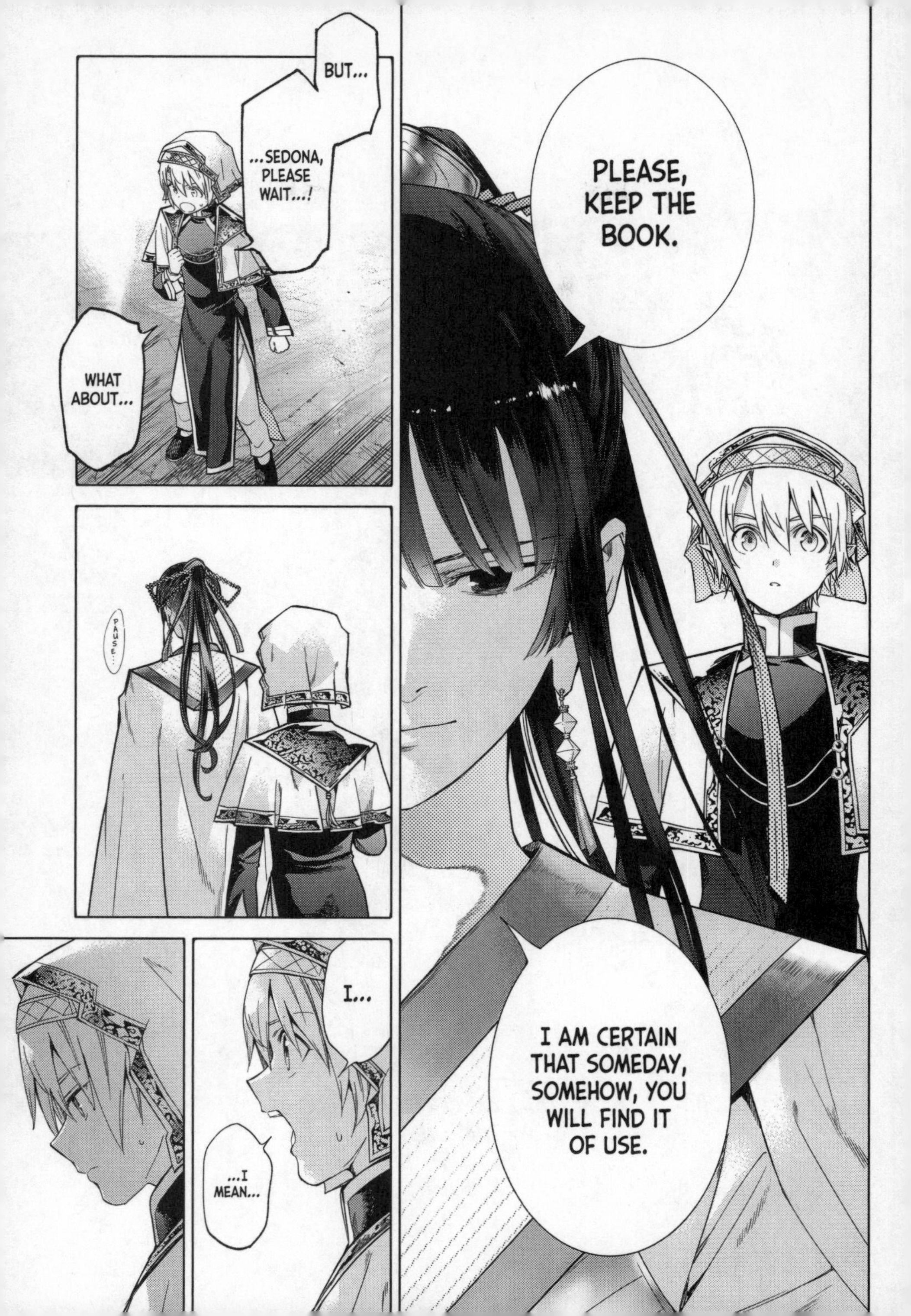
PLEASE, KEEP THE BOOK.
I AM CERTAIN THAT SOMEDAY, SOMEHOW, YOU WILL FIND IT OF USE.
BUT...
...SEDONA, PLEASE WAIT...!
WHAT ABOUT...
PAUSE...
I...
...I MEAN...

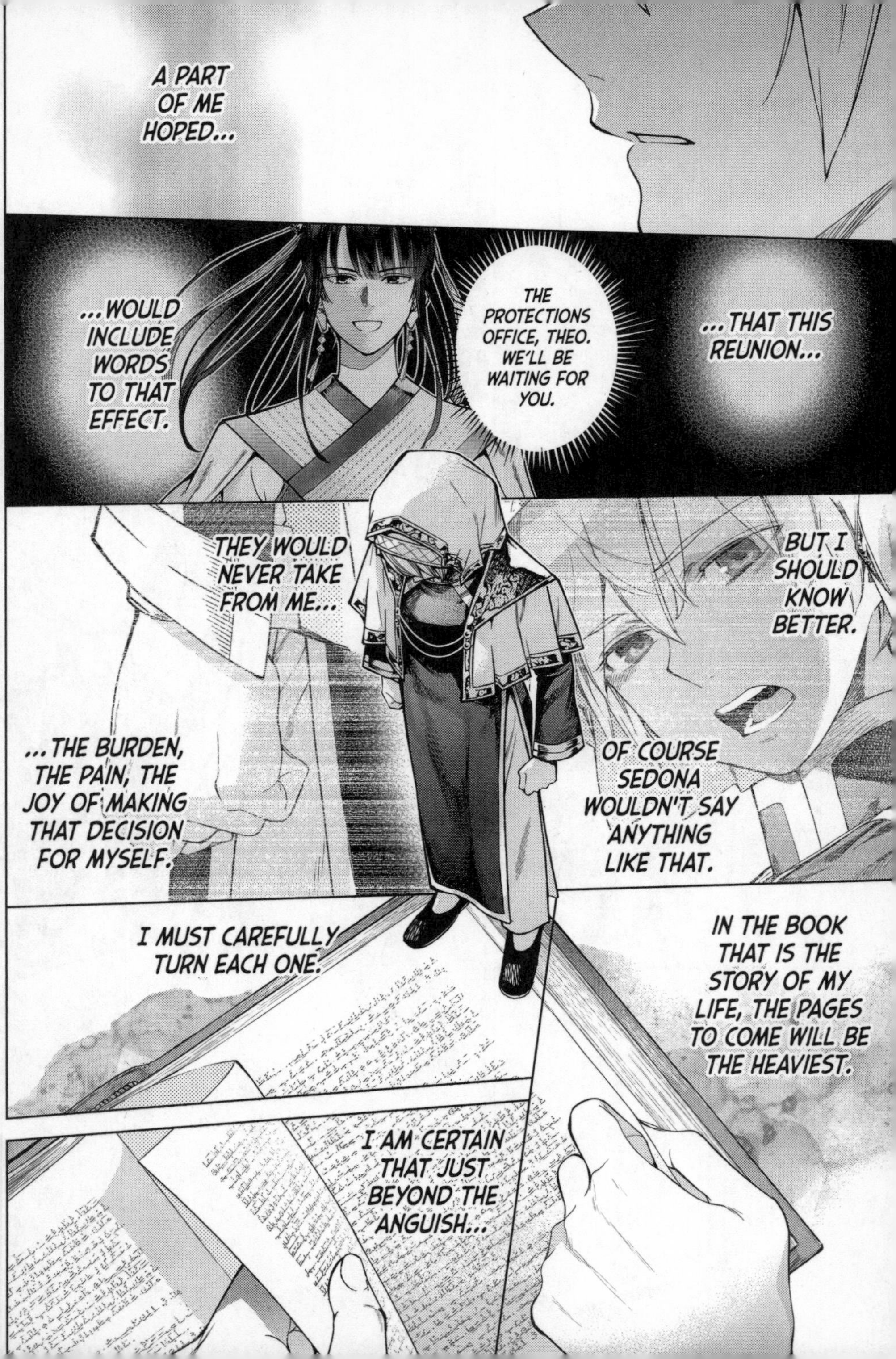
A PART OF ME HOPED...
...THAT THIS REUNION...
THE PROTECTIONS OFFICE, THEO. WE'LL BE WAITING FOR YOU.
...WOULD INCLUDE WORDS TO THAT EFFECT.
BUT I SHOULD KNOW BETTER.
OF COURSE SEDONA WOULDN'T SAY ANYTHING LIKE THAT.
THEY WOULD NEVER TAKE FROM ME...
...THE BURDEN, THE PAIN, THE JOY OF MAKING THAT DECISION FOR MYSELF.
IN THE BOOK THAT IS THE STORY OF MY LIFE, THE PAGES TO COME WILL BE THE HEAVIEST.
I MUST CAREFULLY TURN EACH ONE.
I AM CERTAIN THAT JUST BEYOND THE ANGUISH...

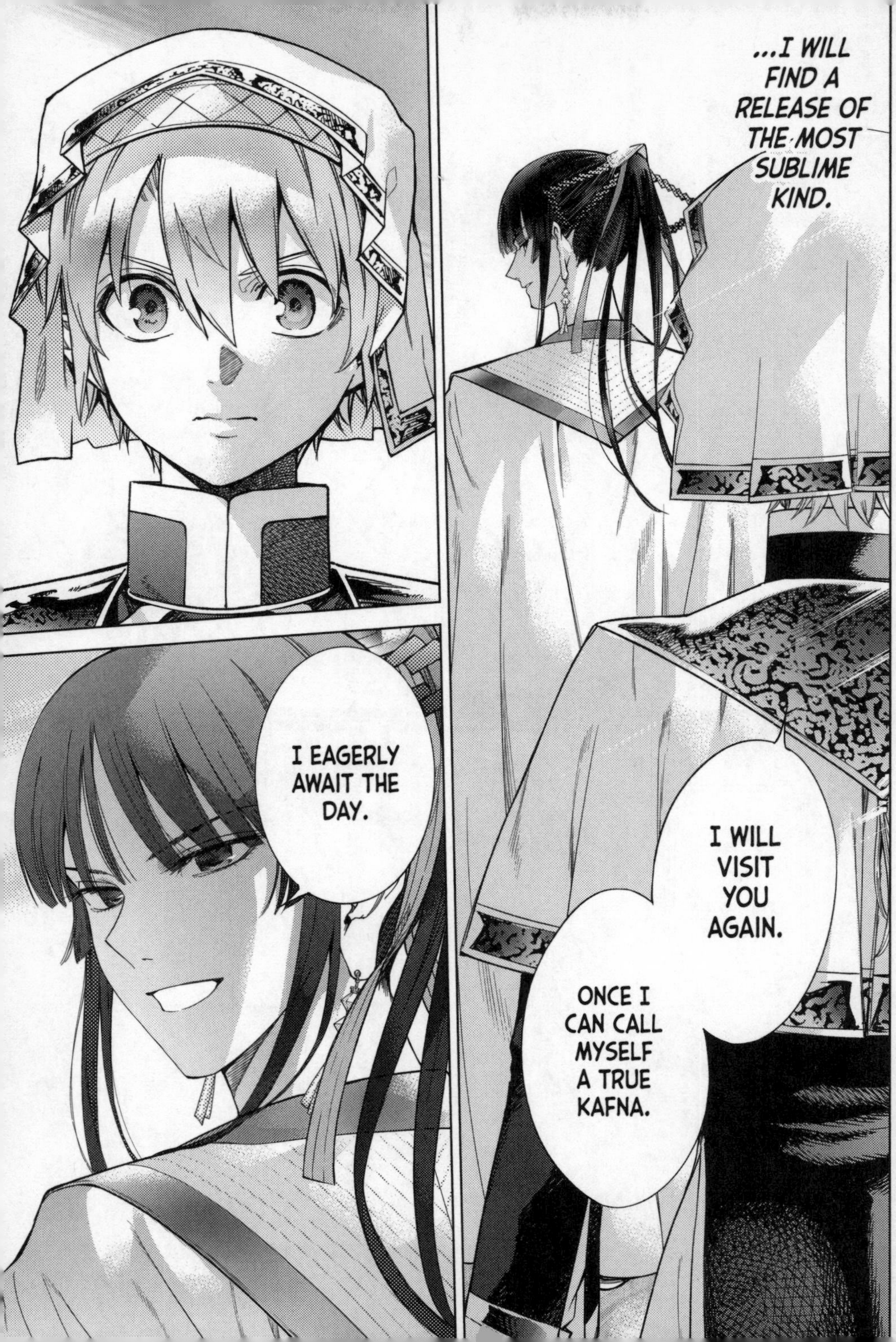
...I WILL FIND A RELEASE OF THE MOST SUBLIME KIND.
I WILL VISIT YOU AGAIN.
ONCE I CAN CALL MYSELF A TRUE KAFNA.
I EAGERLY AWAIT THE DAY.

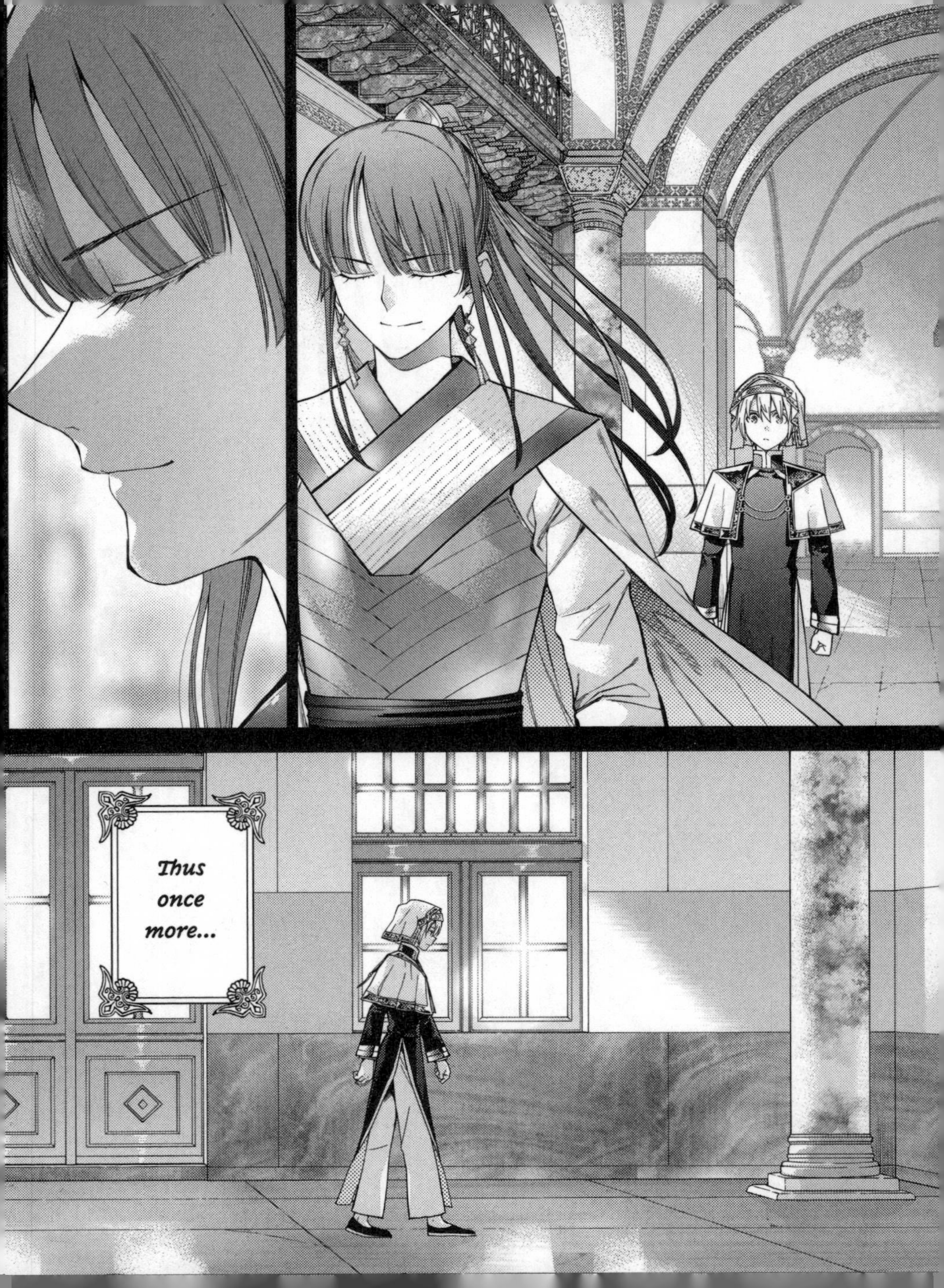
Thus once more...

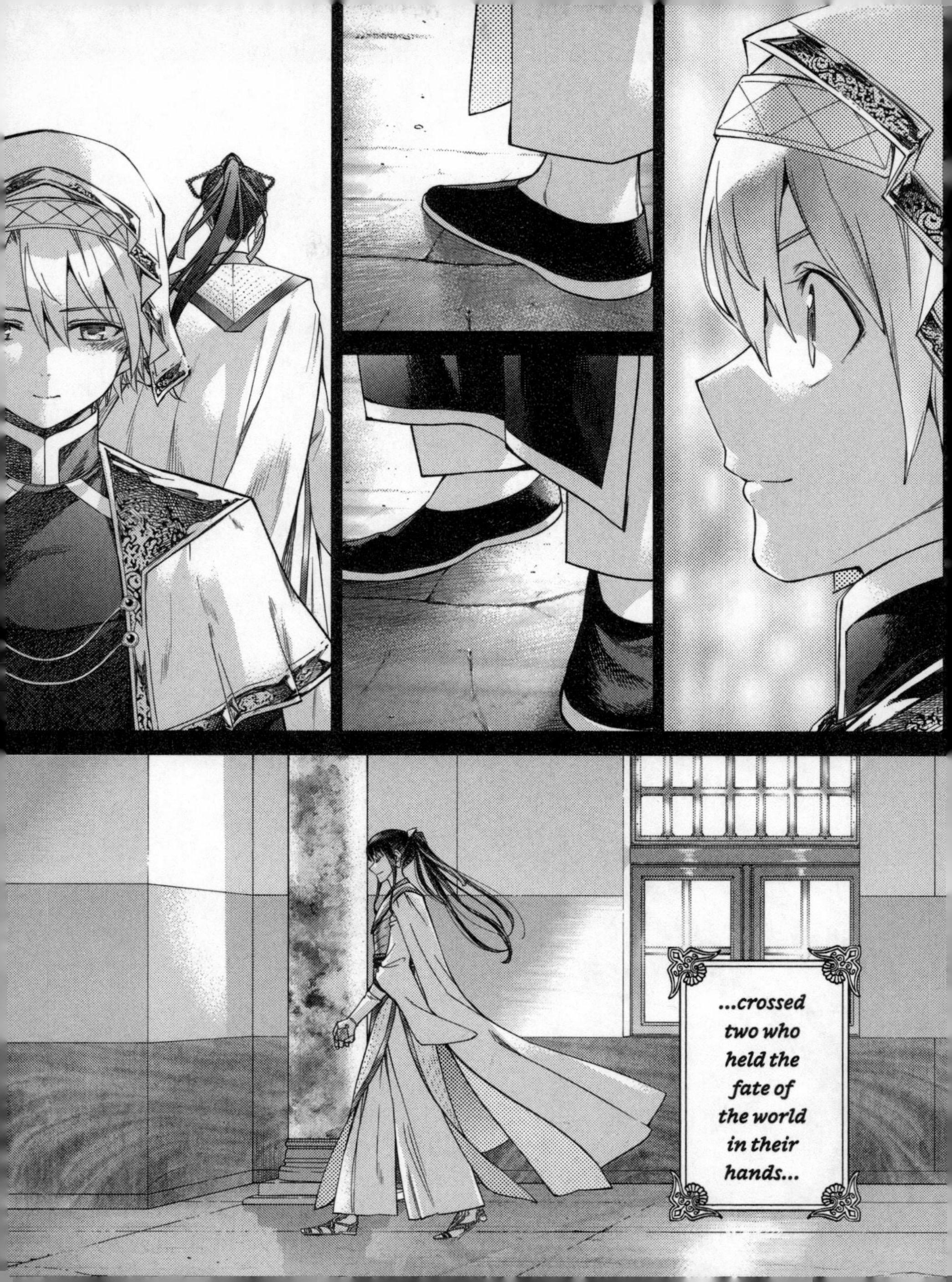
...crossed two who held the fate of the world in their hands...

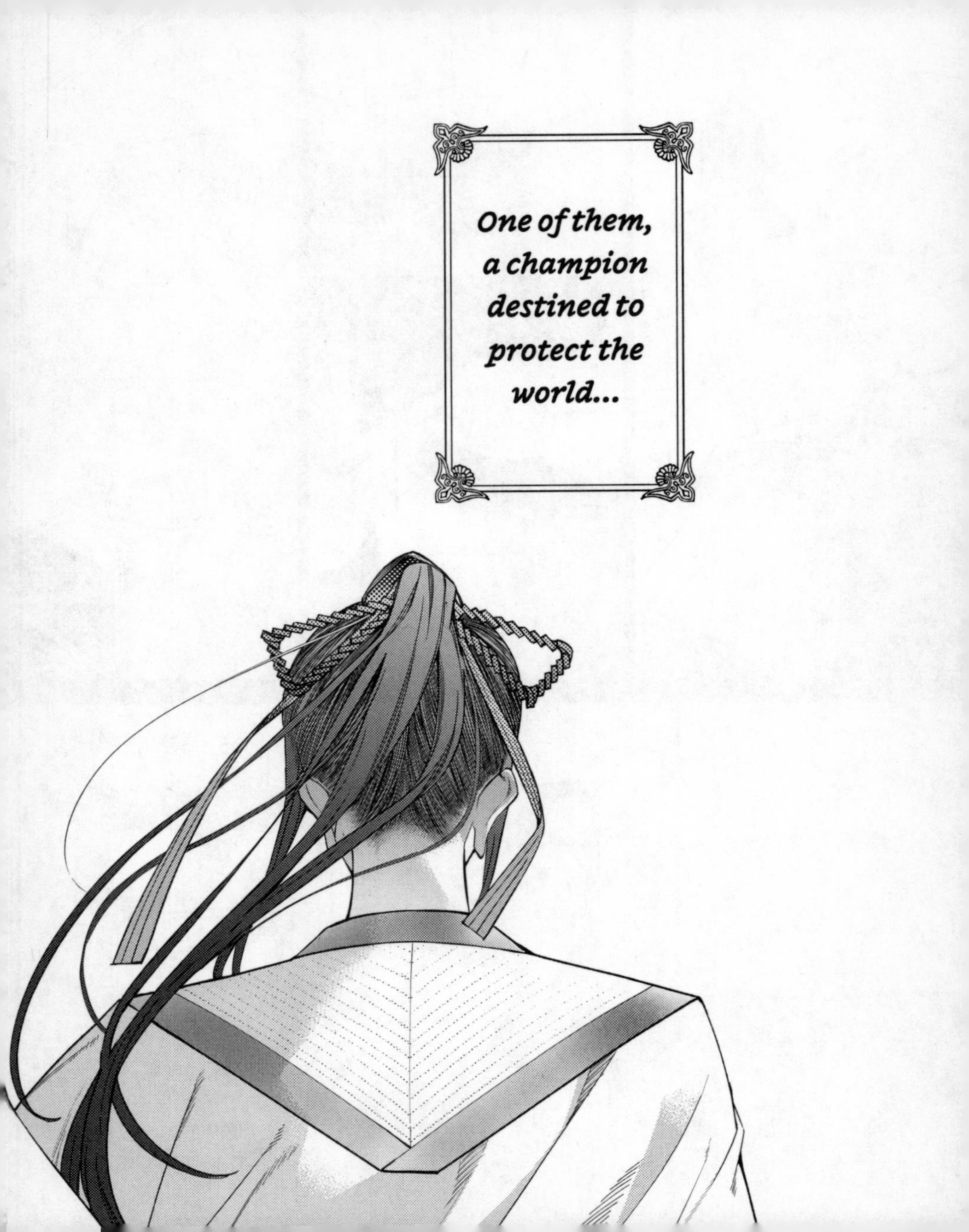
One of them, a champion destined to protect the world...

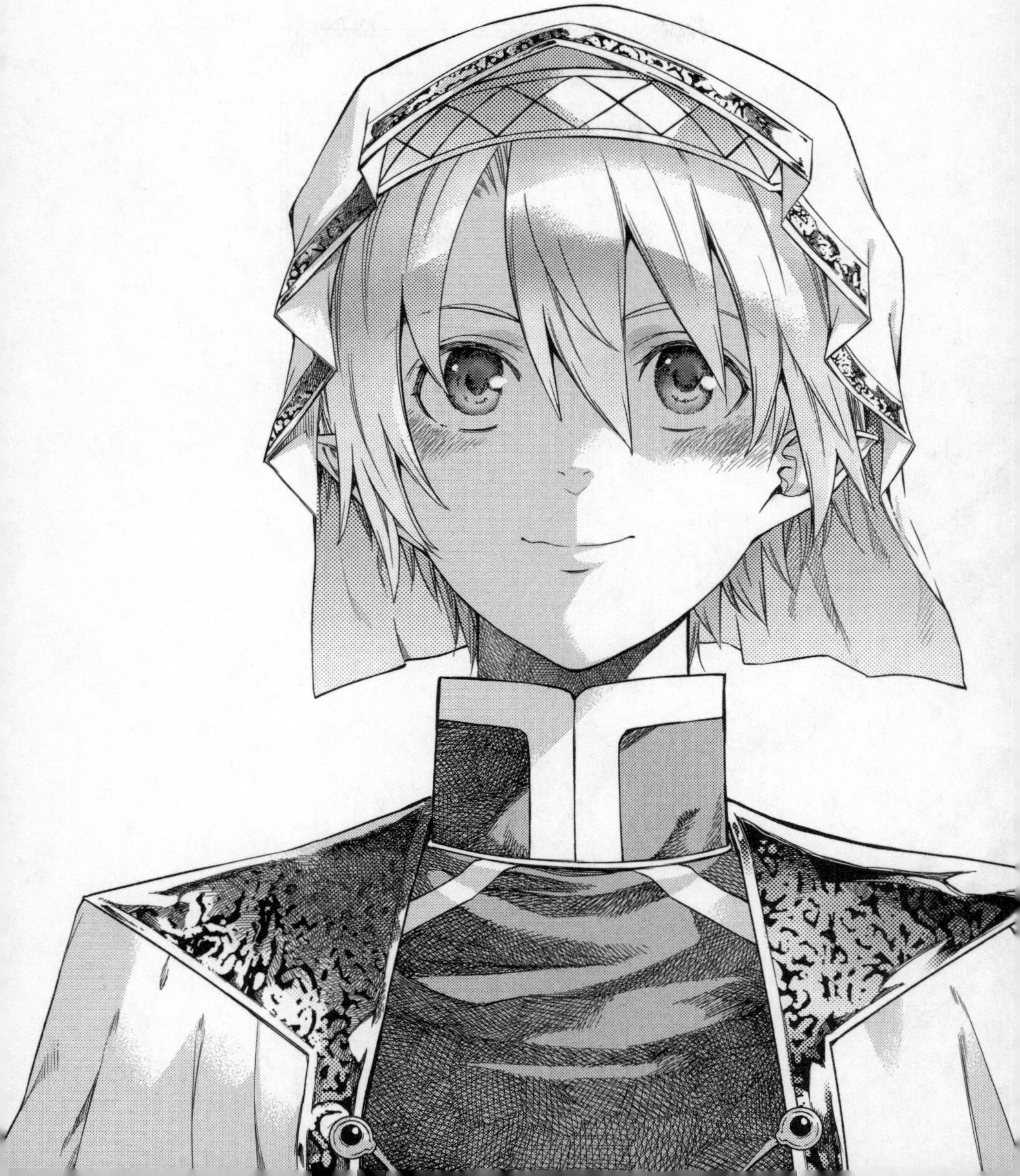

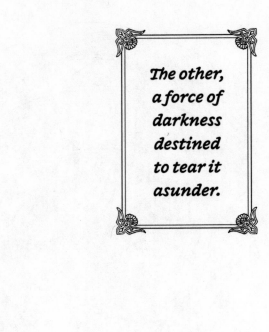

The other,
a force of
darkness
destined
to tear it
asunder.

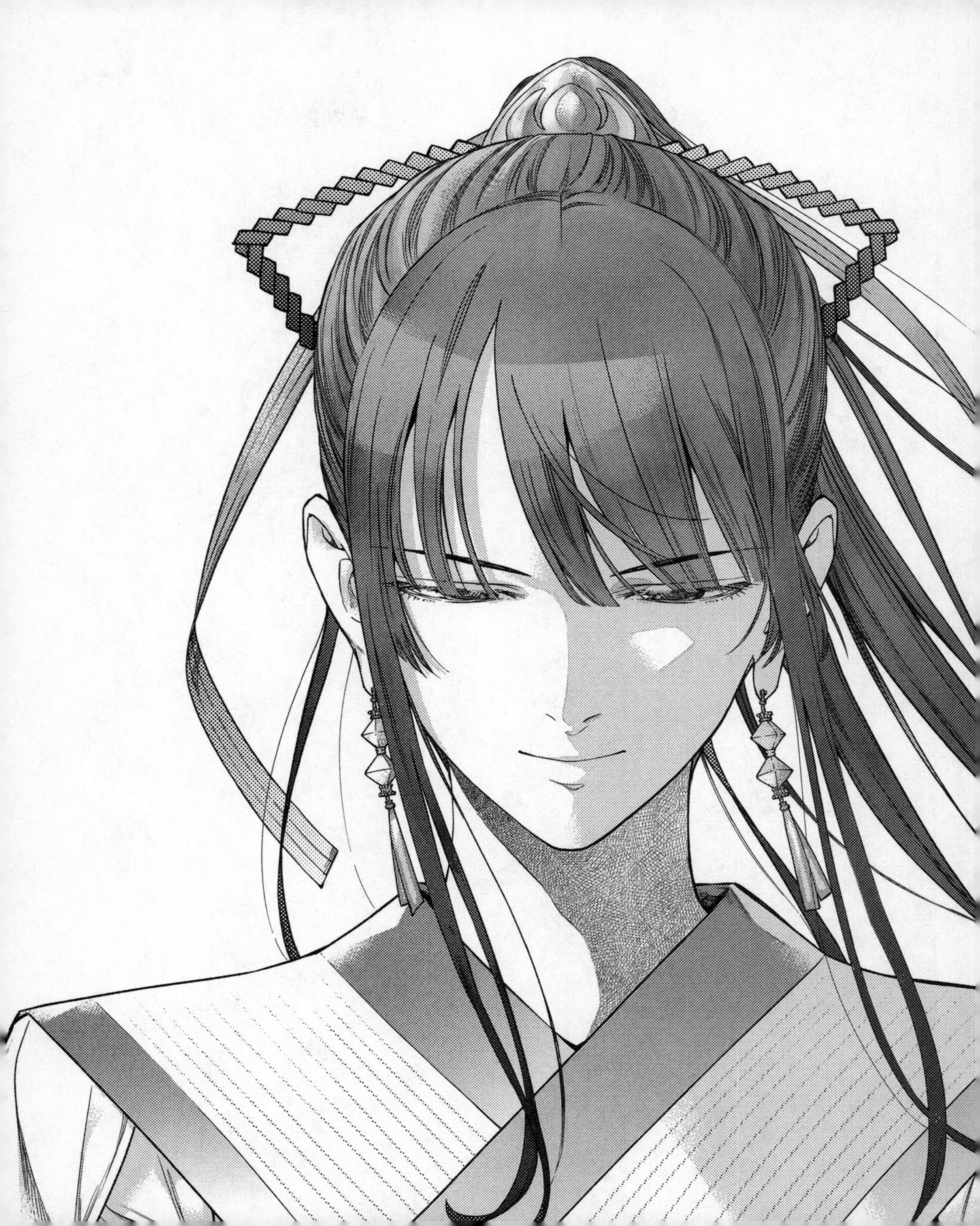

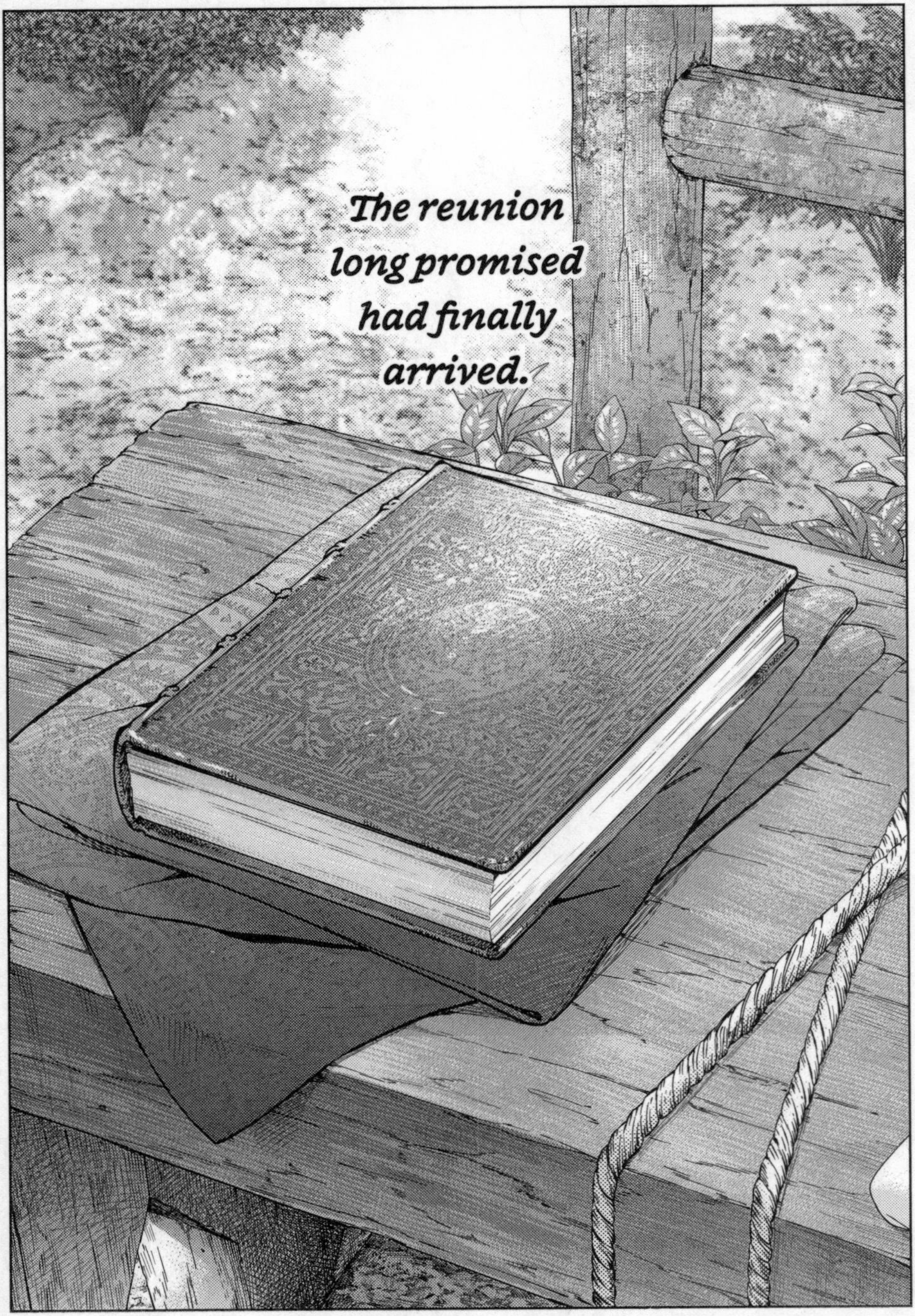
The reunion long promised had finally arrived.

To be continued.

Young characters and steampunk setting, like *Howl's Moving Castle* and *Battle Angel Alita*

Beyond the Clouds © 2018 Nicke / Ki-oon

A boy with a talent for machines and a mysterious girl whose wings he's fixed will take you beyond the clouds! In the tradition of the high-flying, resonant adventure stories of Studio Ghibli comes a gorgeous tale about the longing of young hearts for adventure and friendship!

The adorable new odd-couple cat comedy manga from the creator of the beloved *Chi's Sweet Home*, in full color!

Sue & Tai-chan

Konami Kanata

Sue is an aging housecat who's looking forward to living out her life in peace... but her plans change when the mischievous black tomcat Tai-chan enters the picture! Hey! Sue never signed up to be a catsitter! *Sue & Tai-chan* is the latest from the reigning meow-narch of cute kitty comics, Konami Kanata.

KC KODANSHA COMICS

CUTE ANIMALS AND LIFE LESSONS, PERFECT FOR ASPIRING PET VETS OF ALL AGES!

For an 11-year-old, Yuzu has a lot on her plate. When her mom gets sick and has to be hospitalized, Yuzu goes to live with her uncle who runs the local veterinary clinic. Yuzu's always been scared of animals, but she tries to help out. Through all the tough moments in her life, Yuzu realizes that she can help make things all right with a little help from her animal pals, peers, and kind grown-ups.

Every new patient is a furry friend in the making!

SAINT ☆ YOUNG MEN

A LONG AWAITED ARRIVAL IN PREMIUM 2-IN-1 HARDCOVER

After centuries of hard work, Jesus and Buddha take a break from their
heavenly duties to relax among the people of Japan, and their adventures in this
lighthearted buddy comedy are sure to bring mirth and merriment to all!

"Brilliant...the physical comedy
and facial expressions will
make you literally LOL."
—Sam Humphries
(host of *DC Daily*;
writer, *Green Lanterns*,
Legendary Star-Lord)

Saint Young Men © Hikaru Nakamura/Kodansha

The art-deco cyberpunk classic from the creators of *xxxHOLiC* and *Cardcaptor Sakura*!

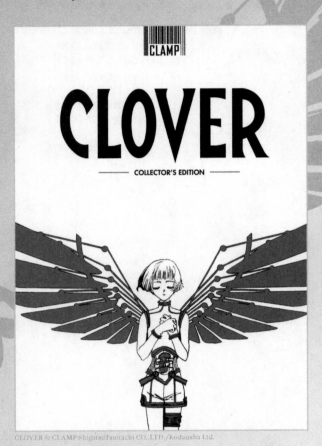

CLOVER © CLAMP·ShigatsuTsuitachi CO.,LTD./Kodansha Ltd.

Su was born into a bleak future, where the government keeps tight control over children with magical powers—codenamed "Clovers." With Su being the only "four-leaf" Clover in the world, she has been kept isolated nearly her whole life. Can ex-military agent Kazuhiko deliver her to the happiness she seeks? Experience the complete series in this hardcover edition, which also includes over twenty pages of ravishing color art!

KC
KODANSHA
COMICS

The beloved characters from *Cardcaptor Sakura* return in a brand new, reimagined fantasy adventure!

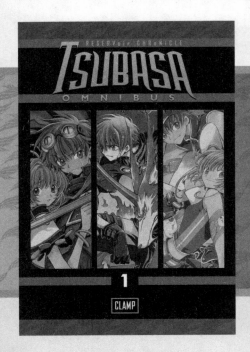

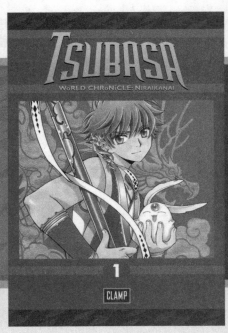

"[*Tsubasa*] takes readers on a fantastic ride that only gets more exhilarating with each successive chapter." —Anime News Network

In the Kingdom of Clow, an archaeological dig unleashes an incredible power, causing Princess Sakura to lose her memories. To save her, her childhood friend Syaoran must follow the orders of the Dimension Witch and travel alongside Kurogane, an unrivaled warrior; Fai, a powerful magician; and Mokona, a curiously strange creature, to retrieve Sakura's dispersed memories!

"Clever, sassy, and original....*xxxHOLiC* has the inherent hallmarks of a runaway hit."
—NewType magazine

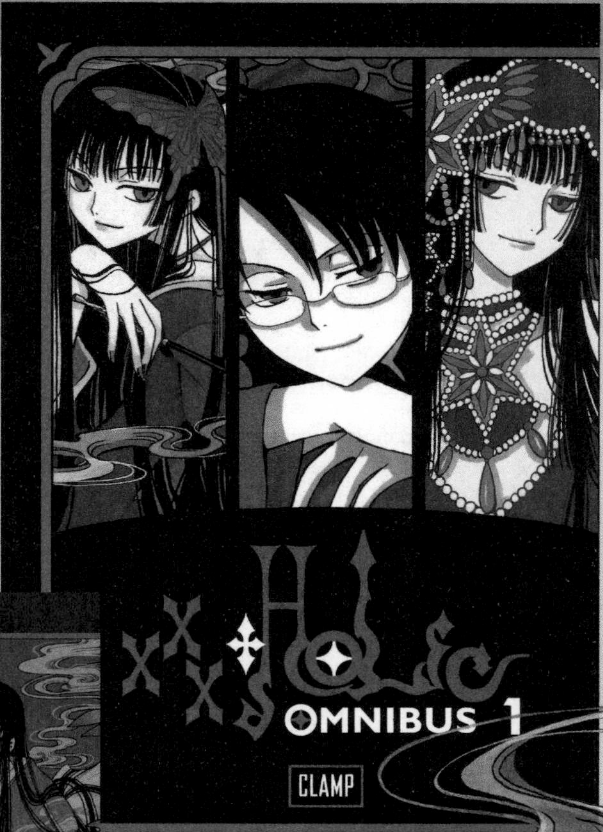
xxxHOLiC
OMNIBUS 1
CLAMP

Beautifully seductive artwork and uniquely Japanese depictions of the supernatural will hypnotize CLAMP fans!

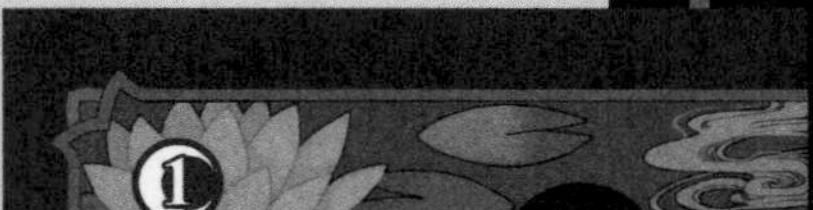
1
xxxHOLiC Rei
From the creators of
Tsubasa and *Chobits*
CLAMP

Kimihiro Watanuki is haunted by visions of ghosts and spirits. He seeks help from a mysterious woman named Yuko, who claims she can help. However, Watanuki must work for Yuko in order to pay for her aid. Soon Watanuki finds himself employed in Yuko's shop, where he sees things and meets customers that are stranger than anything he could have ever imagined.

KC KODANSHA COMICS

Magus of the Library 4 is a work of fiction. Names, characters, places, and incidents are the products of the author's imagination or are used fictitiously. Any resemblance to actual events, locales, or persons, living or dead, is entirely coincidental.

A Kodansha Comics Trade Paperback Original

Published in the United States by Kodansha Comics, an imprint of Kodansha USA Publishing, LLC, New York.

Publication rights for this English edition arranged through Kodansha Ltd., Tokyo.

First published in Japan in 2020 by Kodansha Ltd., Tokyo as *Toshokan no daimajutsushi*, volume 4.

ISBN 978-1-63236-916-1

Printed in the United States of America.

www.kodanshacomics.com

9 8 7 6 5 4 3 2 1
Translation: Stephen Kohler
Lettering: Paige Pumphrey
Editing: Ryan Holmberg
Kodansha Comics edition cover design by Phil Balsman

Publisher: Kiichiro Sugawara

Director of publishing services: Ben Applegate
Associate director of operations: Stephen Pakula
Publishing services managing editor: Noelle Webster
Assistant production manager: Emi Lotto, Angela Zurlo